Traces of Contamination

Traces of Contamination

Unearthing the Francoist Legacy
in Contemporary Spanish Discourse

Edited by
Eloy E. Merino and H. Rosi Song

Lewisburg
Bucknell University Press

Associated University Presses
2010 Eastpark Boulevard
Cranbury, NJ 08512

The paper used in this publication meets the requirements of the American National Standard for Permanence of Paper for Printed Library Materials Z39.48-1984

Library of Congress Cataloging-in-Publication Data

Traces of contamination : unearthing the Francoist legacy in contemporary Spanish discourse / edited by Eloy E. Merino and H. Rosi Song.
    p.   cm.
Includes bibliographical references and index.
ISBN 0-8387-5596-8 (alk. paper)
 1. Spanish prose literature—20th century—History and criticism.
2. Francoism in literature.   3. Spain—In literature.   I. Merino, Eloy E.
II. Song, H. Rosi, 1970–   III. Title.
PQ6134.F73T73   2005
860.9′358—dc22

                                        2004015231

Contents

Acknowledgments

THIS VOLUME WOULD HAVE NOT BEEN POSSIBLE WITHOUT THE HELP OF our contributors and our many generous colleagues who have supported us throughout this project. Special thanks go to those who listened, took the time to read the several versions of the manuscript, and provided much welcomed guidance: Jessamine Cooke-Plagwitz, Frank Graziano, Andrea Lanoux, Monique Lemaitre, Michael Mazzola, María Cristina Quintero. To J. M. Capozzola and C. Colbath for their editing skills. Many thanks to Connecticut College and the University of Northern Illinois (especially the late Raymond Tourville) for their support to fund several translations for the manuscript. Special thanks to the Office of the Provost at Bryn Mawr College for its generous support to finalize the preparation of the manuscript. To the editorial board of Bucknell University Press and its anonymous reader, who have helped us to successfully complete this project. And finally, many thanks to our friends and colleagues who believed in this project from the beginning and have accompanied us with their unconditional support: each one of our contributors, Duncan Black, María Fernanda Lander and Aida Heredia.

The editors wish to thank the following for their permission to reproduce the material needed to vertebrate our analysis: Ms. Beatriz Coll from RDC Literary Agency on behalf of writer Antonio Muñoz Molina, Ms. Mercedes Casanovas, Literary Agent for novelist Javier Marías, Ms. Cristina Mora from Grupo Planeta (to quote from the works of Carmen Martín Gaite, Gonzalo Torrente Ballester, and Federico Jiménez Losantos), Ms. María Vadillo, daughter of the late Fernando Vadillo to quote from his publications. A version of the essay by Patrick Paul Garlinger previously appeared in *Revista de Estudios Hispánicos*. We thank Akiko Tsuchiya for her kind permission to authorize its reproduction. The essay by Ulrich Winter appeared previously in Spanish in the collection of essays *Vencer no es convencer*. We thank Klaus D. Vervuert for his kind authorization to reproduce it in English in a revised version.

Traces of Contamination

Tracing the Past: An Introduction

In the year 2000 Spain commemorated the twenty-fifth anniver-sary of the death of Francisco Franco. Remembering the end of the Francoist regime marked an occasion to reflect on the silence that followed his death—a silence that reflected the tacit pact among politicians from the Right and Left to forget the past in order to save the future.[1] As Paloma Aguilar has observed, Spain, unlike other countries that have experienced profound political transformations and have dealt with institutions and individuals linked to the previous regime, witnessed no purge of civilian or military institutions inherited from the dictatorship.[2] Aguilar notes that the Spanish case became "the paradigm of a peaceful transition from an authoritarian to a democratic regime" and that other countries tried to emulate the "Spanish model."[3] In spite of this model of nonviolent political change, some critics started to question the consequences of the country's politics of consensus, especially in regard to its treatment of the past. They viewed the lack of memory as an "active erasure of the social memory that has been hegemonic up to 1975"[4] and a "deliberate turning-off of the collective memory" motivated by fear of repeating the country's troublesome past.[5] Once critics recognized society's disavowal of the past, they began to question the narrative constructed around Spain's democratization and to focus on the recovery of what for more than thirty years had been repressed or subdued in the country's ideologically polarized cultural landscape.[6]

The retrieval of this past left the remains of the authoritarian regime and the ideology it embraced during Franco's dictatorship from 1939 to 1975 largely unexplored. Motivated by an ethical imperative to redeem and preserve the memories and experiences of those persecuted under Francoism, scholars of the period neglected to inquire into what happened to the hegemonic ideology that had shaped the nation's culture for almost four decades. In other words, beyond what had been suppressed, erased or ignored, the question of what Spaniards integrated and normalized during the dictatorship had been overlooked. As Teresa Vilarós suggests in her study of post-Franco Spain, the past cannot be so easily undone, especially taking into account the patriarchal and repressive structure to which the Spanish collective was addicted before and during the country's transition from dictatorship to democracy.[7] The problem with omitting the less palatable aspects of the past is the implication that its ideological practices have ceased to exist and are no longer relevant in the democratic Spain of the present.[8]

Traces of Contamination explores the remnants of Francoist and Falangist ideology in contemporary Spain. The essays in this volume examine current fictional and intellectual discourses that relate the past to the present; they locate these ideological traces—be they veiled or visible, conscious or unconscious—in the concrete experiences and expressions of the dictatorship. The purpose of this collection is not to disclose instances of extreme ideologies still in practice, but to scrutinize the ways in which their legacy continues to complicate already thorny relations with the present. Our contributors demonstrate how the past still endures in the Spanish psyche in a variety of texts: memoirs, historical novels, testimonial literature, democratically reformed political proselytism, journalism, popular culture, and fiction. As these texts are in some cases concerned with fascist alliances and authoritarian rule, the essays in this volume analyze how authors negotiate their burdensome past—a past struggling to find its place in the present, stigmatized by the world and still divisive for Spaniards.[9] In contrast to the morally justified recovered memories of those who lost the Spanish Civil War (1936–1939), the texts under discussion present a highly conscious approach to memory by either diverting or revealing unexpected aspects of their authors' experiences. These texts, when read against the apparently seamless narrative that tells the successful story of the Spanish transition to democracy, and that in turn projects an inflexible frame of interpretation, offer another perspective into the experience of the political transformation and the country's unavoidable ties to the past.

The period that followed the death of Francisco Franco in 1975, known as the "Transición" [Transition], was defined by Spain's political and cultural transformation from an authoritarian regime to a democracy. All political parties were legalized, including the PCE (the Spanish Communist Party); the 1978 Constitution recognized the Comunidades Autónomas [autonomous communities] while laying out a new concept for *nacionalidades* [nationalities]; and Spanish workers were granted the right to unionize and strike.[10] The complexity of these phenomena, however, was later reflected in criticisms of their actual accomplishments.[11] The political reforms failed to address the divide between Spaniards and their expectations after the death of the Caudillo. This period was supposed to be the beginning of a new era of freedom and equality for the country—a departure from the antiquated Francoist cultural and political machinations to which it had been subjected since the end of the Spanish Civil War in 1939. At the same time, there was hope that the victors and losers of this historical conflict would resolve their differences, putting to rest divisive ideologies while collectively embracing democracy. However, the compromise reached after the death of the dictator by those who wished for a *reforma* [reform] within the old regime and those who demanded a clean *ruptura* [break] with it, proved incapable of fully resolving these issues.

According to Juan Luis Cebrián, the problem with this settlement was that the *Transición* meant leaving intact the fundamental structure of Francoist power through democratic legitimization, and abandoning the objective of transforming the country. Noted historians Raymond Carr and Juan Pablo Fusi view the criticism of this period as a result of unrealistic expectations that arose from Spaniards' inexperience with democratic practices,[12] although the scholars do recognize the continued hierarchical distribution of power in the democratic government of Spain. For Cebrián, the former director of *El País*, the biggest problem of the political transition was that "no se estaba procediendo a una reconciliación fundamental entre españoles, mediante el cambio cualitativo del tejido social, sino a una aminoración de tensiones que permitiera la reacomodación del viejo poder a las nuevas instancias y modas de la política" [there was no process toward a fundamental reconciliation between Spaniards, achievable through a qualitative change of the social fabric, only a reduction in tension that could allow the reaccommodation of the old power within a new political context and fashion].[13] The process of political transformation became one of continuation, in which the goal was to disguise the past and to adapt it to the present.[14]

The persistence of earlier practices (despite intentions to break with the past only within the *ruptura pactada* [compromised break]) begs the question: What cultural and social practices remain after nearly four decades of a culturally and socially manipulative authoritarian regime? Detecting the remains of the regime and pointing out its concrete traces—those that still exist or that have taken a very long time to disappear—are indispensable tasks. Fernando Jáuregui and Manuel Ángel Menéndez, in their aptly entitled study *Lo que nos queda de Franco* (1995) [What is Left of Franco], remind us that only in 1995 were coins with Franco's effigy finally taken out of circulation and the Instituto Nacional de Industria [National Institute of Industry] (INI), one of the last formal institutions of Francoism, closed down.[15] They contrast these disappearances to the permanence of Franco's statues in parks and small cities, and the numerous members of his government still working in Spanish politics and society. They depict a current landscape of Spain that retains many aspects of the past, suggesting that these concrete vestiges imply the existence of a Francoist substratum in the consciousness of Spaniards.[16] The authors themselves question the significance of the Radio Nacional de España's [Spanish National Radio] 1995 use of words like "victory" or "liberation" to commemorate 18 July 1936.[17] Is it intentional or simply carelessness? Is it an unconscious reflex that comes from more than three decades of routine?

Despite their skeptical regard for negative accounts of the political process of the *Transición,* Carr and Fusi agree that Spaniards' attitudes toward politics have clearly been influenced by more than three decades of an authoritarian rule.[18] The cultural primitivism that was enforced during the dictatorship (e.g., Tridentine Catholicism, Manichaeism, miracles and mysteries) to bolster the government's power and cultural control promoted conformity in generations of Spaniards.[19] Apathy, passivity, and the belief that politics is reserved for a minority group left in charge constitute much of the legacy of the Francoist regime. In fact, this "excesiva confianza de los españoles en un 'papá Estado'" [excessive trust in a "father State" on the part of Spaniards] described by Jáuregui and Menéndez carried over into the negotiated transition, consolidating institutional frameworks that had been established under the regime.[20] At the same time, this attitude fostered a political practice that avoids open discussion and lacks transparency, which can "impose serious limits on accountability."[21] And finally, in the current political context Spaniards' proclivity to accept political measures without contestation has produced what Cebrián calls a "fundamentalismo democrático" [democratic fundamentalism], which has converted democracy (and consensus) into the ideology practiced until recently by the governing conservative party Partido Popular.[22]

Even if it is possible to speak of a legacy of Francoism, its social and psychological substrata are harder to pin down. As the essays in this volume reveal, however, they are still present in post-Franco Spain the same way the concrete social and political vestiges mentioned by Jáuregui and Menéndez remain. Noël Valis, following Vilarós's reading of the period following the end of the dictatorship, identifies the death of Franco with a "loss of oppositionality."[23] The deep fissure in the social imagination is for this critic fundamental to understanding post-Franco society. While the cultural underground movement, or *la movida,* that followed the end of the dictatorship attracted the postmodern label, Valis proposes an alternative understanding for this movement, one that focuses on the "relentless insistence on the present as a refusal and inability to come to terms with the past" and which points to the process of rupture itself. For Valis, the hedonism, anarchy, aestheticism, and consumerism that marked the cultural revolt of the *movida* ultimately speak to the failure of resolving the past in the present.[24]

What Valis describes is the revelation of a complicated relation between the present and the unavoidable past, and the breakdown of a utopian vision of the future.[25] Taking into account this experience, she suggests viewing post-Franco Spain "as a displaced, ruptured narrative of identity diffusely structured through complexly ambivalent feelings," where invisible meta-narratives act simultaneously as forms of denial and acknowledgment.[26] The essays in this volume suggest that this sometimes repressed displacement becomes more noticeable in memories and experiences associated with Francoism, for their traditional domains under democracy have been transformed into non-places. While undoubtedly remaining in the social and political structures left behind by the dictatorship, experiences *of* the dictatorship have been historically or culturally alienated. Addressing the effects of this displacement, Valis warns about the difficulty of identifying the "dis-ease and rupture" of post-Franco Spain.[27] The inability to recognize the Francoist legacy might well account for this hardship, especially when accompanied (consciously or unconsciously) by a repression of the fear that the experience might recur. The break with the past, while masked by temporal and cultural strategies such as the *movida,* is exposed as a complex task which keeps insisting on its own unfinished nature, and its simultaneous (dis)continuity within the social collective of all Spaniards.

The purpose behind this volume is two-fold: first, to reveal the artificiality of the break with the past, that is, Franco's death, as a paradigmatic moment of change, a historical narrative of the end of Francoism; second, to understand the prior alliance of the authoritarian regime with fascist ideology and Falangism, and the latter's connections to the present. The essays here explore the enduring connections between past experience and contemporary Spanish society, while raising some questions about the challenges that Spaniards face when confronted with this historical legacy.[28] The essays move beyond traditional approaches to the topic of fascism in Spain and to the literary and cultural study of post-Franco Spain. Such approaches tend to isolate fascism as a historical phenomenon and its ideology as represented in particular texts, or a dialectic between victors and losers. Collectively, the work of our contributors reveals the various moments after the death of Franco when both right- and left-wing ideologues made discernible efforts to break with the country's fascist past. As each analysis demonstrates, an unambiguous intellectual divide between present and past and a rewriting of historical, cultural, and generational antecedent can only exist in the imagination.

According to the Real Academia Española, the term "contamination" refers not only to the polluting effects on a particular environment (when it becomes contagious, infectious, corrupted, or perverted) but also to the result of mixing discordant models. In the context of this volume, the term alludes to those integral elements of post-Franco Spanish narrative, in dissonance with one another, while appearing on the surface to be in accord. As noted earlier, the purpose of the book and its use of the term "contamination" is not to identify malignant and perverse manifestations of Falangist or Francoist ideology in contemporary culture, but rather, following David Carroll's study of French literary fascism, to explore the internal connection between the consecutive periods of extreme ideologies and programmatic democracy and how one survives into the other in varying degrees.[29] The purpose of revealing this dissonance is to reinforce our awareness of the complexity involved when making a historical or ideological assessment of the past from the present, while taking into account the ways in which one still affects the other. If there is a cautionary corollary to the approach offered here, it is that we should keep a critical eye on the democratic rhetoric of complacency.

The articles in this volume share as a premise the perseverance of Spain's right-wing past. In this sense they add to recent scholarship on contemporary Spanish culture that exposes the impossibility of suppressing the social memory of the dictatorship. At the same time, the collection departs from previous studies framed from the standpoint of the ideological Left and focuses on the Right's repressed experiences and memories in order to demonstrate the link between Francoism and the *Transición*—a link that continues to be relevant today. Some of the volume's essays analyze cultural artifacts that lend themselves as an ideal vehicle for the preservation or dissemination of the Francoist legacy; they detect certain attitudes that societies inherit from their past, causing them to fall back on old and condemned practices that become current through an updated rhetoric and a renewed target for attacks.[30] Several of our contributors shift their focus to the "ghostly traces" of this right-wing ideology.[31] In these studies, it becomes obvious that temporal distance transforms ideological militancy, relegating it to an inaccessible non-place while leaving behind only traces of its past tangibility. Because these residual functions are internalized and rewritten into reality, identifying them results in an examination of what already exists below the surface in various, context-dependent articulations. The latent nature of these specters recalls the previously mentioned (dis)continuities in the social collective of post-Franco Spain. Ironically, as Tacussel has observed, "only the transmission of the intransmissible seems [to] be an operation worthy of solidarity."[32] It is the prohibited nature of these traces that gives them their ghostly quality, so that they function undetected, unnoticed, and banned from normal communication by their own historical destiny.

From this perspective, the essays that constitute this volume become pieces of a puzzle in which the reader can follow the traces of Francoism in their concrete or ghostly instances into the present. These traces are found in the ideological residue of the past regime, specifically in the legacy of their cultural objects and rhetorical practices that have distanced themselves from past affiliations. This distance in part accounts for their currency in contemporary Spain. Yet the difficulty in approaching them either by expunging or exposing their historical past calls into question Spain's purported success in overcoming the experience of its recent dictatorship. This unrelenting past is also found in the trauma of those who experienced it, which is in turn passed on to generations that cannot precisely point to reasons for their affliction. The persistence of an ill-fated past creates a challenging problem for the authors of our essays, who attempt to articulate the reasons behind the complexity of the study of this legacy.

The essays in this collection do not represent an exhaustive or unique analytical perspective; they are instances of different approaches to the various traces located by our collaborators. Together, the essays analyze the manifestations of the Francoist and Falangist past that influence the present. Structured around three working themes that touch the many aspects of their experiences, from public to private, our collaborators examine the ways this past is still relevant in the field of contemporary Spanish literature, culture and politics. First, to identify the ideological residue of this past, there is a study of how this past is being recovered and recreated through nostalgic memory or anecdotal recreation, which in turn, fictionalizes history. Second, considering the legacy of the dictatorship as a distressing conditioner of the present, there is a focus on how the past haunts and produces victims, whose world view is mediated by his or her historical experience. Finally, there is an analysis of the traces of a past ideology that resists obliteration and resurfaces unexpectedly in discourses reenacting past rhetorical and social practices. The collection ends with a postscript that explores how literary legacies are necessarily bound by historical specificities, which in turn, determine their interpretation and preservation.

We start the volume with an essay that exposes the tension that exists between the Francoist past and the present democracy. Patrick Paul Garlinger analyzes the uses of the cultural icon of the Transition, Bibi Andersen, to illustrate the conflict between *ruptura* and *reforma* that took place during the country's democratization. He parallels this political debate with the public discussion surrounding Bibi's life as a transvestite and subsequently as a transsexual. Analyzing transvestism from the perspective of artifice and masquerade, his essay questions the political changes in post-Franco Spain in the context of the *movida* and its newfound freedom and apparent embrace of social, cultural, and sexual pluralities as they materialized in the collective obsession with Bibi. However, as Garlinger reflects, the misconceptions surrounding her sexual identity parallel the common misunderstandings of the political process that took place after the end of the dictatorship.

Having established the problematic nature of the political transition after the death of Franco, the first group of essays addresses the ambiguity of the regime's ideological residue—a passive yet active influence of the past—in several works. The activation of the ideological content of these texts would depend on their readership. Ricardo Krauel studies how Giménez Caballero's open affiliation with the fascist movement is reaffirmed in his autobiographical text published in 1979. The title of this book, *Memorias de un dictador,* suggests the memories are those of the Caudillo, but the reader quickly discovers the play on words. Krauel contends that by having been dispatched to distant diplomatic missions by Franco, Giménez Caballero is enabled, on the dictator's behalf, to redefine the controversial relationship between himself and the regime. Giménez Caballero's physical distance from Spain in the 1950s and 1960s allowed him in 1979 to act as a chronicler of the fascist movement in Spain. Using the memoir as a literary vehicle, Giménez Caballero recovers the history of the Falangist movement while re-examining its relation to the dictatorship; the end result is a revisionist picture of Spain. The process through which this project is carried out, however, becomes questionable since one must weigh between the literary quality of the memoir and the ideological purpose behind it. As Krauel himself concludes, the ambivalence of the text itself makes it difficult to discern its intended purposes. Left to the interpretation of the reader, the text allows for multiple readings that depend on the reader's approach to the texts as either literature or historical document.

In a similar vein, Dionisio Viscarri's essay tells us that the rewriting of the Falange's history is characteristic of a particular type of contemporary narrative. Analyzing the works of Falangist Fernando Vadillo, Viscarri demonstrates that, ironically, the loss of political currency reinvigorated Falangist aesthetic militancy in democratic Spain. He also shows how past and current ideologues of the Falange, taking advantage of the freedom of expression under the democratic government, have been publishing a significant number of memoirs, chronicles, and fictional works. Ranging from the testimonial to the nostalgic, these texts serve to revive the Falangist past by conferring popularity to its rhetoric, which, according to Viscarri, has trickled into the literary mainstream. The line between historical revision and ideological recruitment is blurred in these texts because, on the one hand, they recover the forgotten history of the Falangists who fought in World War II; but on the other, they rewrite this history in an attempt to cast it in a more favorable light, possibly winning popularity and sympathizers for their cause.

The rewriting of the fascist past is also the focus of Ana Gómez-Pérez's analysis of well-known Spanish author and intellectual, Gonzalo Torrente Ballester. Following the official demise of Franco's regime, this writer felt profoundly guilty about his political affiliations which, coupled with his subsequent social rejection, worked to create a personal literary theory that distanced his creative work from reality and any type of political ideology. Gómez-Pérez explains that the motive behind creating a self-contained form of literature that avoids any reference to reality was to keep his work separate from politics; for to do otherwise would have run the risk of bringing up his fascist past. Gómez-Pérez concludes that, paradoxically, Torrente Ballester's works only become fully comprehensible when taking into account and understanding his previous political affiliations. The impossibility of breaking free from the past is evident in this author who, by either anecdotal references or fiction, managed to create a new history for himself and a new context for his work.

Carmen Moreno-Nuño, Louise Ciallella, and Ulrich Winter explore the idea of the conditioned subject affected by the passive influence of the past. Their analyses reveal the lingering repression that affects the subject consciously or unconsciously and shapes irremediably his or her outlook of life. Moreno-Nuño's essay is structured around the memory of the Spanish Civil War and its destructive influence on those who were born after the event and who came to know about it through later references. Studying how these memories are often present through the experiences of close relatives or the collective echo that naturally endured in Spanish society during the first two decades of the regime, Moreno-Nuño suggests that this shared memory is individually channeled into a traumatic personal experience. Focusing on the novels of the popular contemporary writer Javier Marías, she isolates war as one of the leitmotifs in all of his writing. She notes that war is often metaphorically presented as a ghost or specter, which irrupts into Javier Marías's discourse, dictating its bearing and reach and victimizing his characters.

Louise Ciallella explores the subjugation of women as it relates to one of the cliché icons of Francoism: the image of the protecting father. This image, projected through the person of the dictator, is a metaphor that, like many other Falangist concepts, was borrowed from Italian fascism. Franco-as-father-figure was presented as benefactor of the new Spanish land born of the Civil War, and the traditional motherland became the dictator's daughter. Keeping in mind this Francoist formula, Ciallella investigates the aftermath of Franco's death in the imaginary equation of father-daughter that the regime created. Ciallella studies *El cuarto de atrás,* whose main character, C., nostalgically equates herself with the dictator's real daughter, Carmencita Franco. Ciallella detects a subtle mourning and pain caused by Franco's passing, suggesting that what is superficially rejected (Francoism) is at the same time desired; C. misses her Father. A victim of the dictatorship while it lasted, she is now once more traumatized by its loss.

What these essays detect in particular works and authors, Ulrich Winter discovers in the collective effect of Francoist repression. Articulating the tension between the Francoist past and the democratic present, Winter argues that many contemporary Spanish novels position themselves between historical reference and the aesthetization of history. He examines how their authors portray Francoism through polyphonic memory or through the conceded impossibility of representing the era altogether. Winter proceeds to analyze a mode of historical rewriting on the part of a generation of writers, including José María Guelbenzu, Juan José Millás, and Antonio Muñoz Molina. In their works the past appears unbidden and artificially implanted, splitting the subject (into self and double, a phantasmagoric other) while fragmenting memories of the past into a myriad of details. As Winter states in his conclusion, these works point to the existence of a subject whose identity is lost in his/her negotiations with the past—lost between a failed evasion from the past and a false hope in the future.

The persistence of certain ways of thinking about Franco's regime is discussed by Jacqueline Cruz, Eloy Merino, and H. Rosi Song.

These analyses reveal an active rehabilitation or reenactment of previous practices that betray the endurance of the past. Jacqueline Cruz, studying the work of one of the best selling Spanish contemporary writers, Antonio Muñoz Molina, asks why the ideological implications in this author's work are often ambiguous to his readers. In Cruz's view, this writer reflects the recent intensifying right-wing transformation of Spanish society (to which no intellectual was immune). She delineates in the novelist's work a rewriting of recent history that directly touches on the role the dictatorship and its opponents played. Centering her analysis on *Plenilunio* [Full Moon] (1997), Cruz demonstrates that in the democratic period political inertia, public indifference, skepticism, and tacit complicity eventually reproduce some of the worst traits of the totalitarian regime. Documenting Muñoz Molina's intellectual participation in Spanish political debate, Cruz discovers a new formulation of familiar conservative views hidden behind an apparently progressive rhetoric. She concludes that his novel implicitly cultivates and perpetuates a simplistic vision of fascism behind an explicit condemnation of Francoism.

The rehabilitation of fascist ideals and their concurrent political aspirations find a new venue of dissemination through modern technology. Eloy Merino offers a study of the nature, scope, and significance of a Falangist website, illustrating how FE de las JONS has adapted to the current national context and the European reality at the beginning of the twenty-first century. He identifies the original tenets of Falangism that persist in their current ideological discourse, and the ones articulated from the need to adjust Spain's reality. He offers a historical perspective on this party, exposing the limitations and deviations that have been imposed on Falange after the dictator's death. While the purported rehabilitation of Falangist political ideals is easy to identify in the case of FE de las JONS, there is another discursive stream in contemporary Falangist rhetoric that, under the disguise of modernization—the image of an "open" and "progressive" Falange—still manages to circulate the same historical blinders. Merino explores how these ideas might remain hidden for a Spanish electorate because of the way they are reformulated in the present.

H. Rosi Song focuses on the criticism of a widely published and popular journalist known for his antagonistic view of Spanish politics: Jiménez Losantos. She looks at how this political columnist, in his criticism of the socialist government and denunciation of the trend toward regional self-determination, creates a moralizing message of the doomed identity and future of the Spanish nation. As a preventive measure, he embarks on a literary project to rescue the "idea" of Spain to assure its survival in the future. Song reveals that this rewriting of history echoes attitudes toward the concept of nation and culture that are clear remnants of past rhetorical (and ideological) practices.

As a way of tying together some of the recurrent themes in the collection, we offer a narrative essay by Jordi Gracia as a postscript. Gracia revisits the recent but timid effort in Spain to reintroduce to the public the works of several fascist authors who had been forgotten during the last years of the dictatorship and the advent of democracy. He offers a panoramic vision of this effort, initiated by academics and publishing houses, with limited success despite the interest of younger writers who wish to reevaluate the literary legacy of Franco's regime objectively, aided by a historical and political distance. Confronted with a literature that was committed politically to the regime, Gracia asks why these works are not being evaluated. He wonders whether their failure has to do with their intrinsic literary value or if it is because Spanish society is not sufficiently comfortable with its democratic experience to approach them. He hints that the answer might be a combination of both poor literary quality and an enduring fear of the past, and suggests that we have to wait for Spain's democracy to reach maturity before we can take a closer look at this literary past.

In an essay written around 1980, the philosopher Julián Marías wonders what scholars in the year 2000 might focus on when looking into what happened in Spain between 1976 and 1979. He predicts that the incredible changes that took place during the scarce forty months following the death of dictator Francisco Franco, might first generate a state of disbelief or scepticism. Then, confronted with all the existing criticism surrounding these changes, a state of incredulity in the form of a burning question: *How was all this possible?*[33] At the end, Marías endorses an inquiry into the study of post-Franco Spain. Focusing on a particular aspect of the experience of the dictatorship, the essays in the volume follow his recommendation examining the traceable remnants of Francoism and Falangism in the country's democratic present. They explore ways in which the past can be freed from earlier interpretations that tended either simply to categorize a specific brand of aesthetics and thematic recurrences, or to disdain past culture as a whole. By focusing on the residual legacy of the country's authoritarian past, the essays in this book read anew Spain's modern history and culture in an effort to recognize how the present still negotiates, consciously or not, with the traumas, cultural practices, and mind-shaping ideologies of the past. In the end, the volume reveals the continuities and discontinuities between historical periods, offering a new perspective for understanding the country's experience, not as one finished and limited to the past, but ongoing and still relevant to contemporary Spain.

Notes

1. Teresa Vilarós, *El mono del desencanto. Una crítica cultural de la transición española (1973–1993)* (Madrid: Siglo XXI, 1998), 8.

2. Paloma Aguilar, "Justice, Politics, and Memory in the Spanish Transition," in *The Politics of Memory*, eds. C. González-Enríquez, Paloma Aguilar, and Barahona de Brito (Oxford: Oxford University Press, 2001), 92.

3. Ibid., 93.

4. Salvador Cardús i Ros, "Politics and the Invention of Memory. For a Sociology of the Transition to Democracy in Spain," in *Disremembering the Dictatorship. The Politics of Memory in the Spanish Transition to Democracy*, ed. Joan Ramon Resina (Amsterdam and Atlanta: Rodopi, 2000), 19.

5. Joan Ramon Resina, "Short of Memory: The Reclamation of the Past Since the Spanish Transition to Democracy," in *Disremembering the Dictatorship*, 90.

6. The projection of a coherent historical narrative of the *Transición* is challenged by Teresa Vilarós in *El mono del desencanto* (6). She criticizes the artificial break with the past offered by the account in which Franco's death is a final point and the start of new era for Spain. In the same vein, two recently published collections of essays about modern Spain and its transition to democracy shift their attention to what is not there, that is, to the vacuum created by what has been forgotten, ignored or silenced in the process of its formulation. What both Resina, op. cit., and Jo Labanyi (*Constructing Identity in Contemporary Spain. Theoretical Debates and Cultural Practice* [Oxford: Oxford University Press, 2002]) lay out is a re-examination of the legacy of the narratives brought forth, on the one hand, during modernity's continued project of nation-building (as suggested by Labanyi), and on the other, the political construct surrounding Spain's transition from dictatorship to democracy (as underscored by Resina). These two volumes stress the importance of recovering the absent experiences of the country's past to critically examine the present.

7. Vilarós, 20.

8. Although Mechthild Albert addresses this question in her edited volume *Vencer no es convencer* [Winning is not Convincing] (Frankfurt: Vervuert, 1998), it shares the historical perspective of the other works that study the relationship between literature and culture and fascism, Falangism and Francoism, in Spain. The other previously published works are José-Carlos Mainer's *Falange y literatura* [Falange and Literature] (1971); Julio Rodríguez-Puértolas's *Literatura fascista española* [Spanish Fascist Literature], vols. 1 (1986) and 2 (1987); and Ángel Llorente's *Arte e ideología en el franquismo* [Art and Ideology in Francoism] (1995). Unlike these works, which offer a historical study of fascism and its influence on literature, our volume addresses the legacy of this experience in the present.

9. The history of fascism in Spain is in itself very complicated. Fascism in Spain, embodied in the Falangist movement *Falange Española* (FE) was articulated in the early 1930s under the leadership of José Antonio Primo de Rivera, who was inspired mainly by Mussolini's party, as well as by the Nazis. However, his early disappearance at the beginning of the Spanish Civil War meant the later transformation of the party into a political tool of Franco who seized its control on the defeat of the Axis powers as an opportunity to *defascistize* his regime, reiterating Spain's neutral stance dur-

ing the conflict. Moreover, to ensure his power he declared that FE had not been a political party in Spain, only an administrative tool for the obtainment of national cohesion and unification. The historian Stanley Payne has the standard account of the history of fascism in Spain in his book *Falange. A History of Spanish Fascism* ([Stanford: Stanford University Press, 1961] and its updated version, *Fascism in Spain, 1923–1977*, from 1999). Another complete study is *Historia de Falange Española de la JONS* [History of Spain's Falange and the JONS] (Madrid: Alianza, 2000) by José Luis Jiménez Rodríguez. Ultimately, the conflictive relationship between Franco and FE had the side effect of partially purging Spain of its fascist identity and traits. One of its most direct consequences is that specialists like Payne regard fascism in Spain as a historical phenomenon and a particularization of Spanish experience within the context of the country's past, labeled as "Falangism" and "Francoism." These terms are generally used instead of "fascism" when referring to the period between 1939 and 1975 in Spain, which distances the country from the other European nations with fascist antecedents in the first half of the 20th century.

10. For a detailed and concise narration of the political changes that took place during this period, see Ramón Arango's *Spain. Democracy Regained* (Boulder, CO: Westview Press, 1995).

11. See for example the writings of Juan Luis Cebrián ("La experiencia del período constituyente" [The Experience of Writing the Constitution]) in *España 1975–1980: Conflictos y logros de la democracia*, eds. John Crispin, Enrique Pupo-Walker, and José L. Cagigao [Madrid: José Porrúa Turanzas, S.A., 1982] and, with Felipe González (*El futuro no es lo que era. Una conversación* [The Future Is Not What It Was. A Conversation] [Madrid: Taurus, 2001]); Fernando Jáuregui and Manuel Ángel Menéndez (*Lo que nos queda de Franco. Símbolos, personajes, leyes y costumbres, veinte años después* [What's Left of Franco among Us. Symbols, People, Laws, and Customs After Twenty Years] [Madrid: Temas de hoy, 1995]); Salvador Cardús ("Politics and the Invention of Memory, op. cit.); Joan Ramon Resina ("Short of Memory: The Reclamation of the Past since the Spanish Transition to Democracy," in Resina, op. cit.) and Aguilar, op. cit., among others.

12. Raymond Carr, "El legado franquista," in *España 1975–1980: Conflictos y logros de la democracia*, 134; 172–173.

13. Cebrián, "La experiencia," 15.

14. Ibid., 18.

15. Jáuregui and Menéndez, 17–18.

16. Ibid., 18–20.

17. Ibid., 47. The date of the military uprising against the Republican government that marks the start of the Spanish Civil War.

18. Carr, 135; Juan Pablo Fusi, "España: el fin del siglo XX" [Spain: At the End of the 20th Century] in *Visiones de fin de siglo* [Visions at the End of the Century], ed. Raymond Carr (Madrid: Taurus), 172.

19. Helen Graham and Jo Labanyi, *Spanish Cultural Studies. An Introduction* (New York and Oxford: Oxford University Press, 1995), 170.

20. Jáuregui and Menéndez, 52.

21. Aguilar, 118.

22. Cebrián and González, 14. The Partido Popular lost the general elections of 14 March 2004, even though polls taken close to the election date showed them being favored to win. After the terrorist bombing of the trains in Madrid on 11 March 2004, the government of José María Aznar tried to blame the attack on ETA. Despite evidence that linked the bombings to Islamic terrorist groups, the government, in its investigation and communications to the press, continued to focus on the Basque

terrorist group. When this manipulation of information became known to the public, an unexpectedly large number of Spaniards showed up to the polls and voted against the conservative party. The socialist party PSOE and its leader, José Luis Rodríguez Zapatero, emerged as the winner of the election.

23. Noël Valis, *The Culture of Cursilería. Bad Taste, Kitsch, and Class in Modern Spain* (Durham and London: Duke University Press, 2002), 282.

24. Ibid., 282–283.

25. By evoking the phenomenon of the *movida,* which ended around 1986, we are not suggesting a discussion of the lasting effects of its suspected excesses in the continuing decades. We refer to this cultural experience as an example of Spain's inability to address the past and how the difficulty of this task still resonates within its society.

26. Valis, 285.

27. Ibid., 286.

28. The works that deal with the literature of fascist and Francoist Spain have been, at most, scarce and sporadic. Jordi Gracia revisits the existing studies on the topic in the postscript for this volume.

29. David Carroll, *French Literary Fascism. Nationalism, Anti-Semitism, and the Ideology of Culture* (Princeton: Princeton University Press, 1995), 7.

30. Richard Golsan's *Fascism's Return: Scandal, Revision, and Ideology Since 1980* (Lincoln: University of Nebraska Press, 1998) is a good collection of detailed studies of this tendency, especially as manifests itself in Western Europe. Although presently the extreme Right does seem to have a negligible strength in Spain, with the recent political invigoration of the nationalist parties in France and Italy, this scenario could change. Although none of the essays contained in Golsan's book deals directly with the situation in Spain, the description of the interests that unite these radical parties also fits the country's current problems. Some of the essays in this volume lay out the ideas and attitudes that could serve to energize these political movements, especially as they find the appropriate channeling for their interests. For example, it is interesting that Peter Davies writes that the National Front in France "has involved itself in both high-brow and low-brow publicity offensives. For the educated and literary, there is now a lecture series, a pseudo-academic review, *Identité,* and a publishing house, *Editions nationales,* committed to 'cultural combat through literature'" (Davies, 6). These efforts can also be found in lesser degree in Spain, as exemplified in Dionisio Viscarri's essay contained in this book.

31. We borrow from Labanyi's use of Derrida's historical-materialist reading of ghosts (Labanyi, 1).

32. Patrick Tacussel, "The Laws of the Unspoken: Silence and Secrecy," *Diogenes* 144 (1998): 30.

33. Julián Marías, *Cinco años de España* (Madrid: Espasa-Calpe, 1982), 138.

BIBLIOGRAPHY

Aguilar, Paloma. "Justice, Politics, and Memory in the Spanish Transition." In *The Politics of Memory. Transitional Justice in Democratizing Societies.* Edited by C. González-Enríquez, Paloma Aguilar and Barahona de Brito. Oxford: Oxford University Press, 2001.

Albert, Mechthild, ed. *Vencer no es convencer. Literatura e ideología del fascismo español.* Frankfurt: Vervuert, 1998.

Arango, E. Ramón. *Spain. Democracy Regained.* Boulder, CO: Westview Press, 1995.

Cardús i Ros, Salvador. "Politics and the Invention of Memory. For a Sociology of the Transition to Democracy in Spain." In *Disremembering the Dictatorship. The Politics of Memory in the Spanish Transition to Democracy.* Edited by Joan Ramon Resina. Amsterdam and Atlanta: Rodopi, 2000.

Carr, Raymond. "El legado franquista." In *España 1975–1980: Conflictos y logros de la democracia.* Edited by John Crispin, Enrique Pupo-Walker, and José L. Cagigao. Madrid: José Porrúa Turanzas, S.A., 1982.

Carroll, David. *French Literary Fascism. Nationalism, Anti-Semitism, and the Ideology of Culture.* Princeton: Princeton University Press, 1995.

Cebrián, Juan Luis. "La experiencia del período constituyente." In John Crispin, Enrique Pupo-Walker, and José L. Cagigao, op. cit.

Cebrián, Juan Luis and Felipe González. *El futuro no es lo que era. Una conversación.* Madrid: Taurus, 2001.

Davies, Peter. *The National Front in France. Ideology, Discourse and Power.* New York: Routledge, 1999.

Fusi, Juan Pablo. "España: el fin del siglo XX." In *Visiones de fin de siglo.* Edited by Raymond Carr. Madrid: Taurus, 1999.

Golsan, Richard J. *Fascism's Return: Scandal, Revision & Ideology since 1980.* Lincoln: University of Nebraska Press, 1998.

Graham, Helen and Jo Labanyi, eds. *Spanish Cultural Studies. An Introduction.* New York and Oxford: Oxford University Press, 1995.

Jáuregui, Fernando and Manuel Ángel Menéndez. *Lo que nos queda de Franco. Símbolos, personajes, leyes y costumbres, veinte años después.* Madrid: Temas de hoy, 1995.

Jiménez Rodríguez, José Luis. *Historia de Falange Española de la JONS.* Madrid: Alianza, 2000.

Labanyi, Jo, ed. *Constructing Identity in Contemporary Spain. Theoretical Debates and Cultural Practice.* Oxford: Oxford University Press, 2002.

Marías, Julián. *Cinco años de España.* Madrid: Espasa-Calpe, 1982.

Payne, Stanley G. *Falange.* Stanford: Stanford University Press, 1961.

———. *Fascism in Spain, 1923–1977.* Madison: University of Wisconsin Press, 1999.

Resina, Joan Ramon. "Short of Memory: The Reclamation of the Past Since the Spanish Transition to Democracy." In Joan Ramon Resina, op. cit., 83–125.

Tacussel, Patrick. "The Laws of the Unspoken: Silence and Secrecy." *Diogenes* 144 (1988): 16–31.

Valis, Noël. *The Culture of Cursilería. Bad Taste, Kitsch, and Class in Modern Spain.* Durham and London: Duke University Press, 2002.

Vilarós, Teresa. *El mono del desencanto. Una crítica cultural de la transición española (1973–1993).* Madrid: Siglo XXI, 1998.

Sex Changes and Political Transitions;
Or, What Bibi Andersen Can Tell Us
about Democracy in Spain

Patrick Paul Garlinger

CHIC, SEXY, AND STATUESQUE, BIBI ANDERSEN IS A HOUSEHOLD NAME in Spain. She became an iconic film star and "chica Almodóvar" [Almodóvar girl] in the 1980s and even reached prime-time television as the host of "Sábado Noche" [Saturday Night], a short-lived but successful night-time television show. Outside of Spain, the name "Bibi Andersen" is most likely to evoke the face of the Swedish star of Ingmar Bergman films, "Bibi Andersson." Andersen borrowed the movie star's name from a list given to her at the *Starlett* cabaret, not knowing the name was misspelled. The provenance of her name is significant as it marks the beginning of Bibi's career as a cabaret performer, and later, a post-operative transsexual. The press coverage has by turns celebrated and exploited her legendary status. Her bodily transformations are so highly publicized that her sex reassignment surgery was national news in 1993. Interviews in the Spanish newspaper *El País* and counterculture magazine *La Luna* [The Moon] have attempted to provide some insight into Bibi's background and professional aspirations, while other tabloids such as *Interviú* [Interview] magazine have focused almost exclusively on her corporeal changes. In 1994 *Interviú* published an interview with Andersen and Pedro Almodóvar along with a long-awaited nude spread of thirteen pictures that provided visual confirmation of her sex change. Her civil marriage ceremony in 2000 was covered by *Hola* [Hello] magazine, complete with enthusiastic proclamations from guests who testified that Bibi was a beautiful bride.

Andersen's public image is indelibly tied to the concept of transition—both physiological and political. Her ascent to fame began shortly after the death of the dictator with the publication of *El sexo del franquismo* [The Sex of Francoism] in 1977, a study of the sexual conditions under the Franco regime by Óscar Caballero. In a chapter on transvestism, Caballero describes Andersen (written "Anderson") as a twenty-two year old from Málaga with a sensational body. At this point in her life, Bibi performed nightly in the Barcelona cabaret *Starlett* in which her erotic strip-tease ended with the explosive exposure of her penis to the audience's delight. As if that were not sufficient proof that Bibi was "packing," Caballero cannot resist reminding the reader that Bibi is after all a *caballero* [gentleman] herself; he writes that she refuses to get a sex-change operation because she's young and lives well performing in cabarets.[1] From 1977 to 1993, however, Bibi underwent the necessary operations and hormone regimens to make the "transition" to womanhood, corroborated by the layout in *Interviú*. Her role in Almodóvar's 1993 movie *Kika,* in which she appears completely nude on the balcony of a penthouse apartment, made it clear to the Spanish viewing audience that her days of panty-dropping cabaret performances with phallic finales were, in fact, finally over. Bibi's name ironically reflects this shifting corporeal status. Earlier documents tend to write her name with an accent mark. Later, the diacritical mark is erased, as if the very writing of her name were indicative of her corporeal changes. The irony of her name does not end there, however, as Andersen's birth name is Manuel Fernández Chica (*chica* means "girl" in Spanish).

John Hooper has argued that Bibi's fame is "evidence that the Spanish feel a need for some sort of antidote to the rigid gender stereotyping which is still so much a part of their culture."[2] As an antidote, she is far more than just a beautiful body for the obsessive Spanish press. Like Esther Newton's claim in *Mother Camp* that drag queens "say a great deal about America,"[3] transgenderism has become symbolic of national political changes in Spain after the death of Francisco Franco in 1975. In José Luis Gallero's 1990 oral account of "la movida," *Sólo se vive una vez* [You Only Live Once], Pablo Pérez Mínguez said that any book about the period would have to have Bibi Andersen's vagina on the cover.[4] In fact, she has commented on the intellectual interest in her transsexuality: "La gente que escribe tiende mucho a teorizar sobre mí, a considerarme un fenómeno que hay que explicar, sobre el cual elucubrar y trasladar sus propias obsesiones" [People who write tend to theorize a lot about me, treating me like a phenomenon that needs to be explained, to be pondered and on which they project their own obsessions].[5] Indeed, Andersen's transgendered body has come to stand as a material emblem of Spain's own transition to democracy and postmodernity. In his 1996 *Los cuerpos gloriosos* [Glorious Bodies], for example, Francisco Umbral described Andersen's transformation as symbolic of political changes in Spain by calling her "la asignatura pendiente de la democracia" [the unresolved matter of the democracy].[6] Presented as the last step in a political movement from fascism to democracy, Bibi's technologically altered and spectacularized body bears the burden, at least for some writers, of embodying the political and social changes that have occurred since the demise of the Franco regime.

What does a symbolic use of transgenderism tell us about democratic Spain? The rhetorical use of transgenderism and the symbolic value of Andersen in particular may be less indicative of an obsession with her and her bodily transformations, as she puts it, than they are a manifestation of broader discursive tendencies that continually resurface in discussions of contemporary politics and culture in Spain. Although the use of transgenderism as a rhetorical trope might indicate an increasing acceptance of transgenderism in Spain, it tends to reiterate a discourse of masquerade and inauthenticity that perceives transgendered people as artificial or, conversely, portrays a celebratory mode of transsexualism as the epitome of postmodern ambiguity, failing at the same time to attend to the real-life legal and economic difficulties that afflict many transsexuals. In fact, the discourse of transgenderism depends upon incoherent and incompatible definitions of transvestism and transsexuality, often used indiscriminately. The confusion and misunderstandings about transvestism and transsexuality are significant in and of themselves. But additionally, the recourse to Bibi Andersen and to transgenderism in general is symptomatic of the continuing presence of a binary mode of conceptualizing the Spanish national panorama in terms of *las dos Españas* [the two Spains]. This perpetual conflict between "two Spains" can be perceived in recent critical assessments of the state of the Spanish democracy that view the corruption of the Socialist Party and the 1996 victory of the right-wing Popular Party as signs of a lingering Francoism.

BIBI ANDERSEN AND THE "TWO SPAINS"

The symbolic value of Andersen's transsexual body is the logical extension of a discourse of transvestism that has surfaced as a means of conceptualizing the transition to democracy. In Spain, the fall of the dictatorship brought with it the hope of a radical rupture with the Francoist structure. Nevertheless, the struggle between the Left and the Right during the early years of the transition to democracy—a tug of war between *ruptura* and *reforma*, between a clean break and reformation—forced both the Right and the Left to assume a politics of consensus. Rather than force a clean break with the Francoist structures still in place, the Left and the Right engaged in a *ruptura pactada,* or negotiated break, in which both sides shared power and responsibility for overturning the Francoist policies, as a way to ameliorate the differences between them and to secure their place in the fledgling democracy. Although many politicians from the Franco period were still involved, a rhetoric of "a new beginning" circulated as a means to promote the alliance between Left and Right. At times, it appeared that radical change would take place, at others, superficial reforms seemed to carry the day. In 1996 the Socialist government lost the national elections to the right-wing party, the Popular Party, as a result of a series of scandals that came to light (in particular, a government-sponsored anti-terrorist group to eliminate Basque terrorists). Addressing these scandals, Umbral referred to Felipe González as a "political transvestite."[7] Transvestism functions rhetorically as an artifice or masquerade, a reflection of the surface changes in the national body that are little more than a travesty. In other instances, a rhetorical use of transsexuality indicates a celebratory escape from the past, a sign of authentic and profound cultural and political transformation. For example, in an analysis of Antonio Giménez Rico's 1983 documentary of transgendered subjects in Madrid, *Vestida de azul* [Dressed in Blue], Marsha Kinder proposes that transgenderism has become the new cultural stereotype, replacing the Andalusian images of flamenco dancers that once emblematized Spain for the rest of the world: "The film's structure encourages us [to] read these six portraits as part of a national discourse on Spain's 'cultural transformation' from fascism to democracy;"[8] she reiterates this argument by similarly describing the effect of Almodóvar's movies as "perform[ing] a sex change on Spain's national stereotype."[9]

Among cinematic portrayals of transsexualism, Vicente Aranda's 1977 *Cambio de sexo* [Sex Change] is a salient example of the use of transsexualism to reflect social change. Not incidentally, it is also Bibi Andersen's first movie, in an autobiographical role. *Cambio de sexo* dramatizes the development of the *destape* [taking the lid off]—the period in the late 1970s and early 1980s characterized by a much more open portrayal of sex in the press, literature, and film. The film recounts the story of José María, a young effeminate boy played by Victoria Abril, who lives in the outskirts of Barcelona and escapes to the city in order to explore his desire to cross-dress. His father, seeing him as a young homosexual, strives to make him into a man by taking him to a night club. There, among the various performers, is Bibi Andersen, who plays herself and ends her performance by revealing her penis. Dubbed an "enigma," her final revelation only enhances the young José María's desire to cross-dress. The film ends when José María falls in love with the night club owner, and (s)he goes to Morocco for her sex reassignment surgery.

Kinder offers an insightful interpretation of the film's portrayal of transsexuality as symbolic of the political transformations of late twentieth-century Spain. She situates *Cambio de sexo* within the broader context of post-Franco cinema, since the film is followed by another filmic rendition of transvestism: Ventura Pons's 1978 documentary *Ocaña, retrat intermitent* [Ocaña: Intermittent Portrait] recounts the performances of the Catalan transvestite in the public space of *Las Ramblas* in Barcelona. In her analysis, Kinder perceives an underlying wariness of Spain's newfound freedom in the film's reserved eroticism. Aranda's portrayal of transsexuality is a sign of increasing sexual liberty marked by reservation and discretion: *Cambio de sexo* hints that political change may have been more superficial than real. Kinder argues that the film foreshadows more ambivalent representations from the 1980s "which all show how the legacy of Francoist repression is still internalized within a supposedly hyperliberated Spain."[10] There is a danger here of reinstalling a dialectic between opposing poles of authentic change and deceitful masquerade by arguing that the movie suggests that beneath the surface of an ostensibly liberated Spain lies the former Francoist repression. At the outset, Kinder avoids this pitfall by viewing the transsexual performance as inherently rife with contradiction and instability. The complexity of transsexuality makes it a rather ambiguous symbol of the changes in social and sexual attitudes in Spain. Nevertheless, this nuanced approach to the film's portrayal of transsexuality gives way to an increasingly sharp distinction between two opposed Spains: "It is this intensity that enables [Victoria Abril] to embody the proverbial two Spains with their opposing extremes of uncompromising orthodoxy and unrestrained anarchy."[11]

The rhetoric of "the two Spains" in Kinder's analysis is significant for it points to the ways in which transgenderism surfaces as a binary means of conceptualizing social and political transformation. In many respects, the emergence of the term "transgenderism" in critical discourses has responded to the need to overcome the simplistic modes of conceptualizing transvestism and transsexuality. For many, transvestism would seem to be more superficial precisely because it does not entail the more intricate process of surgery. By contrast, then, transsexuality entails an anatomical change involving radical surgery, hormone treatments, and name changes—a host of alterations that may appear far more profound physiologically than the sartorial changes involved in transvestism. The conception of transsexuality as a more profound, permanent mode of transvestism posits transvestism and transsexuality as a continuum from clothing to the flesh itself, in which transsexuality is an extension of transvestism. Yet many transvestites neither are nor plan to become transsexuals, whereas many transsexuals begin their transitions by cross-dressing, as did Bibi Andersen. Transgender discourses call attention to this complexity and refuse to divide transvestism and transsexuality in a reductive, binary fashion. Transvestism is not reducible to a superficial, willful performance that privileges the body as the underlying true identity nor is transsexuality simply a more profound psychic identification that views the body as nothing more than a corporeal mistake that surgery can correct.

The meaning of "transgenderism" decidedly complicates the significance that may be adjudicated to Andersen's transgendered body as a trope for conceptualizing the political and social changes of Spain's body politic. In his characteristically direct style, for example, Francisco Umbral foregrounds the desire that Andersen's sex reassignment surgery has produced in him: "Yo lo que quiero es tirarme a Bibí Andersen, ahora que es hembra total, completa, ahora que tiene una vagina, ahora que gusta del hombre/hombre, ahora que el unicornio ha perdido el cuerno y la mujer ha ganado el derecho a ser follada" [what I want is to screw Bibí Andersen, now that she is a total woman, complete, now that she has a vagina, now that she takes pleasure from real men, now that the unicorn has lost its horn and the woman has earned the right to be fucked].[12] Bibi is now a complete woman, a woman whose erotic potential can be fulfilled by Umbral himself. The image of the unicorn—that mythic creature whose most visible difference is the long phallic-shaped horn protruding from its forehead—is remarkable for its transparency, but what is more important here is how Umbral proceeds to allegorize Bibi in relation to Spanish democracy calling her "la asignatura pendiente de la democracia."[13] Umbral's open declaration of erotic interest in Bibi evinces a conceptualization of transgenderism as a profound change, one that marks a complete break from the past. As such, does Bibi Andersen's sex change signify the complete transition to democracy? Based on this paradigm the transition would be conceptualized through the figure of a cabaret drag queen whose ambiguous gender play is suddenly stopped—severed, as it were—by taking that final step and undergoing sex reassignment surgery. And if this is so, how are we to understand the modern Spanish state as somehow transsexual? Does the now surgically removed penis stand as an emblem of the lost but not entirely forgotten Franco regime? Is Spain a "transgender nation"?

THE POSTMODERN FANTASY OF TRANSGENDERISM

The use of transgenderism, and of Bibi Andersen in particular, as symbolic of a national transition from dictatorship to democracy reiterates a rhetorical framework in which the nation is gendered female. Moreover, there is a striking resemblance between transsexual narratives and national narratives that depend upon the mythic construction of an authentic point of origin. At the turn of the century, writers of the Generation of 1898 and the "regenerationists" sought to overcome the ills plaguing the nation: the loss of the empire, the perception of *atraso* or backwardness in comparison with the rest of Europe, and the general state of political upheaval all contributed to the belief that Spain as a nation was a "problem." Read from a transgender perspective, Joaquín Costa's 1901 call for "an iron surgeon" to engage in "a true politics of surgery" takes on the trappings of a transsexual narrative.[14] This narrative alignment between individual and national bodies can be perceived as well in how Jay Prosser's account of altering his corporeal sex from female to male draws on a rhetoric of transition that is reminiscent of political transitions: "I was going through some kind of significant transition."[15] Indeed, the discourse of regeneration prevalent at the turn of the century in Spain is strikingly similar to the medicalized discourses of transsexuality: a body whose "ills" can be corrected with the aid of a surgeon's knife and modern technology.

Umbral's writings on Bibi Andersen not only underscore the metaphorical connection between her bodily changes and the nation, but they also laud her transgendered status as symbolic of the arrival of postmodernity in Spain. Indeed, one of the principal uses of the rhetoric of transgenderism has been to lay claim to Spain's entrance into postmodernity, in which "post-Franco" and "postmodern" are coeval historical periods. Kathleen Vernon and Barbara Morris discuss the transition and rise of youth culture as "cultural transvestism," which they note is later conflated with postmodernism by foreign journalists.[16] Jo Labanyi extols Ventura Pons's aforementioned documentary as the "ultimate postmodernist product,"[17] and David Garland describes *Vestida de azul* as the "epitome of postmodern sexuality: transsexualism."[18] Both critics align the radical ambiguity and self-conscious constructedness of gender with the significant political and social changes taking place in Spain during the years following Franco's death. In theoretical discussions, the same association between transgenderism and postmodernism is rehearsed time and again in such pithy statements as "What is more *postmodern* than transsexualism?"[19]

Yet it is Umbral, once again, who makes the most daring assertion about transsexualism and Andersen. In an interview with Andersen in 1984, Umbral went so far as to write: "Bibi es la posmodernidad unisexual que, con un poco más de imaginación y de libros, andaría hoy de musa de todas las postmodernidades horteras (sexos variados)" [Bibi is the unisex postmodernity who, with a little more imagination and study, would be today the muse of all the vulgar postmodernities (various sexes)].[20] Ambivalent words, to be sure, as Umbral both exalts Andersen as the muse of postmodernity, at the same time as he appears to criticize various strands of postmodernity for being "vulgar." Moreover, the link between postmodernity and Bibi Andersen ought to be understood within the larger context of the cultural phenomenon of *la movida madrileña* that emerged in the early years of the transition to democracy. The international media's sudden attention to Madrid as the new European cultural capital established the link between the explosion of fashion, art, and music with discourses of postmodernity. Gianni Vattimo in turn baptized Spain as the quintessential postmodern society when he wrote: "[L]a España de hoy es sin duda uno de los modelos de sociedad *posmoderna,* donde el carácter social parece brindarse también como *chance* de emancipación" [The Spain of today is without a doubt one of the models of *postmodern* society, whose social nature appears to afford the opportunity for emancipation].[21] While not everyone has agreed with Vattimo's valorization, there is little doubt *la movida madrileña* was intimately connected with the discourse of postmodernism from the outset. Many of the participants of the period referred to themselves as "moderns" (not necessarily distinguishing between modernity and postmodernity), and Spanish intellectuals viewed their exploration of sex, drugs, and "frivolous" night life as a postmodern rejection of politics. As Gallero writes: "Con el tiempo, esa actividad quedaría englobada bajo el epígrafe de *movida madrileña,* identificando un fenómeno tan ambiguo e impreciso como su nombre sugiere, pero que de la noche a la mañana convirtió a una ciudad agotada en emblema máximo de la modernidad" [with time, that activity would become included under the epigraph of *movida madrileña,* identifying a phenomenon as ambiguous and imprecise as its name suggests, but which overnight would convert a wasted city into the greatest emblem of modernity].[22] Hence, Carlos Ferrando asked Andersen in an interview from 1986 in the magazine associated with *la movida, La Luna:* "¿Cómo descubres la modernidad y te conviertes en una de sus musas?" [How is it that you discovered modernity and became one of its muses?].[23]

As a muse of (post)modernity, Andersen would appear to embody the new spirit of Spain's sexual freedom and multiplicity. Unfortunately, the association of transgenderism with postmodernity leaves out the political and juridical impediments that many transsexuals face. It was not until 1983 that reforms of the Penal Code decriminalized transsexual surgery, and the first transgender organization, *Transexualia,* was not formed until 1987.[24] In Alfonso Villagómez Rodil's *Aportación al estudio de la transexualidad* [Contribution to the Study of Transsexuality], he delineates the juridical decisions surrounding legal appeals to have transsexuals change their names legally in the civil register. The watershed case took place on 2 July 1987, when the Spanish Supreme Court overturned a lower court's ruling that the transsexual did not meet legal criteria for being considered a woman. In general, legal debates on transsexualism focus on the criteria for deciding between registering someone as a man or a woman and on the necessary limitations that must be imposed if a transsexual (in all of these cases, male-to-female) is allowed to register as a woman. In nearly all of the cases that Villagómez Rodil discusses, the tenth article of the Spanish Constitution is cited: the freedom of the individual to develop his or her personality without constraint (except in the cases where this would do harm to others). Yet Villagómez Rodil notes that there is a considerable lack of legislation on transsexualism that would answer questions about marriage and child-raising. At the time of his publication, transsexuals were not granted all of the rights of the sex for which they were legally registered. In other words, although a male-to-female transsexual was registered as a woman and her identification card listed her as female, she could not marry a man. The final case that Villagómez Rodil includes, from 4 April 1991, declared that marriages involving transsexuals would be considered null and void.

In recent years the legal situation has improved. Bibi Andersen's civil marriage is one of the few transsexual weddings to date that have legal backing. It is now the case in Spain that some transsexuals who have successfully completed a sex change, along with the legal change of name and sex in civil registers, may marry a member of the opposite sex.[25] Nevertheless, those transsexuals who are unable to complete a sex change—for financial or health reasons—are still denied such a possibility (the PSOE has repeatedly put forth proposals to grant such rights to transsexuals who have not undergone a sex-change operation).

The legal situation for transsexuals in Spain is, to say the least, hardly indicative of postmodern fluidity. Moreover, the determination of sex for legal purposes has yet to include intersexuality, and thus a binary model continues to operate. Indeed, the difficulty lies not only in the legal need to choose between two strict options, male and female—"intersex" being noted several times as an impossibility for the legal world, or "tercium non licit"—but in the weight accorded to the various factors that make up gender. In spite of the emphasis on psychic identifications and the external gender attributes, the legal discourse around transsexualism continually reinforces the superficiality of the changes: from a juridical perspective, the external changes reflect a psychic disposition, yet genetically there are no "profound" changes. In another case from 1989, the dissenting voice of the court, which approved the transsexual's request for a legal name change, argued that society had no obligation to acknowledge the transsexual's choice to change his or her sex.[26] Moreover, he asserted that the decriminalization of transsexual surgery did not constitute its legalization: "Despenalizar no es legalizar" [decriminalization is not the same thing as legalization], placing the transsexual in a legal no-man's-land. From this point of view, transsexuals and the right to sex reassignment surgery (and a host of other legal changes that would ensue) occupy a third dimension of law, neither legal nor illegal. The same judge also quotes the European Court of Human Rights: "La jurisprudencia del Tribunal Europeo de Derechos Humanos, cuyas decisiones son criterio de interpretación, no consta que haya reconocido como derecho inherente a la persona la aspiración al cambio de sexo" [the case law of the European Court of Human Rights, whose decisions are the criteria for interpretation, does not state that it has recognized the desire for sex change as an individual's inherent right].[27]

Although the Spanish Supreme Court may have allowed for some transsexuals to change their names legally in civil registers, to date they are still denied many of the rights that accompany the sex change. In this respect, the legal system in Spain continues to operate under a rather rigid definition of gender as chromosomal sex, and therefore morphological changes are only seen as superficial. In a 1999 volume that reviews the legal proceedings on this topic, María Elósegui Itxaso reiterates that for the Spanish legal system, there is no evidence that psychic dispositions or identifications carry any more weight for determining gender. Citing Merleau-Ponty and Bergson as her authorities on gender, she writes that "toda nuestra conducta está condicionada por nuestra configuración genética" [our entire conduct is conditioned by our genetic configuration].[28] Particularly disturbing, for this author at least, is that Elósegui Itxaso is not the least bit critical of the decisions reached by the Supreme Court. In contrast with Villagómez Rodil, she claims that transsexuals would benefit from therapy and that allowing transsexuals to enter into marriage would subject children (assuming adoption were permitted) to an environment that lacks the "complementary relationship of a man and a woman," the lack of which is, she adds, one of the primary causes of both transsexuality and homosexuality.[29] Such legal limitations—and the attitudes that often accompany or justify them—are a stark reminder of the pitfalls of using a transsexual discourse to describe cultural change in a nation that continues to oppress transsexuals and ignore their material concerns. Nor is it difficult to see a thinly veiled homophobia lurking beneath Elósegui Itxaso's rhetoric of tolerance.

The absence of any true engagement with transgenderism in Umbral's brief text is fundamentally linked to his treatment of Bibi as a figure of postmodernity's fantasy. Umbral states clearly that he wants her as a woman, and he continually refers to her as "hembra total" [complete woman].[30] This point is by no means insignificant, as the tropological use of transsexuality depends almost exclusively on male-to-female transsexuals. Rarely are female-to-male transsexuals given equal attention in theoretical discussions, and almost never are they evoked in the rhetorical strategies I have been outlining here. Nevertheless, Andersen's transformation into a woman is not as simple as Umbral would portray it, and his text reveals this in a subtle manner. For while she now has the genitalia of a woman, her former status as a man is what makes Bibi desirable to Umbral: "Todas las mujeres me saben a poco desde que Bibí Andersen es mujer. A todas les falta ese toque de unicornio. . . . Uno busca la mujer que nos dé algo más de lo que da de sí cualquier mujer, y yo creo que con Bibí ese plus está garantizado" [all women taste less now that Bibí is a woman. All of them lack that touch of unicorn. . . . One searches for a women who can give us something more than the average woman, and I think that with Bibí that extra is guaranteed].[31] Bibi Andersen is thus another mythic body achieved through the advances of technology. That touch of unicorn, that extra something that Umbral fetishizes, is that virtual phallus that Umbral seeks in his mythic union with Bibi. *She,* as the virtual phallus for Umbral, is the fantasy of a postmodern, technologically crafted, phallic woman—a myth transformed into reality.

The fantasy of the complete woman, the one who does not lack, is often associated with transsexualism. While Umbral expresses his personal fantasy, he is not the first to describe Andersen in such terms. In her 1980 *¿Tiempo de mujer?* [Woman's Time?] Catalan feminist Montserrat Roig criticizes Andersen's image as a fantasy creation who attempts to move beyond sexual difference. Referring to her as a "bella con pene" [a beauty with a penis],[32] she remarks on the reactions of the spectators who have gathered for the opening of Aranda's *Cambio de sexo:*

> Desafiante, mostró su trofeo: un pene rosado, largo y hermoso como un badajo de campana mayor de catedral. Los intelectuales contemplaron en silencio la octava maravilla, el sexo completo. La perfección. La mujer, pues, no era mujer y, por lo tanto, no era sexo puro. La mujer era como ellos. La mujer era el falo. Ellos eran la mujer. ¡Excitante simbiosis!

> [Defiantly, she showed her trophy: a pink penis, long and beautiful like the clapper of a large cathedral bell. The intellectuals contemplated in silence the eighth wonder of the world, the complete sex. Perfection. The woman, well, wasn't a woman and therefore, wasn't pure sex. The woman was like them. The woman was the phallus. What an exciting symbiosis!][33]

Roig's image of Bibi focuses on how the transvestite body, only female in appearance, is completed by the unveiling of the penis. Creating a mirror in which men can view themselves and their own desires, Bibi's body offers up a Lacanian fantasy of having and being the phallus all in one complete package. For Roig, who reiterates that Bibi was not born a woman, the penis continues to operate as the true object of desire, in spite of (or perhaps because of) the fact her feminine appearance makes Bibi an object of desire for the mostly heterosexual male audience. Roig perceptively notes that transgenderism in this context functions as a masculine attempt to usurp a feminine space for other men. Her remarks are not so much directed at Andersen as at the audience, which only focuses on the penis, thus eliminating any identification with femininity: the masquerade falls by the wayside, and the intellectuals in the audience, implicitly all men in Roig's passage, can identify with Andersen now that she is once again a man. In a sense, Roig stands in opposition to Umbral, for she does not overtly criticize what the transvestite performance might mean for Andersen. Instead, she interrogates the fantasy on the part of the audience that the complete woman is no longer a woman at all, but rather another man.

There is no doubt that Bibi Andersen's presence on television and film underscores her symbolic status as a fantasy figure. Appearing on screen, Bibi's body is stripped of its materiality and rendered a glossy image. But Andersen is not representative of most transsexuals in Spain, many of whom have not had successful sex changes and do not enjoy the fame and money she has acquired. Most suffer from social stigma and find themselves either unemployed or working in prostitution. Safe and secure in the virtual world of television and film, the spectator need not think of those concerns or even of the fact that Bibi is a real woman in the flesh while viewing her as the simulacrum of a woman, as a signifier that is transmitted through images. To a certain degree, Andersen's public life confirms the belief that transsexuals construct an idealized female image. Yet Bibi's photo spread in *Interviú* also troubles our capacity to know fully the psychic identifications and desires that motivated her sex change. The photo spread bears witness to her sex change (i.e., she is now a woman) and at the same time reifies her image as not a woman (i.e., she was once a man) in that the very framing of her photography session reinscribes her status as "transsexual." Bibi's image pivots on both her appeal as a transsexual, as a sign of Spain's postmodernity vis-à-vis gender, and as a "woman," by her ability to pass. As Prosser asks, "for if the aim of transsexual reassignment is to erase the visible markers of transsexuality from the body, to erase the trace of the former sex as to leave the body unremarkably resexed, how can transsexuality as such be represented through the medium of the photograph?"[34] Andersen's public revelation of her sex change operation could be read as yet another version of a cabaret performance—the "perfect woman," to paraphrase Roig, being created out of a man. On the other hand, it is equally viable to claim that her decision stemmed from the need to declare her psychic identification as a woman to a public that would only be satisfied by visual confirmation; the multiple scenes of her nude body are certainly a testament to the public desire to *see* her as a woman. Reaffirming the narrative construction of herself as a "new" woman, Bibi's decision to appear nude was predicated on *Interviú* magazine's returning all of the photographs taken of her prior to her sex reassignment surgery; *Interviú* paid Andersen 20 million pesetas (less than $200,000 at that time). The visual evidence of her male past was to be destroyed, and the new photographs were given the headline "Bibi, al natural." In a sense, her own efforts to erase the past are reminiscent of the political "desmemoria" [amnesia] following the Franco regime. Still, the reader's knowledge of her male past makes the *Interviú* magazine spread so compelling, because it is precisely the ambiguity of Bibi Andersen's sexuality that Umbral lauds as "postmodern."

The association of transsexuality with fantasy and ambiguity has implications for the concept of postmodernity that Umbral avers in Andersen's corporeal transformation: she reflects a postmodern society invested in spectacle and representation, in design and style—a society in which modern technology and medicine can render myth reality. Indeed, Bibi's symbolic status as a postmodern muse of ambiguity is itself highly ambiguous for it brings into relief the possibility that Spain's postmodernity and democratic transition are exactly that—a fantasy. In other words, Umbral's exaltation of her as a mythic construction made real, a fantasy brought to life, exposes the possibility that the remarkable change is a masquerade that hides the fact that underneath the surgical operation, Bibi is still really a man. As such, the sex-change operation signifies an inauthentic transformation in which the surgical procedures only modify the surface of the body, leaving her "true" masculine psyche intact. Translated onto the national body, the transgender metaphor argues that Spain's postmodernity is a cheap masquerade—a fantasy image—under which lies the Spain of the past, whose relationship to modernity is weak and uneven.

Political Masquerades and the Specter of Francoism

Eduardo Subirats has articulated just such a claim by recourse to the rhetoric of transvestism. During the transition to democracy, Spain's shifting sense of national identity was thus intimately linked to its embrace of postmodernity. As noted earlier, the Left and Right in Spain colluded in an erasure of historical memory, a deliberate refusal of the past, in order to initiate political reform with an eye to the future. Vernon and Morris comment that for Subirats the celebration of postmodernity brought with it potential dangers: "the surrender of historical memory, viewed as the great liberation of mankind, to the simulacrum of technological perfection could only lead to an ecstatic fascination with the dissolution of the subject and the spectacle of the end of the world."[35] In *Después de la lluvia* [After the Rain], Subirats launches a vitriolic attack on the superficial postmodernity that Umbral extols in Bibi Andersen. For Subirats, the Baudrillardian vision of media technology and simulacra exemplifies the delusive mirage that Spain has constructed for itself and for international media: "Desde las señalizaciones de las carreteras hasta las sonrisas de los líderes políticos, la faz de la sociedad española ha sido, en efecto, *travestida íntegramente en superficie,* sin que sus formas de vida hayan tenido que experimentar por ello una reforma más íntima, ni la *ideología española* cambios más sustantivos" [From the signposts to political leaders' smiles, the face of Spanish society has been, in effect, *entirely cross-dressed on the surface,* without its forms of life having to experience any intimate changes nor *Spanish ideology* more substantial changes].[36] In a vein similar to other critics who have used transvestism to signify superficiality and masquerade, Subirats's vision of Spanish modernity argues for a continuity between the authoritarian model of modernization imposed by Franco and the "democratic" model espoused in the post-Franco period.[37]

Debunking *la movida* as a fiction and "un movimiento mágico-realista de modernización global" [a magical-realist movement of global modernization] in a recent article,[38] Subirats similarly describes the transition to democracy as "un proceso de modernización institucional que, sin embargo, *mantenía una ciega continuidad simbólica e intelectual con la España tradicional*" [the process of institutional modernization that, nevertheless, maintains a blind symbolic and intellectual continuity with traditional Spain].[39] Thus Subirats perceives Felipe González and the scandal-ridden Partido Socialista Obrero Español (PSOE) [Spanish Socialist Workers Party] as authoritarian vestiges of the Francoist past, encapsulated in the term "nacionalfelipismo." Subirats thus casts the years of Socialist dominance in a decidedly negative light, as if they were an artifice that harbored an underlying Francoism. By extension, he essentially argues that Spain's 1996 election of José María Aznar, the candidate of the conservative Partido Popular (PP) [Popular Party], and the nation's subsequent shift to the Right marked a return to Franco, or, at least, was symptomatic of the fact that "Franco" as a political institution had never been fully dismantled. Indeed, during the electoral campaigns, supporters of PSOE did not refrain from associating a potential return to the Right with a return to Francoism: Sinova and Tusell, for example, cite Carmen Romero, who stated that "el PP no se merece gobernar porque tiene actitudes que rozan el fascismo" [the PP does not deserve to govern because it has attitudes that border on fascism].[40] It becomes clear from Subirats's article, however, that there are two distinct arguments for a continuity with the past, for a contamination of democracy by Francoism: first, that there is a continuation of Francoism during the Socialist era, and second, that the victory of the Popular Party over the Socialists in 1996 is also a reflection of the specter of Francoism in contemporary politics.

Subirats is not alone in drawing attention to what may be seen as a lingering totalitarianism in contemporary politics. Juan Luis Cebrián also acknowledges this tendency in his published exchange with Felipe González, *El futuro no es lo que era* [The Future Is Not What It Was]. Yet if Subirats emphasizes the corruption and masquerade of the Socialist party, Cebrián emphasizes (as expected, given his interlocutor), the links between the Right and fascism:

En muchas columnas y artículos de la prensa de la derecha se asegura—incluso por voces que se autoproclaman progresistas—que en la transición no se hizo una verdadera democracia, según ellos por varios motivos.

Primero, porque en realidad el proceso estaba dirigido por los franquistas, que sólo pretendían mantener su legitimidad, a través de reformas
legales complicadas; y segundo, porque, mediante la política de con-
senso, lo que hizo la clase política fue blindarse para crear una especie de
superestructura que dirigiera la evolución del régimen.

[In many editorial columns and articles in the right-wing press they affirmed—even by voices that proclaim themselves to be progressive—that
in the transition a true democracy was not created, according to them for
various motives. First, because in actuality the process was undertaken by
the Francoists, who only wanted to maintain their legitimacy by means of
complicated legal reforms; and second, because, what the political class
did through a politics of consensus was to reinforce itself by creating a
superstructure that would supervise the evolution of the regime][41]

Denouncing the refusal to engage the past and the historical erasure
that characterizes a large part of the populace, he claims that the failure to recognize that Franco's regime was a disgrace is owed to the
fact that the right wing is the heir of Francoism, the Francoism of the
1960s and 1970s.[42] In his discussion of the lack of power of opposition parties to the PP, he goes on to say that "los PP están felices
porque son la derecha de siempre, la que colaboró con la dictadura
decididamente porque la engendró, pero encima, legitimada demo-
cráticamente. *De algún modo es como si Franco se hubiera presentado a las
elecciones y las hubiera ganado*" [The members of the PP are happy because they are the same right wing as always, the one that collaborated decidedly with the dictatorship because it gave birth to it, but
even more, because they are legitimated democratically. *In some ways
it is as if Franco had run for office and won the election*].[43] What becomes
increasingly clear from Cebrián's argument is that the labeling of one
political party as "fascist" or the "heir of Francoism" is a rhetorical
strategy adopted by either party to discredit the other.

For Elías Díaz, this type of debate is symptomatic of the "attitudes,
mentalities and ways of thinking [that] surfaced at the time and have
continued to haunt Spanish political culture and practice ever
since."[44] Díaz exposes in his analysis the shortcomings of ideological
postures that, for him, have contributed little to the development of
democracy in Spain, and whose limitations therefore undermine our
capacity to grapple with the contradictions and paradoxes that characterize Spain's democracy as currently practiced. He not only rejects
the long-held belief that a complete break from the past was necessary to establish a working democracy but also the ideology of *desencanto* [disillusionment] that emerged at in the late 1970s and lasted
until the Socialist victory in the 1982 elections. Díaz is not denying

the historical reality of these attitudes, but rather, their efficacy in contributing to the consolidation of a healthy democracy. He argues instead that the prevailing desire for a complete break with the past— what he dubs the ideology of *rupturismo*—fails to account for the ways in which negotiation, pacts, and consensus were necessary for the transition from dictatorship to democracy to take place. In other words, what characterizes genuine *ruptura* for Díaz is in fact the collaboration between Right and Left that was necessary achieve any political transformation.[45] As he points out, however, the belief that a clean break has not taken place surfaces time and again as an explanation for the failures of democratic politics in Spain: "Rather than attempting to identify and analyse the real and objective causes of Spain's problems (including those related to the origins of the democratic regime), all too often they resort to the trite, simplistic explanation that 'of course, since there was no rupture. . . .'"[46] Díaz logically follows from this argument to show that the corollary of this position is that if there was no break with the past, the only other possibility was absolute continuity. In other words, the transition from dictatorship to democracy may have brought change, but "the fundamental, essential characteristics of the previous regime have survived."[47] This posture, he argues, leads to the conclusion that the Francoist dictatorship and the current democratic government are, in spite of superficial differences, essentially the same entity.

The concrete changes to political infrastructures, the increasing politicization of the judiciary, the close relationships between political parties and systems of media communication such as television and newspapers, the various scandals involving party finances and state-sponsored terrorism (FILESA and the "caso Gal," respectively) are the chief areas that are scrutinized for continuity with the past.[48] With the exception of Cebrián, more recent evaluations of the first and so-called "second" transitions have emphasized the weaknesses of Spain's democracy but have resisted any perceived continuity with the Francoist regime. Javier Tusell, in distinguishing between a PP that is "derecha de confrontación" [a confrontational right-wing Popular Party] and a PP that is "derecha democrática" [a democratic right-wing Popular Party], argues that "nada tienen que ver el hecho de que muchos de quienes la protagonizan sean personas con conexiones familiares con el pasado o que no exista una extrema derecha, como resultaría lógico, dadas las peculiaridades de nuestro país y los paralelismos con otros países europeos. Lo primero no implica *perduración de un ideario autoritario* y lo segundo es *consecuencia del recuerdo del franquismo*" [it's irrelevant that many of the main figures of the right wing are people with family connections to the past or that there is no extreme right wing, as would be expected given the peculiarities of our country and the parallels with other European countries. The first does not imply the *perpetuation of an authoritarian ideal* and the second is the *result of the memory of Francoism*].[49] Tusell essentially points out that although the current PP is not a centrist party as it claims, but in fact, a right-wing party, its membership cannot be reduced to the origins in Franco's party (the majority of its members entering politics after the transition to democracy),[50] and therefore cautions against interpreting their political activity in terms of "authoritarianism." Tussell argues that the very lack of an extreme right-wing party responds to the historical memory of Francoism, and as such is a deliberate avoidance of an image of authoritarianism. The authors of *Lo que nos queda de Franco* [What's Left from Franco among Us], Fernando Jáuregui and Manuel Ángel Menéndez conclude that cultural legacy of forty years cannot be erased completely in the twenty years that transpired at their time of their publication. But the premise of their work is not that nothing has changed. Quite the opposite. Jáuregui and Menéndez emphasize the profound changes that have taken place in the areas of the law and of the media, to offer two examples.[51] Similarly, in their diagnostic analysis of the problems of Spanish democracy, Sinova and Tusell argue that the Socialist government from 1982 to 1996 constituted a step backwards in the development of a healthy democracy.[52] Not unexpectedly, they also focus on the political scandals that have marked the Socialist government, the close ties between the government and the judiciary, and the control and use of the media by politicians as symptoms of the current "illness" of Spain's democracy. While their use of terms such as "regeneration" and "infirmity" are reminiscent of similar rhetorical strategies from the late nineteenth century, they refute the argument the current situation approximates or is reminiscent of the Francoist dictatorship: "considerar que en España en los ochenta el régimen se había convertido en una dictadura no era un diagnóstico que contuviera una mínima dosis de veracidad, a pesar de la supuesta radicalidad del juicio" [to consider that in the Spain of the 1980s the political regime had become a dictatorship was a diagnosis that did not contain the slightest bit of truth, in spite of the claim's supposed radicality].[53]

Díaz's persuasive argument cautions us from assuming that all of the plights of the present democratic government are reducible to the origins of democracy and the supposed lack of a clean break. This is not to deny that there may be identifiable vestiges of the Franco regime or that the Spanish government has failed in redressing the historical legacy of fascism. As Joan Ramon Resina points out, the PP rejected a motion in 1999 to officially denounce the military uprising against the Second Spanish Republic.[54] Resina makes a strong case for the need to demythify the transition to democracy and pay attention to the deleterious effects of the *ruptura pactada* on the various nations within the Spanish state. He is right to ask: "Was not the transition, as well as the thing in transit, the result of tinkering, not only with the state's political and economic structures but also with the official memories of that very process?"[55] My point is not to deny the critical import of questioning the historical process by which Spain engaged in a transition from dictatorship to democracy. Rather it is that the rhetorical appeal to fascism to characterize all signs of corruption or flaws in the present democracy obscures the concrete conditions that have produced them by treating them uncritically as if they were an inherited legacy of the Franco regime. To my mind, Díaz is right to warn against the facile assumption that a failure to engage in a full rupture with the past can only mean a total continuity in the present, but he leaves out an important aspect in his analysis: why these "ideologies," as he calls them, continue to surface even now. For although there may not be complete continuity with the past, the arguments made by Subirats and Cebrián reflect a prevailing tendency to align rhetorically contemporary manifestations of corruption and political scandal with the specter of Franco. Moreover, the very need on the part of writers such as Tusell to dispel any links between the present and the past suggests that the association of violence, political corruption, and the Right with the Francoist past endures even today. The crucial point that emerges in these assessments of the transition is not that Francoism is, in fact, alive and well or that Spain's democracy is fundamentally authoritarian, but rather, the concept of *las dos Españas,* in spite of the fact that the dictatorship has been over for nearly 30 years, continues to dominate our conceptual frameworks. Franco and Francoism may be dead and Spain may be a full-fledged democracy, but the past continues in the present as a discourse to interpret (at times for political gains) the contradictions and faults of democracy as practiced in Spain.

CODA: BIBI, *ENCORE UNE FOIS*

I have argued in this essay that the transgender metaphor—in its various guises—reflects the persistence of a conceptual framework that persists from the early years of the transition that can only view the contemporary political landscape in terms of a celebratory but deluded fantasy of authentic change (Umbral) or a pessimistic vision of masquerade and inauthentic transformation (Subirats). Umbral's vision of Andersen epitomizes the new "postmodern" Spain, whereas Subirats sees Spanish modernity as merely a thin veneer of glitzy media images—nothing more than a superficial artifice of transvestism. As it has been deployed, the use of the transgender metaphor reveals both misconceptions about transgenderism and the inadequacy of its use for understanding contemporary Spain. The construction of transgenderism as "fantasy" on the one hand, and as "masquerade" on the other, seems to designate two opposing poles between a positive embrace of transgenderism and a negative rejection of it. Nevertheless, fantasy and masquerade both see transgenderism as something not quite real, as a gender that is not as real as the transgendered person's "original" gender. It is this conception of transgenderism which undermines the efforts of transsexuals to legitimate their identifications with the opposite sex and to change their names through proper legal channels upon completing sex reassignment surgery. At the same time, there is a way in which the complexity of transgenderism, when understood in terms other than a strict binary, can be useful in conceptualizing the current relationship of the democratic present with its dictatorial past.

In short, a final word on Bibi's story may offer us an avenue out of the impasse of the rhetorical uses of transsexuality. At the end of the interview with Almodóvar in *Interviú,* Andersen states that she is thinking of changing her name again, to which he responds that it is too late, that her legend is already made. Bluntly, Bibi retorts: "Nunca es tarde para cambiar, si uno de verdad lo desea" [It's never too late to change if you really want to].[56] Bibi Andersen did, in fact, change her name. She now goes by "Bibiana Fernández." If her name originally tied her to the Swedish film star, and the loss of the deictic marker in the transition from Bibí to Bibi somehow reflected her corporeal changes, "Bibiana Fernández" is a sign that her own transition continues. Bibi has broken with the name that has made her an iconic film star and has attempted to recapture a bit of her own past by using her family name. "Bibiana" suggests that she is now more than the Bibi of the silver screen, and the use of "Fernández" implies that her past is still an integral part of her present identity. Her return to the past further suggests that she cannot completely eschew her former male identity, but the return does not posit that past as the underlying core or foundation of her sexual identity. By refusing to see transgenderism in a dialectic between masquerade and fantasy, on the one hand, and authenticity on the other, we too might avoid seeing Bibi's ambiguous body in the temporal frame of masculine, Francoist past and feminine, postmodern present.

By extension, the transition from dictatorship to democracy and postmodernity might be better conceptualized by not falling back into an untenable dichotomy between past and present, dictatorship and democracy, ambiguous modernity and celebratory postmodernity, in which any sign of the past is an indication that the present is a mere ideological façade hiding an underlying Francoist self. As discussed earlier, a transsexual subject-position points to the future, to the moment of realization, when the past will be eliminated through a sex reassignment procedure. Yet to exist as a transsexual, the past must be maintained, for only the juxtaposition of the masculine past and the feminine present bring transsexuality into relief (or the female past and the male present in the case of female-to-male transsexuals). For the transsexual, the past can never be fully eliminated, for it persists in the perpetual "transitioning" of the transsexual, yet neither does the past persist as the "authentic" identity against which the transsexual crosses gender "inauthentically." As Andersen's own story affirms, transsexual subjectivity cannot be reduced either to the sexed body prior to surgery or to the psychic identification with the opposite gender. Read in this manner as symbolic of Spain's own transformations, Andersen's own transgender narrative potentially allows us to think of Spain's relationship to its past in a way that avoids seeing every instance of authoritarianism, violence, and corruption as the sign of a "travestied" democracy. At the same time, however, her subjectivity as a transsexual reminds us that historical memory is essential, that the dictatorship should not be forgotten. Bibi has, in a sense, moved beyond the binarism between past and present, tradition and postmodernity, Franco and post-Franco. Bibi's own transgendered transition offers us a valuable lesson: in questioning the conceptual frameworks that continue to mark discussions of Spanish national identity—the "two Spains," the continuity of the present with the past as a form of masquerade—we can perhaps begin to see that the legacy of Francoism is not to be found only or even primarily in the vestiges of the regime waiting to be exposed in contemporary politics but in our own critical discourses.

NOTES

An earlier version of this essay appeared as "Transgender Nation: Bibi Andersen, Postmodernity, and the Spanish Transition to Democracy," *Revista de Estudios Hispánicos* 37 (2003). My thanks to the editors for permission to use material from the original publication. All translations of citations from Spanish are my own, unless otherwise noted. The earlier version focused more on the theoretical debates around transgenderism and the insufficiency of the rhetorical uses of transgenderism, given their ignorance of the material conditions under which real transsexuals live. In this version, I am more interested in the ways in which the recurrence of transgenderism as a discourse for describing the political transformations in Spain is a manifestation of a critical and political discourse tied to Franco and Francoism.

1. Óscar Caballero, *El sexo del franquismo* (Madrid: Cambio 16, 1977), 219.

2. John Hooper, *The New Spaniards* (London: Penguin, 1995), 163.

3. Esther Newton, *Mother Camp: Female Impersonators in America,* 2nd ed. (Chicago: University of Chicago Press, 1979), xvii.

4. José Luis Gallero, *Sólo se vive una vez: esplendor y ruina en la movida madrileña* (Madrid: Ardora, 1991), 87.

5. Jorge Berlanga, "Una noche con Bibi," *La Luna de Madrid,* 19 June 1985.

6. Francisco Umbral, *Los cuerpos gloriosos: memorias y semblanzas* (Barcelona: Planeta, 1996), 177. Umbral's own name underscores the connection to the transition, as *umbral* in Spanish refers to a passage, entrance, or threshold and thus connotes a transition from one space to another. His name alludes to both the concept of the political transition to democracy and crossing the barrier to Bibi's newly constructed body.

7. Paul Julian Smith, "Modern Times: Francisco Umbral's Chronicle of Distinction," *Modern Language Notes* 113 (1998), 335.

8. Marsha Kinder, "Documenting the National and Its Subversion in a Democratic Spain," in *Refiguring Spain: Cinema/Media/Representation,* ed. Marsha Kinder (Durham, NC: Duke University Press, 1997), 78.

9. Kinder, "Refiguring Socialist Spain: Introduction," in Kinder, ed., op. cit., 3.

10. Kinder, "Sex Change and Cultural Transformation in Aranda and Abril's *Cambio de sexo* (1977)," in *Spanish Cinema: The Auteurist Tradition,* ed. Peter Williams Evans (Oxford: Oxford University Press, 1999), 133.

11. Ibid., 145.

12. Umbral, *Los cuerpos gloriosos,* 177.

13. Ibid.

14. Joaquín Costa y Martínez, *Oligarquía y caciquismo como la forma actual de gobierno en España, urgencia y modo de cambiarla* [Oligarchy and Caciquism as the Current Form of Government in Spain, the Urgency and Means of Changing It] (Madrid: Biblioteca Nueva, 1998), 115.

15. Jay Prosser, *Second Skins: The Body Narratives of Transsexuality* (New York: Columbia University Press, 1998), 3.

16. Kathleen M. Vernon and Barbara Morris, "Introduction: Pedro Almodóvar, Postmodern Auteur," in *Post-Franco, Postmodern: The Films of Pedro Almodóvar,* eds. Kathleen M. Vernon and Barbara Morris (Westport, CT: Greenwood Publishing Group, 1995), 7.

17. Jo Labanyi, "Postmodernism and the Problem of Cultural Identity," in *Spanish Cultural Studies: An Introduction,* eds. Helen Graham and Jo Labanyi (Oxford: Oxford University Press, 1995), 399.

18. David Garland, "A Ms-Take in the Making? Transsexualism, Post-Franco, Post-Modern, Post-Haste," *Quarterly Review of Film and Video* 13.4 (1991), 16.

19. Julia Epstein and Kristina Straub, "Introduction: The Guarded Body," in *Body Guards: The Cultural Politics of Gender Ambiguity,* eds. Julia Epstein and Kristina Straub (New York: Routledge, 1991), 11.

20. Umbral, "Bibi Andersen," *El País,* 24 December 1984.

21. Gianni Vattimo, *La sociedad transparente* (Barcelona: Paidós, 1990), 67.

22. Gallero, 9.

23. Carlos Ferrando, "La última romántica: Bibi Andersen," *La Luna de Madrid* 33 (December 1986), 18.

24. Beginning in the 1990s, transgender organizations began to form in Catalonia, Asturias, Andalusia, and Galicia, and in 1996 the Federación de Asociaciones de Transexuales del Estado Español [Federation of Transsexual Associations of the Spanish State] was constituted. At the end of the 1990s, political parties such as the PSOE and Izquierda Unida [United Left] created subsections of their parties devoted to the interests of transgendered people, gays, and lesbians. The most significant advance in transgender rights has been the successful effort of the Asociación de Identidad de Género [Association of Gender Identity] first in 1999 to get the PSOE in Andalusia to include transsexuality among the services covered by state health care.

25. Another transsexual marriage, which took place in Catalonia in September 2001, received (erroneous) national headlines as "the first transsexual wedding in Spain." *El Mundo* published an article with the title "Celebran en Cataluña la primera boda transsexual de España" [Catalonia Celebrates the First Transsexual Wedding in Spain]. Accessed from www.elmundo.es/elmundo/2001/09/09/sociedad/100050061/html (8 April 2004). It is perhaps a testament to the success of Bibi's transformation that the press would overlook her civil ceremony as the first transsexual marriage in Spain.

26. The Ley de Identidad de Género [Law of Gender Identity] proposed by the PSOE in 1999 would allow preoperative transsexuals to legally change their names. Under current law, name changes are contingent upon completion of sex reassignment surgery. As a result, many who identify as transsexuals yet cannot afford surgery or do not wish to entail the risks (particularly for female-to-male transsexuals for whom the necessary medical technology is still underdeveloped) must continue to use their legal birth names in spite of the fact they live their lives as the other gender. Approval of the law has been delayed for years and has undergone numerous emendations. At the time of writing, it is under opposition from the conservative Partido Popular [Popular Party].

27. Alfonso Villagómez Rodil, *Aportación al estudio de la transexualidad* (Madrid: Tecnos, 1994), 60. In one of the findings, there was considerable concern for the effects on genealogy: with sex reassignment surgery, fathers could become mothers, and children from that marriage could potentially have two mothers, thus producing, from a certain perspective, a lesbian marriage. In such cases, the marriage would be declared null and void (Villagómez Rodil, 36–37). For an extended discussion of the legal issues around marriage and paternity, see Javier López-Galiacho Perona, *La problemática jurídica de la transexualidad* [The Juridical Issue of Transsexuality] (Madrid: McGraw Hill/Interamericana, 1998), 297–346, and María Elósegui Itxaso, *La transexualidad: Jurisprudencia y argumentación juridical* [Transsexuality: Jurisprudence and Juridical Argumentation] (Granada: Comares, 1999), 21–28.

28. Elósegui Itxaso, 48.

29. Ibid.

30. Umbral, *Los cuerpos gloriosos,* 177.

31. Ibid., 179.

32. Montserrat Roig, *¿Tiempo de mujer?* (Esplugues de Llobregat: Plaza & Janés, 1980), 123.

33. Ibid., 124.

34. Prosser, 209.

35. Vernon and Morris, 10.

36. Eduardo Subirats, *Después de la lluvia: sobre la ambigua modernidad española* (Madrid: Temas de hoy, 1993), 206.

37. Ibid., 28–29.

38. Subirats, "De la transición al espectáculo," *Quimera* 188–189 (2000), 23.

39. Ibid., 26. Emphasis mine.

40. Justino Sinova and Javier Tusell, *La crisis de la democracia en España: Ideas para reinventar nuestro sistema político* [The Crisis of Democracy in Spain: Ideas for Reinventing Our Political System] (Madrid: Espasa Calpe, 1997), 43.

41. Felipe González and Juan Luis Cebrián, *El futuro no es lo que era: una conversación* (Madrid: Suma de Letras, 2002), 24–25.

42. Ibid., 39.

43. Ibid., 53. Emphasis mine.

44. Elías Díaz, "Ideologies in the Making of the Spanish Transition," in *Politics and Policy in Democratic Spain: No Longer Different?*, ed. Paul Heywood (London and Portland: Frank Cass, 1999), 26.

45. Ibid., 32.

46. Ibid., 33.

47. Ibid.

48. See Fernando Jiménez, "Political Scandals and Political Responsibility in Democratic Spain," in Heywood, ed., op. cit., for a concise overview of the spate of scandals that have marked Spain's democracy, which he remarks, citing Heywood, have been "the single most salient issue in Spanish politics" (80).

49. Tusell, "Entre el centro y la derecha: El PP, desde la oposición al poder," in *El gobierno del Aznar: Balance de una gestión,* 1996–2000 [Aznar's Government: An Assessment of an Administration], ed. Javier Tusell (Barcelona: Crítica, 2000), 20. Emphasis mine.

50. Ibid., 18.

51. Fernando Jáuregui and Manuel Ángel Menéndez, *Lo que nos queda de Franco: Símbolos, personajes, leyes y costumbres, veinte años después* (Madrid: Temas de hoy, 1995). One of the areas in which they do perceive a continuity with the forty years of the dictatorship is in cultural production, in which they affirm that "no resulta demasiado exagerado afirmar que el sistema cultural sigue siendo básicamente el mismo de antes, con las excepciones e incorporaciones—sobre todo, por lo que se refiere a museos—de rigor" [it would not be an exaggeration to affirm that the cultural system is basically the same one as before, with the usual exceptions and additions—above all, with regards to museums] (316). Although the debate over the supposed lack of a masterpiece of literary fiction awaiting the freedom of democracy to come to light has abated, it strikes me that the continued evaluation of contemporary culture vis-à-vis the dictatorship is perhaps itself a sign of a residue of a cultural framework, apparent in the use of the term "post-Franco" by literary and cultural critics alike, that stresses such a continuity with the past.

52. Sinova and Tusell, 24.

53. Ibid., 226.

54. Joan Ramon Resina, "Short of Memory: the Reclamation of the Past Since the Spanish Transition to Democracy," in *Disremembering the Dictatorship: The Politics of Memory in the Spanish Transition to Democracy,* ed. Joan Ramon Resina (Amsterdam: Rodopi, 2000), 106.

55. Resina, "Introduction," in Resina, ed., op. cit., 8. Cebrián adopts a similar position by arguing that there is a prevailing silence about the past, about Francoism and the transition to democracy. The silence cloaks, for Cebrián, any debate about the historical significance of Francoism for Spain. The right refuses to condemn the regime for being fascist, and the left refuses to acknowledge that the economic developments in the 1960s paved the way for democratic change (González and Cebrián, 32–33).

56. Pedro Almodóvar, "Bibi, al natural," *Interviú,* 10 October 1994, 23.

BIBLIOGRAPHY

Almodóvar, Pedro. "Bibi(r su Vida) Andersen." *La Luna de Madrid* 33 (December 1986): 17.

———. "Bibi, al natural." *Interviú* 10 October 1994: 12–23.

Aranda, Vicente, dir. *Cambio de sexo.* Sogepaq, 1977.

Berlanga, Jorge. "Una noche con Bibí." *La Luna de Madrid* 19 (June 1985): 75.

Caballero, Óscar. *El sexo del franquismo.* Madrid: Cambio 16, 1977.

"Celebran en Cataluña la primera boda transsexual de España." *El Mundo.* 9 Sept 2001. Available at www.elmundo.es/elmundo/2001/09/09/sociedad/ 100050061/html. Accessed on 8 April 2004.

Costa y Martínez, Joaquín. *Oligarquía y caciquismo como la forma actual de gobierno en España, urgencia y modo de cambiarla.* Madrid: Biblioteca Nueva, 1998.

Díaz, Elías. "Ideologies in the Making of the Spanish Transition." In *Politics and Policy in Democratic Spain: No Longer Different?* Edited by Paul Heywood. London & Portland: Frank Cass, 1999.

Elósegui Itxaso, María. *La transexualidad: Jurisprudencia y argumentación jurídica.* Granada: Comares,1999.

Epstein, Julia, and Kristina Straub. "Introduction: The Guarded Body." In *Body Guards: The Cultural Politics of Gender Ambiguity.* Edited by Julia Epstein and Kristina Straub. New York: Routledge, 1991.

Ferrando, Carlos. "La última romántica: Bibi Andersen." *La Luna de Madrid* 33 (December 1986): 16–18.

Gallero, José Luis. *Sólo se vive una vez: esplendor y ruina en la movida madrileña.* Madrid: Ardora, 1991.

Garland, David. "A Ms-Take in the Making? Transsexualism, Post-Franco, Post-Modern, Post-Haste." *Quarterly Review of Film and Video* 13.4 (1991): 95–102.

Garlinger, Patrick Paul. "Transgender Nation: Bibi Andersen, Postmodernity, and the Spanish Transition to Democracy." *Revista de Estudios Hispánicos* 37 (2003): 1–28.

González, Felipe, and Juan Luis Cebrián. *El futuro no es lo que era: una conversación.* Madrid: Suma de Letras, 2002.

Hooper, John. *The New Spaniards.* London: Penguin, 1995.

Jáuregui, Fernando, and Manuel Ángel Menéndez. *Lo que nos queda de Franco: Símbolos, personajes, leyes y costumbres, veinte años después.* Madrid: Temas de Hoy, 1995.

Jiménez, Fernando. "Political Scandals and Political Responsibility in Democratic Spain." In *Politics and Policy in Democratic Spain: No Longer Different?* Edited by Paul Heywood. London & Portland: Frank Cass, 1999.

Kinder, Marsha. "Documenting the National and Its Subversion in a Democratic Spain." In *Refiguring Spain: Cinema/Media/Representation.* Edited by Marsha Kinder. Durham, NC: Duke University Press, 1997.

———. "Refiguring Socialist Spain: Introduction." In *Refiguring Spain: Cinema/ Media/Representation.* Edited by Marsha Kinder. Durham, NC: Duke University Press, 1997.

———. "Sex Change and Cultural Transformation in Aranda and Abril's *Cambio de sexo* (1977)." In *Spanish Cinema: The Auteurist Tradition.* Edited by Peter William Evans. Oxford: Oxford University Press, 1999.

Labanyi, Jo. "Postmodernism and the Problem of Cultural Identity." In *Spanish Cultural Studies: An Introduction*. Edited by Helen Graham and Jo Labanyi. Oxford: Oxford University Press, 1995.

López-Galiacho Perona, Javier. *La problemática jurídica de la transexualidad*. Madrid: McGraw Hill/Interamericana, 1998.

Newton, Esther. *Mother Camp: Female Impersonators in America*. 2nd ed. Chicago: University of Chicago Press, 1979.

Prosser, Jay. *Second Skins: The Body Narratives of Transsexuality*. New York: Columbia University Press, 1998.

Resina, Joan Ramon. Introduction. In *Disremembering the Dictatorship: The Politics of Memory in the Spanish Transition to Democracy*. Edited by Joan Ramon Resina. Amsterdam: Rodopi, 2000.

————. "Short of Memory: the Reclamation of the Past Since the Spanish Transition to Democracy." In Joan Ramon Resina, op. cit., 83–125.

Roig, Montserrat. ¿*Tiempo de mujer?* Esplugues de Llobregat: Plaza & Janés, 1980.

Sinova, Justino, and Javier Tusell. *La crisis de la democracia en España: Ideas para reinventar nuestro sistema político*. Madrid: Espasa Calpe, 1997.

Smith, Paul Julian. "Modern Times: Francisco Umbral's Chronicle of Distinction." *Modern Language Notes* 113 (1998): 324–38.

Subirats, Eduardo. "De la transición al espectáculo." *Quimera* 188–189 (2000): 21–26.

————. *Después de la lluvia: sobre la ambigua modernidad española*. Madrid: Temas de hoy, 1993.

Tusell, Javier. "Entre el centro y la derecha: El PP, desde la oposición al poder." In *El gobierno de Aznar: Balance de una gestión, 1996–2000*. Edited by Javier Tusell. Barcelona: Crítica, 2000.

Umbral, Francisco. "Bibi Andersen." *El País*, 24 December 1984.

————. *Los cuerpos gloriosos: memorias y semblanzas*. Barcelona: Planeta, 1996.

Vattimo, Gianni. *La sociedad transparente*. Barcelona: Paidós, 1990.

Vernon, Kathleen M. and Barbara Morris. "Introduction: Pedro Almodóvar, Postmodern *Auteur*." In *Post-Franco, Postmodern: The Films of Pedro Almodóvar*. Edited by Kathleen M. Vernon and Barbara Morris. Westport, CT: Greenwood Publishing Group, 1995.

Villagómez Rodil, Alfonso. *Aportación al estudio de la transexualidad*. Madrid: Tecnos, 1994.

(Im)Memorable Memoirs:
Ernesto Giménez Caballero's
Memorias de un dictador

Ricardo Krauel

Even if he lacked many other qualities, ernesto giménez ca-ballero (1899–1988) possessed a sharp imagination and intuition and an unrestrainable creativity. The confluence of these traits would pre-dispose him to be a "pioneer" in the use of forms and ideas—or, as he liked to put it, to be a "visionary poet." With his proverbial ten-dency to exaggerate, he boasted of having introduced Surrealism in Spain. He would also attribute to himself the dubious honor of hav-ing initiated—with his "Carta a un compañero de la Joven España" [Letter to a Comrade of Young Spain]—the "fascist Revolution" in that country, although admitting the impossibility of importing Ital-ian fascism to the Iberian Peninsula without "anarchizing" and na-tionalizing it within Spain's Catholic tradition (that is, without mak-ing it a synthesis between authoritarianism and libertarianism). Recognized by José Antonio Primo de Rivera (according to Giménez himself) as his "precursor," Giménez declares himself to be one of the "ideological founders of Falangism," to the extent that, he says, the dictator's son would offer him Falange's number one member-ship card, although he would decline the offer and keep card num-ber five. He claims to have anticipated King Juan Carlos's "liberal democracy" and Santiago Carrillo's "Eurocommunism." When eval-uating himself as a writer, he highlights, above all, his condition as an avant-garde author, as an *"adelantado."*[1]

Although perhaps not as much as Giménez might have liked, there is some—if not quite a bit—of truth in all of these claims. The writ-ing of his memoirs is based on premises that correspond with this atypical and innovative character. Giménez begins by questioning the very notion of writing memoirs: his memoirs have not been written directly onto paper by their author, but rather "dictated" to a stenog-rapher. Besides the play on words that the term "dictator" suggests

when it refers to a figure with a political trajectory such as that of
Giménez Caballero, the fact that these memoirs have been dictated
will have important consequences for the configuration of the text,
its generic definition, and its relation with orality. The work begins
by refuting the genre to which it is ascribed: "Las Memorias son siempre falsas porque si se acude a los documentos históricos dejan de ser
Memorias y se convierten en pasajes eruditos. Y si no hay esa comprobación la mayoría de tales Memorias se hacen *narcisismos del que escribe* y por tanto falseamientos de la verdad" [Memoirs are always false
because if they are based on historical documents they are no longer
memoirs and become erudite passages. And if they are not backed
up by evidence, most memoirs become *narcissisms of the writer* and
therefore falsifications of the truth].[2] Moreover, he attacks memoirs
as a "non-Spanish literary genre," not so much because of what Ortega y Gasset argued (i.e., that the cultivation of memoirs bears a direct proportion to the joy of living that a people feel, and that
Spaniards experience life "as a universal toothache"), but rather because of the influence of Arabic culture on Spanish tradition.[3] He argues that essentially individualistic literary genres—those that exalt
personal freedom (i.e., epic, tragedy, memoirs)—are foreign to oriental cultures.[4]

Based on these affirmations, Giménez launches into the dictation
of his memoirs with a will to redefine the genre. And with a purely intuitive impulse, he coincides with—and, in many cases, perhaps anticipates—some of the main lines of contemporary theoretical reflection on autobiography. That is so not only because of the hybridity
from which he conceives the genre ("unas veces soliloquios, otras
rapsodias, otras anales" [sometimes soliloquies, others rhapsodies,
others annals]); or because he inserts himself within the picaresque
tradition ("en la tradición de un Lázaro o un Don Pablos o un Este-
banillo" [in the tradition of a Lázaro or a Don Pablos or an Esteban-
illo]), thus convoking, along that same "dialogic" vein, the concur-
rence with novelistic discourse; but, above all, because of his will to
"poeticize" his memoirs while calling for the active participation of
the reader.[5] In this sense, once again Giménez Caballero is both a visionary and a pioneer. Yet once again, Giménez Caballero is caught
in a contradiction: for his *Memorias* will be a kind of death certificate,
proof that fascism in Spain (in the strict sense of the term) is something which inevitably pertains to the past, the offspring of unrepeat-
able historical circumstances, an impossibility for the future. Fascism,
in short, became something as anachronistic in times of democracy—
in spite of some more or less partial or picturesque efforts—as
Giménez Caballero himself, who, as one of his main biographers has

pointed out, began to "outlive himself" ["sobrevivirse"] even before the end of the Civil War.[6]

The innovative impulse that characterizes Ernesto Giménez Caballero's intellectual activity has complex implications for the elaboration of his *Memorias*—implications which are only intensified by the text's self-reflexivity. Such an impulse places us before one of the fundamental problems raised by autobiographical works: namely, the role assigned in them to "creativity." Since the mid 1950s, in the foundational theoretical texts of contemporary criticism on autobiography, two directions appeared that apparently would not contradict each other but which implied two different conceptions of the genre. The first line of thought might be represented by a statement by Georges Gusdorf to which we have already indirectly alluded in part: "The significance of autobiography should [be] sought beyond truth and falsity. [It] is unquestionably a document about a life. . . . But it is also a work of art."[7] The second direction could be synthesized in this statement by Northrop Frye: "Most autobiographies are inspired by a creative, and therefore fictional, impulse."[8] It might well be thought that we are facing two versions of the same idea, but an important discrepancy lies behind that similarity—a discrepancy bound up in the remark "and therefore fictional." Such a remark not only problematizes the uniqueness of autobiography as a genre, but also has important implications for the way in which the reader of autobiography interacts with the text.

In the wake of the first critical position, we encounter other approaches such as that of Louis Renza, who sees autobiography as "neither fictive nor nonfictive, not even a mixture of the two;"[9] or that of Elizabeth Bruss, who contributes the notion of "autobiographical act," an act invested with an inherent ability for redefinition and relocation that allows it to maintain its autonomy before the fictional text;[10] or that of Jerome Bruner, who deepens the consideration of autobiography as a "constitutive act," an act open to negotiation with an interlocutor situated "on the other side of the text;"[11] or, finally, even that of Paul de Man (after Bruss and Renza), who underscores the existence of a reciprocal current of generativity between life and autobiography, and insists that a distinction between fiction and autobiography is "undecidable."[12]

However, in de Man, unlike in the contentions of Gusdorf and Renza, the fact that the distinction between fiction and autobiography is "undecidable" does not necessarily imply that the fiction/reality axis of autobiographical writing becomes displaced or inoperative. The road is thus cleared for the association between autobiography and fiction that we found in Frye, insofar as it would later be sanctioned by Lejeune and continue to be favored (maybe even become dominant with the influence of postmodern mentality) by authors like Olney, Eakin, Smith, or Benstock. Few figures within the context of twentieth-century Spanish literature—excluding the insurmountable case of Ramón Gómez de la Serna—make us think as much as Giménez Caballero does of a confusion or inversion between life and fiction. Gecé (a pen name he would sometimes use by spelling out the initials of his surnames) gives the impression of being a fictive character and, as of the 1930s, maybe a character of a nightmarish fiction. If his *Memorias* seem fabulous (he explains how he tried to arrange the marriage between Hitler and Pilar Primo de Rivera) it is not because what they refer to appears implausible or incredible, but because the author himself is the one who seems to be fabulous or implausible. But the fact that the subject of enunciation may look like the character in a novel, or that he never stops infusing creativity into his writing, does not mean that his autobiographical account (as any autobiographical account would be according to the authors to whom we have just referred) becomes permeated with fictionality.

To write a life is to recreate it and, therefore, to lose it. Life, in its irreducible multiplicity, in its thickness and sphericity, is subjected to the sequentiality, linearity, and finiteness of language, and becomes something different: the *version* of a life. No matter how "sincere" and "objective" the recounting of a life tries to be, its writing implies its transformation—and probably more so the more sincere and objective it intends to be. As Michael Sprinker observed, autobiography "is always circumscribed by the limiting conditions of writing, of the production of a text," and he reminded us that such an idea was already pre-formulated in Vico, Kierkegaard, Nietzsche, and Freud.[13] We are not facing, as Ángel Loureiro has pointed out, a mimetic transposition but rather "a *constructed* sense of reality," "a *discursive creation* of reality."[14] We witness the founding of a universe of meaning with its own solidarities and its own demands for aesthetic coherence, a universe that is endowed with autonomy and originality as it is configured, and that is defined by the means through which it is expressed. Life is re-formulated when it is written; no matter what the intention, experience is rectified. The retelling cannot help but generate, necessarily, innumerable fundamental modifications based on the selection of events, their rearrangement, the setting up of logical links, the handling and design of temporal and spatial variables, etc. Life is also subjected to an explicit or unavoidable process of *interpretation,* which immediately results in an infusion of ideology. From the outset, life is not only transformed into writing but also, simultaneously (and with no less relevance), into a reading, in this case the reading of the autobiographer.

The writer will likely notice that he is facing a fascinating possibility: to reorient a life that has already elapsed, with the purpose of becoming reconciled with it and also with a view to its future interpretation. It is, though, a possibility of which it is very difficult to take advantage with complete efficacy—and more so because of the suspicions that the autobiographer's perspective on his own life will probably generate. This seems to be extremely problematic in Giménez Caballero's case; for many readers may be predisposed to think that a tendency toward imposture prevailed in him as a natural companion to his ideological position. The autobiographer's version does not invalidate others' versions—it could even validate them further, especially when we are dealing with a work like Gecé's, a work of exaggerated rhetorical apparatus. For that reason, an autobiography may also discredit coinciding versions provided by others when the frequently related marks of fear and adulation (particularly in biographies contemporary to their protagonist) can be found.

The fact that someone narrates his life declaring a commitment to veracity will, in effect, always inspire skepticism, and more so because autobiographical texts tend to present many *excusationes non petitae*. But that criterion of "empirical" veracity will seldom deeply affect the value of autobiographical activity. A meticulous factual verification may rapidly become an exercise in futility: the "raw material" of events is infinitely dilatable in extension and intensity; the verification will always be incomplete and objectionable.[15] The "mode" of presentation is much more relevant, and that is where the core of the distinction between autobiography and fiction may lie. As a textual construction, autobiography not only can, but should, in order to obtain a better result, make extensive use of narrative artifice (even if this may yield an extreme formal simplicity). Fiction, however, not only implies a different attitude toward referentiality, but also induces a different reading position. The channeling of the interpretive process varies from an autobiographical text to a fictional text, though they may finally converge in a very similar aesthetic or cognitive experience.

Considering a text like Giménez Caballero's, it is important to distinguish, with respect to autobiographical writing, what could be called an "ironic mode" from a fictional mode. Perhaps the best definition of "ironic memoirs" would be that they are memoirs which consciously reveal or assume their own cognitive and representa-

tional limitations. As I have indicated, the fictional mode would en-
danger the distinctiveness of autobiographical writing—and it seems
that the hypothesis of this lack of distinctiveness is refuted by experience itself. With the preservation of their distinctive identity (i.e.,
without being absorbed by fiction's "way of perceiving"), ironic memoirs (or autobiography) are perhaps the ones that end up offering
the most reliable perspective on "reality," since they undo the illusion
of some hypothetical "truthful" memoirs that are able to "establish
the truth."[16]

From this point of view, Giménez's *Memorias* appear full of authenticity and verisimilitude. The privileged space that is reserved in them
for dreams and even deliriums strongly contributes to this end.
Dreams and deliriums were a fundamental aspect of Ernesto
Giménez Caballero's life; it would be impossible to recognize him
fully in his own self-portrait without their presence. These *Memorias*
metaphorically contain and reduplicate the referent on which they
are centered. They are nervous, hallucinated, and megalomaniacal,
just like the life to which they refer. If the autobiographer is at the
same time painter and model, Gecé is a model in constant motion—
a model for whom it is impossible to remain still in a position that
allows a measured and defined portrait of him to be drawn.[17] And,
simultaneously, he is a painter of uncontrollable pulse: he can pro-
long the most imaginative, delicate, and inspired stroke into the most
careless and coarse smudge. If these memoirs function as a mirror it
is not because they offer a reproduction of factual information but
because they establish a sort of symbolic equivalence between form
and content, signifier and signified. They represent a perfectly coherent addition to the incoherent life they aspire to reflect. Ultimately,
they are redundant (as are almost all memoirs), a lens that dupli-
cates, another episode to be added to the memoirs. Life and autobiography become linked in a completely solidary relationship; as an
artist full of intuitive sense, Giménez dreams of the best possible end:
"Cuando voy terminando estas *Memorias* dictándolas. . . . [C]elebraría
que mi vida también terminase. No por desesperación o decrepitud,
sino por amor a la perfección literaria: para [hacer] coincidir el fin
de las evocaciones de mi vida con mi vida misma" [When I finish dictating these *Memorias*. . . . I would be glad if my life would end as
well—not because of desperation or decrepitude, but rather out of
love for literary perfection, for having made the end of the evocation
of my life coincide with the end of life itself].[18] In another passage of
the text he already had drawn the reader toward the suggestion of
the almost impossible perfection of memoirs that end at the moment
the author dies—we can imagine a dying man dictating or writing

about his experience just as he is beginning to die.[19] The eighth chapter of the book is entitled "Mi fusilamiento" [My Execution], and only a few lines before its conclusion the reader discovers that the execution (which, from a narrative point of view, seemed to be an inevitable consequence of the compositional tension created throughout the chapter) will not take place.

In "Some Principles of Autobiography," William Howarth presented three perspectives of the genre which he titled, respectively, "Autobiography as Oratory," "Autobiography as Drama," and "Autobiography as Poetry." Gecé's *Memorias* belong to all three of these categories in similar proportion. These categories correspond to the three main registers we encounter in the text: the persuasive, the pathetic, and the poetic. The vehemence and eloquence of Gecé's discourse—an unrestrained verbal torrent in which the subject himself often drowns—both move and disturb the reader, inducing in him an effect that combines the pathetic and the persuasive moods. The ironic condition to which we referred before also helps to saturate the work with poetic meaning. The textual construction becomes constantly permeated with playfulness and self-reflexivity. The use of ambiguity and playfulness opens up a line of communication with his fictional work. For instance, the second chapter of the text is taken, in large part, from the literal transcription of fragments of Lucy Tandy's study *Ernesto Giménez Caballero y "La Gaceta Literaria"* [Ernesto Giménez Caballero and "The Literary Gazette"].[20] The chapter bears the title "Lucy Tandy's memories," thus incorporating a parodic reflection on the exercise of autobiography which, perhaps necessarily—the text may be wanting to tell us—in some way acquires a kind of apocryphal condition. There is always, in any autobiography, a breach between the I of (hi)story and the I of discourse, such that it could be thought that there is a lack of legitimacy for the proper use of the term "*auto*biography." When inscribed verbally, the I becomes "an-other."

Self-reflexivity is not only augmented with multiple direct appeals to the reader, but also with the dialogue (dialogue of just one voice) that the dictator establishes with the stenographer or with himself about the act of dictation. For example, at the beginning of chapter 8 Giménez writes: "Recordemos al lector, querida taquimeca, dictada mía: A mediados de octubre de 1936, pude evadirme de Madrid. . . ." [Let's remind the reader, my dear stenographer, my dictated one: By mid October, 1936, I managed to escape from Madrid. . . .].[21] And later we find yet another example: "(Me interrumpen en mi dictación.) Perdonadme un instante, ¿dónde iba yo? ¡Ah, sí! *Los Combatientes* [a journal he published during the war]: el primer número apareció por la Navidad del 37. . . ." [(My dictation was interrupted.) Excuse me a minute. . . . Where was I? Ah, yes! *The Fighters:* the first issue appeared around Christmastime, 1937. . . .].[22] It is interesting to compare this second example with a "narrative incident" from Giménez's short story entitled "Infancia de don Juan," [Don Juan's Childhood] found in *Yo, inspector de alcantarillas* [I, Sewer Inspector] (1928). In the course of the story, after a parenthetical digression, the narrative voice asks itself: "Bueno, ¿dónde estaba? . . . Lo que es no tener costumbre de escribir. . . . estos sucesos . . . Perdí el hilo, sin saber rescatarlo. . . . Releeré desde aquel párrafo. . . . " [Well, where was I? . . . Since it is not my habit to write. . . . these events . . . I've lost the narrative thread and don't know how to recover it. . . . I'll reread from that paragraph. . . .]. He then inserts into the text a copy of the paragraph that preceded this digression, and concludes in this way: "(Bueno. . . . Ya sé lo que quería decir . . .)" [(Ah, yes. . . . Now I know what I wanted to say . . .)].[23]

In the cases of both the memoirs and the story the compositional process is "revealed" and becomes completely conscious. As I have studied in the section I devote to "Infancia de Don Juan" in *Voces desde el silencio* [Voices from Silence],[24] the rhythm of the narrative suggests a correspondence with the masturbation on which the story is focused thematically. The notion of the writing process as a masturbatory process can be extrapolated to *Memorias de un dictador.* The narcissistic component that underlies masturbatory activity ("masturbation is sex with someone you love," the proverb says) finds a perfect symbolic correlation in the "recreation" the writer enjoys by recreating his own life. Memoirs are the onanistic genre *par excellence.* In the case of *Memorias de un dictador,* though, it might be better to speak of fellatio, since Gecé dictates his memories to a beautiful girl ("linda muchacha"[25]), who, in turn, serves as kind of receptacle for his "seminal" or signifying emission. (She seems, by the way, to be enthusiastic about her task, even to have a physical enthusiasm which is very delicately suggested: "Observo con emoción que [mi taquígrafa] se ha ido apasionando por lo que dicto. Y ello me anima a sentir que no es vano y lleva música a sus oídos y se abre el corazón en mis labios" [I observe with emotion that my stenographer has become increasingly impassioned about what I am dictating. And that makes me feel that what I am dictating is not in vain, that it is like music to her ears; and my heart opens up through my lips].[26]

The text's orality takes on new dimensions this way—and so does the reader's participation, since the reader bears witness to this contact, being "forced" to intervene vicariously or by substitution in the submissive practice of "oral" sex. However, he is offered a possible reward that goes beyond hypothetical aesthetic or cognitive pleasure. Within a tradition of "redemptive" writings whose origins can be traced back to *A Thousand and One Nights,* the speaking subject hopes to attain his personal "salvation" through his discourse, justifying his life in the act of verbalizing it, in a Dante-like journey toward self-knowledge. The reader, as a companion on this exemplary journey, is offered the opportunity to benefit from such redemption. Giménez Caballero concludes his memoirs by celebrating the ultimate success of his own writing: at last, the autobiographer finds peace in having become reconciled unto himself, in having been capable of giving "sense" to his life, in having written his autobiographical "poem."[27] And perhaps—the text seems to suggest—having borne witness to this process can, in turn, inspire the reader to become reconciled with his own life.

We must wonder, though, if Gecé's memoirs, in the context of the new democratic regime in which they appear, are trying to find accommodation for their author in the new circumstances, as many important *falangistas*—and, more broadly, *franquistas*—would do after the dictator's death. However, far from trying to conceal his historic trajectory (and, for that matter, also his responsibility), Giménez Caballero maintains his ideological fidelities to the end, and even concludes his memoirs cherishing the dream of being buried near José Antonio Primo de Rivera and Franco in the Valle de los Caídos [Valley of the Fallen: monastery and mausoleum]. Throughout the book he softens, of course, the edges of his most aggressive rhetoric—that which was produced within the context of the war years.[28] Giménez speaks enthusiastically of having been the author of the "first nationalist manifesto" ("En torno al casticismo de Italia. Carta a un compañero de la Joven España" [On Italian Traditionalism. Letter to a Comrade of Young Spain]);[29] of having inspired Ledesma Ramos, José Antonio Primo de Rivera and Franco with his ideas; of having attempted to invent a patently Spanish brand of fascism;[30] of having been entrusted, during the war, the position of head of Franco's Propaganda; of having authored the speech Franco delivered in 1937 to announce the unification under his command of all the forces fighting against the Republic; of having been part of the first Franco government; of having been designated Secretary General of the "Movimiento" [Movement] in 1942; and so on. Before the Civil War, such a résumé had already gained him fierce animosity from the most progressive and revolutionary circles of the Left. The verbal attacks he would receive once the War had begun could be illustrated by the following lines threateningly addressed to him in *El Mono Azul* [The Blue Overall], the journal of the Alliance of Antifascist Intellectuals.

Attacks such as this one could be seen as the counterpart of those fiery texts he would publish later on, also during the Civil War. The quotation comes from *El Mono Azul*'s second issue—appeared on 3 November 1936—and was included in a section bearing the startling title of "A paseo":[31]

> Giménez Caballero, el hijo del lío, de sus líos, de la confusión, de la mixtificación de todos los tópicos españolistas; mercachifle, orgulloso de serlo; degenerado hasta la exaltación histérica de las más viles explotaciones de empresa; el que llevaba su adulación a todos los poderes constituidos a términos de indignidad humana, de bajeza, jamás conocidos (recuérdense sus adulaciones personales a Azaña). Giménez Caballero, el famoso "chulo azteca," ¿dónde está? Giménez Caballero, "inspector de alcantarillas," cloaco máximo, coco mínimo, estará en los vertederos, en los pozos negros de sus generales atacados por la disentería del miedo.

> [Giménez Caballero, offspring of this mess, of his own messes, of confusion, of the falsification of every Spanish cliché; a profiteer, and proud to be so; a degenerate to the extent that he exalts hysterically the vilest employers' exploitations; he who admired the establishment to unheard of extremes of human indignity and baseness (remember his personal admiration of Azaña). Giménez Caballero, the famous "Aztec ruffian": Where might one find him? Giménez Caballero, the "sewer inspector," with his big "drain" and his small brain. He'll be hanging around the trash dumps, around the cesspools of his generals, who have been attacked by fear's dysentery.][32]

Although limited in this quotation to the denigratory sentence "remember his personal adulations to Azaña" (in reference to the book *Manuel Azaña* which he published in 1932), Giménez Caballero's attitudes and relations with the Left introduce a component of atypicality and complexity in the design of his ideological profile. In 1918, he was one of the co-founders of the Grupo de Estudiantes Socialistas [Group of Socialist Students]—an organization which has been called a forerunner of the Spanish Communist Party, established in 1920. In the "Carta a un compañero de la Joven España," Gecé defends the need to reconcile the elements that liberal and traditionalist Spain shared in common—to reconcile, as he says, "Moscow's cosmopolitan current" ("la corriente cosmopolita de Moscú") with "Rome's purist current" ("la corriente casticista de Roma").[33] Giménez was also deeply empathetic toward the principles that inspired anarchism—an empathy which he symbolically translated into the design he gave to Falange's flag.[34] In the journal that would succeed *La Gaceta Literaria, El Robinsón literario* [The Literary Robinson] (which he virtually penned by himself), he would write remarks of this kind: "Los anarcosindicalistas siguen en España dando el pecho. Ellos siguen siendo los heroicos, los protagonistas de los movimientos, con su mito revolucionario y místico de la 'huelga general'" [Anarchist-unionists continue to show courage in Spain. With their revolutionary and mystical myth of the "general strike," they are still the heroic ones, the protagonists of the movement], and he alluded to the common anarchist origin of fascism and the "Soviets"].[35] In the same journal, he attacked clericalism, calling it "el caparazón de toda religión sin vida" [the shell of every lifeless religion].[36] Moreover, he used the pages of *La Gaceta* as well as his personal trips to promote interest in the study of Sephardic culture—something rather peculiar for a person with Gecé's ideological background.[37] Furthermore, after the War, he defended the need to expedite reconciliation with Republicans.[38] And finally, in his *Memorias,* he expresses his admiration for figures like Lenin, Mao, and Fidel Castro.

Certainly, all the "heterodoxies" of his ideological formation and transformation, together with his intellectual idiosyncrasy, could not but make him an uncomfortable figure for Franco's regime over the course of the years. He was progressively ostracized by the regime in a manner also consistent with the changes in orientation that would affect it.[39] By the 1950s, his ostracism was in fact so extreme that he observes in his memoirs: "Vi que en España o me quedaba de profesor de Instituto, o aprendía a tocar la guitarra" [I realized that if I stayed in Spain I would either wind up as a high school teacher or have to learn to play guitar].[40] By 1955, though, the regime would offer him a "way out" by naming him Cultural Attaché in Paraguay and Brazil;[41] in 1958 he becomes "estranged" for good when he is named Ambassador in Paraguay—a position he would hold for more than a decade, until his retirement.

Memoirs may perhaps be the nostalgic genre *par excellence.* As he reaches the final pages of his *Memorias,* Giménez Caballero begins to vanish in his text like a nostalgic shadow, like a shadow that seems to have lost its foundations and motivation in reality. In spite of having been an avant-gardist and an *hombre de avanzada* [progressive man], as soon as the effects of his ideology were confronted with reality, he rapidly became a man of the past, of a totally outdated past, a past that would almost seem imaginary in its anachronism, although, at the same time, would be sadly present and alive for some decades during the last century. The history of fascism, Falangism, and even *Franquismo* in contemporary Spain cannot be accurately traced without considering the life and writings of Ernesto Giménez Caballero. His *Memorias* help us reconstruct the itinerary of that historical cycle, from its beginnings to its final derivations—selectively, of course; and from the extreme peculiarity of his personal perspective. Mussolini once noted that "Life is all gesture." Faithful to the inspiration of he who, in more than one sense, would be for him an ideological—and even behavioral—role model, Giménez reveals himself as an ever gesticulative and histrionic figure—even (or maybe especially) in his writing, or in his dictation/-orship. His memoirs are the final convulsion of the histrion, the symbolic closure of a life that, probably to his chagrin, would be prolonged in an almost ghost-like way for a decade beyond the end of writing, beyond the composition of the final verse of "his poem." In fact, we might say that both Giménez's political and emotional lives really ended with Franco's regime. In that sense, these memoirs are also a metaphoric memorandum of the dying out in Spain of those endless "forty years," or even forty-five or fifty, if we consider the most immediate antecedents of the Civil War. These are, in effect, "immemorable memoirs," as he himself (showing, as always, his capacity for ironic self-distance) refers to them at some point. Are they immemorable because they make him feel ashamed? Are they immemorable because they are vulgar? Are they immemorable because the attempt to apprehend or register reality in memory is always in vain, because—as we discussed before—reality ceases to be so when it is inscribed in memory? Probably there is some truth in all of these claims. Yes, in many ways, Gecé's memoirs are indeed "immemorable"; but, as we have seen, they are able to revive and innovate, to always add an original and imaginative touch, to infuse the genre of memoirs with a stimulating freshness, putting into practice a purely intuitive theorization about its renovation. They are, thus, memoirs that project themselves into the future, even though they are constituted, for many reasons, by an almost inert past.[42]

NOTES

1. All these initiatives and innovations are recapitulated in the *Memorias* we are studying: Ernesto Giménez Caballero, *Memorias de un dictador* (Barcelona: Planeta, 1979) at, respectively, 14, 296, 85, 88, 74, and 15.

2. Ibid., 15. As we shall see below, this narcissism, which is alluded to here with a somewhat pejorative tone, opens up a suggestive approach—different from the criterion of truth and falsehood—for reading his *Memorias*.

3. The reference from Ortega he is talking about comes from "Sobre unas memorias" [On Some Memoirs]. In *Obras completas* [Complete Works], vol. 3. Madrid: Alianza Editorial, 1983, 590.

4. With this observation, Giménez adds his name to the long tradition of Spanish autobiographers who, as James D. Fernández has noted, underscore (though, at the same time, contradict with their practice) that autobiography is a genre that Spaniards do not cultivate. Fernández adduces the examples of Alcalá Galiano, Be-

navente, González Ruano, and Juan Goytisolo (*Apology to Apostrophe: Autobiography and the Rhetoric of Self-Representation in Spain* [Durham, NC: Duke University Press, 1992], 1–2). See, in reference to this, Ángel G. Loureiro, "La autobiografía española: actualidad y futuro" [Spanish Autobiography], *Anthropos* 125 (Octubre 1991), 18–19.

5. *Memorias,* 15, 19.

6. Enrique Selva, *Ernesto Giménez Caballero entre la vanguardia y el fascismo* [Ernesto Giménez Caballeo between Fascism and Avant-garde] (Valencia: Pre-Textos, 2000), 18.

7. Georges Gusdorf, "Conditions and Limits of Autobiography," in James Olney, ed., *Autobiography: Essays Theoretical and Critical* (Princeton: Princeton University Press, 1980), 43.

8. Northrop Frye, *Anatomy of Criticism: Four Essays* (Princeton: Princeton University Press, 1985), 307.

9. Louis A. Renza, "The Veto of the Imagination: A Theory of Autobiography," in Olney, ed., 295.

10. Elizabeth W. Bruss, *Autobiographical Acts: The Changing Situation of a Literary Genre* (Baltimore: Johns Hopkins University Press, 1976).

11. Jerome Bruner, "The Autobiographical Process," in Robert Folkenflik, ed., *The Culture of Autobiography: Constructions of Self-Representation* (Stanford: Stanford University Press, 1993), 38–56.

12. Paul de Man, "Autobiography as De-Facement," in *The Rhetoric of Romanticism* (New York: Columbia University Press, 1984), 69–70.

13. Michael Sprinker, "Fictions of the Self: The End of Autobiography," in Olney, ed., 342.

14. Loureiro, *The Ethics of Autobiography: Replacing the Subject in Modern Spain* (Nashville, TN: Vanderbilt University Press, 2000), 19. Emphasis mine.

15. "Events" should be understood here in the broadest sense of the word as anything that happens or attains existence, even immaterially (feelings, ideas, impressions, etc.).

16. As may be noted, I am using the terms "memoirs" and "autobiography" almost interchangeably. The precise delimitation of the conceptual difference between both genres has been attempted repeatedly. For example, Philippe Lejeune argued that both genres can be distinguished according to the "subject treated," which in autobiography would be "[an] individual life, [a] story of a personality," while memoirs would not focus on the subject himself but on public life (*On Autobiography.* Katherine Leary, trans. Paul John Eakin, ed. (Minneapolis: University of Minnesota Press, 1989), 4. Darío Villanueva refers to the different consideration of the receiver: as confident in autobiography and as public in memoirs ("Realidad y ficción: la paradoja de la autobiografía" [Reality and Fiction: The Paradox of Autobiography], in José Romera, Alicia Yllera, Mario García-Page, and Rosa Calvet, eds., *Escritura autobiográfica. Actas del II Seminario Internacional del Instituto de Semiótica Literaria y Teatral* [Madrid: Visor, 1993], 19). Giménez Caballero, as we have indicated, impugns the concept of "memoirs" and approaches emotionally that of "autobiographical narration or picaresque novel" (*Memorias,* 20); nonetheless, he titles his work *Memorias de un dictador* (although that is what opens for him the door to his innovative labor). But leaving aside the most prototypical or visible cases, the distinction between memoirs and autobiography vanishes in innumerable intermediate cases, especially when there is not a clear consciousness of these "technical" definitions at the moment of writing. One of the main formalizers of the distinction, Georges May, after exploring in depth the nuances that apparently invite to maintain it, ends up referring to it as "artificiel et . . . trompeur" [artificial and deceptive]; his more than ten pages

in search for distinct criteria of separation lead him to this conclusion: "Plus on cherche les frontières qui séparent l'autobiographie et les mémoires, plus on s'aperçoit donc qu'elles sont floues, fuyantes, mouvantes et subjectives" [The more one searches for the limits that separate autobiography and memoirs, the more one realizes that they are vague, elusive, shifting, and subjective] (*L'Autobiographie* [Paris: Presses Universitaires de France, 1979], 124; 128).

17. The painter-model analogy is developed by William L. Howarth in "Some Principles of Autobiography," in Olney, ed.

18. *Memorias*, 295.

19. Let us imagine for a moment the possibility of a situation similar to the one portrayed in the final pages of Carlos Fuentes's *La muerte de Artemio Cruz* [Death of Artemio Cruz].

20. The study was originally written in English as a doctoral dissertation in 1932, and its translation was included, along with María Sferrazza's work *Ernesto Giménez Caballero en la literatura española de la dictadura a la República* [Ernesto Giménez Caballero in Spanish Literature, from the Dictatorship to the Republic] (written in 1964), in the volume entitled *Ernesto Giménez Caballero y "La Gaceta Literaria" (o la generación del 27)* [Ernesto Giménez Caballero and "The Literary Gazette" (or the Generation of 1927)], published by Ediciones Turner.

21. *Memorias*, 82.

22. Ibid., 115.

23. Giménez Caballero, *Yo, inspector de alcantarillas (Epiplasmas)* (Madrid: Turner, 1975), 71.

24. Ricardo Krauel, *Voces desde el silencio. Heterologías genérico-sexuales en la narrativa española moderna (1875–1975)* (Madrid: Libertarias, 2001), 172–188.

25. *Memorias*, 12.

26. Ibid., 33.

27. Ibid., 300.

28. Some samples of it can be found in the newspaper articles compiled by Julio Rodríguez Puértolas in the second volume of *Literatura fascista española* [Spanish Fascist Literature] (Madrid: Akal, 1986–1987).

29. *Memorias*, 11. The complete text, initially published in *La Gaceta Literaria* no. 52 (February 15, 1929), is also reproduced in the Bassolas anthology, *La ideología de los escritores* [The Ideology of Writers].

30. *Memorias*, 68.

31. As is well known, "dar el paseo" (or "el paseíllo") to someone implied to detain or kidnap him in order to take him by car to an isolated place where he would be executed without any kind of previous trial.

32. Selva, 275.

33. Giménez Caballero, "En torno al casticismo de Italia. Carta a un compañero de la joven España," in Bassolas, ed., 150–151.

34. "Yo encontré la fórmula ideal de la que surgiría el Falangismo viendo por 1929 en mi barrio de Delicias su Ateneo Libertario o anarco-sindicalista, con su bandera roja y negra, proponiendo 'nacionalizarla' con el Yugo y las Flechas, el Haz o Fascio de los Reyes Católicos" [I found the ideal formula from which Falangism would arise when I saw in my district of Delicias, around 1929, its Libertarian or anarchist-syndicalist Athenaeum, with its red and black flag, which I proposed to "nationalize" with the Yoke and Arrows, the Fasces or *Fascio* of Isabella and Ferdinand] (*Memorias*, 84). Fernando Sánchez Dragó comments in this vein: "Ernesto Giménez Caballero [se] hizo falangista sin dejar de ser anarquista y hasta se permitió la sublime impertinencia de teñir con los santos colores de la anarquía la bandera de Falange" [Ernesto

Giménez Caballero became a Falangist without ceasing to be an anarchist, and he even allowed himself the sublime impertinence of dying Falange's flag with the holy colors of anarchism] ("Prólogo a *Genio de España,* de Ernesto Giménez Caballero," in Rodríguez-Puértolas, op.cit., 1271).

35. Giménez Caballero, "El anarquismo y España," in Bassolas, ed., 493–494.

36. Giménez Caballero, "Tipos y tipismos de la República," in Bassolas, ed., 459.

37. For example, he referred to Sephardim in declarations to *La Gaceta Literaria* in 1929 as "nuestros antiguos compatriotas que tras casi cuatro siglos de apartamiento casi absoluto mantienen heroicamente nuestro idioma" [our old fellow citizens who, after almost four centuries of nearly complete estrangement, heroically still speak our language] (Selva, 135). Regarding this question of *La Gaceta*'s "philo-Sephardism," see Norbert Rehrmann, "Los sefardíes como 'anexo' de la Hispanidad: Ernesto Giménez Caballero y *La Gaceta Literaria*" [The Sephardim as "Annex" to Hispanicity: Ernesto Giménez Caballero and *La Gaceta Literaria*], in Albert, ed. See also Douglas W. Foard, *The Revolt of the Aesthetes: Ernesto Giménez Caballero and the Origin of Spanish Fascism* (New York: Peter Lang, 1989), 98–100, and Lucy Tandy and María Sferrazza, *Ernesto Giménez Caballero y "La Gaceta Literaria" (o la generación del 27)* (Madrid: Tuner, 1977), 50.

38. "España la habíamos deshecho entre todos los españoles, divididos en dos bandos. Había que reedificarla sin más victoria que la moral de abrazar al derrotado" [All of us Spaniards, divided into two bands, had destroyed Spain. We had to rebuild it with no other victory than the moral triumph of embracing the defeated] (reference to a speech given after the end of the conflict, *Memorias,* 141); "[Y]o inicié inmediatamente ['la apertura democrática'], ¿os importa recordarlo?, fundando una Cripta, la de Don Quijote, en ese antiguo Café de Levante, para que acudieran a ella los que fueron nuestros adversarios y con los que urgía reconciliarse. [Y] allí vinieron desde antiguos comunistas liberados de la cárcel, a escritores tenidos por adversarios, como Buero Vallejo, al cual le dediqué toda una sesión sobre los ciegos, por su 'ardiente oscuridad'" [If you'll be so good as to remember, I immediately initiated the democratic opening by founding a Crypt—that of Don Quijote—in that old Café de Levante, so that our former adversaries, with whom we urgently needed to be reconciled, could come. And they all came—everyone from former Communists who had been let out of jail to writers who were our adversaries: like Buero Vallejo, to whom I dedicated a session about the blind because of his "ardiente oscuridad"] (Ibid., 23).

39. With regard to this "evolution," see Walther L. Bernecker, "El debate sobre el régimen franquista" [The Debate about the Francoist Regime], in Albert, ed.

40. *Memorias,* 101.

41. 1955 is the year indicated on page 308 of *Memorias;* on pages 225 and 242, however, Giménez mentions the year 1956.

42. I would like to thank Michael Lazzara for his assistance during the preparation of this article.

BIBLIOGRAPHY

Albert, Mechthild, ed. *Vencer no es convencer. Literatura e ideología del fascismo español.* Frankfurt: Vervuert, 1998.

Bassolas, Carmen, ed. *La ideología de los escritores. Literatura y política en "La Gaceta Literaria" (1927–1932).* Barcelona: Fontamara, 1975.

Benstock, Shari. "Authorizing the Autobiographical." In *The Private Self: Theory and Practice of Women's Autobiographical Writings*. Edited by Shari Benstock. Chapel Hill: University of North Carolina Press, 1988.

Bernecker, Walther L. "El debate sobre el régimen franquista: ¿fascismo, autoritarismo, dictadura de modernización?" In Albert, op. cit.

Bruner, Jerome. "The Autobiographical Process." In *The Culture of Autobiography: Constructions of Self-Representation*. Edited by Robert Folkenflik. Stanford: Stanford University Press, 1993.

Bruss, Elizabeth W. *Autobiographical Acts: The Changing Situation of a Literary Genre*. Baltimore: Johns Hopkins University Press, 1976.

Eakin, Paul John. *Fictions in Autobiography: Studies in the Art of Self-Invention*. Princeton: Princeton University Press, 1985.

Fernández, James D. *Apology to Apostrophe: Autobiography and the Rhetoric of Self-Representation in Spain*. Durham, NC: Duke University Press, 1992.

Foard, Douglas W. *The Revolt of the Aesthetes: Ernesto Giménez Caballero and the Origins of Spanish Fascism*. New York: Peter Lang, 1989.

Frye, Northrop. *Anatomy of Criticism: Four Essays*. Princeton: Princeton University Press, 1990.

Giménez Caballero, Ernesto. "El anarquismo y España." In Bassolas, op. cit.

———. "En torno al casticismo de Italia. Carta a un compañero de la joven España." In Bassolas, ed., op.cit.

———. *Memorias de un dictador*. Barcelona: Planeta, 1979.

———. "Tipos y tipismos de la República. Yo soy un rabioso anticlerical." In Bassolas, ed., op. cit.

———. *Yo, inspector de alcantarillas. (Epiplasmas)*. Prologue by Edward Baker. Madrid: Turner, 1975.

Gusdorf, Georges. "Conditions and Limits of Autobiography." Translated by James Olney. In James Olney, ed., op. cit.

Howarth, William L. "Some Principles of Autobiography." In Olney, ed., op. cit.

Krauel, Ricardo. *Voces desde el silencio. Heterologías genérico-sexuales en la narrativa española moderna (1875–1975)*. Madrid: Libertarias, 2001.

Lejeune, Philippe. *On Autobiography*. Translated by Katherine Leary. Edited by Paul John Eakin. Minneapolis: University of Minnesota Press, 1989.

Loureiro, Ángel G. "La autobiografía española: actualidad y futuro." *Anthropos* 125 (Octubre 1991): 17–20.

———. *The Ethics of Autobiography: Replacing the Subject in Modern Spain*. Nashville, TN: Vanderbilt University Press, 2000.

Man, Paul de. *The Rhetoric of Romanticism*. New York: Columbia University Press, 1984.

May, Georges. *L'Autobiographie*. Paris: Presses Universitaires de France, 1979.

Olney, James. "Autobiography and the Cultural Moment: A Thematic, Historical, and Bibliographical Introduction." Olney, ed., op. cit.

———, ed. *Autobiography: Essays Theoretical and Critical*. Princeton: Princeton University Press, 1980.

Ortega y Gasset, José. "Sobre unas memorias." In *Obras completas*. Vol. 3. Madrid: Alianza Editorial, 1983.

Rehrmann, Norbert. "Los sefardíes como 'anexo' de la Hispanidad: Ernesto Giménez Caballero y *La Gaceta Literaria*." In Albert, ed., op. cit.

Renza, Louis A. "The Veto of the Imagination: A Theory of Autobiography." In Olney, ed., op. cit.

Rodríguez Puértolas, Julio. *Literatura fascista española.* 2 vols. Madrid: Akal, 1986–1987.

Sánchez Dragó, Fernando. "Prólogo a *Genio de España,* de Ernesto Giménez Caballero." In Rodríguez Puértolas, op. cit., vol. 2.

Selva, Enrique. *Ernesto Giménez Caballero entre la vanguardia y el fascismo.* Foreword by Juan Manuel Bonet. Valencia: Pre-Textos, 2000.

Smith, Sidonie. *A Poetics of Women's Autobiography: Marginality and the Fictions of Self-Representation.* Bloomington: Indiana University Press, 1987.

Sprinker, Michael. "Fictions of the Self: The End of Autobiography." In Olney, ed., op. cit.

Tandy, Lucy, and María Sferrazza. *Ernesto Giménez Caballero y "La Gaceta Literaria" (o la generación del 27).* Madrid: Turner, 1977.

Villanueva, Darío. "Realidad y ficción: la paradoja de la autobiografía." In *Escritura autobiográfica. Actas del II Seminario Internacional del Instituto de Semiótica Literaria y Teatral.* Edited by José Romera, Alicia Yllera, Mario García-Page, and Rosa Calvet. Madrid: Visor, 1993.

Preserving the Falangist Myth
in the Post-Franco Era:
The Case of Fernando Vadillo's
Los Legionarios and *Los Irreductibles*

Dionisio Viscarri

WITH THE ABORTED 1981 COUP OF "23–F" AND THE PSOE'S LANDSLIDE victory in the 1982 national elections, the political aspirations of Spain's extreme right, and with them the principles of the Movimiento Nacional [National Movement], were decisively rendered ineffectual. Unable to legitimize its previous hegemony and lacking popular support, the far-right was forced to go on the defensive. Even during the late Franco era, disenchanted groups had splintered into numerous factions of more symbolic value than political effectiveness. The regime's demise increased the balkanization of extremist associations. Spanish politics became a heterogeneous landscape of ultra-right organizations ranging from the Neo-Nazi and Europeanish Círculo Español de Amigos de Europa [Spanish Circle of Friends of Europe], originally established in 1966, to more autochthonous groups like Falange Española Auténtica [Authentic Spanish Falange], the Frente Nacional Español [Spanish National Front] and the Junta Coordinadora Nacional Sindicalista [Syndicalist National Coordinating Junta] among others. The last three groups competed to appropriate the ideology, symbols, rituals, historical legacy, and identity of the Pre-Civil War Falange Española de las JONS [Spanish Falange of the JONS]. As Sheelagh Ellwood explains, "[e]ach claimed to be the direct descendant of the party founded in 1933 and accused the other of having 'betrayed' the original doctrine by their collaboration with the Franco regime."[1] Better supported, comparatively less violent, and much more Francoist in outlook was Fuerza Nueva [New Force], led by the flamboyant Blas Piñar López.[2] The party would dissolve following the debacle of the 1982 elections, only to return in 1986 under the mimetic title of Frente Nacional

[National Front].[3] However, all attempts by the radical Right to reinvent and redefine itself proved futile. The bulk of the Spanish electorate perceived these political groups as anachronistic representatives of an exhausted authoritarian era. Most Spaniards wanted a clean break with the past; they demanded democratic change.

In an often-repeated historical paradox, the loss of political currency reinvigorated Falangist aesthetic militancy. A significant number of memoirs, chronicles, and fictional works, ranging from the testimonial to the nostalgic, trickled into the literary spectrum.[4] Many of these texts were published by obscure, ideologically committed presses dedicated to the preservation and propagation of the Franco–Falangist legacy, or in some cases to the disassociation of Falangism from Francoism. Small literary enterprises like Ediciones Dyrsa [Dyrsa Editions], Editorial Barbarroja [Barbarossa Publishing], and the Fundación Nacional Francisco Franco [Francisco Franco National Foundation] responded to counter the limited access afforded to reactionary writings by conventional publishing houses in post-Francoist Spain. Generally speaking, ultra-right presses have had an ephemeral existence. Highlighting their own desire to project a semi-clandestine, anti-establishment image of staunch resistors beleaguered by the outside world, some publishers have resorted to frequent name changes of their firms. Furthermore, they have catered to a limited readership of similar political views and/or interest (including military aficionados, veterans, and current members of the Armed Forces), creating what can be loosely termed an underground for an ideologically driven literary culture. Although many of these publishers were backed by political or military organizations, or by private benefactors, the issuing of a limited number of copies was the norm.

A significant share of the literary activity engaging rightist authors of this period has centered around Falangist participation in the Second World War. According to Carlos Caballero and Rafael Ibáñez this proliferation, "choca al propio tiempo con el profundo desinterés por parte de las casas editoriales, lo que lleva a los excombatientes a editarse sus propios libros, a hacerlo a través de sus Hermandades o con la mediación de editoriales pequeñas, con un estilo literario y de edición muy desigual" [conversely collides with the profound disinterest from publishers, which drives many of the veterans to self-publish their manuscripts, and/or have them distributed by their veteran organizations, or through smaller publishing houses, however with inconsistent quality in terms of style and format].[5]

In 1984, Fernando Vadillo Ortiz de Guzmán (1923–2001), a once fervent Falangist and veteran of the Russian campaign, and later a

renowned sports writer, published *Los Legionarios* [The Legion-
naires], the first installment in a three volume series of thematically
similar but independent narratives, under the encapsulating title
"Balada final de la 'División Azul'" [The 'Blue Division's Final Bal-
lad].[6] Following a fairly strict chronological sequence and dependent on first-hand accounts, each book presents a particular episode
of Spanish involvement in World War II, after the repatriation of the
Blue Division.

In June of 1941, after being officially informed of the launching of
Operation Barbarossa, Ramón Serrano Súñer, Secretary General of
the Falange and brother-in-law of General Franco, proclaimed before
a fanatic audience, "la destrucción del comunismo es condición
necesaria para la supervivencia de una Europa libre y civilizada" [the
destruction of Communism is mandatory for the survival of a free and
civilized Europe].[7] Soon afterwards, a volunteer expeditionary force
consisting primarily of professional soldiers, but also including a
large contingent of ardent young Falangists, was organized and
dispatched to fight on the Eastern front. In this manner the 250th Division of the Wehrmacht was created, later to be commonly designated the 'Blue Division' because of the Falangist blue shirts worn by
its members.

Hitler's Spanish contingent fought extensively in the northern sector of operations in the areas surrounding Leningrad.[8] Due to Allied
political pressure and to a redirection in Spanish foreign policy, the
unit was reduced and transformed into the Blue Legion in November 1943 and eventually repatriated in March 1944. Several hundred
Spanish soldiers remained and were incorporated into other
Wehrmacht and Waffen-SS units. In fact, several Falangists, among
the last defenders of the Reichstag, were interned after the war, joining other comrades who had been in Russian prison camps since
1941. However, the saga of the Falangist volunteers did not end until 1954, when, on board the Liberian vessel "Semíramis," they
reached the port of Barcelona, thus ending their captivity.

Vadillo's post-Francoist trilogy narrates the final chapters of the
Russian expedition and other instances of Spanish assistance to the
Axis war effort. As suggested by its title, *Los Legionarios* focuses on
the reduced force of volunteers that opted to continue the struggle
against Communism in 1943.[9] Its chronological sequel, *Los Irreductibles* [The Unyielding] (1993), is centered around the several
hundred Spaniards who joined the Nazis for a final stand throughout Europe and ultimately in Berlin, while the final volume, *Los Pri-
sioneros* [The Prisoners] (1996), depicts the daily life and hardships
of the Spanish POW's in the Stalinist gulag.[10] Although they form au-

tonomous narrative constructs, they all share identical ideological strategies of representation. Because the first two texts contain several elements illustrative of orthodox Falangist discourse, this study focuses exclusively on them. Adding to their interest is the fact that they are paradigmatic of other works on the same topic published in the post-authoritarian era.

To a large extent, the series retains the Falangist model of representation. It shares ideological, stylistic, and interpretative components that firmly place it within the fascist literary tradition. Julio Rodríguez Puértolas underlines the anachronistic nature of *Los Legionarios*, "con idénticos tonos a los empleados cuarenta años atrás—se trata, contra lo que pudiera parecer, de un libro de 1984" [with identical tones to those used forty years ago—it is, contrary to what one would expect, a book from 1984].[11]

The diegetic components of this fictionalized chronicle rest on a series of segmental episodes that, imitating the movement of a camera lens, focus on different aspects of the Legion's performance. Attempting to create an epic style, the text alternates scenes of collective and individual action with references to the historical context and panoramic views of the Russian landscape.[12] After an initial chronological jump forward in the presentation of events, the text immediately settles into a linear pattern that corresponds to the timeline of the unit's existence.

Speaking in the third person, the narrative voice reconstructs the past with the mediation of official documents and other historiographic sources. A palimpsestic effect results and is evident in the meticulous attention afforded to chronological, geographic, and statistical data. Beneath the fictionalized narrative layer one detects the presence of Franco–Falangist historiographical discourse, which had been the pervasive representational referent for scholars while the Regime was in power. In fact, in the prologue the author highlights the academic approach that mediates the portrayal of events, "[t]ampoco la presente obra es de carácter imaginativo. Hombres, nombres, fechas, paisajes, acciones y cuanto en ella se narra es fruto de recopilación de documentos oficiales, testimonios personales y manejo de una extensa bibliografía" [this is not a work of fiction. The men, names, dates, setting, and actions that appear in this story are the product of the compilation of official documents, personal accounts, and the use of extensive bibliographical sources].[13] Well aware of the fictional properties of this work, a clarification is made "[t]odo debidamente cotejado para no incurrir en errores de fondo ni defectos de forma" [everything has been aptly integrated in order to avoid background errors and structural shortcomings].[14] Factual accuracy hence becomes the facilitator and guarantor of ideological veracity.

To this end, the text fuses fiction with historiography, maintaining the Falangist conceptualization and interpretation of their version of History as a sacred, transcendental space. Unavoidably, content is subordinated to political–didactic interests. Traditional military narrative strategies are integrated with bits of mythologized discourse. The images of war are presented in a combination of gripping combat action, tension-building interims which describe the military situation and off-duty escapades of the enlisted men, and preparatory maneuvers that focus on the hardships and dangers of daily life in a war zone.[15] These genre-specific elements are interspersed with political referents that underline the historical significance of the events taking place. A "realistic" effect is steadily pursued immersing the reader into the center of the action, and making him/her part of the historical experience through direct address. By exercising a highly referential concept of language the text purports to frame the past in a veracious and supposedly objective manner. The result is a monologic construct, constrained by its overtly ideological pretensions and the overwhelming presence of minute historical detail that restricts the development of a consistent story-line. A concern for fealty to facts is the underlying premise that provides a degree of unity to the narrative. Discerning historical from fictional characters, for example, becomes an impossible task, attesting to the effectiveness of a narrative strategy designed to reduce reader ambiguity toward the events that unfold. It is precisely in the overlapping confines of fiction and historical chronicle that the author/narrator articulates his ideological message. By resorting to a fictionalized form, in what intends to be an otherwise factual account, the text enjoys the imaginative and representational flexibility, albeit in a limited fashion, connected with novelistic production, while simultaneously convincing the reader that verisimilitude and veracity are conjoined.

The text does not, however, possess palimpsestic characteristics at an ideological level. It does not propose a recycled, elaborate reconsideration of Falangist ideology in order to make it more palatable to a post-Francoist audience. In other words, it does not pursue reader adherence to a refurbished political program. Had the Franco regime produced a unitary, systematic ideology loyal to the original principles of Falangism, then perhaps we would be looking at an attempt to articulate a redirected political discourse. Rather, what the narrative evinces is the practice of discursive archeology—that is, the restoration of an authentic, purist vision of Falangism in its ideological and aesthetic manifestations.[16] The text offers a nostalgic revisiting of the past to inscribe the protagonists and events of the Eastern Front into the annals of Falangist myth. Loyal to its Romantic elements, *Los Legionarios* exhibits a tension between present reality and frustrated desire in the form of a longing for a lost heroic era, when the fantasies and hopes of a veritable Falangist future for Spain were still being contemplated. Clearly, the sub-textual Odysseyan properties inherent in an account involving the perilous journey of idealistic warriors to a foreign land and their return home reinforce Falangism's quest to represent universal values.[17]

As in other works of the series, the narrative's primary objective is to mythicize Falangist involvement in the Second World War as "el episodio bélico más destacado de la reciente historia de España" [the most outstanding military episode in recent Spanish history].[18] From the outset a persistent and direct correspondence is established between the Legion and its predecessor. Repeated references to the continuation of an heroic legacy, already cemented in Vadillo's previous works, abound. He characterizes them as "los legionarios, herederos de la gloria de los antiguos divisionarios" [the legionnaires, heirs of the glory attained by the Blue Division].[19] Early in the plot, the narrator explains that the new regiment's first position in the northern sector of operations is very near to the area "donde luchara la ya fabulosa División Azul" [where the fabulous Blue Division once fought].[20] In this manner a precarious syllogism is constructed, equating and bestowing the assumed magnificence of one military unit to the other.[21] If the Blue Division's performance was as the adjective suggests, legendary and fantastic, and if the Legion is the natural inheritor of its epic past, then the latter is equally glorious and deserving of the reader's admiration. Of course, the logical soundness of the initial premise is dependent on the unconditional acceptance of the principle that the Blue Division was indeed deserving of the superhuman attributes derived from the term chosen by the narrator. This exaltation extends to the individual soldier, adding an identifiable human component, which serves to personalize the deeds presented. Men like Captain Urbano are described as "[u]no de los oficiales falangistas que se libraron, a precio de sangre, una leyenda de heroísmo en la batalla de Krasny Bor" [one of the Falangist officers who forged in blood a legend of heroism at the battle of Krasny Bor],[22] the Blue Division's hardest fought engagement. He is a hero because the narrator tells us that he is, thus creating a tautology typical of Falangist discourse that relies on the persistence and repetition of an assertion in order to make it factual. The intention is to historicize the human component, while simultaneously humanizing the historical event.

A recurrent theme, evident in the previous quote, is the stoic acceptance of suffering and danger by the legionaries for the sake of the fatherland.[23] There is a calculated attempt to obtain the recognition and sympathy of the Spanish general public for the sacrifices incurred on the battlefield. Blood is the symbolic, mythical, cultural, religious, and biologic agent that bonds the contemporary Spanish reader to the Falangist volunteers. From a Fascist perspective, it is only through the ritualistic individual and collective offering of blood that a return to spiritual origins and national totality can be achieved, after generations of internal decomposition:

> ¡Que la sangre de nuestro primer oficial caído en combate, alférez Antonio de Palma, fortalezca el espíritu que a todos nos anima en esta lucha ideológica! ¡Que su sacrificio nos estimule para combatir el comunismo! ¡Su muerte no será estéril, y de su sangre brotarán las cinco rosas de una primavera triunfal . . . !

> [Let the blood of our first officer fallen in battle, Second Lieutenant Antonio de Palma, fortify the spirit that encourages us in this ideological struggle! Let his sacrifice incite us to fight Communism! His death will not be fruitless, and from his blood will sprout the five roses of a triumphant Spring . . . !][24]

Thus is reiterated the antithetical concept of a national rebirth inseminated by sacrificial death. The martial metaphors and euphemisms used by militant Catholicism are literalized and synthesized with Falangist discourse, which in turn is given a more subliminal semantic referent in the imagery of the "five roses." An obvious reference extracted from the Falangist anthem, the flowers are the superior symbols of ideological victory, which as the song suggests is attained through armed struggle, as represented by the "five arrows" (the emblematic icon of the Falange) that lie beneath the plants. Spain's regeneration is therefore only possible through a cleansing process entailing the reinscription of heroic action into national myth and the rejection of an inauthentic historical trajectory.

"La España verdadera, la España auténtica, se siente gozosamente implicada en su bella y patriótica aventura" [The real Spain, the authentic Spain, feels itself to be engaged in this beautiful and patriotic adventure],[25] asserts a Falangist envoy delivering the troops' Christmas bonus. His powerful statement uncovers a persistent myth in Spanish Fascist ideology. The idea that Spain had deviated from its logical historical destiny, a concept appropriated from Regenerationists and Generation of 98 intellectuals alike and interpreted to fit into the Falangist ideological mold, became the justification to undercut all political opposition. Authenticity is defined by Falangists as a conglomerate of traits that, proclaiming its superiority among other nations, identify Spain as indivisible, militaristic, nationalistic, socially harmonious, imperialist, culturally Catholic, and endowed with a universal mission to propagate its cultural and spiritual essence.

The book meets (as does *Los Irreductibles*) the fundamental criteria demanded from a Falangist work of art. According to this model, aesthetic value is determined by its utilitarian function. It upholds the concept of art as propaganda (interestingly, a trait also evident in Stalinist art), whose transcendence relies on its spiritual essence, as a manifestation of the national will (as defined by the State) and its interests. Based on these premises, "[e]l primer 'servicio' que el artista debía rendir a España, el primer 'deber' a que le obligaba su condición de artista español y católico era el de recuperar un lenguaje artístico referencial o, lo que es igual, subordinar la forma, el estilo, las cuestiones técnicas del arte a su elemento esencial, el contenido" [the first 'service' that an artist should render Spain, the first 'duty' to which he was bound as a Catholic and as a Spaniard was that of regaining an artistic and referential language, that subordinates artistic form, style, and technique to its essential element: content].[26] The application of these aesthetic principles in the context of a non-supportive State apparatus is what explains the extreme reliance on historical materials for legitimization. Implicitly, national history is made to compete with current national politics. In the polyphonic, decentered discursive practices made possible by the democratic change, the agency previously enjoyed by nationalist writers could no longer be taken for granted. Claims on the truth were now favorable to the previously suppressed voices of the Civil War vanquished. In order to undermine the new democratic context, major emphasis is placed on the ennobling attributes of armed conflict and of personal sacrifice in the pursuit of higher ideals, "algo que hoy no entendería la juventud de porro y discoteca," [something that today's drug and discotheque-driven youth could not understand], while simultaneously maintaining the cult of youth (that is Falangist youth) and the anti-bourgeois rhetoric of revolutionary Falangism, "ni acaso tampoco la clase madura y materializada" [neither perhaps could the older and materialistic classes].[27] Ironically, the emphasis on the generational conflict that had prompted the exaltation of youth in the seminal years of Fascism, was now realigned to contrast the idealism of the Falangist generation with the decadent habits of democratic Spain's youth. By chastising the hedonistic predisposition of the new youth culture, Vadillo insinuates a doubtful future for the new society. On the other hand, the text seeks to vindicate the historical significance of the Falangist movement, while subtly distancing itself from the Franco regime. It offers a counter discourse to democratic Spain's now recuperated dissident voices and to the detractors of the Falangist past.

Although almost identical to its predecessor in perspective and ideological content, *Los Irreductibles* is less dependent on fictionalized enhancement, relying instead on a more traditional form of historical narration. It also lacks the thematic and structural unity that the Legion's role provides the other text. Much more fragmented, each chapter identifies a particular theater of operations or military unit and gives an account of the extent of Spanish involvement. Dialogue and character development is even more subordinated to historical content than in *Los Legionarios*. History, mutated or not, and ideology are given the role of protagonists. Nevertheless, the narrator appears to delight in revealing the intense and colorful roles played by Falangists in the service of the Third Reich, who knowingly risked losing their Spanish citizenship to affirm their ideological convictions. Anecdotal sequences involving prominent figures of the Axis powers, such as Otto Skorzeny and Léon Degrelle, seek to rehabilitate their images, stressing their links to the Spanish belligerents and, by extension, to Spanish history, and simultaneously contesting their demonizing by historians.[28] In fact in the prologue, the author explains that the reconstruction of the events presented in the text was made possible by their testimonial collaboration. Both had settled in Spain after the war and were active in Nazi revivalist movements.[29] By consciously associating the content of his book with the historical memory of unrepentant, die-hard Nazis, the author/narrator utterly demystifies his historical perspective, while paying homage to their experience by implicitly including them among the "unyielding" warriors alluded to in the title.

It is, however, in the recuperation of Adolf Hitler's legacy that the author/narrator exercises his most controversial rewriting of history. The German Führer's death is recounted in apocalyptic terms. He is viewed as a martyr, a creative genius, popularly sanctioned and responsible for the regeneration of Germany after World War I. Conceived as a man of action, a larger-than-life hero, he embodies values of service and sacrifice, values associated with Christian morality. Avoiding references to the disastrous consequences and suffering stemming from his quest for European domination, including the Holocaust, emphasis is placed on his qualities as a statesman and his importance as a national icon, remembering that he was (and implying that he should be) the object of adulation:

> Su ídolo supremo, su héroe popular, el hombre que desempolvó los viejos laureles del ejército prusiano, que forjó el III Reich sobre los cimientos de una sociedad depauperada, de una economía en bancarrota, [que] elevó a sus compatriotas desde el hambre y la miseria hasta el hartazgo y la prosperidad, y que creó un nuevo ejército, unas nuevas armas y tácticas de combate, y de la humillación de la derrota elevó a los ciudadanos al orgullo de las victorias . . . situando a Alemania a la cabeza de las naciones europeas . . . ¡Ese hombre ya no existe!

> [Its most supreme idol, its popular hero, the man that shook the dust off the old laurels of the Prussian army, who forged the Third Reich upon the foundation of an impoverished society, of a bankrupt economy . . . who elevated his countrymen from hunger and misery to plentifulness and prosperity, and who created a new army, new weapons and battle tactics, and who out of the humiliation of defeat, elevated the citizenry to the pride of victories . . . placing Germany at the head of the European nations . . . That man no longer exists!].[30]

An anonymous, collective cry follows the narrator's eulogy, suggestively opening to interpretation the identity of the intended receptor, "¡luchemos en su memoria, defendamos sus ideas!" [let's fight for his memory and defend his ideas!].[31] From the intended ambiguity emerges the unanswerable question of whether the message is contextually derived or esoterically directed to the reader. By positioning the meaning of the expletive in an atemporal context, the mythical inscription of ultra-rightist history is reinforced. Thus the symbolic value of the icons of the far-right, in this case Hitler, is enhanced by their sacrificial death, while the ideological content of their programs acquires chronological impermeability.

In a notable deviation from the tone set in previous works, including *Los Legionarios,* a conciliatory gesture is detected in *Los Irreductibles* in the respectful, even favorable representation of former Spanish Republicans fighting with the Allied forces. Acknowledging their contribution to the French Maquis and the Red Army, they are described as "bravos y resistentes voluntarios españoles fieles a la extinguida República" [the brave and resistent Spanish volunteers, loyal to the deceased Republic].[32] Maintaining this perspective, the narrator alludes to the emotional impact experienced by a Falangist spy, to whom "a pesar de los pesares [se] le agita su corazón de gallego" [in spite of everything . . . his Galician heart is touched],[33] as he witnesses Spanish crews operating tanks through the streets of recently liberated Paris, tanks whose metallic surfaces bore familiar names hand-written in chalk. Names like "Santander," "Guernica," and "Belchite," which were provocative reminders of the Spanish conflagration.[34] Although this episode reinforces the concept that Nationalists and Republicans alike considered the Second World War to be the continuation of the ideological confrontation that had enveloped Spain in the previous decade, the author/narrator is well aware that the divisive memory of the Civil War would detract from his nationalistic, image-rebuilding account. Therefore, Vadillo incorporates the exploits of his former enemies into the fabric of Spanish military history. This recognition somewhat ameliorated the fact that the Falangist volunteers had been defeated by foreign troops. National pride and historical leadership could be salvaged if other Spaniards were counted among the victors.

By the early 1990s, a pronounced generational schism separated the supporters of the ultra-right. Having perennially identified themselves with the spirit of the "National Crusade" of 1936, many older Falangists, and Franco–Falangists in particular, were incapable of renouncing what they considered to be the foundation of their political reality. Younger activists whose historical memory was unburdened by the direct influence of the Franco regime, and even less by the specter of the Civil War, realized the limits such a heritage imposed in attracting new followers, and consequently removed from their official discourse references to Francoist Spain.[35] Vadillo's attempt at historical rapprochement indicates a partial modification of the prevailing view in traditional Falangist circles. An important development influencing the author/narrator's perspective was the fact that the perceived threat of the Spanish far-left had greatly diminished, since even the incumbent Socialists had settled comfortably into a centrist position. Furthermore, the demise of the Soviet Union and its satellites was interpreted in Falangist circles as a belated ideological victory. Only in this contextually conditioned, limited sense does *Los Irreductibles* depart from earlier texts. Vadillo's interest in overcoming the traditional antagonism expressed towards the stereotypically maligned Loyalists is overshadowed by his overtly sympathetic predisposition toward Nazi Germany. Gravitating from national to continental concerns, Falangism, Nazism, and Italian Fascism are projected as overlapping ideological variations of the same belief system, sharing the mutual objective and responsibility of safeguarding European civilization.[36] In a provocative stance, Francoism is deliberately excluded from this grouping.

Vadillo accuses the Franco government of usurping the identity of the original Falange, in order to provide a veneer of ideological cohesion to what otherwise was little more than a nineteenth-century-styled "Pronunciamiento" (military rebellion) and "a falta de ideas programáticas y símbolos propios, adoptara la doctrina de José Antonio, recitara sus frases más luminosas, exhibiera sus guiones, sus yugos y flechas" [lacking a political program and symbols of their own, they adopted the doctrine of José Antonio, recited his most splendid phrases, exhibited his banners, his yokes and arrows].[37] Conveniently, he fails to mention that many of the ideological features and style of the Falange had in turn been adopted from Ramiro Ledesma's JONS, when the two groups merged in 1934. These appropriated components remained in the party even after Ledesma's dissent prior to the Civil War. Furthermore, he perpetuates the idea that orthodox Falangism was betrayed by the disloyalty of opportunistic party members who embraced Francoism and served to consolidate its powerbase, mainly the Church, the Army, and the capitalist upper classes.[38] Nevertheless, Vadillo's argument is undermined by its inability to disassociate itself from Franco's patrimony, a situation which mirrors the political limitations of non-conformist Falangism. On the one hand, the party owed its access to power and the implementation of part of its ideological program to the regime instituted in 1939. The poor showing of Falangist candidates in national elections during the Republic demonstrated that they lacked the popular and organizational support to represent a genuine challenge. It was only after Franco pronounced his Decree of Unification in 1937 that the Falange, despite its adulteration, acquired a shared leadership in Spanish politics. On the other hand, the loss of credibility of its dissidents was partly due to their being identified with the same regime they repudiated in the Post-Civil War era. Although several of these non-conformist Falangists (many, although not all, of whom were "Camisas Viejas" [Old Shirts], that is, party members prior to the Civil War were incarcerated repeatedly, they were often reintegrated into the bureaucracy of the regime once released, therefore diminishing their claim to be an oppositional voice. In a similar fashion, Vadillo maintains a contradictory respect for Franco's memory. Despite his criticism, he continues to refer to him as "El Caudillo," and is reluctant to address his role in the death of Primo de Rivera. Instead, the burden of José Antonio's execution and by extension the death of revolutionary Falangism, is attributed to the pillars of the regime: "El capitalismo, la burguesía, y en fin la recelosa derecha, tuvieron parte de culpa del fusilamiento del Fundador" [capitalism, the bourgeoisie, and ultimately the frightened Right, were partially to blame for the execution of the Founder by firing squad].[39] By ignoring what historians have referred to as Franco's "passive negligence" when confronted with the prospect of José Antonio's death sentence, Vadillo exhibits remnants of an emotional attachment to the paternal figure of the Dictator.

A cult of action prevails in the tone and imagery employed. By showcasing military action and its inherent violence, Falangism's romantic irrationalism is exposed. Its implicit manifestations are a disregard for life (one's own as well as the enemy's), an attraction to risk, viewed casually as an adventure, and an understanding that heroic action supersedes intellectual endeavors. Both texts uphold what Mussolini called a *trincerocrazia*, the elitism of the warrior caste. These elements are most clear in the numerous combat sequences, where the narrator focuses on the glamour of the soldiers, stressing their skill, their courage, and their sense of camaraderie. Further enhancement of this effect is provided at the morphological level by the use of present tense verbal forms that give the reader the sensation of witnessing the narrated events. Past and present are fused in the series' insistence on the enduring continuity of the Falangists' mythical actions.

In the prologue to Vadillo's 1991 strictly historical work *División Azul: La gesta militar española del siglo XX* [The Blue Division: The Military Epic of the Twentieth Century], Rafael García Serrano, an equally committed conservationist of the Falangist past, addresses the motives surrounding the marginal importance given to the volunteer contingent in both Francoist and Democratic Spain.[40] He reproaches the negative evolution in their portrayal by the regime's press, adding that its culpability was nevertheless inferior to that "del rumor o el panfleto" [of rumor or of a propagandistic pamphlet] since the former "al menos disponía como única arma en contra de la famosa ley del silencio" [at least had at its disposal as its only weapon the famous law of silence].[41] Undoubtedly, there was an overt effort by Franco's government to distance itself from the implications of having contributed to the Axis war effort.[42] Consequently, the indifferent reception experienced by returning Blue Division and Blue Legion veterans contrasted significantly with the euphoria of their departure.[43] As Germany's defeat became obvious, the regime accelerated the process of defascistization, replacing segments of pro-Axis Falangists, including Serrano Súñer, with more moderate army officers, some of whom had conservative or monarchist sympathies: "Falangists remained in the cabinet but less prominently . . . Catholics rather than Falangists, would carry the burden, with the support of the Vatican, of blunting the enmity of the victorious democracies."[44] The cabinet reshuffles that ensued counteracted attempts of Falangist control of parcels of the state apparatus, such as the move by Antonio Tovar, Press Undersecretary of the Ministry of the Interior, to regulate the FET [Traditionalist Spanish Falange] publications, which would have resulted in "a politically autonomous Fascist press in Spain."[45] Had this measure worked, it would have favored the legacy of the Russian front participants. Conversely, they became an embarrassing liability and were therefore relegated to the marginal realm of their veteran organizations or, in the case of most of the professional soldiers, absorbed quietly back into the armed forces. Relaying the outrage and resentment felt by many of the veterans, García Serrano sardonically questions the patriotism of a sector of the Spanish public, some of whom were now prominent in Democratic Spain: "¿Por qué no reconocerlo?—pensaba con alegría en que bien pudiera considerarse a la División Azul como criminal de guerra, a sus generales, jefes y oficiales como criminales de guerra" [why not admit it?— they thought with glee that the entire Blue Division could very well be considered criminals, and its generals, commanders and officers war criminals].[46]

Responding to an accusation that had reverberated in anti-Franco-Falangist circles increasingly after the revelation of Nazi atrocities, Vadillo reiterates the strictly military nature and spirit of the volunteers. In its initial phase, the Blue Legion was briefly employed to assist the Germans in neutralizing partisan operations, and was assigned the task of dislodging and relocating Russian civilians, burning their homes to the ground in the process. Conscious of the distasteful, anti-heroic impression this action might cause on the reader, the narrator sterilizes the episode, insisting on the discomfort experienced by the soldiers at having to participate in non-combat aggression: "Están la mayoría de los españoles asqueados de la operación Partinsanshtshina . . . la condenada operación de limpieza" [the majority of the Spaniards are sick and tired of the Partinsanshtshina operation . . . the dammed mopping-up operation].[47] The narrator excludes from his depiction the human drama that must have unfolded as the villagers of Ivanoskoye were removed from their homes at a moment's notice and forced at gunpoint to relinquish the affective and geographic ancestral center of their lives. Limiting his omniscient voice, his only observation of the emotional impact of the event on the locals is that they exhibited surprise and fear, a superficial comment considering the tragic situation. On the other hand, the perpetrators are viewed as benevolent victims of circumstance, justifying their actions to the civilians and, most importantly, to the reader. Faced with the Russians pleading denials of collaboration with the partisans, a Spanish officer attempts to offset the negative connotations stemming from the episode:

El alferez daría el brazo derecho por complacerles. Y les habla con tono afectuoso y persuasivo:—[No] os ocurrirá nada malo. ¡Eh! ¡Intérprete! Explícales que no somos enemigos suyos, que los españoles no tenemos nada contra ellos, que les trasladaremos a un lugar mejor que éste, lejos del peligro de la guerra, que les suministraremos comida y ropa y les alojaremos en casas calientes y confortables.

[The lieutenant would give his right arm to please them, and speaks to them in a persuasive and affective tone:—Nothing bad will happen to you. Hey! Interpreter! Explain to them that we are not their enemies, that we Spaniards have nothing against them, that we will take them to a better place than this, far from the dangers of the war, that we will supply them with food and clothes and that we will house them in warm and comfortable homes.][48]

These misleading promises of earthly paradise, intentionally or not, were inconsistent with the reality of the times. More likely, in the final stage of the brutal war in the East, the probable destination of the evicted old men, women, and children would be a work or concentration camp, or perhaps mass execution in a less conspicuous location. As is well documented, Nazi racial policy deemed all Slavic peoples to be *Untermenschen* (subhuman); therefore the fate of Russian villagers, suspected of aiding the enemy, would have been precarious at best. Regardless of whether the actual executions or internment would have been conducted by the Spaniards themselves or by other Wehrmacht or SS units, the impact of the former's passive complicity through apathy and silence is difficult to measure. The narrator's representation of the events is interpreted by the informed, modern reader of Post-Francoist Spain, familiar with images of Holocaust victims, as disingenuous and manipulative. Ironically, the historical argument implied by the author/narrator to explain the behavior of the legionaries is akin to the legal defense used by the surviving German hierarchy at Nuremburg. They were "following orders," and were therefore constrained by the parameters of military discipline. Attempting to muster reader sympathy, the narrator explains: "Descienden ateridos, exhaustos, hambrientos, y soltando tacos contra los malditos doiches que les ordenaron realizar la operación antiguerrillera" [They descend numb from the cold, exhausted, hungry, and uttering profanities against the damned krauts who had ordered them to carry out the anti-guerrilla operation].[49] Notwithstanding the uncomfortable impression left by the fact that the soldiers could have built-up an appetite after their unsavory duties, guilt is placed on the Germans. Instead, the Spanish volunteers are given the role of protectors and care givers. The text propagates the image of the Legion as liberator, a much reiterated theme in Falangist literature of the Russian campaign. In one of these accounts, for example, the mayor of a small Russian town evaluates in a positive light the consequences of a possible Axis victory:

El ruso como ser humano recobrará su dignidad. Por primera vez se sentirá libre como individuo, y de esta libertad espiritual, aun bajo la férula extranjera, espero más para el futuro que de una Rusia independiente, poderosa, y temida dentro de cuyas fronteras los habitantes no sean más que un rebaño de esclavos.

[The Russian will recover his human dignity. For the first time he will feel free as an individual, and from this spiritual liberty, even under foreign rule, I expect more for our future than in an independent, powerful, and feared Russia within which borders its inhabitants would be nothing more than a flock of slaves.][50]

Thus a Manichaean interpretation of reality is developed, promoting a confrontational dichotomy that separates "us" from "them." Accentuating this opposition is the association of Communism with the Asiatic Other. A series of stereotypical images steeped in centuries of Orientalist discourse, describe the Red army as being bloodthirsty, savage, lascivious, and inhumanly destructive. In addition, its uncontrolled ferocity is expressed in terms of a natural disaster: "Un alud tan poderoso, tan arrollador por lo numérico y tan pavoroso por la estela de mujeres violadas y niños y viejos clavados a las puertas de las granjas" [An avalanche, so powerful, so devastating in quantifiable terms and so terrifying as it leaves in its wake a trail of raped women, and of children and old people nailed to the doors of their farms].[51] Communism is viewed as a dehumanizing, atheistic influence subduing the human soul and threatening the underpinnings of European civilization. Stalin's army represents a new "Yellow Peril," "la invasión de los tártaros, kirguises y mongoles que avanzan amenazando encharcar de sangre toda la Europa Oriental, antes de proseguir su galopada por la Europa de occidente" [the invasion of Tartars, Kyrgystanis and Mongols that threateningly advance to drench all of Eastern Europe in blood, before galloping onward towards Western Europe].[52] In a designed maneuver of role reversal, the author/narrator assigns the Axis armies (and the ideology they represent) a defensive identity. In direct opposition to mainstream post-war historiography, which he interprets as tendentious, the Allies are perceived as the aggressors. Alluding to a non-European conspiracy, the narrator indirectly attacks capitalism, blaming the United States for financing the Red Army, "la invasión del occidente europeo por las tropas asiáticas de Stalin, motorizadas y abastecidas por obra y gracia de los Estados Unidos de América" [the invasion of Western Europe by Stalin's Asian troops, motorized and supplied by the grace of the United States of America].[53] To facilitate his task, he resorts to the careful compartmentalization of historical events and their reduction to military matters, without having to reflect on more profound issues of moral or intellectual content. In addition, he expands the concept of an anti-Spain, pervasively employed by the far-Right during the Franco era as an artificial manifestation of menacing otherness, to the more redolent notion of an anti-Europe. Europe becomes an occupied territory resisting the colonizing influences of ideological and military forces from beyond its borders. Interestingly, the same imperialist traits that enjoy a positive connotation in fascist ideology are momentarily displaced and given a negative meaning.[54] Foreign transgression into the geographical confines of what Hitler metaphorically termed as "Fortress Europe" provokes the dutiful self-protective reaction of its ideologically pure. For the author/narrator it is an exemplary endeavor of pan-European cooperation and unity. Therefore, the Falangists engaged in such a struggle are portrayed as "freedom fighters," wishing to maintain the autonomy of their civilization. Ultimately, Vadillo wants the reader to believe that this same civilization to which he/she belongs has endured in part as a result of the volunteers' efforts. Through this strategy the reader is encouraged to associate current prosperity and well-being with the past sacrifices made by an ideologically committed vanguard. Far from being an original representation of historical events, the author/narrator is echoing one of the justifications given by José Antonio to express the Falange's enmity toward Communism:

> Tiene que horrorizarnos a nosotros, europeos, occidentales, cristianos, porque [es] la terrible negación del hombre . . . la asunción del hombre en una inmensa masa amorfa donde se pierde la individualidad, donde se diluye la vestidura corpórea de cada alma individual y eterna . . . somos antimarxistas porque nos horroriza . . . [ser] como un animal inferior, en un hormiguero.

> [It must horrify us as, Europeans, Westerners, and Christians, because . . . it is the terrible negation of man . . . the absorption of man into an immense amorphous mass where individuality is lost, where the corporeal exterior of each eternal and individual soul is diluted . . . we are anti-Marxists because it horrifies us . . . to be like an inferior animal, living in an anthill.][55]

In large part, Falangism exploited public (especially middle and upper class) fears of social revolution, and loss of individual and national identity (much in the same way as the Nazis used suspicion of Jews, Gypsies, and other minority groups) in order to justify the validity of their program, and to mobilize the masses. Defined by a series of antagonisms (making it anti-Marxist, anti-liberal, anti-capitalist, anti-separatist, etc.), Falangism tacitly projects itself as the positive alternative to all other belief systems.

Firmly planted within the confines of Modernity, the author/narrator's concept of ideology is dogmatic and categorical: "[d]os mundos distintos, dos ideologías antagónicas, dos sistemas y conceptos de vida enfrentados" [two different worlds, two antagonistic ideologies, two opposing systems and ways of life].[56] To fight for what he perceives to be a just cause, sanctioned by religious and national imperatives, endows the combatants with moral superiority. All actions carried out by Spanish troops are legitimated by Catholicism, since what is Spanish and what is Catholic are assumed to be one of the same. The narrator insists on defining the war against Soviet Russia as another phase in the "Crusade" against Marxism that started in 1936. In sharp contrast to the "godless," "immoral" Russian hordes, the Spanish fighting men are represented as a community steeped in family and religious values, a view that reiterates the universal role assigned to Spanish history. Resorting to a topical image of Falangism (although inverting the order of the nouns, giving primacy to the military image), Vadillo defines them as "mitad soldados y mitad monjes" [half-soldiers and half-monks], for whom José Antonio Primo de Rivera in a messianic role "profetizase un paraíso de ángeles con espadas" [prophesied a paradise of sword-bearing angels].[57] In this struggle between the forces of "good and evil," Falangism becomes the standard bearer representing the former.

The text clings to the Franco-Falangist notion, borrowed from Romanticism, of History as a continuum of great events consciously forged by principled, driven men who are endowed with an acute sense of patriotic mission. History is represented from a tightly centered perspective that is monophonic and indisputable. The narrative voice exerts complete control over the text it produces, mirroring the authoritarian properties of the ideology it holds infallible. The text parts from the overwhelming assumption that the events of the past can be organized and presented as reality. Hence the belief that a tightly constructed historical metanarrative could deliver a single and uniform chronological perspective, closed to multiple interpretations.

Although the Falangist components constituted a significant number of the volunteer forces, they were nevertheless a minority. Concerned with the importance of ensuring the unit's military effective-

ness, which he hoped would serve as a deterrent to prospective enemies, including Germany, and in order to avoid the possible threat
of an entire Division under Falangist control, Franco opted for a
mixed force selecting most of the officer corps from Army volunteers.
However, the text gives the impression that it was an entirely Falangist
enterprise, underscoring the idealism with which it was undertaken.
Continuous references equate the soldiers' actions to their ideological purity. Moreover, the novel seems to abandon one of the myths of
revolutionary Falangism, that it was a mass movement, revealing instead what had been apparent since the post-Civil War era, that a
group of select idealists had been the motivating force behind a lost
cause. News that the Legion was to be withdrawn led to feelings of betrayal and disappointment for the lack of solidarity with the Germans,
"[s]e regresa en contra de nuestra voluntad y en la pesadumbre de
la parte selecta de nuestro país" [we are returning against our will and
with the regret of the best and brightest of our country].[58] For the
narrator, these chosen few are the committed Falangists, who regret
having to abandon the struggle to establish a New European Order.
Even more esteemed and admired are those who refuse to accept and
understand the contingencies of Francoist diplomacy, risking it all in
their utopian pursuits, "[s]on los últimos combatientes idealistas de
la llamada Nueva España. Son los últimos combatientes románticos
y soñadores. Y también, quizá, los últimos ingenuos, los aguerridos y
limpios de corazón" [they are the last of the idealistic fighters of the
so-called New Spain. They are the last of the romantic fighters and
dreamers. And also, perhaps, the last of the naive, of the bold and
pure of heart].[59] Again, ideological purity is defined in terms of a collective European ideal, while Francoism is viewed as a contaminating,
corrupting force.

Avoiding an emphasis on individuality that could be construed by
focusing on a central character, it elevates the Blue Legion and the
other volunteers to the role of collective protagonists, icons of national sacrifice and heroism. The deeds presented are property of the
national community. Character development is limited to delineat-
ing the political antecedents and affiliations of the soldiers presented. A brief mention of familial relationships, profession, and
birthplace is usually the only other information provided. Providing
the place of origin of the volunteers, however, encloses a disguised
ideological message. The narrator insists that Catalans, Basques,
Castilians, Galicians, and others are harmoniously united under a
common cause. By giving a superficial sense of regional diversity and
adherence to national unity and absolutism, relativity and plurality
are effectively suppressed.

Part of the rhetorical offensive displayed is in the form of speeches, claimed to be extracted from official records or reconstructed from eyewitness accounts, delivered to the troops by Spanish or German officers during ceremonial occasions. These discursive fragments are filled with the semantic topoi of Falangist rhetoric. Numerous scenes have a ritualistic communal function that incorporate the reader into the mass spectacle of fascist liturgy. A detailed description of the stage where one such ceremony was held reaffirms the importance of facilitating reader visualization and emotional participation in an effort to achieve ideological submission: "flamean la bandera de Falange, la alemana de guerra, la nacional española y la nacionalsocialista, se alza un altar flanqueado por un púlpito y el águila alemana" [fluttering are the flag of the Falange, the German battle flag, the Spanish national flag, and the National Socialist flag; an altar is raised which is flanked by a pulpit and the German eagle].[60] The narrator's enumeration of the contemporary national icons of both nations serves to deliver a metonymical symbolic progression that suggests their sacralization. Through the juxtaposition of the flags, Falangism and Spain, and Nazism and Germany, are amalgamated into a single conceptual construct implying their shared identity. The sanctity of the union on a national (fascism and the nation) and international level (Spain and Germany) is consecrated by the presence of the altar. Culminating this iconographic code is the eagle (also a symbol of Franco-Falangist Spain but forbidden under democracy), which possesses imperial and martial connotations, as well as representing the cultural continuity of Imperial Rome. Moreover, references in some of the speeches to the legion's duty to maintain "[l]a gloria del país más rico del orbe en laureles militares" [the glory of the country richest in military honors on the globe],[61] aspires to seduce the reader by appealing to his/her sense of national pride, while simultaneously forcing an identification of the volunteer force with the preservation of Spain's historical legacy. By evoking images of martial patriotism the author/narrator seeks to accentuate values that he believes have become obfuscated in the present. Values like a respect for hierarchy, honor, discipline, and bravery, become, as he sees it, the relinquished unifying symbol of Spanish communal culture.

Also integrated into the texts are sporadic interruptions in which verses of Falangist songs and poems are uttered either by an individual soldier or more frequently by a group. In *Los Irreductibles,* for example, the predominant stanzas that recur belong to "Cara al Sol" [Facing the Sun] the Falangist anthem, and their position in the narrative frame, in some instances, is random and unrelated to the event that is unfolding. This procedure, already practiced in pre-Falangist texts like Luys Santa Marina's *Tras el águila del César: elegía del tercio, 1921–1922* [Behind the Caesar's Eagle: The Legion's Elegy, 1921–1922] (1924), seeks to inscribe presumably real actions into the realm of the poetic and transcendental. By alternating the prosaic daily events of military life and the action-packed combat scenes with emotionally charged lyrical images of patriotic fervor and ideological commitment, the intent is to immerse the reader in a whirlwind of inflated lexical and syntactic structures compounded by their metaphorical suggestiveness. Of course, reader familiarity with the formulaic applications inherent to Falangist discourse impinges on the originality and effectiveness of the message produced. In this vein, José Antonio Pérez Bowie has identified the limitations of ultra-rightist artistic representation:

> En los textos literarios sólo en muy contadas ocasiones se deja oír una voz personal y sentir un destello de emoción sincera: la uniformidad se extiende no sólo a los temas sino también a su tratamiento y la individualidad del escritor desaparece para dejar lugar a una voz omnipresente y monocorde que reitera con machaconería los mismos mensajes.

> [In these literary texts seldom is a personal voice heard or a sincere sparkle of emotion felt: uniformity extends not only to the themes, but also to their representation, and the individuality of the writer disappears and is replaced by an omnipresent and monotone voice that reiterates the same messages with insistence.][62]

Ironically, this application of prescribed language, with its inability to regenerate its own representational model, is ultimately responsible for the undoing of the homogeneous discourse of Spanish fascism. In spite of its novel thematic content, Vadillo's message is undermined by his reliance on an obsolete system of representation. Of course, it is impossible to determine what long-term significance his attempt at historical reinscription may acquire among future far-Right nationalists as they undoubtedly look to expand the ideology's myths.[63]

Although writing for historical posterity, Vadillo is very concerned with modifying contemporary attitudes. Implicated in the 1981 coup were several veterans of the Russian campaign, including the Captain General of Valencia, Jaime Milans del Bosch, and the second-in-command of the general staff, Lt. General Alfonso Armada Comyn, both of whom were court-martialed, convicted, and discharged from the Armed Forces.[64] As Pedro Vilanova has pointed out, "[t]he Army was the institution which was at the same time tied by its nature and structure most closely to the previous régime, and the one having the greatest reservations when confronted with the democratic change."[65] Therefore, the presence of other high ranking "Blue" veterans, sympathetic to, if not directly involved in, subversive activities was perceived by the general public as a threat to the stability of the constitutional monarchy. Since the appointment in 1976 of the democratic General Manuel Gutiérrez Mellado to Vice-President of Defense Matters, a gradual expunging of Falangist officers had followed. The presence of liberal factions within the armed forces, evident in groups like the Unión Militar Patriótica [Patriotic Military Union], increased the siege mentality in extremist military circles. The fact that the more conservative elements of the Union of the Democratic Center Party (UCD), the first democratically elected party in power, were referred to as "the new Blue Division," underscoring their fondness of the old regime, further illustrates the negative connotations associated with the volunteer forces. To accentuate the reactionary and demonic nature of the ultra-rightist elements in the Army, the Press frequently resorted to assigning them the stigma of their association with Hitler's Third Reich. It is in an effort to rescue and cleanse the image of the Blue contingents that Vadillo resumes his purportedly genuine version of events. In 1991, he would summarize, in usual hyperbolic terms, his defensive posture before historical revisionists: "La historia reciente es innamovible, vivimos millares de los que protagonizamos la gesta de la División Azul y no podrán difamarla, por mucho que se lo propongan algunos historiadores de pacotilla que escriben al dictado del rencor personal, al dictado de sus dueños y señores políticos" [Recent history is unchangeable; thousands of us who took part in the epic of the Blue Division are still alive and they will not be able to defame its memory, despite the efforts of some shoddy historians who write under the influence of personal grudges, under the dictates of their masters and political bosses].[66] This rebuttal is directed to all detractors of the volunteer forces launching their criticism before or after 1975.

Vadillo's trilogy reflects the displacement of Fascist thought from contemporary, tangible reality to the literary as a mode of preserving Falangist orthodoxy, and as an outlet for fascist views in the context of democratic Spain. Once the signs of impotence in the political arena were evident, artistic representation became the refuge of Falangist ideology and nostalgia. From its inception, José Antonio Primo de Rivera had declared his movement as poetic.[67] He envisioned his political program as transcendent of the un-heroic existence of bourgeois man. Only an aesthetically appealing, action-promoting ideological program could, in his view, redeem the spiritual vacuum left by centuries of historical decadence. Ironically,

Falangism's "principled amoral commitment to violence, war, and destruction of its enemies,"[68] was reduced to the rhetorical expression of its style, its symbolism, and its nostalgia.

Yet even in present-day Spain, as the relative safety of chronological distance and the inevitability of mortality have set in, a resurgent body of works authored by former Falangist volunteers continue to voice their claim to a solid and respectable place in History. It is the final appeal by those who forfeited their youth and innocence chasing an ideological chimera that Franco and historical circumstance had conspired to dissipate.

NOTES

1. Sheelagh Ellwood, "The Extreme Right in Spain, a Dying Species," in Lucian Cheles, Ronnie Ferguson, and Michalina Vaughn, eds., *Neo-Fascism in Europe* (New York: Longman, 1991), 149. In 1976 the issue was resolved in favor of the Frente Nacional Español, which officially assumed the name of José Antonio's organization.

2. Like many other fascist groups in Spain, Fuerza Nueva began as a political publication with Blas Piñar as its editor. He was connected to Mariano Sánchez Covisa, leader of the terrorist organization Los Guerrilleros de Cristo Rey [Warriors of Christ the King], which had evolved from Defensa Universitaria [University Defense], a campus-based anti-leftist association made up of radical Catholics and Falangists.

3. A few months prior to the elections, plans for another coup involving several military officers linked to Fuerza Nueva were foiled by intelligence services loyal to the government.

4. An active newspaper and periodical establishment had always been central to the dissemination of radical Right political views in Spain. In fact, several early publications of the 1930s, including *El Fascio* and *La Conquista del Estado* [The Conquest of the State], became springboards for organized Spanish fascism. With the folding in 1987 of *El Alcázar* [The Citadel], the most influential and popular of all far-Right newspapers of the post-Franco era, the forces of reaction suffered a serious setback. Although attempts were made to launch similar publications, like *España Express, El porvenir de la nación española*, [The Future of the Spanish Nation], *Mundo Informativo* [Informative World], and *La Nación* [The Nation], none equaled the success of the defunct daily, which, incidentally, was controlled by the National Organization of Combatants. The vacuum left by the diminished ultra-right press was filled by the publication of new books and the reissuing, also in book form, of the canonical works of Spanish fascism.

5. Carlos Caballero and Rafael Ibáñez Hernández, *Escritores en las trinchera: La División Azul en sus libros, publicaciones periódicas y filmografía (1941–1988)* [Writers in the Trenches: The Blue Division in its Books, Journalistic Publications and Filmography] (Madrid: Ediciones Barbarroja, 1989), 19.

6. In October 1967 Vadillo published *Orillas del Voljov* [Shores of the Wolchow] (Barcelona: Marte) his first novel dealing with the Blue Division. As he explains in the preface, his intention was to gradually narrate in novelistic form the entire saga of the 250th Division, from its inception to its dissolution. By 1975, the three-volume set (due to their length, in later editions each novel was divided into two volumes)

dedicated exclusively to the Blau and entitled "La gran crónica de La División Azul" [The Great Chronicle of the Blue Division] was complete. Added to the initial work were *Los Arrabales de Leningrado* [The Outskirts of Leningrad] (Barcelona: Marte, 1971), and *Y lucharon en Krasny Bor* [And They Fought in Krasny Bor] (Barcelona: Marte, 1975). Nine years after the death of Franco, Vadillo would extend his already gargantuan account, now tracing the adventures (or misadventures) of the remaining Spanish volunteers, in the already mentioned "Balada final de la 'División Azul'."

7. Gerald R. Kleinfeld and Lewis A. Tambs, *La división española de Hitler. La División Azul en Rusia* (Madrid: San Martin, 1984), 22.

8. Soldiers of the Blue Division earned a total of 2,497 Iron Crosses of various classes. The unit was also the only non-German volunteer force to have a specific military medal created by Hitler on its behalf, the Medal of the Spanish Volunteers in the Struggle Against Bolshevism [Erinnerungsmedaille für die Spanischen Freiwilligen' im Kampf gegen den Bolschewismus]. In addition, eleven Crosses of St. Ferdinand [Cruz Laureada de San Fernando], the most prestigious of Spanish military medals, were also awarded by the Franco government to the Blau.

9. The Blue Legion was created on 17 November 1943. About the size of a regiment, it consisted of 2,133 men (including 103 officers), recruited from volunteers of the Blue Division. It was divided into two infantry and one mixed battalions, and placed under the command of Colonel Antonio García Navarro. Following a brief training period it was deployed to counter guerrilla attacks near Hamburg, then it was dispatched to the Liuban sector, where it covered an eleven-mile front supporting the Werhmacht's 121st Division. With the Russian Winter offensive, the Legion was responsible for protecting the rearguard of the German retreat towards Luga. Scarcely three months after its formation, Hitler authorized the withdrawal of the Legion in order to avert a possible Allied invasion of Spain.

10. Many of these men fought in Léon Degrelle's Friwilligen Legion Wallonie, or in Otto Skorzeny's SS Jagdverbände, whereas others formed part of the Einheit Ezquerra (named after its commander Miguel Ezquerra Sánchez), all were Waffen-SS units and included soldiers of other nationalities (Belgians, Frenchmen, Lithuanians, Croatians, Italians, and even a Guatemalan). These units were independently allocated to various fronts and fought against both regular army and partisan forces in Normandy, Northern Italy, Croatia, Romania, Slovakia, Austria, and finally, in Germany. Furthermore, several Spaniards served in the Abwehr, the German intelligence agency, as radar and radio specialists and as saboteurs.

11. Fernando Vadillo, *Los Legionarios* (Madrid: Dyrsa, 1984), 1201.

12. The integration of poetic and military images is constant:

El centinela dispara el ametrallador, pero casi nunca hace blanco. Lo aconsejable es permanecer inmóvil, acurrucado y silencioso, y no abrir fuego hasta el momento propicio.— ¡Atrás, muchachos! La sección de enlaces da media vuelta, se reagrupa y retrocede en columna de a uno. Pronto se apagará la tarde. Un raudo crepúsculo, un resplandor anaranjado en las copas nevadas de los árboles y, después, un oscurecimiento progresivo. Hasta que la luna se levante por el pantano Kobryina y empiecen a canturrear las primeras ametralladoras de la noche."

[The sentry fires with his machine gun, but seldom hits his target. The advisable thing is to remain motionless, crouching and silent, and not open fire until the most propitious moment.—Back up, boys! The section of couriers turns around, regroups and retreats in a single column. Soon the afternoon will end, first will come an impetuous twilight, an orange brightness on the snow-capped trees and, later, progressive darkness, until the moon rises above the Kobryina swamp and the first machine guns begin to hum in the night.] (*Los Legionarios*, 33)

13. Ibid., 14.

14. Ibid.

15. "Patrulleos, descubiertas, golpes de mano, escaramuzas, fuegos y contrafuegos. Lo de siempre. Soledad, monotonía, sobresaltos y bajas. Muertos y heridos en el frente de la Legión Azul" [Patrols, reconnaissance missions, sudden attacks, ambushes, defensive and offensive fire. Always the same. Loneliness, monotony, nerves and casualties. Dead and wounded soldiers on the Blue Legion's front] (*Los Legionarios,* 76).

16. When describing the ideological conversion experienced by several previously uncommitted volunteers, Vadillo focuses on the aesthetic appeal of the party, stressing that content and style were equally important: "[C]ontagiados del ideal falangista, del romanticismo de sus canciones, y de la poesía de sus consignas, y del heroísmo de sus gestas, y del halo deslumbrante del Fundador . . . porque advirtieron que la Falange era, o lo había sido en sus orígenes y sus dogmas, un movimiento nacional equidistante de las derechas y de las izquierdas tradicionales, una empresa renovadora y movida por hermosos fines" [Inspired by Falangist ideals, by the romanticism of their songs, and the poetry of their slogans, and the heroism of their deeds, and by the dazzling aura of the Founder . . . because they realized that the Falange was, or had been in its origins and dogma, a national movement equally distant from the traditional Left and Right, a regenerative enterprise moved by a beautiful purpose] (*Los Legionarios,* 10).

17. Vadillo himself refers to the narrated events as "la odisea española" [the Spanish odyssey], in both a figurative and literal sense.

18. *Los Legionarios,* 9.

19. Ibid., 223.

20. Ibid., 22.

21. Although the fighting zeal and valor of the Blue Division are generally acknowledged by historians, even by those writing out of Soviet Russia, the Blue Legion's military legacy is much more dubious. The fact that the Legion was formed after the course of the war in the east had taken a turn for the worse for the Axis, its desertion rate, and its limited life-span, partially account for its unimpressive history. In fact, part of the argument used in 1944 by Spanish Minister of Foreign Affairs, Count Jordana, to justify its withdrawal was the fear that it would taint the reputation of its predecessor.

22. *Los Legionarios,* 51.

23. The Falangist Code of Conduct emphasized the relationship between self-immolation and the sanctity of patriotic duty, "[h]acerse militante de la Falange, es entregar todos los actos útiles de la vida para un servicio sagrado; el de España. [El] militante tendrá siempre presente que la prisión, las heridas y aún la misma muerte, son meros actos de servicio" [becoming a member of Falange is to relinquish all useful acts in life to a sacred service, that of Spain. The party member will always keep in mind that prison, injury and even death, are mere acts of service] (Eduardo Álvarez Puga, *Historia de la Falange* [Barcelona: Dopea, 1969], 90).

24. *Los Legionarios,* 25.

25. Ibid., 78.

26. Sultana Wahnón, *La estética literaria de la posguerra* (Atlanta: Rodopi, 1998), 130.

27. *Los Legionarios,* 10

28. Otto "Scarface" Skorzeny (1908–1975) had been a member of Hitler's personal bodyguard and an SS officer when in September 1943 he led a group of commandos on a successful rescue mission using gliders to free Benito Mussolini, who

was being held by Italian Partisans in the Abruzzi Apennines. The undoubtedly courageous Austrian later kidnaped Miklós Horthy, Hungary's premier, who wanted to surrender to the Soviets. At the end of the war, Skorzeny established a clandestine escape network for SS officers aptly named Die Spinne [The Spider]. Léon Degrelle (1906–1994) founded the fascist-inspired Rexist party in his native Belgium and after 1940 collaborated with the German occupation forces. Dubbed the Walloon Quisling, he fought on the Eastern front and was sentenced to death for treason by a Belgian court. In 1945 he settled in Madrid under the protection of the Franco regime, which refused his extradition.

29. Martin A. Lee in his indispensable study, *The Beast Reawakens* (Boston: Little Brown & Co., 1997), points out that Degrelle's summer retreat in Málaga became a shrine for neo-Nazis worldwide. A reconstruction of the old Waffen SS General's interview with the radical German leader Michael Künen in the 1980s shows the former's nostalgic use of traditional fascist rhetoric (in a similar fashion as Vadillo), with rekindled expectations for a New World Order, "[t]rue elites are formed at the front . . .a chivalry is created there, young leaders are born. . . . [W]hen we see a young revolutionary, from Germany or elsewhere, we feel that he is one of ours, for we are one with revolution and youth. We are political soldiers . . .we prepare the political cadres of the postwar world. Tomorrow, Europe will have elites such it has never known. An army of young apostles, of young mystics, carried by a faith that nothing can check" (203–4).

30. Fernando Vadillo, *Los Irreductibles* (Alicante: Garcia Hispán, 1993), 274.

31. Ibid., 274.

32. Ibid., 41.

33. Ibid., 46.

34. Further evidence of the author/narrator's calculated rapprochement can be found in Vadillo's reconstruction of the troops marching into the French capital: "Pero sólo una de las columnas marcha perfectamente alineada y a paso rítmico. La encabeza la bandera tricolor de la República española que, sostenida por tres mástiles, ocupa la ancha avenida de lado a lado. Se trata de los españoles en el exilio, que desfilan con el puño cerrado al grito de UHP! UHP . . . !, entre las más atronadoras ovaciones que la multitud dedica a esta marcha triunfal" [but only one of the columns marches perfectly aligned and at a rhythmic pace. It is headed by the tricolor flag of the Spanish Republic which, supported by three masts, fills the wide avenue from side to side. They are exiled Spaniards, who march with their raised, clenched fist yelling UHP! UHP . . . !, they receive from the crowd one of the most thunderous ovations given in this triumphant march] (*Los Irreductibles*, 47).

35. Immigration, globalization, the European Union, and American cultural imperialism have become the new targets of contemporary far-right Spanish movements. Although more anti-Semitic than ever, they propose a contradictory elimination of the traditional division between right and left political ideologies. As in other European countries, the new radical Right has also adopted an ecologist agenda.

36. "¡Españoles! . . . ¡Berlín está a punto de ser totalmente cercado! Los que deseéis luchar en su defensa, que es la defensa de Occidente, de nuestra cultura, de nuestra religión, de nuestros antecesores, de nuestras mujeres y de nuestros hijos, que me sigan al combate. . . . En estos momentos, las palabras sobran. ¡Arriba España!" [Spaniards! . . . Berlin is about to be surrounded! Those who wish to fight in her defense, which is the defense of the West, of our culture, of our religion, of our ancestors, of our women and children, follow me into battle. . . . At a time such as this few words are needed. Long live Spain!] (*Los Irreductibles*, 183).

37. *Los Irreductibles*, 17.

38. Alluding to Franco's betrayal, he explains that the disheartened Falangists joining Hitler's armies against the Regime's wishes, are the genuine representatives of José Antonio's doctrine, "la Falange original está malherida y desarmada. . . . [E]l ánimo de robustecerla, y de emprender la demorada revolución nacionalsindicalista, es la espuela que mueve a cruzar la frontera a muchos jóvenes idealistas por el aspecto lastimoso que les ofrece su Patria, todavía escasa de pan y de justicia" [the original Falange is wounded and disarmed. . . . [T]he spirit to restore it, and to initiate the delayed National-Syndicalist revolution, is the incentive that moves many young idealists to cross the border, given the pitiful sight of their Fatherland, still devoid of bread and justice] (*Los Irreductibles,* 18).

39. *Los Irreductibles,* 17.

40. Regarding efforts stemming from official sources to erase the legacy of the Blue Division, Sergio Alegre Calero notes: "El deseo de *olvidar* la División fue tan pronunciado que ningún miembro de la misma pudo ver publicadas sus memorias durante muchos años. . . . Destaca y sorprende enormemente, al mismo tiempo que corrobora nuestras afirmaciones, que la vuelta de la División y la estancia y repatriación de la llamada Legión Azul no mereciera ni un metro de película de los noticiarios españoles" [The desire to *forget* the División was so pronounced that none of its members was able to publish his memoirs for many years. . . . It is highly notable and enormously surprising, while meanwhile supporting our point, that the return of the Division and the tour and repatriation of the so-called Blue Legion did not warrant a single meter of film footage in Spanish broadcasts]. "Las imágenes de la División Azul: Los vaivenes de la política exterior e interior de Franco a través del cine" [The Images of the Blue Division: The Wavering of Franco's Exterior and Interior Politics Through Film] in Aitor Yraola, ed., *Historia contemporánea de España y cine* (Madrid: Ediciones de la Universidad Autónoma de Madrid, 1997), 73.

41. Rafael García Serrano, Prologue to *División Azul: La gesta militar española del siglo XX* (Madrid: Este Oeste Editorial, 1991), 5.

42. In Paul Preston's words (*Franco: A Biography* [New York: HarperCollins, 1994], 532): "The weight of Franco's propaganda machine was thrown into the task of rewriting the history of his role in the Second World War. For the rest of his life, he would assert that he had never contemplated entering the war," a claim otherwise contradicted by the secret protocol signed at Hendaye.

43. "Maldicen a los políticos, a los chaqueteros de retaguardia, a los emboscados, a los que ayer les empujaban al combate y hoy les ordenan regresar a España, a una España [que] no les recibirá como a héroes que arriesgaron su vida por defender la paz de la patria. Por eso maldicen a los disidentes y cantan con voces quebradas de ira: falangista soy, falangista hasta morir o vencer" [They curse the politicians, the turncoats in the rear, the behind-the-scenes manipulators, those who yesterday pushed them into battle and today order them to return to Spain, to a Spain that will not receive those as heroes, who risked their lives to defend the peace of the Fatherland. That is why they curse all dissidents and sing as their voices tremble with anger: I am a Falangist, a Falangist until death or victory] (*Los Legionarios,* 204).

44. Preston, 538–39.

45. Stanley Payne, *Fascism in Spain 1923–1975* (Madison: University of Wisconsin Press, 1999), 258.

46. García Serrano, 6.

47. *Los Legionarios,* 47.

48. Ibid., 46.

49. Ibid., 49.

50. Ángel Ruiz Ayucar, *La Rusia que yo conocí* (Madrid: Fuerza Nueva, 1976), 75.

51. *Los Irreductibles,* 95.

52. Ibid., 56.

53. Ibid., 22.

54. "Allí, en Narva, baluarte de Europa, donde el Ejército rojo pusiera en retirada al Ejército del Kaiser en 1918, se puede repetir ahora el desenlace de la Primera Guerra Mundial. Allí, en Narva, se agrupan unidades de voluntarios estonios, noruegos, holandeses, daneses y de otros países, que simbolizan la defensa de Occidente contra el imperialismo marxista" [There, in Narva, bulwark of Europe, where the Red Army forced the Army of the Kaiser to retreat in 1918, the outcome of the First World War could now repeat itself. There, in Narva, units of Estonian, Norwegian, Dutch, Danes, as well as volunteers from other countries have gathered, symbolizing the defense of the West against Marxist imperialism] (*Los Legionarios,* 179).

55. Puga, 17–18.

56. *Los Legionarios,* 179.

57. *Los Irreductibles,* 315.

58. *Los Legionarios,* 199.

59. *Los Irreductibles,* 18.

60. *Los Legionarios,* 220.

61. Ibid., 79.

62. José Antonio Pérez Bowie, "Retoricismo y estereotipación, rasgos definidores de un discurso ideologizado. El discurso de la derecha durante la Guerra Civil" [Rhetoric and Stereotype, Defining Characteristics of an Ideologized Discourse. The Discourse of the Right during the Civil War], in Julio Aróstegui, ed., *Historia y memoria de la Guerra Civil,* vol. 1 (Valladolid: Junta de Castilla y León, 1988), 363.

63. In an uncharacteristic reference to Falangism's future, the author acknowledges the inspirational contribution of young party members to his writings, "esa parcela de juventud española que, al cabo de medio siglo, rinde culto a la División Azul y a sus caídos cuando a éstos les canta o les reza las bellas estrofas del Cara al Sol. Estos jóvenes falangistas actuales son los llamados a tomar el relevo de la antorcha divisionaria. Es un consuelo que Dios ha concedido a quienes no merecen el silencio y el olvido de la Patria por la que lucharon y cayeron" [that segment of Spanish youth, who after half a century, worships the Blue Division and their fallen in battle as they sing or pray for them with the beautiful stanzas of the "Cara al Sol." These young Falangists of today are called upon to take the Blue Division's torch. It is a consolation that God has granted to those who do not deserve the silence and the disregard of the country for which they fought and they died] (*Los Irreductibles,* 10).

64. Milans del Bosch received 30 years, and Armada Comyn was sentenced to six years. After a brief period of incarceration, both sentences were commuted. The following year, military intelligence discovered that Milans del Bosch also had close ties to the three colonels implicated in a 1982 plot. Both Milans del Bosch and Armada Comyn had participated in subversive activities prior to 1981, including the so-called "Operation De Gaulle," a projected attempt, never carried through, to replace the UCD government with a military junta, and the thwarted "Galaxia" coup of 1978.

65. Pedro Vilanova, "Spain: the Army and the Transition," in David Bell, ed., *Democratic Politics in Spain: Spanish Politics After Franco* (London: Frances Pinter Publishers, 1983), 156.

66. *Orillas del Voljov,* 7.

67. See José Antonio Primo de Rivera, *Obras completas de José Antonio Primo de Rivera* (Madrid: Publicaciones Españolas, 1952), 69: "En un movimiento poético, nosotros levantaremos este fervoroso afán de España; nosotros nos sacrificaremos; nosotros renunciaremos, y de nosotros será el triunfo" [As a poetic movement, we will raise

this fervent zeal for Spain; we will sacrifice ourselves; we will not relinquish, and victory will be ours].

68. Juan Linz, "Some Notes Toward a Comparative Study of Fascism in Sociological Historical Perspective," in Walter Laqueur, ed., *Facism, A Reader's Guide: Analysis, Interpretations, Bibliography* (Berkeley: University of California Press, 1976), 104.

BIBLIOGRAPHY

Alegre Calero, Sergio. "Las imagénes de la División Azul: Los vaivenes de la política exterior e interior de Franco a través del cine." In *Historia contemporánea de España y cine.* Edited by Aitor Yraola. Madrid: Ediciones de la Universidad Autónoma de Madrid, 1997.

Álvarez Puga, Eduardo. *Historia de la Falange.* Barcelona: Dopesa, 1969.

Caballero Jurado, Carlos and Rafael Ibáñez Hernández. *Escritores en las trincheras: La División Azul en sus libros, publicaciones periódicas y filmografía (1941–1988).* Madrid: Ediciones Barbarroja, 1989.

Ellwood, Sheelagh. "The Extreme Right in Spain, a Dying Species." In *Neo-Fascism in Europe.* Edited by Luciano Cheles, Ronnie Ferguson, and Michalina Vaughn. New York: Longman, 1991.

García Serrano, Rafael. Prologue to *División Azul: La gesta militar española del siglo XX.* Madrid: Este Oeste Editorial, 1991.

Kleinfeld, Gerald R. and Lewis A. Tambs. *La división española de Hitler. La División Azul en Rusia.* Madrid: San Martin, 1984.

Lee, Martin A. *The Beast Reawakens.* Boston: Little Brown & Co., 1997.

Linz, Juan. "Some Notes Toward a Comparative Study of Fascism in Sociological Historical Perspective." In *Fascism, A Reader's Guide: Analyses, Interpretations, Bibliography.* Edited by Walter Laqueur. Berkeley: University of California Press, 1976.

Payne, Stanley. *Fascism in Spain 1923–1975.* Madison: University of Wisconsin Press, 1999.

Pérez Bowie, José Antonio. "Retoricismo y estereotipación, rasgos definidores de un discurso ideologizado. El discurso de la derecha durante la Guerra Civil." In *Historia y memoria de la Guerra Civil,* vol I. Edited by Julio Aróstegui. Valladolid: Junta de Castilla y León, 1988.

Preston, Paul. *Franco: A Biography.* New York: HarperCollins, 1994.

Primo de Rivera, José Antonio. *Obras completas de José Antonio Primo de Rivera.* Madrid: Publicaciones Españolas, 1952.

Rodríguez Puértolas, Julio. *Literatura fascista española,* vol II. Madrid: Akal, 1987.

Ruiz Ayucar, Ángel. *La Rusia que yo conocí.* Madrid: Fuerza Nueva, 1976.

Santa Marina, Luys. *Tras el águila del César: elegía del tercio, 1921–1922.* Barcelona: Planeta, 1980.

Vadillo, Fernando. Prologue. *Orillas del Voljov.* Alicante: García Hispán, 1991.

———. *Los Legionarios.* Madrid: Dyrsa, 1984.

———. *Los Irreductibles.* Alicante: Garcia Hispán, 1993.

Vilanova, Pedro. "Spain: the Army and the Transition." In *Democratic Politics in Spain: Spanish Politics After Franco.* Edited by David Bell. London: Frances Pinter Publishers, 1983.

Wahnón, Sultana. *La estética literaria de la posguerra.* Atlanta, GA: Rodopi, 1998.

Torrente Ballester and the Specter of Fascism:
Fragmentos de Apocalipsis

Ana Gómez-Pérez

"Fiat ars–pereat mundus," says Fascism, and, as Marinetti admits, expects war to supply the artistic gratification of a sense perception that has been changed by technology. This is evidently the consummation of "l'art pour l'art." Mankind, which in Homer's time was an object of contemplation for the Olympian gods, now is one for itself. Its self-alienation has reached such a degree that it can experience its own destruction as an aesthetic pleasure of the first order. This is the situation of politics which Fascism is rendering aesthetic. Communism responds by politicizing art.

(Walter Benjamin, "The Work of Art in the
Age of Mechanical Reproduction")

El cerco, sin embargo, que me han puesto unos y otros, es más amenazador que en otras ocasiones, y por eso me he refugiado en el interior de esta novela, mero conjunto de palabras, como el gusano se esconde en el ovillo que él mismo se fabrica

[The siege, however, to which I have been subjected by these and others, is more threatening than on previous occasions, and that is why I have found refuge in the interior of this novel, a mere group of words, the way the worm hides in the cocoon he himself has made]
—(Gonzalo Torrente Ballester, *Fragmentos de Apocalipsis*)

THE SPANISH CIVIL WAR AND ITS CONSEQUENCES LEFT A PERMANENT mark on the generations which lived through the conflict conscious of the ideological compromises and conflicts which would determine the course of their lives from that point on. Those who chose exile retained a vague feeling of guilt about their escape and, in particular, their survival. Those who remained were burdened as well by what Aranguren defined in 1976 as "a guilty conscience":

The best Spaniards of our time have been unable to avoid a "guilty conscience" because of their passivity—imposed nevertheless, and, as we have already seen, politically irremediable—towards the Regime, a passivity lived, in fact, as a *structural complicity* with it. All Spaniards of a certain age and still in Spain, are responsible for the Regime which is, if not the one we deserve, the one that, at a certain point, we deserved.[1]

Aranguren refers to the "best Spaniards," establishing a clear difference between those who feel guilty and those who do not and never did. The philosopher situates himself in opposition to the dictatorship of Franco, in a position of dissidence that allows him to redeem himself by means of an admission of his own participation in the political structure erected following the Civil War. Implicit in his position is the idea that only the person who recognizes and confesses to the "'culpa' contraída" [acquired guilt][2] can attain the necessary ethical ground from which to recover not only his or her dignity, but also a certain credibility and freedom from the ideological scars that mark any survivor of the Franco regime.

Gonzalo Torrente Ballester, publicly identified with the Falange during the Civil War and the first few years of the post-war period, refused to make a public admission of this type. Although the period of his support for the fascist movement can be seen as relatively brief from the point of view of his overall trajectory as a writer and private citizen, his obstinacy has motivated a long-standing reaction on the part of readers and critics against his subsequent novels, a reaction which in turn has had such an effect on his artistic development as to suggest that most of the author's work is haunted by the specter of fascism. When confronted with the unerasable paper trail documenting his involvement with fascism, Torrente Ballester remained evasive and began to elaborate a very personal theory of literature that denied the relationship between fiction and reality so he might continue to develop as a writer without the constant reminder of his earlier ideological commitments. In the long run, however, the refuge of the novel became a new form of imprisonment that he then attempted to tear apart in his most metafictional novel, *Fragmentos de Apocalipsis* [Fragments of Apocalypse], in order to regain the pleasure of literary creation. Linda Hutcheon has written regarding metafiction: "There can be no 'theory' of metafiction, only 'implications' for theory; each self-informing work internalizes its own critical context. To ignore that is to falsify the text itself."[3] The theoretical implications of the metafictional novel for Torrente Ballester have as their basis the existential anxiety of the author, who insisted with such force on a strictly literary self-interpretation that it served only to underline his own fear of ideological debate.

At the beginning of the Spanish Civil War, Torrente Ballester was forced to enter the Falange in order to save himself from certain death for his affiliation with the *galleguista* [Galician nationalist] movement.[4] It was in Salamanca that he met Pedro Laín Entralgo and Antonio Tovar at a conference of journalists,[5] and through them became a member of the "Burgos group." His active participation in the Press and Propaganda branch of the Falange goes no further than the early 1940s, although he maintained strong ties with the "grupo de Burgos," especially Laín Entralgo and Dionisio Ridruejo, for the rest of his life. In Galicia, after returning from the war, he confirmed his role as ideological representative of Spanish fascism by giving talks on various occasions to members of the Falange and even participating in a Falangist delegation sent to Germany to confer with high Nazi officials in 1942.[6] During this period he had already begun contributing to *Arriba,* a journal founded by José Antonio Primo de Rivera that later would support the Francoist hard line over the course of the dictatorship. Around 1947 he obtained, through close contacts, a position as professor of History in the Naval Academy of Madrid, where he would live until 1964. In 1962, after signing a manifesto protesting the manner in which the government had attempted to cover up recent events in the mines of Asturias, he was expelled not only from the Naval Academy, but also from his positions as theater critic of *Arriba* and at Radio Nacional.

The literary and intellectual ambition that drove him to accept such ideologically committed positions in Madrid over the course of nearly fifteen years, a period during which he was able to act independently of any direct political pressure, contrasts sharply with his insistence years later that fear was his only motivation for having joined the Falange during the Civil War.[7] With his writings of the time, the documented alibi of his official censure in 1962, and a vague relationship with anarchist and *galleguista* groups before the war as proof of his dissent, Torrente Ballester rejected any form of public repentance, in contrast to other important figures such as his friend Dionisio Ridruejo. However, it is also true that a one-sided interpretation of the events of his own life has provoked an effort by many left-wing intellectuals to erase him from Spanish culture and history, and has served to obscure the work of political criticism of the Franco regime developed by the author beginning in the mid 1940s. It is not surprising that since the 1950s Torrente has felt the need to defend himself both against Francoist propaganda and leftist intellectuals who never forgot his early commitment to the Spanish fascist party.

Torrente Ballester often situates the moment of his initial disenchantment near the beginning of the decade, when Ridruejo was placed in internal exile for having told Franco in a letter that his regime was not the goal for which the Civil War had been fought and that he should renounce control of the government. Although by 1940 he had already written *República barataria* [Barataria Republic], a play in which he begins to question political and historical myths (what he called "destripar el mito," literally, "gutting the myth"), he would do it again in a much more comprehensive and conscious manner in *El golpe de estado de Guadalupe Limón* [Guadalupe Limón's Coup d'État] (1946), *El retorno de Ulises* [Ullyses' Return] (1946), and *Ifigenia* (1950). The urge to bring to light the mechanisms of political and ideological manipulation in order to eliminate their power to persuade is the most direct and violent consequence of this first stage of political disenchantment. The fascist and Francoist mechanisms of mythification taught Torrente Ballester to reflect carefully on the manipulation of history and its written record, and the political disillusionment he suffered forced him toward the literary expression of this historical insight. The annihilation of the myth, from this point of view, arises from the author's experience with fascism in two different but complementary ways. On the one hand, it is an intellectual necessity provoked by a discovery of the creation and manipulation of the Falangist myth of José Antonio Primo de Rivera. On the other, this demythification has its origin, ironically, in the fascist aesthetic of purification through destruction, a concept that always fascinated Torrente and whose mechanisms we will observe again in his experiments with the metafictional novel.

The author's metahistorical experiments with political criticism came to an end towards the middle of the 1950s, and he began to develop a theory of the novel impervious to ideological concerns. One of the reasons for this retreat was the increasing politicization of literature and literary criticism, which had become an important source of opposition to the Franco regime. In the words of José María Castellet: "Political concerns converted literature into an instrument of substitution for that which did not exist: a conscious and combative politics of effective civil rebellion against the Regime. It seemed as if, suddenly, the weak Spanish Left had grown and was about to take power."[8] After the initial lack of success of *Los gozos y las sombras* [Pleasures and Shadows] (1957, 1960, and 1962), novels through which Torrente attempted to reconcile himself to the dominant aesthetics of social realism (although later he would deny any interpretation of that novelistic cycle's central conflict as class-based),[9] and especially after the total silence that accompanied the publication of *Don Juan* (1963), a work which lost a competition of the Real Academia to a novel by Ángel María de Lera, *Hemos perdido el sol* [We Have Lost the Sun], defined sarcastically by Torrente as "a report on the life of emigrants in Germany,"[10] the author realized he was being marginalized by two opposing groups: the Francoists, for whom he had become an uncomfortable figure (as evidenced by the violent official reaction of 1962), and the literary left, which found itself unable to forgive either his Falangist past or his obvious incapacity to adapt to the ideological exigencies of contemporary literature in Spain.[11]

In the United States, where he sought economic and psychological refuge in 1966, he enjoyed the comfort of his position as professor at the State University of New York at Albany, with plenty of time not only to write but also to bring himself up to date on the literary criticism of the moment in order to resolve some of the pedagogical problems that arose with his American students, "given that, as far as literary questions were concerned, the Americans were only interested in ideological content."[12] The triumph of structuralism during this period provided him the means to counteract any form of ideological criticism: "He says he was able [to interest his students] thanks to a new slant that, taking advantage of fashionable theoretical trends; he gave to his lessons by means of methods of literary analysis from which were excluded all ideological factors."[13] However, in the course of his critical incursions he avoided structuralism proper (which he had always criticized as excessively schematic when describing literary work), focusing instead on obtaining a thorough knowledge of Russian formalism with which he felt identified and, indirectly, on Spanish stylistics, the dominant critical school during his years of literary apprenticeship. Despite the differences of perspective between the two movements, one feature they had in common was the isolation of literary structures and the rejection of any attempt to analyze literature from a point of view external to literature or linguistics. According to Blanco Aguinaga, for Dámaso Alonso, in contrast to the less extreme opinions of Leo Spitzer or Amado Alonso:

> The literary work is a reality in itself, the interpretation of which (its meaning) must be sought through strictly internal analysis, everything else—biography, sources, themes, etc.—being material that is useful but secondary and which, although it helps us to approach the poem, loses all importance when we come to understand—as Edgar Allan Poe already did—that the poem, because of its unique reality, is an object that must be isolated, as if in parentheses, in order to be studied "scientifically."[14]

This would mean that Spanish stylistics could be considered "our version of the formalism which has dominated criticism in the West until recently."[15] The interest of Torrente in formalism could in this context be seen as related to his early assimilation of the theories of his friend Dámaso Alonso, who would later visit him at Albany during his years there.

It is important to consider carefully the possible attraction of the school of Spanish stylistics for Torrente. In 1954, Dámaso Alonso admitted to Max Aub: "I have not been the writer that I should have been because of Franco. I hid myself in Romance linguistics, just in case. It was what could compromise me the least."[16] The goal of analyzing poetic expression without reference to any external context is at the same time a refuge for the critic from the ideological climate of the times.[17] Torrente Ballester declares himself "formalist" in the "Prólogo a la segunda edición" [Prologue to the Second Edition] of *Fragmentos de Apocalipsis*,[18] and in his particular case the approximation to formalism has a clear relationship to the political disillusionment of the forties and the political and cultural repression of the Franco regime, but it arises fundamentally from a desire to defend himself from the ideological persecution by the Left of those accused of collaboration with fascism and Franco. Pressured by the ideological conflicts that arose in Spain in the late 1950s, Torrente's insecurity produced a certain sense of regret for his fascist past, and this lingering unease drove him little by little to raise the novel to the category of myth through a conception of literature as a closed universe free from ideological concerns. Central to this conception is a theory of literature in which he affirmed the existence of a "realidad suficiente" [sufficient reality] in the novel:

Yo llamo *realidad suficiente* a ese mínimo de fuerza necesaria para que la narración o el drama nos impongan su realidad, la suya específica, precisamente, y no la de lo que está pasando en la calle o en la conciencia de mi vecino de piso. La constancia, la operatividad de esa realidad suficiente tampoco se obtiene por cotejo, sino que se advierte meramente por sus efectos. Conviene insistir, hasta la pesadez, en que la obra poética es autónoma y dotada de una realidad *sui generis*.

[I call *sufficient reality* that minimum of effort necessary for the narrative or the drama to impose its reality upon us, its own specific reality, precisely, and not that of what is happening in the street or in the mind of my next-door neighbor. The constancy, the operativity of that sufficient reality cannot be achieved by comparison, but rather is noticed only in its effects. It is important to insist to the point of boredom that the poetic work is autonomous and endowed with a reality *sui generis*.][19]

Although he does not reject the connections which may exist between the "realidad suficiente" and lived human experience, on many occasions, as we will see below, the intention is clear on the part of the author of separating his work from its ideological background, thereby revealing precisely that the ghost of fascism still haunts him.[20]

The rise of the metafictional novel during the 1970s included considerable contributions by Torrente, thus opening a new phase of his artistic evolution. This literary movement was often interpreted as heralding the destruction of the novel as a genre: "Many reviews of new metafiction, especially in the early 70s, were negative: cries of lamentation over the death of the novel genre abounded."[21] Although we can find metafictional elements in much of his earlier work, we can only speak of a completely metafictional novel in the case of *Fragmentos de Apocalipsis* (1977). The project, which forms the basis for the further metafictional experiments of the author, is a continuation of the attempt to demythify history and ideology with which he began his literary career. The "novela destripada" [disemboweled novel], considered at the beginning as a type of self-destructive novel, fulfills its purpose for Torrente, who comes to believe that *Fragmentos de Apocalipsis* is the "diario de un fracaso" [diary of a failure].[22] The failure is that of the attempt to write a novel. The critical exploration of metafiction does not produce a novel, according to Torrente, but rather something else: "no es propiamente hablando una novela, al menos según mi modo de concebir y practicar el género" [It is not, strictly speaking, a novel, at least according to my way of conceiving and practicing the genre].[23] In the prologue he constantly refers to *Fragmentos* as a "book" or "work", never as a novel, but on another occasion he has commented that *Fragmentos* is "a critical novel, about the novel itself as an object, and it tells the story of how I, having decided to write a novel, failed to do so, and the story of how I failed constitutes the novel."[24] This terminological ambiguity corresponds to the double purpose that guided Torrente during the composition of *Fragmentos de Apocalipsis:* the destruction of the genre of the novel on the one hand and at the same time the demonstration, by exposing its conventions, that literature functions as a closed universe. The question remains: why propose to destroy the novel if the true intention is to affirm the autonomy and vitality of the genre? What seems to be a contradiction is in reality a demonstration of the manner in which Torrente remained faithful to his own intellectual and artistic trajectory. Just as the discovery of the fascist manipulation of collective reality led him to attempt a general demythification of history, the negation of ideological concerns as central to literary discourse produced his own myth of the novel: However, after obsessively parodying the techniques and tendencies of literary criticism in *La saga/fuga* [The Saga/Fugue] (1972), he reached the limit of his own conception of literature and was unable to find any escape other than to destroy the myth of the novel which he himself had created. As the author himself remarks in an interview with Carmen Becerra:

> In order to demythicize one needs an awareness of the myth and my first response to this awareness is demythification because, of course, the myth irritates me; I don't realize, on my first understanding of the myth, its value and extent; I believe that I simply feel deceived by things which have happened around me, and my answer is irritation, but later reflection allows me to understand that the myth is an inevitable reality, and that when one initiates the process of demythification it is simply in order to substitute one myth for another.[25]

Although this comment refers to historical myths, the mechanism proves appropriate as a conceptual thread that unites the trajectory of Torrente from fascism to metafiction. Historical demythification and the memory of his fascist youth lead Torrente to idealize literature as a balanced universe free from ideology. Upon recognizing this, he attempts to destroy and purify at once his literary work. As we have seen above, this mechanics of destruction (annihilation as purification to reach beauty) is related directly to fascist politics and aesthetics. In the Spanish Falange we can find examples of this tendency in the rhetoric of the last stage of the Civil War, a discourse that was used by the Francoists to construct a mythology that would help to win the war. The well-known Falangist writer Agustín de Foxá declared in an article: "Necesitamos ruinas recientes, cenizas nuevas, frescos despojos. . . . Pero ya está Toledo destruido, es decir, edificado" [We need recent ruins, new ashes, fresh plunder. . . . But Toledo is already destroyed, that is, constructed].[26] Álvaro Cunqueiro, friend and countryman of Torrente, let himself get carried away by the apocalyptic passion of the Falange: "Se contará en los tiempos venideros de esta guerra de España como de una cabalgada de fiebre y de incendio, victoria inmortal de un espíritu" [In future times this war in Spain will be told of as a fevered and fiery raid, the immortal triumph of a spirit].[27] Again, it is ironic that Torrente's fear of facing the specter of his fascist past compelled him to use such an ideologically marked strategy. The external signs of this destructive tendency can be seen in the metafictional dissection of *Fragmentos de Apocalipsis* and in the selection of the apocalypse as a central theme.

In *Fragmentos de Apocalipsis,* the title itself indicates the theme of apocalypse will be a constant presence. Over the course of the work, the reader encounters not only a cathedral in which "[se] custodia un manuscrito famoso, *Los comentarios al Apocalipsis,* de San Beato de Liébana" [is kept a famous manuscript, *Commentaries on the Apocalypse,* by the Beato of Liébana],[28] but also the apocalyptic writings of Justo

Samaniego, systematically compiled by the narrator. These "secuencias proféticas" [prophetic sequences], as they are called in the novel, are, according to their author, Samaniego: "símbolos y alegorías de un futuro inmediato del que he tenido revelación. . . . Le aconsejo que se prepare con una lectura previa del Apocalipsis, pues, *mutatis mutandis,* tienen mucho en común, si no es la inspiración, que aquella fue divina y ésta más bien pertenece al orden de la intuición histórica" [symbols and allegories of the near future of which I have had a revelation. . . . I advise you to prepare yourself by a previous reading of the Apocalypse since, *mutatis mutandis,* they have much in common, if not the inspiration, because the first was divine and the second more clearly pertains to the order of historical intuition].[29] The historicity of this apocalypse has to do with the fact that "se va a cumplir el milenario [desde] que las tropas de Olaf huyeron tras la batalla de Catoira. El rey juró volver a los mil años y arrasar la ciudad de Villasanta" [the millennium will arrive since the troops of Olaf retreated following the battle of Catoira. The king swore he would return after a thousand years and destroy the city of Villasanta].[30] Samaniego begins to compose a prophecy that will be fulfilled in the novel. Both apocalypses, the Christian and the historical, are combined through the work of John of Patmos:[31] in addition to the text of the Beato, we are told of the reign of the Vikings (the third reign before the final judgement, also used by the Nazis, with intentionally apocalyptic connotations, as the source for the concept of the "Third Reich") just before the destruction of Villasanta; the erotic female automaton created by them "que en tan mala hora había inventado el señor Samaniego para su profecía (la supongo inspirada en la Gran Ramera Babilónica del Apocalipsis)" [that Señor Samaniego had so unfortunately invented for his prophecy (I assume her to have been inspired by the Whore of Babylon)];[32] and finally the destruction of Villasanta de la Estrella by the sound of the Vikings' bells, a clear reference to the apocalyptic trumpets of the Book of Revelation.

The theme of apocalypse extends as well to the metafictional structure of *Fragmentos.*[33] For Torrente, a novel represents a pact between the author and the reader, "un pacto tácito que puede resumirse (o expresarse) en estas pocas palabras: *mientras dura la operación de leer haz como si lo que lees fuera cierto*" [a tacit pact that can be summarized (or expressed) in these few words: *while the operation of reading lasts, act as if what you read were true*].[34] In *Fragmentos,* however, Torrente's proposal to the reader: "*fue justamente la contraria,* quiere decirse ésta: *Todo lo que te cuento en este libro es rigurosamente cierto*" [was precisely the opposite, that is to say the following: Everything that I tell you in this book is strictly true].[35] The breaking of the pact is what differentiates

Fragmentos from a standard novel. The novel, from a certain point of view, is a closed and ordered structure which produces in modern man, according to Hutcheon, "a certain curiosity about art's ability to produce 'real' order, even by analogy, through the process of fictional construction."[36] The impulse to reveal the process of the creation of a novel is, however, a result of a felt need for its destruction, although this does not imply the destruction of the novel as a genre in the case of Torrente, but rather produces a liberating catharsis in the author. This is precisely the feeling produced in him by the destruction of one of the most important characters in the novel, Lénutchka. The author says in the "Prólogo a la segunda edición": "Jamás me sentí más cerca del demonio como al escribir aquella escena (páginas 386 a 388). Si crear es placentero, la sensación (o el sentimiento) que se experimenta cuando se destruye, si pertenece por su naturaleza al orden de lo tenebroso, no deja por ello de conducir igualmente al placer, aunque al oscuro, aunque al diabólico" [I never felt myself to be closer to the Devil than when I was writing that scene (pages 386 to 388). If creation is pleasurable, the sensation (or emotion) one experiences in the act of destruction, while it belongs by nature to the realm of darkness, does not therefore fail to lead equally to pleasure, although of the dark and diabolical sort].[37] As noted earlier, this aesthetics of destruction, provoked by the self-alienation of Torrente in a hostile environment, has a virtual relationship with the politics and aesthetics of destruction that characterizes fascism.[38] Walter Benjamin has suggested that "[fascism's] self-alienation has reached such a degree that it can experience its own destruction as an aesthetic pleasure of the first order. This is the situation of politics which fascism is rendering aesthetic."[39] It seems particularly significant that the author refers to the pleasure of literary destruction as "dark" and "diabolical." These adjectives indicate the reproduction of fascist mechanisms from the other side of the mirror, in other words, from the reinterpretive distance of a politics and aesthetics in which he no longer believes but which still exerts a certain fascination on him based on its "predominantly negative character."[40] It is a trace that confirms the trajectory from the aesthetic and political destruction of the Civil War, according to fascist mythology, to a newer aesthetic and surreptitiously political destruction of the novel at the hands of Torrente Ballester.

From the beginning of *Fragmentos* the narrator advises the reader as to his intentions: "Nada de lo que escribo ni de lo que he escrito tiene que ver con la realidad. Su espacio es mi imaginación, su tiempo el de mis pulsos. Si con ciertas palabras intento configurar imágenes de hombres, es por seguir la costumbre, pero que nadie lo tome en serio" [Nothing of what I write or have written has to do with reality. Its space is my imagination, its time is that of my heartbeats. If with certain words I attempt to construct images of men, it is only by custom, but no one should take it seriously].[41] He pauses carefully in order to name Villasanta de la Estrella, its cathedral and its people, always insisting that the existence of this entire world depends directly on his own will and word: "He nombrado la torre, y ahí está. Ahora, si nombro la ciudad, ahí estará también. Entonces, digo: catedral, monasterios, iglesias, la universidad, el ayuntamiento, el palacio del arzobispo; y digo: columnas, pórticos, bóvedas, ángeles, santos, profetas, volutas, pilastras, pináculos" [I have named the tower and there it is. Now, if I name the city, there it will be as well. So, I say: cathedral, monasteries, churches, the university, the city hall, the palace of the archbishop; and I say: columns, porticos, vaults, angels, saints, prophets, spirals, pilasters, pinnacles].[42] But in the middle of this literary genesis, immediately following the previous statement, an enigmatic warning appears without any apparent or obvious recipient: "No te olvides de que eres un conjunto de palabras, lo mismo da tú que yo, si te desdoblas somos tú y yo, pero puedes también, a voluntad, ser tú o yo, sin otros límites que los gramaticales" [Do not forget that you are a group of words, you are the same as me, and if you split we are you and me, but you can, at will, be you or me, with no other limit than grammar].[43] What follows may indicate the meaning of the message: "Gracias a eso, respondo, puedo, si quiero, descender de la torre, atravesar las plazas, guarecerme de la lluvia bajo los soportales y preguntar qué hora es al sereno de comercio" [Thanks to that, I answer, I can, if I wish, descend from the tower, cross the squares, take shelter from the rain beneath the archways and ask the time of the night watchman].[44] We find, therefore, that the enigma refers to the author-narrator relationship, that it is a coded message from Torrente Ballester with the purpose of including himself as narrator and protagonist in the novel. Thus multiplied, he may accomplish all manner of narrative sleight-of-hand within the work in order to illustrate by means of multiple stories, at times failed or truncated, a pedagogy of novelistic method. At the same time, this link between the author and the narrator has connotations of authority for the reader. The reader must at all times know who is the motive force (the author, conveniently reproduced in the narrator for greater expository clarity) and how literary creation functions (as the exclusive result of an independent imagination). The only limits he accepts are grammatical, reinforcing in this way a formalist vision which, in the words of Jakobsen, considers the literary work "as a verbal message whose aesthetic function is its dominant."[45]

At the same time, however, this author-narrator apparently abhors solitude and therefore creates a character whose function is to underline the critical aspects of the metafictional mode in *Fragmentos,* but who reveals herself to be a curiously sharp indication of the critical and existential tensions of the author. I am referring to Lénutchka, the young Russian professor the narrator introduces into the novel in order to have a "compañera en una narración erótica" [companion in an erotic narrative].[46] This is the only purpose admitted by the narrator, although over the course of the narration we discover that he also converts Lénutchka into a critical interlocutor, significantly educated in "el marxismo-leninismo más ortodoxo" [the most orthodox Marxism-Leninism],[47] despite her espousal of a view of literature which fluctuates between social realism and formalism. She even, once in a while, expresses rather paradoxical opinions, such as suggesting to the narrator that he write various complementary stories in his novel in three parallel columns,[48] an avant-garde experiment difficult to reconcile with her defense of social realism, and which contrasts with her later criticism of the narrator's idea of writing without any regard to punctuation.[49] In the "Prólogo a la segunda edición" the author writes:

> lo que en mí puede haber de crítico, no sólo no se repliega y enmudece, no sólo no se oculta, deslumbrado por mi potencia imaginativa, sino que está siempre presente, y atento, y actuante, y muchas veces mete el freno, cuando no arroja encima de mi entusiasmo (transitorio) eficaces dosis de agua fría. Para dejar constancia de esta realidad, recurrí a un procedimiento figurativo, es decir, objetivé mi raciocinio estético y lo confié, como función justificante, a la figura de Lénutchka.

> [What I might have in me of the critic not only does not retreat and fall silent, not only does not hide itself, but rather is always present, and watchful, and active, and many times puts on the brakes, when it is not throwing effective doses of cold water on my (temporary) enthusiasm. In order to leave a record of this reality, I resorted to a figurative procedure, that is to say, I objectified my aesthetic reasoning and entrusted it, as a justifying function, to the figure of Lénutchka.][50]

This affirmation has caused Herzberger to characterize the amorous and critical relationship between the narrator and Lénutchka in the following manner: "If on the one hand she functions as the narrator's existential Other, on the other she serves as his creative Other during the process of writing. Together, the two form a dialectic of reason and imagination: Lénutchka insists on the rational structure of fiction, the narrator engages the free play of his imagination."[51] It is important to dwell briefly on this supposed dialectic, beginning with the critical doubling of the author, in order to reconsider the negative implications arising in the text from a link which is constantly established between the erotic or pornographic and the image of a literary criticism contaminated by political interests.

It is doubtful that the "aesthetic reasoning" of Gonzalo Torrente Ballester would be objectified in the figure of a Marxist critic. A man who has constantly emphasized the great harm done by Marxist critics to contemporary Spanish culture and who, as we have already seen, brought himself up to date toward the end of the 1960s in contemporary literary criticism in order to counteract the ideological preoccupations of his students, is unlikely to consider Lénutchka, "muchacha soviética educada en el materialismo histórico y dialéctico" [a Soviet girl educated in historical and dialectical materialism],[52] as his critical alter-ego in the novel.[53] It is possible that the necessity of a critical interlocutor drove him to invent her in order to present his literary reflections in a manner more attractive than the continuous narratorial monologue, but the selection of his counterpart, her characteristics and treatment are necessarily significant, and more so in this case, in which he surprises us by presenting a Marxist critic who is at the same time a young, beautiful, and seductive woman. Continuing a practice of political sexualization that considers the feminine intellect inferior and the female body as an object of male conquest, Lénutchka is a perfect example of how fascist ideology persists as a specter in the writing of Torrente. Nonetheless, it is important to underscore the fact that, although the strongly sexist nature of fascist propaganda has been well documented, and according to which women are reduced to the roles of mother and pillar of the home, discursive feminization of political adversaries has been a common practice of all political groups since the early twentieth century. This strategy of denigration and humiliation of the enemy is the result of an extreme misogynistic, sexist, and homophobic attitude which arose out of a "crisis of male identity brought on throughout Europe by the ravages of World War I [that] clearly transcended the political and ideological categories of Left and Right . . . making any definite conclusions concerning fascism's exclusive and defining link to sexism untenable."[54] Sartre, in "Qu'est-ce qu'un collaborateur?" [What is a collaborator?] and Adorno, in *Minima Moralia,* characterize fascists as "feminized males." According to Adorno: "In the end the tough guys are the truly effeminate ones, who need the weaklings as their victims in order not to admit they are like them."[55] Both thinkers thereby achieve a position of political dominance through phallic dominance by reestablishing their virility when faced with an aggressive political adversary. In attempting to regain control of his novel from the recurrent specter of his fascist past, it is not surprising that this is exactly the ideological strategy which Torrente employs when he represents his Marxist critics by means of a feminine character, Lénutchka.

From the very first, the narrator is surprised that the supposedly real Lénutchka would decide to participate in the game that *Fragmentos* is, transforming herself into his literary mistress, because "hasta entonces, nuestras ideas literarias no habían concordado mucho a causa de su formación marxista, que la llevara a profesar el social realismo" [until that time, our literary ideas were not very much in agreement because of her Marxist education, which led her to defend social realism].[56] The goal of the narrator is to write an erotic novel in which he is the protagonist, but Lénutchka makes it a condition of her presence in the novel "'que halles la manera de que la intimidad de nuestro amor no se publique.' . . . Lo cual, por lo pronto, limitaba bastante mi propósito" ['that you find a way for the intimacy of our love to escape disclosure.' . . . Which, for the moment, rather limited my purpose].[57] As a solution, they decide to write "una segunda novela, esta secreta, en la que se contase con pelos y señales lo que pasaba a solas" [a second novel, this one secret, in which would be told what happened in private, warts and all].[58] This erotic novel is suppressed in the published text along with the "discusiones teóricas en las cuales jamás nos poníamos de acuerdo" [theoretical arguments in which we never agreed][59] which are mentioned at various moments. Torrente has said in *El País:* "I think it is obvious that there are two symptoms to watch for in order to tell a bad writer: if he falls back on either ideology or pornography."[60] The figure of Lénutchka represents both tendencies in the text and with them bears certain sinister connotations the novel manipulates until the moment of her destruction. As many critics have observed, despite Lénutchka being the critical presence within the novel, she does not seem to have a very great influence on the narrator, who rejects almost all of her suggestions, insinuating in this way the inviability of her opinions and, indirectly, those of the social realists in general.[61] The narrator believes himself to be the representative of "la escritura en libertad" [writing in freedom], in contrast to the "realismo social" of Lénutchka.[62] And although he recognizes the critical learning of the Russian woman, he does so by means of paternalistic exclamations such as "-qué minucioso es su talento, qué avispada!" [how thorough is her talent, how clever!] and insists this talent is the product of careful training by her teachers: "Se ve que sus maestros han sido concienzudos y que le han enseñado cómo se analiza una página" [One can tell that her teachers were conscientious and that they have taught her how to analyze a page].[63] This elicits the observation: "Cuando habla, parezco su discípulo" [When she speaks, it is as if I were her disciple],[64] a fairly significant expression, given the fact he only "seems" to be her disciple, obviously implying he is not and does not want to be. He constantly maintains a position of superiority by silencing the arguments of Lénutchka in the text and, near the end, he condenses into a single phrase everything that he feels regarding the young Soviet critic: "Lénutchka tiene una gran experiencia crítica, pero lo ignora todo de la invención" [Lénutchka has great critical experience, but she is completely ignorant of the workings of invention].[65] With this condemnation, which includes both Lénutchka and the ideological criticism of the Marxists, the novel begins the task of destroying the character of the young interlocutor.

But before proceeding to analyze the destruction of Lénutchka, it is important to reconsider the attitude of the narrator towards his character with regard to sex and gender. In naming those details that incite his love for the Russian woman, the narrator pauses to consider the purely physical aspects of her person, which for him serve to overcome his misgivings about her profession and beliefs: "Es muy notable su postura en el diván, cuando más intelectual se siente, cuando más profesora: se sienta, entonces, con las piernas cruzadas, mete los brazos por debajo de los muslos y baja la cabeza: entonces es temible y le fluyen las citas de Tynianov. Sería insoportable de escuchar sin aquella postura tan escasamente convencional" [Her posture on the couch is quite striking when she feels herself to be most intellectual, most like a professor: she sits, then, with her legs crossed, she puts her arms beneath her thighs and lowers her head: then she is truly frightening and quotes from Tynianov come flowing out of her. It would be unbearable to listen to without that unconventional posture].[66] Further on, he remembers the personal graces which "precisamente le brotan espontáneas y jamás repetidas cuando se olvida de que yo soy escritor, de que ella ejerce la función crítica en una universidad y quedamos reducidos a varón y mujer. ¿Se me ofenderá mucho si menciono, sin comentarios, sus tetas respingonas? Caso de que lo haga, con tacharlo está listo" [flow from her spontaneously and without repetition precisely when she forgets that I am a writer, that she is a critic in a university, and we are reduced to a man and a woman. Will she be offended if I mention, without commentary, her perky breasts? If she did, I could correct it by simply crossing it out].[67] All of the negative characteristics that could disturb their sexual relations are concentrated in the critical work of Lénutchka. She is the one who has to forget that the narrator is a writer and repress her own professional training in order to seem enticing to the narrator. Moreover, in the second example her charms are again represented strategically by her "perky breasts," by her anti-intellectualized body, the only way in which the narrator can express the attraction he feels for her. Even when he tries shortly after to demonstrate to the reader the admiration which her "seriedad profunda" [profound seriousness] and her psychological equilibrium produce in him, the only significant example which he can give is the following statement made by Lénutchka: "'Admito sin turbación que mi madre haya gozado el engendrarme, y el buen trato, el afecto tranquilo que siempre advertí en mis padres lo atribuyo a un buen entendimiento sexual'" [I admit without any hesitation that my mother enjoyed herself while I was being conceived, and the good relationship, the tranquil affection which I always noticed between my parents I attribute to good sexual understanding].[68] The paternalistic and arrogant reduction of Lénutchka to an attractive body, young and sexualized—particularly when her intellectual accomplishments are silenced or censured—suggests a subtle revenge on Marxist critics through the textual and sexual subjection of the Russian woman, who in the final analysis is no more than a character manipulated by the author and the narrator.

The novel then turns to the annihilation of Lénutchka. In order to accomplish this, the Russian is transformed definitively into a mere pornographic body in one of the prophetic sequences of Samaniego, the second most important narrator of *Fragmentos*. Lénutchka appears in his writings as a lesbian who sleeps with one of the mechanical dolls constructed by the Vikings. The principal narrator goes to see Justo Samaniego in order to ask him to erase that part of his story: "'Estoy persuadido de que, en este caso, su imaginación falseó la realidad sin razón suficiente' '-Oh, a mí la realidad me trae sin cuidado! Invento lo que se me ocurre y escribo lo que invento'" ["I am persuaded that, in this case, your imagination falsified reality without sufficient reason." "Oh, reality doesn't matter to me at all! I invent whatever I come up with and I write what I invent"].[69] Torrente Ballester defends through Samaniego the principal reasons for the composition of *Fragmentos*. When the narrator insists that the anecdote about Lénutchka is a lie, Samaniego replies by giving a definition of literature as it is understood by Gonzalo Torrente Ballester: "¿Mentira? La literatura, como usted debe saber, no es mentira ni verdad, no es más que eso, literatura" [A lie? Literature, as you should know, is neither lies nor truth, it is no more than that, literature].[70] Despite the good intentions of the principal narrator, it is significant to note that he does not insist more on the destruction of this part of the prophecies when Samaniego says the final word about the matter: "Bueno. . . . Pero no las romperé [las páginas]. A lo mejor, cualquier día cambia de opinión. Es de sabios cambiar. De manera que si usted es sabio . . . me las puede pedir" [Well. . . . But I won't destroy them [the pages]. You might change your mind any day. Wise men change their mind. So if you are wise . . . you can ask me for them].[71] The pornographic sections remain then intact, while the erotic tale of the narrator's relationship with Lénutchka is burned shortly before the end of the novel in a bonfire which also appears to destroy Lénutchka herself,[72] and its destruction is complemented by that textual blackmail the narrator allows through, leaving virtually intact the pornographic text which testifies to his unequivocal attitude of sexual and textual domination. If we recall the "Prólogo a la segunda edición" and the passage that refers to the destruction of Lénutchka ("Jamás me sentí más cerca del demonio como al escribir aquella escena. . . . Si crear es placentero, la sensación [o el sentimiento] que se experimenta cuando se destruye, si pertenece por su naturaleza al orden de lo tenebroso, no deja por ello de conducir igualmente al placer, aunque al oscuro, aunque al diabólico" [I never felt myself to be closer to the devil than when I was writing that scene. . . . If creation is pleasurable, the sensation (or emotion) that one experiences in the act of destruction, while it belongs by nature to the realm of darkness, does not therefore fail to lead equally to pleasure, although of the dark and diabolical sort]), we can now not only perceive the relationship between her annihilation and the destructive mechanics of the aesthetics and politics of fascism, but also, and closely related to it, the diabolical joy produced by Torrente's personal vengeance upon ideological criticism and its representatives by feminizing, sexually subduing, and finally destroying them.

Regarding the relationship between the author and Lénutchka, Spires has suggested: "Lénutchka is simultaneously an obstacle and a creative impulse; her constant objections to his metafictional mode lead him to the point of destructive exasperation, but she also provides the very reason for the being of the text."[73] The critic relates Lénutchka to the role of the reader in general, whose relationship with the author of a novel is always problematic: "They simultaneously work for and against one another in a dynamic process of creation-destruction, a creative-destructive process."[74] Santiáñez Tió extends this interpretation by considering that with Lénutchka "the act of reading and the critical commentary born of that act are textualized."[75] In reality, with Lénutchka the author dramatizes the personal and literary conflict with his own critics, with what he refers to as "la vigilancia crítica" [critical vigilance] that organizes and controls "la imaginación en libertad" [the imagination in freedom].[76] His problems with the critics began with Franco's system of censorship, but they evolved during the constant public airing of his past ideological commitments which created a permanent sense of insecurity and which provoked in him a reaction that was to become the project of *Fragmentos:* the demonstration, once and for all, that literature is only that, literature. But the realization that he had been hiding within the novel forced him to attempt a form of destructive therapy, a demonstration of "la virtud catártica de la palabra" [the cathartic virtues of the word],[77] in the words of Justo Samaniego, who also violently exorcized his personal demons through his prophecies.[78]

Fragmentos de Apocalipsis, as Loureiro correctly suggests, is "a descent into the hell of the word, a frustrating experience for both author and reader, but a necessary purification in order to recuperate the pleasure of narration, in order to find once again a balance: upon return from that voyage to the other side of the word *La isla de los jacintos cortados* [The Island of Chopped Hyacinths] will arise."[79] The tension provoked in the author by a feeling of ideological persecution concentrated itself in his act of literary refuge. Fascism becomes as much the specter that brings the novel to a dead end as the way out of stagnation by means of a purifying act of destruction. It is significant that it is the Vikings, representatives of the fascist political project, who destroy with a bell the entire novelistic framework of *Fragmentos de Apocalipsis,* an act of destruction that concludes with the last thoughts of the narrator: "Yo, por mi parte, empecé a pensar en otra cosa" [I, for my part, began to think of something else],[80] thereby indicating a certain textual complicity between the Vikings and the narrator. By facing his fears through the dissection and "death" of his novel (a process mirrored internally by that of Lénutchka), Torrente is able to liberate himself from his ghosts in several ways. On the one hand, he destroys the myth of the novel, perceived by him as a prison, a constant reflection on the need to defend himself from ideological attack provoked by the anxiety that arises from his early affiliation with the Falange.[81] On the other hand, he avenges himself textually on his literary adversaries, the Marxist critics, through the manipulation and destruction of Lénutchka in the novel. Thus, Torrente subjects literature and literary criticism to a process of constant destruction, and from then on feels free to create at will without reference to the ghosts of his past. Another question entirely is the sinister repetition of a fascist mechanics of destruction that continued to fascinate Torrente and which appears in the process of his ideological struggle as something beyond his control.

This is another specter of fascism that remains in the author's writing process and becomes transparent to the critical gaze.

[Translation by Ramón Espejo-Saavedra]

NOTES

1. José Luis Aranguren, "Testimonio y símbolo democráticos de Dionisio Ridruejo," in *Dionisio Ridruejo, de la Falange a la oposición* [Dionisio Ridruejo, from Falange to the Opposition], ed. Juan Benet (Madrid: Taurus, 1976), 214–15. Translation from the original Spanish. Unless otherwise noted, all translations are by Ramón Espejo-Saavedra.

2. Ibid., 215.

3. Linda Hutcheon, *Narcissistic Narrative. The Metafictional Paradox* (Waterloo, Ontario: Wilfrid Laurier University Press, 1983), 155.

4. About this episode Gonzalo Torrente Ballester later told his son, Gonzalo Torrente Malvido: "There must have been a piece of paper loose somewhere relating my name to some recent ideological activity, my Galleguism at that time, or about earlier associations that in the context of the war had acquired a greater and much different meaning than is truly the case. The fact is that father Fermín, after a long conversation, asked me to wait for his return, and left. It would be very convenient, he said after returning an hour later, for me to register with the Falangist party the next day. Imagine, that was the real reason for my getting into the whole mess. What do you think? Simply to be able to feel safe" (Gonzalo Torrente Malvido, *Torrente Ballester, mi padre* [Torrente Ballester, My Father] [Madrid: Temas de Hoy, 1990], 33). See also: Torrente Ballester, "Prólogo a la obra completa" [Prologue to the Complete Work], in *Obra completa*, vol. 1 (Barcelona: Destino, 1997), 49–50; Carlos Reigosa, *Conversas de Gonzalo Torrente Ballester con Carlos Reigosa* [Talks between Gonzalo Torrente Ballester and Carlos Reigosa] (Vido: S.E.P.T.: 1983), 45, 88; Carmen Becerra, *Guardo la voz, cedo la palabra. Conversaciones con Gonzalo Torrente Ballester* [I Keep the Voice and Yield the Word. Conversations with Gonzalo Torrente Ballester] (Barcelona: Anthropos, 1990), 101; Francisca Miller and Stephen Miller, "Lo político-literario en Gonzalo Torrente Ballester: entrevista con el escritor en Salamanca el 20 de junio de 1987," [The Political-Literary Side of Gonzalo Torrente Ballesteril; Interview with the Writer] in *Critical Studies on Gonzalo Torrente Ballester*, eds. Janet Pérez and Stephen Miller (Boulder, CO: Society of Spanish and Spanish-American Studies, 1989), 184–86; and Javier Villán, ed., *Gonzalo Torrente Ballester* (Madrid: Ediciones de Cultura Hispánica, 1990), 61–63.

5. Reigosa, 89.

6. Torrente Malvido, 57, 59. According to his son, Torrente stopped giving these talks in 1951: "That November Uncle Jaime and I accompanied GTB to Salamanca where he had been invited by Taboada, a friend and civil governor of the town, to talk about José Antonio on the twentieth—the last of all of his political talks —; and we stayed there a couple of days, invited by the Falangist hierarchy" (Ibid., 128).

7. In this context the following statement to Alicia Giménez about his political past is particularly significant: "I don't have any reason to repent, and there is nothing that I can be accused of. Besides, he who is free from sin can cast the first stone. For circumstantial reasons (my family was there at the time), I chose one of the two Spains. I was under a conditional obligation, and I fulfilled it as long as my con-

science would permit. When I began to see certain things, serious things, my conscience would not allow me to continue, and I withdrew from my obligation in the best way possible without risking my life, that is to say, in an indirect and literary way. But I think that my dissent is clear in all of my works of the period" (Giménez, "Llegados los gozos, alejadas las sombras: Entrevista con Gonzalo Torrente Ballester," [Pleasure Arrived, Shadows Dispersed: Interview with Gonzalo Torrente Ballerster] *Quimera* 21–22 [1982]: 14).

8. José María Castellet, "Tiempo de destrucción para la literatura española," [Time of Destruction for Spanish Literature] in *Literatura, ideología y política* [Literature, Ideology and Politics] (Barcelona: Anagrama, 1976), 141–42. Martín Vilumara, in his review of *La saga/fuga de J.B.* [The Saga/Fugue of J.B.], gives a more negative interpretation of this phenomenon: "In the Spain of the post-war period, political action, impossible on its natural and logical grounds, was surreptitiously and castratingly displaced to other fields that, under normal conditions, should remain, if not neutral or above such considerations, at least free from the Manichaeism typical of parliamentary speeches and party manifestos, and much more so of the cheap demagoguery of libel" (Martín Vilumara, "El desafío de Torrente Ballester," [The Challenge of Torrente Ballester] *Camp de l'arpa* 6 [1973]: 22). Of course by this time—the review is from 1973—disillusionment with social realism and its excesses is generalized.

9. He states in an interview from 1974: "The trilogy *Los gozos y las sombras* is a social novel published in the age of the social novel. It is not a socialist novel; that is another question. But it is a social novel in which the basic problems that are presented are basic problems of the social and even the economic situation. I do not know where, on some occasion I have said that the greatest influences on me in writing that novel are Ortega y Gasset and Karl Marx. Nevertheless, since it wasn't a novel that fell within the canonical rules of the social novel at that time, no one paid attention to it as a social novel. It was called a psychological novel, an intellectual novel. In short, nonsense like that" (Villán, 15–16). But when in 1990 Carmen Becerra asks him if he thinks that in *Los gozos y las sombras* the theme of class struggle is developed, Torrente answers: "Well, as background, yes. The relationship, the typical framework (the class struggle) is changed a bit in order to make it a conflict between people" (Becerra, 99), denying in this way any attempt to study the fundamental problem of the social and economic situation of the characters. He misinterprets in his own fashion the famous phrase of Engels "typical events in typical situations" (in other words, the exploration of quotidian reality) and in contrast to this literary and ideological position he decides to demonstrate "that what I see in my experience is not that: they are individual cases in individual situations" (Becerra, 100).

10. Villán, 63.

11. Vilumara comments: "For readers of my, let us say 'ideological,' background, the marginality of Torrente Ballester was probably motivated by the political connotations suggested by his name." (Vilumara, 22). This continues to be true, even knowing, as the author's son informs us, that he attempted to approach some of the social realists of the fifties, especially after his fall from favor in 1962 (Torrente Malvido, 205). Torrente Malvido points out that "for the first time he found himself included in a political *status* that was very favorable given the winds that were beginning to blow from the East" (Ibid.), an observation which is sufficiently significant to give us an idea that, at least before 1962, he was far from being well received. At the same time, in the following paragraph he states that: "*Don Juan* exploded on the scene [with] neither shame nor glory: no one seemed to understand a word of it, and no one showed the least surprise at the feat" (Ibid.). No one, not even his new contacts

among the social realists, pays attention to his favorite work, and he decides to leave Madrid for Pontevedra in 1964, from where he will leave for the United States in 1966.

12. Torrente Malvido, 228.

13. Ibid., 230–231.

14. Carlos Blanco Aguinaga, "La estilística hispanística: esquema para un estudio de su rechazo de la historia," [Hispanic Stylistics: Notes toward a Study of its Rejection of History] in *Actele celui de al XII-lea congres international de lingvistica si filologie romanica*, eds. Alexandru Rosetti and Sanda Reinheimer-Ripeanu, (Bucharest: Editura Academiei Republicii Socialiste Romania, 1971), 694.

15. Ibid., 695.

16. Max Aub, *Diarios (1939–1972)* [Diaries], ed. Manuel Aznar Soler (Barcelona: Alba Editorial, 1998), 247.

17. See Carlos Blanco Aguinaga, "La estilística hispanística: esquema para un estudio de su rechazo de la historia." Blanco Aguinaga explains the historical and ideological motivations for this withdrawal in the following manner: "the most important stylistic studies appear between 1940 and 1951, and they have exerted an influence until very recently. [In] order to understand this historical peculiarity of stylistics one must take into account what has been forgotten for being so well known: that for Spain and for the world the years from 36 to 45 are a terrible story which leads many to believe that it is not worth it to worry about History (always the same in what it reveals about human brutality, etc.); that during those years the sociological criticism which broke out in the thirties attempting to rethink the relationship between the literary work and History disappeared. [Given] which, insofar as the criticism produced in Spain is concerned, it is important to remember, in this context, that these were the years in which it was more convenient not to have a particular individual history and not to write history in a particular way; under this pressure of a historical reality that only favored historical examination of what was most remote in time, it should not surprise us that theoretical declarations and formalist studies with grand 'scientific' pretensions should appear and hope to connect at such an inopportune moment with avant-garde principles whose true value should have already been rethought and surpassed" (Blanco Aguinaga, 695–96).

18. Torrente, "Prólogo a la Segunda edición" [Prologue to the Second Edition], in *Fragmentos de Apocalipsis* (Barcelona: Destino, 1997), 23.

19. Torrente, "De la realidad suficiente," [About the Sufficient Reality] in *Cotufas en el golfo* [Impossible Things] (Barcelona: Destino, 1990), 67–68.

20. In "Hay una realidad que urge" [There is an Urgent Reality] the author writes: "Yo nunca he creído en la obligación del artista de convertir su arte en testimonio, pero jamás se me ha ocultado que, de un modo o de otro, el arte es siempre testimonio, directo o indirecto" [I have never believed in the obligation of the artist to transform his art into testimony, but I have never ignored the fact that, in one way or another, art is always a form of testimony, whether direct or indirect] (Torrente, "Hay una realidad que urge," *Cotufas en el golfo* [Barcelona: Destino, 1990], 51).

21. Hutcheon, 2.

22. "Prólogo," 21.

23. Ibid., 12.

24. Lola Suardíaz Espejo, *Gonzalo Torrente Ballester, evidentemente* [Gonzalo Torrente Ballester, Evidently] (Madrid: j. Noticias, s.l., 1996), 127.

25. Becerra, 84.

26. José Carlos Mainer, *Falange y literatura* [Falange and Literature] (Barcelona: Labor, 1971), 43.

27. Ibid.

28. Gonzalo Torrente Ballester, *Fragmentos de Apocalipsis* (Annotated by Nil Santáñez Tió) Barcelona: Destino, 1997), 49.

29. Ibid., 107–8.

30. Ibid., 49–50.

31. Janet Pérez, in her article "Cervantine Parody and the Apocalyptic Tradition in Torrente Ballester's *Fragmentos de Apocalipsis*" (*Hispanic Review* 56.2 [1988]: 162), studies the Judeo-Christian apocalyptic tradition in the novel. Pérez briefly relates the historical demythification of Torrente with his demythification of millenarianism. She analyzes the influence of Cervantine parody on the metafictional experiments of Torrente (understood as destructive parody) and offers a thorough list of motives taken from the biblical apocalypse that are fundamental in order to appreciate the use of the theme within the present work.

32. *Fragmentos*, 320.

33. Nil Santiáñez Tió, "Introducción," *Fragmentos de Apocalipsis*, lvii.

34. "Prólogo," 13.

35. *Fragmentos*, 14.

36. Hutcheon, 19.

37. "Prólogo," 22.

38. Anarchists believe revolution is an ethical and political means to achieve the realization of the Idea of Anarchy. It would be difficult to find anarchist discourses that exalt a pure aesthetics of destruction in the same manner in which it constantly appears in fascist proclamations.

39. Walter Benjamin, "The Work of Art in the Age of Mechanical Reproduction," in *Illuminations,* ed. Hannah Arendt (New York Schoken Books, 1985), 242.

40. José Ortega y Gasset, "Sobre el fascismo," [About Fascism] *Obras completas,* Vol. II (Madrid: Revista de Occidente, 1946), 496.

41. *Fragmentos*, 33.

42. Ibid., 37.

43. Ibid.

44. Ibid.

45. Roman Jakobson, *Language in Literature* (Cambridge: Harvard University Press, 1987), 43.

46. *Fragmentos*, 161.

47. Ibid., 135.

48. Ibid., 120.

49. Ibid., 283–84.

50. "Prólogo," 17.

51. David Herzberger, "*Fragmentos de Apocalipsis* and the meaning of the Metafictional Character," in *Critical Studies on Gonzalo Torrente Ballester,* eds. Janet Pérez and Stephen Miller (Boulder: Society of Spanish and Spanish-American Studies, 1989), 40.

52. *Fragmentos*, 155.

53. In the interview with Reigosa, from 1983, he makes a very clear statement on this issue: "[Reigosa]—We will speak of this as well, of the *coexistence* with the social realists of our time. [GTB]—There aren't any anymore.—There must still be some, no?—What remains are critics and historians of literature who are involved with Marxism and who never read Marx, because, if they had read him, they would think differently. And, of course, they are doing great damage, great harm" (Reigosa, 122).

54. Richard J. Golsan and Melanie Hawthorne, "Introduction: Mapping the Terrain," in *Gender and Fascism in Modern France,* eds. Richard J. Golsan and Melanie

Hawthorne (Hanover, NH: Dartmouth College/University Press of New England, 1997), 10–11.

55. Quoted in David Carroll, *French Literary Fascism: Nationalism, Anti-Semitism, and the Ideology of Culture* (Princeton: Princeton University Press, 1995), 152.

56. *Fragmentos*, 161.

57. Ibid.

58. Ibid.

59. Ibid., 228.

60. Reigosa, 254.

61. Santiáñez Tió, lxiv; Robert C. Spires, *Beyond the Metafictional Mode. Directions in the Modern Spanish Novel* (Lexington: University Press of Kentucky, 1984), 92–93; and Genaro G. Pérez, "Metaficción en Don Juan y *Fragmentos de Apocalipsis* de Gonzalo Torrente Ballester," *Revista canadiense de estudios hispánicos* 12 (1988): 425.

62. *Fragmentos*, 229.

63. Ibid., 383.

64. Ibid.

65. Ibid., 405.

66. Ibid., 421.

67. Ibid.

68. Ibid., 422.

69. Ibid.

70. Ibid.

71. Ibid., 423.

72. Ibid., 431.

73. Spires, 92.

74. Ibid., 93.

75. Santiántez Tió, lxiii.

76. *Fragmentos*, 23.

77. Ibid., 423.

78. Ibid., 424–28.

79. Ángel G. Loureiro, *Mentira y seducción. La trilogía fantástica de Torrente Ballester* [Lie and Seduction. The Fantastic Trilogy of Torrente Ballester] (Madrid: Castalia, 1990), 110.

80. *Fragmentos*, 437.

81. Santiáñez Tió speaks of the prison of language, but in a different sense than that used here. Referring to the narrator and Lénutchka, he comments: "Only in literary language can these two characters live out a love story. In the expression of Nietzsche adapted lately by Fredric Jameson, the narrator and Lénutchka are confined in the 'prison' of language because it is the only space possible for their love" (lxix). He interprets this relationship as the key to the novel as a whole, by means of the Derridian concept of the supplement (lxxiv): "The supplementarity of the love between the narrator and Lénutchka symbolizes the supplementary character of this novel and, of course, of any literary work with respect to extraliterary reality" (lxxv). This all forms part of the problem of literary referentiality in general, and in the present case I have limited myself to relating the literary refuge of Torrente to his consideration of the novel exclusively as a linguistic system, in this way creating a relationship which, as Jameson has shown, is nothing more than "the application of a metaphor" (viii), and showing at the same time that all forms of ideological criticism frighten him for obvious reasons. The supplementarity of literature with respect to extratextual reality does not imply the need for mutual separation, the constant goal of Torrente Ballester. On the other hand, regarding the positive interpretation Santiáñez Tió and others give of

the relationship between Lénutchka and the narrator, after the above analysis it is difficult, if not impossible, for me to consider it as anything other than problematic.

BIBLIOGRAPHY

Aranguren, José Luis. "Testimonio y símbolo democráticos de Dionisio Ridruejo." In *Dionisio Ridruejo, de la Falange a la oposición*. By Juan Benet et al. Madrid: Taurus, 1976.

Aub, Max. *Diarios (1939–1972)*. Edited by Manuel Aznar Soler. Barcelona: Alba Editorial, 1998.

Becerra, Carmen. *Guardo la voz, cedo la palabra. Conversaciones con Gonzalo Torrente Ballester*. Barcelona: Anthropos, 1990.

Benjamin, Walter. "The Work of Art in the Age of Mechanical Reproduction." In *Illuminations*. Edited by Hannah Arendt. New York: Schoken Books, 1985.

Blanco Aguinaga, Carlos. "La estilística hispanística: esquema para un estudio de su rechazo de la historia." In *Actele celui de al XII-lea congres international de lingvistica si filologie romanica*. Edited by Alexandru Rosetti and Sanda Reinheimer-Ripeanu. Bucarest: Editura Academiei Republicii Socialiste Romania, 1971.

Carroll, David. *French Literary Fascism: Nationalism, Anti-Semitism and the Ideology of Culture*. Princeton: Princeton University Press, 1995.

Castellet, José María. "Tiempo de destrucción para la literatura española." *Literatura, ideología y política*. Barcelona: Anagrama, 1976.

Giménez, Alicia. "Llegados los gozos, alejadas las sombras: Entrevista con Gonzalo Torrente Ballester." *Quimera* 21–22 (1982): 14–19.

Golsan, Richard J. and Melanie Hawthorne. "Introduction: Mapping the Terrain." In *Gender and Fascism in Modern France*. Edited by Richard J. Golsan and Melanie Hawthorne. Hanover, NH: Dartmouth College/University Press of New England, 1997.

Herzberger, David. "*Fragmentos de Apocalipsis* and the meaning of the Metafictional Character." In *Critical Studies on Gonzalo Torrente Ballester*. Edited by Janet Pérez and Stephen Miller. Boulder, CO: Society of Spanish and Spanish-American Studies, 1989.

Hutcheon, Linda. *Narcissistic Narrative. The Metafictional Paradox*. Waterloo, Ontario: Wilfrid Laurier University Press, 1983.

Jakobson, Roman. *Language in Literature*. Cambridge: Harvard University Press, 1987.

Jameson, Fredric. *The Prison-House of Language. A Critical Account of Structuralism and Russian Formalism*. Princeton: Princeton University Press, 1974.

Loureiro, Ángel G. *Mentira y seducción. La trilogía fantástica de Torrente Ballester*. Madrid: Castalia, 1990.

Mainer, José Carlos. *Falange y literatura*. Barcelona: Labor, 1971.

Miller, Francisca and Stephen Miller. "Lo político-literario en Gonzalo Torrente Ballester: entrevista con el escritor en Salamanca el 20 de junio de 1987." In *Critical Studies on Gonzalo Torrente Ballester*. Edited by Janet Pérez and Stephen Miller. Boulder, CO: Society of Spanish and Spanish-American Studies, 1989.

Ortega y Gasset, José. "Sobre el fascismo." *Obras completas*, vol II. Madrid: Revista de Occidente, 1946.

Pérez, Genaro G. "Metaficción en *Don Juan* y *Fragmentos de Apocalipsis* de Gonzalo Torrente Ballester," *Revista canadiense de estudios hispánicos* 12 (1988): 415–28.

Pérez, Janet. "Cervantine Parody and the Apocalyptic Tradition in Torrente Ballester's *Fragmentos de Apocalipsis*," *Hispanic Review* 56.2 (1988): 157–79.

Reigosa, Carlos. *Conversas de Gonzalo Torrente Ballester con Carlos Reigosa.* Vigo: S.E.P.T., 1983.

Santiáñez Tió, Nil. "Introducción." *Fragmentos de Apocalipsis.* Barcelona: Destino, 1997.

Spires, Robert C. *Beyond the Metafictional Mode. Directions in the Modern Spanish Novel.* Lexington: University Press of Kentucky, 1984.

Suardíaz Espejo, Lola. *Gonzalo Torrente Ballester, evidentemente.* Madrid: j. Noticias, s.l., 1996.

Torrente Ballester, Gonzalo. "Prólogo a la obra completa." *Obra completa,* vol. 1. Barcelona: Destino, 1977.

———. "Hay una realidad que urge." *Cotufas en el golfo.* Barcelona: Destino, 1990.

———. "De la realidad suficiente". *Cotufas en el golfo.* Barcelona: Destino, 1990.

———. *Fragmentos de Apocalipsis.* Commented by Nil Santiáñez Tió. Barcelona: Destino, 1997.

———. "Prólogo a la segunda edición." In *Fragmentos de Apocalipsis.* Commented by Nil Santiáñez Tió. Barcelona: Destino, 1997.

Torrente Malvido, Gonzalo. *Torrente Ballester, mi padre.* Madrid: Temas de Hoy, 1990.

Villán, Javier. "Gonzalo Torrente Ballester en la cumbre," *La estafeta literaria* 533 (1974): 14–17.

———, ed. *Gonzalo Torrente Ballester.* Madrid: Ediciones de Cultura Hispánica, 1990.

Vilumara, Martín. "El desafío de Torrente Ballester," *Camp de l'arpa* 6 (1973): 22–23.

The Ghosts of Javier Marías: The Trauma of a Civil War Unforgotten

Carmen Moreno-Nuño

I

According to Raymond Williams's theory, societies are made up of both "residual" elements (which stem from the past and survive in the hegemonic present) and "emergent" elements (new and marginal realms of reality which are not yet dominant in the present).[1] The understanding of the political and cultural present as a structure in constant internal transformation impels the study of the re-structuring effects that historical changes have over time on any society. An analysis of current ideological elements originating in the Francoist dictatorship is therefore required for any inquiry into Spanish contemporary reality. On the one hand, such a study should not be melancholic;[2] it should avoid fixating on the historical tragedies that fascinate subsequent generations. On the other hand, it should not reiterate those ideas (e.g., collective madness) that were important explanatory tools during Francoism or during the Transition to democracy, even if they still enjoy a wide currency in the social imagination.[3] Such explanations shed scant light on the present or the past. Thus, a study of the most recent literature on the Spanish Civil War becomes not only appropriate but necessary, for this new literature is essentially different from the narratives bequeathed by the "children of the war." Most contemporary authors do not belong to that older generation but are its descendants. In the first part of this essay I explore the theoretical implications of the seemingly simple previous sentence (i.e., what it means to be a literary offspring of the children of the war), while claiming a new interpretive paradigm for the literature on the Civil War written during the recent decades of democracy: the paradigm of trauma. The second part of the essay analyzes the work of Javier Marías in the light of this new hermeneutic paradigm of trauma.

A quick glance at contemporary Spain forces one to question the relevance of a study that searches for the survival of "residual" elements that sprang both from a fascist *coup d'état* in 1936 and the following dictatorship. For most Spaniards today the *coup* and Francoism have become only a series of remote images. For the new Spain that satisfactorily recovered its socio-political rights in the 1970s and 1980s, the only vestige of past oppression is the tyrannical power of ETA, whereas the Civil War long ago entered into the realm of memory. However, during the Transition this memory was still both conflicted and painful. Indeed, fear of another civil war conditioned the actions of the political elites, the design of the new democratic institutions, the journalistic discourse of the time, the general attitude of citizens, and even a significant part of cultural production. Political parties often made use of the war, especially during electoral campaigns, as a very efficient weapon to arouse common fears and desires. As the democratic system settled into place, the war little by little lost its value within the political realm as a vital element of decision-making. During the years of Transition, the Civil War posed a problem with no easy or evident solution. Nevertheless, with the passage of time, what was once a difficult political issue became an essential dimension of national memory and also an object of growing cultural interest.[4] So although the Civil War may have lost its dramatic resonance in political forums, it persisted as an important element of national identity and became a constant theme within all realms of cultural production. The Spanish Civil War had been an object of study reserved almost exclusively for foreign scholars, who were less afraid of treading this political minefield.[5] However, since the 1980s and 1990s a growing number of Spanish researchers have delved into the subject in an attempt to understand their own historical origins.[6] The inevitable generational cycle produced younger scholars who could approach the war without suffering the lacerating emotional burden that had beset the previous generation. The intense historical research generated a precious *corpus* of knowledge, while literature and cinema—aided by the official political silence about the war—turned the Civil War into a subjective memory. However, the subjectivization of the memory of the war did not heal its traumatic nature. The division that existed between contradictory social and individual memories has perpetuated, helped by the lack of a full official accounting of the past (a truth commission has never been created in Spain).[7]

As democracy became established in the 1980s, a contradictory tendency grew stronger, one whose survival and continuing importance into the twenty-first century should be questioned. From the late 1970s on, the sheer number of literary, cinematic, and historiographical products that reflect upon the conflict has drastically increased, as cultural producers sought to take advantage of the new political freedom. However, a tacit watchword of social silence was growing against this proliferation of discourses in order to encourage both a peaceful transition to the new political regime and a national reconciliation. The silence was neither explicit nor evident, as is usually the case with regard to absence and lack, especially in times of public rejoicing.[8] But silence, the chosen political strategy to help overcome trauma, began to reign nonetheless. In spite of the abundant cultural production in cinema, literature, and historiography, the mass media (most of which was public at that time in Spain) did not promote debate about the war. Many citizens preferred to displace the shadow of the war, moving it out of the sphere of everyday life and into the anecdotal plane of their grandfather's (at this point no longer even their father's) war stories. Ever since the economic miracle of the 1960s, the unquestioned goal for Spaniards (questioned in its form, but not in its content) had been the incorporation of Spain into a never achieved Modernity associated with Europe.[9] The most assumed and widespread idea was that the Civil War had been the ultimate cause of this historical lag weighing so heavily upon Spaniards. A simple *modus ponens* led to the desired conclusion: if Modernity is the dream, and war is its main obstacle, let us eliminate war in the only realm in which it is still possible, the realm of memory. Only the socially marginalized (the elderly, the insane, and those who otherwise refused to be integrated into the system) could remain obsessed with the conflict. If anyone else dared to scratch the surface of silence, he or she would discover that the Civil War was still a living trauma. The fact that the "Two Spains" still existed just below the façade of the peaceful Transition was immensely worrisome for most Spaniards.[10] And scholars also faced the fear of falling into the same ideological trap of the two Spains and perpetuating old forms of both stereotype and ideology.

Moving from the social plane to a narrower political dimension, we find that the most characteristic trait is, again, silence.[11] The memory of those who died in Nazi concentration camps (some ten thousand were Spaniards) is honored in the monuments built to the victims of Nazism all around Europe, including Germany. However, there is no monument in Spain that pays them homage. Hundreds of thousands of Spaniards were condemned to prisons and concentration camps, and many were forced into hard labor. Many national construction companies took advantage of that free labor force, but

Spain has never contemplated the possibility of indemnifying these prisoners, as Germany did. When the combatants of the International Brigades were finally honored in 1986, neither the Chief of State, King Juan Carlos, nor the President of government, Mr. Aznar, received them, which the international press angrily noted. The last remaining *maquis*[12] are still fighting to overturn the sentences they received during the Franco regime, which condemned them as bandits rather than soldiers. Due to persistent refusal of the right-wing party, the Partido Popular [Popular Party], the Parliament has not been able to condemn the *coup* that unleashed the Civil War until 2002. The millions of people who were assassinated, exiled, fired from their jobs, given unjust criminal records, tortured by the Tribunal de Orden Público [Tribunal of Public Order], or who "disappeared" or were otherwise persecuted, have never witnessed a trial of their oppressors (as has happened in France, Italy, and Germany). There have never been major public displays of retribution because the Francoist regime was never defeated; rather, it has been progressively recycled and adapted to fit the current democracy. As pointed out by Vicenç Navarro, the victors (the Army, the Catholic Church) has never condemned Francoism: "Los vencedores nunca han pedido perdón a los vencidos, condición indispensable para la reconciliación, puesto que la expresión de perdón implica el reconocimiento de un error" [The victors have never apologized to the victims, an essential condition for reconciliation, as the expression of pardon implies the recognition of a mistake].[13] Fear of offending the victors, which was emphasized after the 23 February attempted *coup*, played an essential role in the transition to democracy. And this apprehension transformed the former political strategy of reconciliation into a *modus vivendi* of omissions and silences. This is the situation against which a large portion of contemporary narrative has reacted, raising itself as a voice for the defeated.

One of the consequences of this Pact of Silence[14] is that, in democratic Spain, the Civil War has been displaced as a key reference for understanding the present. The battle against injustice has moved from the narrower political realm of fighting against a dictatorship to a more inclusive socioeconomic realm. Spaniards are now worried about issues such as the future of a socially supportive political system, drug addiction, terrorism, unemployment, immigration, abuse of women, and so on. Political claims from the old-guard leftists against the old-guard conservatives have yielded to other priorities in a new country where intellectuals (as José-Carlos Mainer has pointed out) no longer have to be leftists to be intellectuals. Literature reclaims new topics: historiographical metafiction, postmodern subjectivity, queer and women's writing, and so forth. This new reality emphasizes the common idea that the Spanish war belongs only to a remote past without effect on the present. In fact, literature echoes this common knowledge through the hermeneutic paradigm that prevails in war fiction; literary narratives have transformed the Spanish Civil War into a "myth."[15] Despite the polysemy that the concept of myth evokes, relatively few traits are regularly selected from the various theories of myth for the description of contemporary war fiction. The repeated selection of the same traits leads to the following characterization of recent war narratives: 1) the Civil War, due to its emotional and temporal distance, is no longer a bleeding wound or a source of conflict—it has been forgotten; 2) consequently, war fiction is depoliticized and it is no longer a political discourse; 3) a cyclical conception of time prevails, as stories leave aside any concrete temporal context; 4) spatial context has been substituted by the centrality of *ordo naturalis;* and 5) protagonists are likened to classical heroes from Greek mythology.

As useful as the paradigm of myth may be to understand some particular narratives, it entails numerous problems if we try to extend it as a valid hermeneutic scheme for all, or at least most, of the war fiction written since 1975. Furthermore, the conceptual richness of myth carries with it the danger of grouping together theories that mesh uneasily, such as those of Sigmund Freud, Ernst Cassirer, Lévy-Bruhl, Jung, Mircea Eliade, Northrop Frye, Lévi-Strauss, and Roland Barthes. While the concept of myth is a very powerful explanatory tool, even mythologists themselves have not been able to unify all the different explanations into a single comprehensive theory because of the enormity of dimensions and variety of notions it includes. Moreover, this polysemy gives way to internal contradictions, one of which is the assumed depoliticization of contemporary fiction and the predominance of atemporal heroes. Manuel Vázquez Montalbán's *El pianista* [The Pianist] (1985) illustrates this particular contradiction through a story that combines a clear political content with a mythical hero as the main character.[16] Despite the aforementioned tendency to categorize politicized novels as myth, the larger problem is the acceptance of the idea that the Spanish Civil War has been depoliticized and forgotten when many novels betray a crystal-clear political content. This depoliticization is especially difficult to accept in works such as *Beatus Ille* by Antonio Muñoz Molina (1986), *Largo noviembre en Madrid* [Long November in Madrid] by Juan Eduardo Zúñiga (1980), *Tiempo de cerezas* [Time of Cherries] by Montserrat Roig (1978),[17] *La enredadera* [The Bindweed] by Eduardo Alonso (1980), *El lápiz del carpintero* [The Carpenter's Pencil] by Manuel

Rivas (1998), *El embrujo de Shangai* [The Charm of Shangai] by Juan Marsé (1993), *Libertarias* [Libertarians] by Antonio Rabinad (1996), *¿Qué me quieres, amor?* [What Do You Want Me For, Love?] by Manuel Rivas (1996), *Dios sentado en un sillón azul* [God Seated on a Blue Chair] by Carlos Casares (1997), or *Maquis* by Alfons Cervera (1997).

With regard to the literary representation of the Civil War, the depoliticization and oblivion that myth presupposes should at least be questioned. A brief digression will help to illustrate this point. In a recent summer course on the war (offered by Paul Preston in August 2000 at San Lorenzo de El Escorial), the divergent opinions among students and the frequent conflation of personal and anecdotal memories with scholarly study reveal how depoliticization and forgetfulness are not yet a reality for Spaniards.[18] Enthusiasm for the course transformed into an open and sometimes confrontational skepticism on the part of the young and old alike as they listened to the professor. The emotional reaction of participants revealed the survival of a collective trauma that has not yet been overcome. College students (for whom the pursuit of knowledge should have prevailed) questioned Professor Preston's claims on several different occasions, giving preference to the "truth" of family oral accounts over the scholarly information that the respected researcher offered. A group of elderly people who had lived through the Civil War joined the students in their disregard, bringing to the fore the "truth" of their experiences and testimony. For these older participants, memory meant the last and only bond with their own past, thus overriding any query that would undermine the foundations of their identity. Even though objectivity has always been a goal for people from all different sectors of society, the possibility of achieving objective knowledge was cast aside. The defense of subjective personal accounts illustrates how the war has become, as I pointed out above, a subjective memory. This subjectivism denies the foreigner equal access to historical knowledge, thereby signaling the existence of a never healed national wound, superficially forgotten but never forgiven.

In the literary field, the works of the children of the war have, for a long time now, coexisted with a narrative that is the fruit of the next generation. These younger authors did not live through the Civil War, but they did spend their childhood and adolescence in the harsh Spain of the immediate postwar period, surrounded by deprivation, fear, and silence. Although this generation was not part of the fighting, it has in fact lived through its painful consequences; its members were raised on an oral tradition that rehashed the horror of the conflict. There is an essential difference between this generation and the following ones (the generations of those who were raised and even born during democracy), despite their contemporaneity in the leadership of the current cultural field.[19] The difference can be found in the experience of a historical trauma, orally transmitted through the family or through the more extended social circle. In recent years, after the official recognition of Post-Traumatic Syndrome in 1980, the issue of trauma as a social problem has given rise to a broad-based interest in trauma theory in the disciplines of psychiatry, psychology, neurobiology, literary criticism, cultural studies, and sociology. Trauma first received attention in a strictly therapeutic realm (where it has been very useful in the study of the most common pathologies exhibited by veterans of the wars in Vietnam and Korea), proving to be a very revealing concept for cultural analysis, thanks to such theorists as Cathy Caruth, Dori Laub, Shoshana Felman, Dominick LaCapra, Ruth Leys, Geoffrey Hartman, et al. Trauma is commonly defined as "a wound in memory," a definition shared by these critics and also by the American Psychiatric Association. One of the key elements of trauma is its perpetuation, its power to be orally transmitted to others. The effects of the trauma (or its contagion)[20] influence not only those immediately affected by the experience: "This is its danger—the danger, as some have put it, of the trauma's 'contagion', of the traumatization of the ones who listen."[21] There is no doubt that many children of the war's survivors grew up surrounded by a silence that could never be broken and by a pervasive fear, because anything could bring about a terrible fate. They faced perpetual recrimination because they were not "real men," because they did not eat all the food on their plates, because they dared to waste, because basically they had not lived through the war. The subjectivity of this "second generation of the trauma" has been forged by collective experiences (collective but not identical, as authors suffered them in various degrees depending on their familial and socioeconomic backgrounds). Over the years, many of these writers have echoed this never-healed social wound in their fiction, acting as spokespersons for their generation.

This new literary paradigm based on the concept of trauma allows for an explanation of: 1) the vivid interest that the topic of the Civil War continues to arouse, even for younger generations immersed in a radically transformed reality, and 2) the expansion of a literary genre which has never been more alive despite the predictions that were made some years ago about its imminent demise (and fossilization). Thus, trauma offers an explanatory paradigm for a whole group of novels and short stories, including *Luna de lobos* [Wolf Moon] by Julio Llamazares (1995), *El jinete polaco* [The Polish Horseman] by Antonio Muñoz Molina (1991), *Caballeros de fortuna* [Men with Luck] by Luis Landero (1994), *Ramona, adiós* [Goodbye, Ramona] by Montserrat Roig (1987), *El árbol del bien y del mal* [The Tree of Good and Evil] by Juan José Armas Marcelo (1995), "El sur" [The South] by Adelaida García Morales (1985), "Ucronía" by Manuel Talens (1994), along with the titles previously mentioned. Many contemporary novels about the Spanish Civil War are best understood as a response to a national trauma that persists today in the collective imagination. The politics of silence regarding the war have turned it into a ghost which obsessively reappears to a second generation who seeks its identity in connections with a past that has resisted oblivion. This continuum between past and present holds the key for understanding the cultural production of a generational group that has transformed the residual traumatic memory of the war into a strategy for literary representation.

II

Since the release of his *opera prima, Los dominios del lobo* (1971) [The Wolf's Domains], literary critics have considered the work of Javier Marías to be a central referent for the generation of "los novísimos" [the ultra-new]. In the 1970s, this generation abandoned the traditional "problem of Spain" and sought out topics with more international roots. The goals of *los novísimos* were, first, to break away from the constricting tenets of social realism; second, to overcome the literary establishment's unsuccessful aspiration to change the world through literature; and third, to affirm literature "como algo universal y atemporal que no entiende de barreras lingüísticas ni de fronteras geográficas ni de conyunturas económicas" [as something universal and timeless, that does not recognize linguistic barriers, geographical borders or economic conjunctures].[22] Soon after the publication of his first novel, Javier Marías became a leader of this new literary trend, for which he was accused of being an "escritor británico nacionalizado español" [a British writer with Spanish citizenship].[23] Marías's fiction at first glance seems to be anything but Spanish, since it lacks the referents most traditionally associated with Spain. One explanation of his particular writing style has to do with his taste for and prize-winning translations of Anglophone authors. But beyond this predilection, in many of his writings Marías has attributed his initial rejection of social realism and all things Spanish to what he views as the simplistic and unfair identification of everything Spanish with everything Francoist. Marías recognizes that his gradual literary reconciliation with national reality has been a somehow difficult effort: "Se podría ir viendo una lenta aproximación hacia el mundo español, muy lenta, muy paulatina, como si me costara, como si no me fuera fácil—realmente no me lo ha sido" [It could be seen as a measured approach to Spanish reality, very slow, very gradual, as if it were difficult for me, as if it were not easy—in fact it has not been easy].[24]

Trauma allows for an explanation of the literary evolution of Javier Marías's work and for the growing importance that the representation of the war has held in his literary trajectory. In fact, a search for the Spanish "national" element in Javier Marías's work reveals the landscape of Madrid strongly connected to the Spanish Civil War. He explores the city of his birth and depicts the long siege that the Spanish capital underwent during the conflict. Furthermore, the Civil War has become over time one of the leitmotivs (that is, a recurrent theme) in Javier Marías's literary production as a whole, and it merges, obsessively and repeatedly, with the figure of the traitor. The author's supposed betrayal of Spanish literary tradition is indeed superceded by another treason with much more serious consequences; the treason that sent his father, Julián Marías, to prison right after the war is what nourishes his writing. This treason has never been forgotten by the offspring, for his philosopher father was falsely accused by one of his best friends.[25] Born in 1951, Javier Marías does not belong to the generation of writers who experienced the war and he is not a "child of the war," but he is most certainly part of that generation that lived through the war's severe consequences. Marías belongs to the "second generation of the war," that is, he is among the children of those who lived through the war. In his case, the trauma stems from family circumstances rather than socioeconomic ones, unlike the traumas one could trace in the fiction of other writers, such as Muñoz Molina or Vázquez Montalbán. All of them, however, are victims of the harsh Spain of the 1940s and 1950s and its legacy of suffering.

It is not surprising that as soon as Marías decides to explore the national reality in order to incorporate it into his fiction, a family trauma emerges. He resolves to control his trauma in a reflective and critical way by incorporating it into his writing as a leitmotiv. Traumatic memories (even different in nature from the remembrances of the children of the war) have affected the younger generation of authors who now live in a radically different Spain. This new context is one that allows for the emergence of a spokesperson (even if this person neither desires nor seeks such a role) for the postwar generation, specifically for those who suffered from imprisonment or denunciation. In Javier Marías's writing, the figure of the traitor merges with that of the denouncer; every denunciation is by definition the unveiling of the hidden, and treason is always committed by means of a word that reveals a secret. Word and secret, as fundamental conceptual keys in Marías's work, are intertwined with the figure of the traitor-denouncer. Likewise, the fictionalization of war aligns the traitor-denouncer with the ghost, another recurrent motif in Marías's narratives. The author himself has analyzed this figure many times a propos his own work, and also his favorite movie, *The Ghost and Ms. Muir* (1947), by Mankiewicz.

Scattered reflections about the Civil War, the siege of Madrid, and the figures of the traitor/denouncer and the ghost are plentiful in Javier Marías's work. Limiting ourselves only to the articles and essays specifically devoted to such topics,[26] we can single out the compilations *Vida del fantasma* [Life of the Ghost] (1995), *Literatura y fantasma* [Literature and the Ghost] (1993), *Mano de sombra* [Shadowy Hand] (1997), and *Pasiones pasadas* [Preterit Passions] (1999). In particular, Marías touches on ethical questions in his articles "El artículo más iluso" [The Fanciest Essay], "Pringue" [Greasy Dirt], "Culpable o culpable" [Guilty or Guilty] (in *Vida del fantasma*), "Nada importa" [Nothing Matters] (in *Pasiones pasadas*), "Malas lenguas" [Evil Tongues] (in *Mano de sombra*), and "Malvado gran escritor" [Wicked and Great Writer] (in *Literatura y fantasma*). These writings level serious accusations against a number of renowned intellectuals (philosophers, professors, novelists, journalists) without mentioning names but making identification an easy matter. These intellectuals reaped the rewards of the Francoist regime thanks to their offensive behavior, which could range from enthusiastic support of the political system to the betrayal of acquaintances and friends. Rejecting the benevolent forgiveness of the permissive and forgetful society that the Transition spawned, Javier Marías points again and again to traitors, censors, and other collaborators. His goal is to remind us of the earnestness of actions that are in truth moral faults with serious consequences and not merely little white lies. His call for rectitude intends to bring justice to all of those who both resisted the delinquency of the Francoist era and refused to comply with immoral behavior. All of this took place during a historical period in which it was all too easy to engage in such actions, and yet many people resisted even as they were being forced to become involved in dishonest acts. These honest citizens suffered reprisals because of their integrity, and thus they should not be falsely and unfairly equated with those less honorable. Javier Marías takes his arguments further, claiming that literature cannot be easily separated from the extra-literary. He insists that when a reader is confronted with the work of an author who cooperated with Francoism, there should be no tolerance. He speaks out against the current permissiveness that overlooks the crimes of the dictatorship and casts them into an amnesic oblivion. Further exposing the traces of family trauma, Marías has protested several times against the judicial system of early Francoism, in which mere accusation was equivalent to culpability; the accused had to prove their innocence, while the accusers enjoyed the protection of the system. This situation encouraged all sorts of personal revenge. For Marías, a situation where "la acusación se hace condena . . . constituye la mayor perversión de la idea de justicia" [an accusation becomes guilt . . . constitutes the worst perversion of the idea of justice].[27]

In "Ficción y recuerdo" [Fiction and Remembrance] Javier Marías warns his reader "a propósito de nuestra Guerra Civil, que ese acontecimiento tremendo está a punto de ser olvidado en el mal sentido de la palabra" [regarding our Civil War, this terrible event is about to be forgotten in the bad sense of the word].[28] To avoid the onslaught of a forgetfulness that would make a society ignorant of its own historical past, Marías repeatedly returns to this theme from a number of perspectives. In "Otra vez derrotados" [Defeated Again] (in *Mano de sombra*) Marías criticizes the Socialist Party's unfulfilled promise of granting citizenship to surviving International Brigadiers. Although only a few of these veterans are still alive and are now very old, the government ignored the parliamentary resolution, the end result being good propaganda for the government but a new defeat for the Brigadiers. "No los quiero" [I Don't Want Them] (in *Mano de sombra*) and "Glosario español para extranjeros (o palabras clave al terminar el año que ya terminó)" [Spanish Glossary for Foreigners (or key words when the year already over is about to end] (in *Vida del fantasma*) accuse those who, sheltered by the younger generations' ignorance of the war and Francoism, could insist that the political corruption in democratic times is "equal to or worse than the Francoists." In "Cuando los españoles querían cortarse el cuello" [When Spaniards Wanted to Cut Their Own Throats] (in *Literatura y fantasma*), Javier Marías glosses the results of two almost unknown surveys given to British and North American writers about the Spanish war before it ended. In "La foto" [The Photograph] (in *Vida del fantasma*), Marías attacks Franco and his lieutenant Millán Astray. Finally, a group of articles compiled in *Vida del fantasma* ("Una jornada en Madrid," "La ciudad sin realidad," "Más saña," "Tortura y asedio," and "Lo que no es Madrid"—[A Day in Madrid / The City without Reality / More Cruelty / Torture and Siege / What Madrid is Not]) reflects upon the last war as part of the ineluctable identity of the city;

Madrid has always exhibited a great capacity for resistance to the many outrages that history has forced it to witness.

The traumatic memory of the Civil War is also the object of Javier Marías's fiction. The recurrent, compulsive, and obsessive nature of trauma is represented through the narratological strategy of the leitmotiv, a resource that is fully appreciated by Javier Marías, configuring his peculiar style: the repetition and reworking of multiple and seemingly exhausted leitmotivs, allowing an overflowing that is meticulously controlled at the end. As trauma is defined not so much by its content (suffering), but by the very nature of its structure, it is that structure through which Marías has chosen to represent the memory of the Civil War in his fiction. One of Javier Marías's first novels, *El siglo* [The Century], belongs to those narratives that analyze the nature of fascism after the end of Francoism. *El siglo* was first published in 1983, but unfortunately every edition has suffered a precarious existence. In the prologue to the 2000 edition, the author declares that this has been a novel "sin suerte" [without luck], because "*El siglo* de 1995 había sido secuestrado" [the 1995 *El siglo* was kidnapped], and even that "lo acompañaba la mala fe" [it met with bad faith].[29] Due to its lack of distribution (most copies were rapidly taken off the shelves) *El siglo* remains a shadowy novel within Marías's own *oeuvre*. Nevertheless, as the author himself has so aptly stated, "no creo que se hiciera acreedora *El siglo,* ni en su primera ni en su segunda malhadadas vidas, a tan malos tratos" [I do not think that *El siglo* deserved, either in its first or in its second ill-fated incarnations, such a bad reception].[30] Although it is one of his first novels, *El siglo* is a pointed reflection on a crucial topic in contemporary Spanish history. With this novel, Javier Marías tries to shed light on the questions provoked by the figure of the Franco-era informer. In the prologue, Marías informs the reader of both the family trauma that led him to write this novel and the problem to which he attempts to provide a solution:

> Creo que si me interesó este asunto fue en parte por una cuestión familiar. Como he contado este año en algún artículo, mi padre fue denunciado en 1939, al término de la Guerra Civil, por quien había sido su mejor amigo (incluso habían publicado un libro juntos, con un tercero) y por ello pasó un tiempo en la cárcel. Esta historia siempre me impresionó desde niño, como también la revelación de que uno de nuestros más famosos escritores se hubiera ofrecido como delator, según parece, al "Cuerpo de Investigación y Vigilancia" franquista en plena guerra, para "prestar datos sobre personas y conductas," cuando dar nombres suponía enviar directamente al paredón a sus portadores. Supongo que con esta

novela quise, en parte, intentar explicarme de qué modo personas valiosas o meritorias, de las que en principio era difícil esperar vilezas, podían llegar a cometer la mayor de todas sin verse aparentemente conminadas ni forzadas a ello.

[I think this issue interested me partly because it was a family matter. As I explained this year in an article, my father was denounced in 1939, at the end of the Civil War, by the man who had been his best friend (they had even published a book together, with a third person), and because of that he spent some time in prison. This story made a deep impression on me as a child, as did the revelation that one of our most renowned writers had volunteered as an informer, it appears, to the Francoist "Cuerpo de Investigación y Vigilancia" (Division for Vigilance and Investigation) in the middle of the war, in order to "provide information about persons and behaviors," when giving names meant sending their bearers directly before the firing squad. I suppose that with this novel I wanted, in part, to try to explain to myself how worthy or laudable persons, from whom it was in principle difficult to expect baseness, could commit the worst kind without apparently being called on or forced to do so.][31]

Casaldáliga is the main character and also the informer. Born at the beginning of the century, he now awaits his coming death as the century draws to a close: Casaldáliga thus represents the epitome of an epoch. *El siglo* alternates chapters narrated by an omniscient voice with chapters narrated in the first person. This first person is Casaldáliga himself, who in a farcical tone reconstructs what in his old age he considers to be the outstanding episodes of his life. This division shows how the reality of Casaldáliga's life is different from the vision that Casaldáliga himself has of it. But this device also, and perhaps more emphatically, underlines the dramatic fissure that separates how others see Casaldáliga (as a traitor), and how he sees himself (as an illustrious being who has chosen a heroic destiny). Throughout its pages, *El siglo* articulates an answer to the question: Why would anyone want to be considered a traitor (and face the accompanying social rejection) without being forced to do so? Smells and scatological elements work in this novel as both prophecies of drama and metaphors for treason. The color blue repeatedly points to the fact that we are facing the story of a moribund fascist, who ultimately never dies. The lasting agony illustrates the perpetuation of Francoist elements within the new democracy. Despite that, the intertextuality with Latin poet Sextus Propertius underlines the elegiac nature of this novel and thus, the definitive end of the dictatorship. Finally, the end of *El siglo* fuses Casaldáliga's death with his becoming a denouncer at the end of the Civil War within an ellipsis: an ellipsis represents the unrepresentable, since trauma leads to the limits of representation and understanding.[32]

Javier Marías's novel echoes the distinction between destiny ("destino") and future ("porvenir," literally translated as "what's to come") that Casaldáliga's father teaches his son for years during their Sunday walks. From the opening pages, Marías discards the idea that a person becomes a traitor (that is, the particular type of traitor he is interested in) because he or she is obeying an imperative to survive, that is, succumbing to his or her *porvenir.* Rather, Javier Marías accuses the traitor of using his will and freedom to ruthlessly pursue a promising future (his or her "destino") regardless of whether his means to that end are morally reprehensible. As time unfolds, Casaldáliga learns to view his own existence from an impassive distance, as an entity that does not concern him or at most as something toward which he has an aesthetic (but not ethical) responsibility. Besides, the idea of one's destiny concerning only oneself and not others allows Casaldáliga to exonerate himself from the blame of society.

El siglo is full of intertwined betrayals: the foreign mother who forsakes Casaldáliga when he is just a baby; the governess who tells him secrets she should never have revealed; the father whose destiny was not that of being a grieving Francophile widower but rather an abandoned Germanophile buffoon; the mysterious case of lieutenant Catilina which results in Casaldáliga's promotion, and so on. And during the long final years of Casaldáliga's life, there is the continuous betrayal of the relatives and friends who hope to inherit his fortune, people whose greed and ambition are their only motives for standing by the moribund old man. On the other hand, the foundation of Truth that the main character desperately seeks is reduced to, in Marías's words, "la historia de un abúlico, un cobarde, un pasivo y un indeciso" [the story of a listless, cowardly, passive, and indecisive man].[33] The novel, becoming a moral fable, pays special attention to the consequences of a life full of intolerance and the abuse of power: the isolation of a dying person surrounded by lovers, friends, and relatives who care only about his fortune. At the end of his life, the accuser is accused and the denouncer is denounced once and again by the musical piece that his stepson sings with malicious pleasure: "Llora sin cesar durante la noche, y corren las lágrimas por sus mejillas: no hay quien lo consuele entre sus amadores: todos sus amigos lo han traicionado, y se han convertido en sus enemigos" [He cries without pause in the night, and the tears streak down his cheeks: there is no one to console him among his admirers: all his friends have betrayed him and have become his enemies].[34] In the last pages, the intertwined betrayals metamorphose into a haunting death sentence, which is repeated as a leitmotiv: a first example of a writing style that becomes more prominent later on.

The elegiac nature of *El siglo* apparently allowed Javier Marías to come to terms with the traumatic memory of the war that he had inherited. The topic of the Civil War seemed to disappear during the late eighties and early nineties. However, in 1992, the novel *Corazón tan blanco* [*A Heart so White*] subtly equates war and corruption: Ranz's personal fortune is the result of the corruption unleashed by the Civil War. Corruption (the resulting consequence of the successive betrayals of clients) is located within the political and historical framework of, besides Cuba, the Spanish Civil War and Francoism.[35] The short story "Cuando fui mortal" [When I Was Mortal] (1993), included in the eponymous volume of 1996, again connects themes of treason, war, and now the figure of the ghost. In fact, the narrator is a ghost—the conscience of a dead man who narrates his story as a result of a curse that consists of remembering everything that he and others experienced during his lifetime. His holistic conscience renders his memories repetitive, like the symptoms of a trauma. Betrayal is the hermeneutic kernel of the narration, which unites the two betrayals that have determined the life of the narrator. The first story takes place at the time when the narrator is still a toddler, being raised in a family crushed by the war. His father has to endure the humiliation of conceding to sexual acts between his wife and Doctor Arranz so that the latter will not denounce him. The double humiliation of political defeat and cuckoldry is added to the betrayal of his wife, who also becomes defeated and objectified. The traumatic repetition of remembrances brings about the second story, which the ghost-narrator perceives as memories he had not experienced while he was alive. Already married to Luisa, the narrator has a love affair with María, whom he tries to keep in the strictest secrecy. But when the narrator is murdered—his death by Luisa's hand appearing to be an act of justice for his adultery—it is nothing other than a new betrayal. The murder is planned in cold blood by Luisa and her own lover who, like Arranz, also happened to wear the pencil-thin moustache so popular during Francoism. The instrument for treason in both cases is "the word"—the word never uttered but always threatening in Arranz's postponed denouncement, and Luisa's word agreeing to the murder.

Mañana en la batalla piensa en mí [Tomorrow in the Battle Think On Me] (1994) presents the topic of the Civil War once more as a traumatic memory, which reappears obsessively in Víctor Francés's mind. The reappearance of this memory occurs often as the ghost of Marta, Víctor's one-night stand who dies in his arms while her little son Eugenio sleeps in the next room. Deriving from both this unforeseen

death and the abandonment of two year-old Eugenio in the apartment, the memory of that night becomes an obsession for Víctor. It
leaves him in a state of distress that oscillates between enchantment,
as he experiences the world around him from the emotional distance
of an outsider, and curse, as a parade of ghostly images chases him
incessantly. Such ghosts are the contemporary version of the specters
of Richard III's victims who, in Shakespeare's play, seek out the king
and offend him with accusations and bad omens: "Mañana en la
batalla piensa en mí, y caiga tu espada sin filo: desespera y muere"
[tomorrow in the battle think about me, and fall thy edgeless sword:
despair and die].[36]

Mirroring the chaotic array of figures, the traumatic memory never
appears as an isolated entity, but rather is associated with more traumatic recollections in an asphyxiating totality within which order is
impossible. In the same manner, Marta's ghost is accompanied by the
trauma of the Spanish Civil War. Even when this traumatic memory
embodies different things in the novel, each appearance underscores
the insistence of that which always returns: the traumatic memory is
embodied in the strategy of the leitmotiv. The repetition and reworking of seemingly exhausted leitmotivs are resources that are fully appreciated by Javier Marías, given his love of digression. In *Mañana en
la batalla piensa en mí*, this technique works well with the structure and
recurrent dynamic of post-traumatic thought. Thus the Spanish battle is one of the most important leitmotifs in the novel, and the memory of it adopts various forms that each become a new leitmotiv: 1) a
tombstone inscribed with the year 1914 (the year of Julián Marías's
birth, as his son points out) from where Víctor spies Marta's funeral;
1914 also symbolizes the consecutive wars that, along with the Spanish conflict, have devastated the twentieth century, permanently scar-
ring future generations;[37] 2) the toy planes in Eugenio's room, which
threaten to fly into the peaceful dreams of a child who sleeps quietly,
ignorant of the nearby tragedy; these toy planes are miniatures of
those that threatened and killed so many people during the Civil
War and World War II;[38] 3) the masses of people that seek shelter
from the rain, which evoke the masses that sought shelter from the
continuous bombings in the siege of Madrid between 1936 and
1939;[39] and 4) the contrast between the same places in Madrid today
and those in the old Madrid under siege; there is a deep feeling of
uneasiness that results from facing something which remains the
same but which at the same time becomes something different due
to the passage of time.[40]

The order broken by a traumatic event can be re-established only
through a cathartic discourse that provides the past with both mean-

ing and a sense of necessity. In this novel, such discourse starts with the childish utterance of Eugenio, who recognizes Víctor and calls him by name, repairing the fragmented identity that Víctor had been hiding from Marta's family and that he is also trying to repair. Both the enchantment and the curse vanish with the utterance of the word that needs to be said and wisely heeded. Luisa, Marta's sister, is the understanding person who listens to Víctor, forcing his ghosts away. Deán's ghosts will also disperse after unveiling to Víctor all of the different aspects of the tragedy that affect the widower: during his short trip to London, Deán contributes to the death of his lover by his ignorance of the recent death of his own wife. Catharsis seems possible at the end of the novel: the broken order is being reconstructed and the victim (Víctor) becomes a witness to others.[41]

The most recent novel by Javier Marías, *Negra espalda del tiempo* [Dark Back of Time] (1998), again brings the Civil War to the fore. That the voluminous essay in metafiction culminates with this topic is not arbitrary. The detailed reflection that sustains the narration scrutinizes the relationship between fiction and reality; there is an area, the "dark back of time," where what is real is at the same time fictitious. In this space the strict margins that separate both ontological grounds shatter, making them porous, and what does not exist enters the sort of reality that is open to concepts, ideas, words, and stories. The origin of this idea is the growing sum of real events that the author has experienced since the writing of his novel *Todas las almas* [All the Souls] (1989), and the way in which one part of his life has been influenced and conditioned by the unreal: fiction. Throughout its pages, *Negra espalda del tiempo* accumulates the narration of certain episodes and human lives that will be retold and grouped at the end, forming a comprehensive totality in the manner that the author values so much. In the last chapters the various attempts to decipher the life of the adventurer Oloff de Wett lead to both the scenery of the Spanish Civil War and the inevitable trauma of Marías's imprisoned father; the "acusaciones demasiado improbables y novelescas contra quien no podía ni soñar todavía ser mi padre ni el padre de nadie" [accusations that were finally too improbable and novelistic about the man who couldn't yet even dream of being my father, or anyone's].[42] Such accusations make him admit the motivation for his writing: "por eso estoy aquí yo dando la lata" [and that's why I'm here causing trouble] (367).[43] The choice to use the Civil War to end the essay validates the references to the betrayal suffered by Javier Marías's father (and the suffering of the entire family during the war) that are repeated as a leitmotiv throughout the book.

This metafictional essay, in which the autobiographical flirts with the fictional, includes the Civil War as one of its main topics because of the war's controversial status and its mixing of reality and fiction in contemporary Spain. In the same way that the autobiographical blends with the fictional in the last pages of the essay (despite the author's continuous claims for the independence of the two modes), the reality of the war fuses with its fictional legacy. For Marías, the transformation of the war into an adventure story like Oloff de Wett's is valid and even inevitable, but it should not allow us to cast into oblivion important social, political and ethical dimensions. Since the publication of *El siglo* in 1983, Javier Marías has been pointing out through his articles and novels the imperative of a moral and political dimension that ought to thrive within the teaching and contemporary discussions of the Civil War. Marías has not forgotten the past, and since the 1980s he has been joined by a group of writers who are cultivating the genre of war fiction because they belong to a second, younger generation that has inherited a traumatic memory of the war. In fact, the notion of trauma arises repeatedly not only in Marías's work, but also in most literature and literary analysis that the war has generated since the first years of the Transition and that it continues to generate now, some thirty years later. The current discourse on the war is permeated with all sorts of references to this residual trauma, which are imprecise but constant. It is imperative that we begin to study all of the implications of this concept, which indeed has the explanatory capacity to develop a new paradigm of interpretation for an extensive literary corpus that continues to grow. From the standpoint of the emerging importance that trauma is gaining in very different disciplines, and the increasing knowledge that such disciplines are offering us, the centrality of this theoretical tool should be claimed for the analysis of the literary production of the second generation of the trauma that was the Spanish Civil War.

NOTES

1. Raymond Williams, "Base and Superstructure in Marxist Cultural Theory," in *Rethinking Popular Culture: Contemporary Perspectives in Cultural Studies.* Chandra Mukerji and Michael Schudson, eds. (Berkeley: University of California Press, 1991).

2. For a study on how melancholia has shaped some cultural products in contemporary Spain, see Alberto Medina Domínguez, *Exorcismos de la Memoria* [Exorcisms of Memory] (Madrid: Libertarias, 2001).

3. In *Memoria y olvido de la guerra civil española* [Memory and Amnesia: The Role of the Spanish Civil War in the Transition to Democracy], Mark Oakley, trans. (New York: Berghahn Books, 2002), Paloma Aguilar Fernández has explained the socio-

political implications of the notion of the War of the Insane. The implications of this metaphor, which spread during the Transition, are not trivial, especially with regard to the issue of political responsibility. As mental derangement bestows a considerable exemption of responsibility, "it frees society as a whole from responsibility because it accepts that everyone was equally subject to this madness" (210).

4. Ibid.

5. Some of the most well-known foreign scholars of the Spanish Civil War are Paul Preston, Stanley Payne, Gerald Brenan, Raymond Carr, and Ronald Fraser.

6. To recount the enormous number of fine studies by Spanish historians in these two last decades would prove almost impossible. Many of these studies focus especially on the victims of the war, as Santos Juliá's *Víctimas de la guerra civil* [Victims of the Civil War] (Madrid: Temas de hoy, 1999) epitomizes. The areas that had been markedly silenced under Francoist censorship (especially, the nature of repression) have been finally recovered by Spanish scholarship. The *maquis* is a paradigmatic example of this recovered reality, as proved by Secundino Serrano's *Maquis: Historia de la guerrilla antifranquista* [*Maquis:* A History of the Anti-Francoist Guerrilla Fighters] (Madrid: Temas de hoy, 2001) and Francisco Moreno Gómez's *La resistencia armada contra Franco* [The Armed Resistance to Franco] (Barcelona: Crítica, 2001).

7. Neil Kritz, *Transitional Justice: How Emerging Democracies Reckon with Former Regimes*, vol. II (Washington, DC: United States Institute of Peace Press, 1995), 297–322.

8. See Eduardo Subirats's "Postmoderna modernidad: La España de los felices ochenta," [Postmodern Modernity: Spain in the Happy Eighties] *Quimera* 145 (March 1996).

9. Subirats has underlined how, in Spain, modernity is not a resulting product of democracy, but the paradoxical achievement of a dictatorial regime (*Después de la lluvia* [After the Rain], [Madrid: Temas de hoy, 1993], 27–41).

10. The term "Two Spains" refers to the deep division that has historically separated Spaniards into two violently confronting groups: liberals and conservatives. The term first applied to the division of Spain after the French invasion (1808–14). It also applied to the peripheral regions in their attempts to gain political independence from Madrid. After the Civil War in 1936, the term has sadly been used to describe the deadly opposition between nationalist and republican Spaniards.

11. Vicenç Navarro, *Bienestar insuficiente, democracia incompleta: Sobre lo que no se habla en nuestro país* [Insufficient Well-being, Incomplete Democracy: What is not Talked About in our Country] (Barcelona: Anagrama, 2002), 153–216.

12. The word "maquis" refers to the anti-Francoist guerrilla soldiers who kept fighting against fascism during the 1940s and 1950s.

13. Navarro, 189.

14. The Pact of Silence has been denounced by some intellectuals and literary critics, among others, Alberto Medina Domínguez in *Exorcismos de la memoria* [Exorcisms of Memory] (Madrid: Libertarias, 2001) and Joan Ramon Resina in *Disremembering the Dictatorship: The Politics of Memory in the Spanish Transition to Democracy* (Amsterdam: Rodopi, 2001).

15. The paradigm of myth is accepted by a variety of literary critics, and it is primarily defended by Maryse Bertrand de Muñoz who, through her critical analyses, has produced valuable work on the subject, the fruit of many years' work. In fact, Bertrand de Muñoz has extensively studied the literature on the Spanish Civil War in the two volumes of *La guerra civil española en la novela: Bibliografía comentada* [The Spanish Civil War in Fiction: Annotated Bibliography] (Madrid: José Porrúa Turanzas, 1982). More recently, she has compiled her critical analyses in *Guerra y novela:*

La guerra española de 1936–1939 [War and Fiction: The Spanish War of 1936–1939] (Sevilla: Alfar, 2001).

16. See Carmen Moreno-Nuño's *Las huellas del trauma: El tropos de la guerra española en la ficción de fin de siglo* [Traces of the Trauma: The Trope of the Spanish War in Fiction at the End of the Century] (Ph.D. diss., University of Minnesota, 2000) for a further explanation on how *El pianista* shows an inherent contradiction between non-temporal heroes and non-political narratives.

17. Montserrat Roig's novel *El temps de les cireres* was first published in Catalan in 1977. It appeared in translation in 1978 for the first time in Barcelona (Argos Vergara edition).

18. Juan J. Gómez, "El curso de Paul Preston levanta pasiones" [Paul Preston's Lecture Stirs Up Passions], *El País,* 4 August 2000.

19. I prefer to leave the term "generation" as a wide and open category, and not circumscribe it within any particular theory, in order to stress the enormous internal differences that can be found within the members of any specific historical decade in terms of social, political, economic or family aspects.

20. The concept of the contagion of the trauma has raised a number of critical responses. Instead of "contagion," Dominick LaCapra proposes the idea of the "effect" of trauma on those who listen (*History and Memory after Auschwitz* [Ithaca: Cornell University Press, 1998]).

21. Cathy Caruth, *Trauma: Explorations in Memory* (London: The Johns Hopkins University Press, 1995), 10.

22. Javier Marías, "La nueva máscara de lo de siempre" [A New Mask for the Usual], in *Vida del fantasma* (Madrid: Alfaguara, 1995), 220.

23. Marías, "Javier Marías: El hombre de moda" [The Fashionable Man], in *Qué leer.* Interview with Oscar López. September 1997, 35.

24. Ibid., 10–11.

25. Julián Marías devotes a number of pages of his autobiography to his denouncement and imprisonment in Francoist prisons. For further information, see *Una vida presente* [A Present Life], vol. I (Madrid: Alianza, 1988), 263–78.

26. In "El tabú del franquismo vivido en la narrativa de Mendoza, Marías y Muñoz Molina" [The Taboo of Francoism Lived in the Narrative of Mendoza, Marías, and Muñoz Molina], in Resina, op. cit., Maarten Steenmeijer has analyzed the discourse on the Spanish national reality that frecuently appears in Marías's essays and articles. For Steenmeijer, this discourse does not appear in Marías's narrative.

27. Marías, "Culpable o culpable," in *Vida del fantasma,* 305.

28. Marías, "Ficción y recuerdo" [Fiction and Remembrance], in *Mano de sombra* (Madrid: Alfaguara, 1997), 81.

29. Marías, *El siglo* (Madrid, Alfaguara, 1983), 15.

30. Ibid., 16.

31. Ibid., 12.

32. In *Testimony: Crises of Witnessing in Literature, Psychoanalysis, and History* (New York: Routledge, 1992), Shoshana Felman and Dori Laub have analyzed how traditional means of assessing and narrating human experience have failed to encompass and account for the historical trauma of World War II and the Holocaust.

33. Marías, *El siglo,* 11.

34. Ibid., 259.

35. Oscar Calvelo, "Memoria, olvido e historia en *Corazón tan blanco* de Javier Marías" [Memory, Forgetfulness, and History in *A Heart so White* by Javier Marías] Available at http://www.lehman.cuny.edu/ciberletras/v06/calvelo.html. Accessed on 13 February 2002.

36. I use the translation by Margaret Jull Costa, *Tomorrow in the Battle Think on Me* (New York: Harcourt Brace & Company, 1996), 34.

37. Marías, *Mañana en la batalla piensa en mí* (Madrid: Anagrama, 1994), 91, 92, 100, 160, 226, 321.

38. Ibid., 32, 38, 80, 94, 171, 247, 249, 250, 251, 366.

39. Ibid., 122, 174.

40. Ibid., 25, 29, 46, 71, 90, 161, 197–99, 213–14, 233, 237, 239, 253–54, 312, 315.

41. See Laub for a study of the act of witnessing.

42. Marías, *Negra espalda del tiempo* (España: Santillana, 1998), 391. I use the translation by Esther Allen, *Dark Back of Time* (New York: New Directions, 2001), 314–15.

43. Marías, *Negra espalda del tiempo,* 367, and Allen, 294.

BIBLIOGRAPHY

Aguilar Fernández, Paloma. *Memory and Amnesia: The Role of the Spanish Civil War in the Transition to Democracy.* Translated by Mark Oakley. New York: Berghahn Books, 2002.

Alonso, Eduardo. *La enredadera.* Valencia: Fernando Torres, 1980.

Armas Marcelo, Juan José. *El árbol del bien y del mal.* Barcelona: Seix Barral, 1995.

Bertrand de Muñoz, Maryse. *Guerra y novela: La guerra española de 1936–1939.* Sevilla: Alfar, 2001.

———. *La guerra civil española en la novela: Bibliografía comentada.* Vols. I-III. Madrid: José Porrúa Turanzas, 1982.

Caruth, Cathy. *Trauma: Explorations in Memory.* London: The Johns Hopkins University Press, 1995.

Calvelo, Oscar. "Memoria, olvido e historia en *Corazón tan blanco* de Javier Marías". Available at http://www.lehman.cuny.edu/ciberletras/v06/calvelo.html. Accessed on 13 February 2002.

Casares, Carlos. *Dios sentado en un sillón azul.* Madrid: Santillana, 1997.

Cervera, Alfons. *Maquis.* Barcelona: Montesinos, 1997.

De Azúa, Félix. *Cambio de bandera.* Barcelona: Anagrama, 1991.

Felman, Shoshana, and Dori Laub. *Testimony: Crises on Witnessing in Literature, Psychoanalysis, and History.* New York: Routledge, 1992.

García Morales, Adelaida. *El sur.* Barcelona: Anagrama, 1985.

Gómez, Juan J. "El curso de Paul Preston levanta pasiones." *El País.* 4 August 2000.

Juliá, Santos. *Víctimas de la guerra civil.* Madrid: Temas de hoy, 1999.

Kritz, Neil J. *Transitional Justice: How Emerging Democracies Reckon with Former Regimes,* vol. II. Washington DC: United States Institute of Peace Press, 1995.

Labanyi, Jo. *Myth and History in the Contemporary Spanish Novel.* Cambridge: Cambridge University Press, 1989.

LaCapra, Dominick. *History and Memory after Auschwitz.* Ithaca: Cornell University Press, 1998.

Landero, Luis. *Caballeros de fortuna.* Barcelona: Tusquets, 1994.

Lazo, Alfonso. "¿Franquismo o fascismo?" *La aventura de la Historia.* 16 February 2000: 14–18.

Llamazares, Julio. *Luna de lobos.* Barcelona: Seix Barral, 1995.

Marías, Javier. *Los dominios del lobo.* Barcelona: Edhasa, 1971.

————. *El siglo.* Madrid: Alfaguara, 1983.

————. *Corazón tan blanco.* Barcelona: Anagrama, 1996.

————. *Mañana en la batalla piensa en mí.* Madrid: Anagrama, 1994.

————. *Negra espalda del tiempo.* España: Santillana, 1998.

————. *Cuando fui mortal.* Madrid: Alfaguara, 1996.

————. *Todas las almas.* Barcelona: Anagrama, 1993.

————. *Pasiones pasadas.* Madrid: Alfaguara, 1999.

————. *Mano de sombra.* Madrid: Alfaguara, 1997

————. *Literatura y fantasma.* Madrid: Alfaguara, 1993.

————. *Vida del fantasma.* Madrid: Alfaguara, 1995.

————. "Javier Marías: El hombre de moda." *Qué leer.* Interview with Oscar López. September 1997.

————. *Tomorrow in the Battle Think on Me.* Translated by Margaret Jull Costa. New York: Harcourt Brace & Company, 1996.

————. *Dark Back of Time.* Translated by Esther Allen. New York: New Directions, 2001.

Marías, Julián. *Una vida presente: Memorias,* vol. I. Madrid: Alianza, 1988.

Marsé, Juan. *El embrujo de Shangai.* Barcelona: Plaza y Janés, 1993.

Medina Domínguez, Alberto. *Exorcismos de la memoria: Políticas y poéticas de la melancolía en la España de la Transición.* Madrid: Libertarias, 2001.

Moreno Gómez, Francisco. *La resistencia armada contra Franco: Tragedia del maquis y la guerrilla.* Barcelona: Crítica, 2001.

Moreno-Nuño, Carmen. "Las huellas del trauma: El tropos de la guerra española en la ficción de fin de siglo." Ph.D. Diss. University of Minnesota, 2000.

Muñoz Molina, Antonio. *Beatus Ille.* Barcelona: Seix Barral, 1986.

————. *El jinete polaco.* Barcelona: Planeta, 1991.

Navarro, Vicenç. *Bienestar insuficiente, democracia incompleta: Sobre lo que no se habla en nuestro país.* Barcelona: Anagrama, 2002.

Rabinad, Antonio. *Libertarias.* Barcelona: Planeta, 1996.

Resina, Joan Ramon ed. *Disremembering the Dictatorship: The Politics of Memory in the Spanish Transition to Democracy.* Amsterdam: Rodopi, 2000.

Rivas, Manuel. *¿Qué me quieres, amor?* Translated by Dolores Vilavedra. Madrid: Alfaguara, 1996.

————. *El lápiz del carpintero.* Madrid: Santillana, 1998.

Roig, Montserrat. *Tiempo de cerezas.* Translated by Enrique Sordo. Barcelona: Plaza y Janés, 1996.

————. *Ramona, adiós.* Barcelona: Plaza y Janés, 1987.

Serrano, Secundino. *Maquis: Historia de la guerrilla antifranquista.* Madrid: Temas de hoy, 2001.

Steenmeijer, Maarten. "El tabú del franquismo vivido en la narrativa de Mendoza, Marías y Muñoz Molina." In *Disremembering the Dictatorship: The Politics of Memory in the Spanish Transition to Democracy.* Edited by Joan Ramon Resina. Amsterdam: Rodopi, 2000.

Subirats, Eduardo. "Postmoderna modernidad: La España de los felices ochenta." *Quimera* 145 (March 1996): 11–18.

———. *Después de la lluvia: Sobre la ambigua modernidad española.* Madrid: Temas de hoy, 1993.

Talens, Manuel. "Ucronía". *Venganzas.* Barcelona: Tusquets, 1994.

Vázquez Montalbán, Manuel. *El pianista.* Barcelona: Seix Barral, 1985.

Williams, Raymond. "Base and Superstructure in Marxist Cultural Theory." In *Rethinking Popular Culture: Contemporary Perspectives in Cultural Studies.* Edited by Chandra Mukerji and Michael Schudson. Berkeley: University of California Press, 1991.

Zúñiga, Juan Eduardo. *Largo noviembre en Madrid.* Barcelona: Bruguera, 1980.

The Estranging of Franco's Text and Mourning in *El cuarto de atrás*

Louise Ciallella

> *. . . ese angustioso respiro del aviso, esos instantes para que pueda volver los ojos a un paisaje, a un amigo; todas esas historias y canciones aunque estaban a punto de borrarse definitivamente del archivo de su memoria, tal vez tuvieron un postrer eco en ella todavía cuando supo en su carne que de verdad la muerte avisa. . . .*
>
> *[. . . that anguished breath of warning, those instants in which to turn to look at a landscape, at a friend; all those stories and songs that although they were about to erase themselves definitively from the archive of his memory, perhaps had a last echo in it still when he knew in his flesh that death truly sends a warning. . . .]*
>
> (Carmen Martín Gaite, "Un aviso: ha muerto
> Ignacio Aldecoa," La búsqueda de interlocutor)

THIS STUDY OF CARMEN MARTÍN GAITE'S *EL CUARTO DE ATRÁS* STARTS with Todorov's theory of the fantastic in order to consider Freud's analysis of the uncanny and of mourning as modes of focusing the effects of the dictator Franco's texts on the protagonist C., a woman author who grew up under the Sección Femenina's [Women's branch of the Falangist Party] ubiquitous feminine ideal. I enter here, then, into a specific theoretical dialogue with *El cuarto*[1] in order to show the novel's writing of the uncanny persistence after death of some elements of Franco's texts within an individual psyche, placed in relation to a collective one. Above all, my reading here is principally concerned with the images that arise ambivalently from the past and disrupt the novel's fantastic present.

In this regard, as Manuel José Ramos Ortega wrote in 1996: "The civil war, the postwar, or however it is called has still not ended, its ghost continues to act for the heirs of this historic episode."[2] With respect to both those who lived through that time and to the ghosts that remain, I will first show, through elements of Todorov's fantastic and then Freud's uncanny, together with references to both verbal and vi-

147

sual texts from the Sección Femenina, how *El cuarto* describes a necessary process of estranging familiar elements of Franco's omnipresent, univocal textual corpus.[3]

My reading of the functioning of uncanny images in the novel principally concerns not its questioning of the Sección Femenina's ideal(ized) roles for women but rather its recognition of C.'s internalization of them. As a result of her eventual estrangement of the Sección Femenina's texts, ultimately C. mourns the ideals which have governed her actions for almost forty years. I start by situating my readers, like C., in the fantastic present.

I. Modes of the Fantastic and the Uncanny in *El cuarto*

In Todorov's theory, the pure fantastic rarely exists on its own, but rather is a vacillating dividing line in and of the present between uncanny and marvelous events.[4] In this fantastic present in literature, uncanny ("strange") and supernatural ("marvelous") occurrences are perceived in relation to "the background of what is considered normal and natural."[5] Furthermore, "[f]ar from being a praise of the imaginary [the] literature of the fantastic posits the majority of a text [as] provoked by reality."[6] Thus, in the fantastic, literary and social functions coincide in that the "normal" laws of what is perceived as reality are transgressed, there is "a break in the system of pre-established rules."[7] Transgression in fantastic literature may be as much in terms of institutionalized censorship as of an internalized one which the author had self-imposed in order to avoid speaking of what her/his society considers taboo themes.[8]

For the reader, the fantastic consists of a moment of hesitation upon confronting an extraordinary event governed by laws that can be considered either familiar or unknown.[9] In this sense, if the reader decides for familiar laws, the event pertains to the realm of the uncanny, where "we refer the inexplicable to known facts, to a previous experience, and thereby to the past."[10] In this sense, uncanny events in literature are ultimately explicable by normal reasoning and familiar laws of reality; but they are initially perceived as "incredible, extraordinary, shocking, singular, disturbing or unexpected," and provoke an emotional reaction of fear.[11] The fantastic, present moment of hesitation confronting the extraordinary event, the doubt as to whether it is a product of illusion or a part of referential reality, depends on a reader who identifies with the main character.[12]

In both Todorov's and Freud's terms and consistent with C.'s declared motivation to write a fantastic novel, I consider the most uncanny event, the most extraordinary occurrence in *El cuarto* to be the death of Franco in 1975.[13] As the result of his death, elements from the past surface in a dialogue having both literary and social functions, and taking place as much within the novel between characters as with the reader. This fantastic dialogue results in the expression of both individualized and collective reactions to the event, and which Martín Gaite's C. succinctly describes when she states, "no somos un solo ser, sino muchos" [we are not one single being, but many].[14]

With this last quotation in mind, I find it clarifying to consider Freud's analysis of the literary uncanny double, first in that it functions in part as an expression of "all those strivings of the ego which adverse external circumstances have crushed."[15] From this standpoint, on one hand C.'s affirmation of "we" as many "beings" expresses the plural striving*s* crushed within each individual psyche by Franco's univocal text. In C.'s own case, the man she meets on the beach, the man in black, the Carola who calls C. looking for Alejandro (who may be the "man in black" or not), to cite some examples, all can conceivably function at different points as literary doubles for C. (and/or for each other) in Martín Gaite's text.[16] On the other hand, the protagonist's words also express a collective "we" constituted as a pluralistic group of individuals with common thwarted dreams. With both possible functions in mind, the doubling in *El cuarto* functions as the work of both individual and collective psyches, in the literary act of coming out from under the effects of extraordinarily adverse conditions.

According to the above theoretical orientation, the uncanny event, in that it depends on reader identification and social, emotional interaction, does not stand isolated as an initially incredible yet ultimately reasonable occurrence in one individual's psyche. However, while representing past strivings and the ghosts of past adversity, the Freudian uncanny double also expresses the protagonist's reaction to death, including his/her own: in Freud's words, the double also functions as a "ghastly harbinger of death."[17] In general, in the course of Freud's theory, significant elements of the uncanny are the appearance of death and ghosts and the ambivalent emotion they provoke, the death of the father, and silence, darkness, and solitude as accompanying childhood fear. All these uncanny elements are present in Martín Gaite's 1978 novel.

This is especially evident when C. describes the war years, including her family's general indications to not talk about whatever was discussed at home, and specifically about her uncle Joaquín.[18] Killed by the nationalists at the beginning of the war, the socialist Joaquín is an uncanny ghost from C.'s past—both a near experience of sudden death and a silenced member of the family about whom an adult C. can now speak freely. In individual terms, the repeated, ghostly image of Uncle Joaquín arises from a persistent childhood fear, at the same time as it is a reminder of collective political silence and death.[19]

Once again C. speaks from childhood fear and also solitude, when the dialogue with her principal interlocutor in the novel, the man in black, turns to defending oneself (*defenderse*) versus losing oneself or getting lost (*perderse*). As she speaks, the image arises of a fragile castle built with papers in C.'s handwriting. As the castle grows taller, C. talks about a fear of it falling down on her: "y yo me guarezco en el interior, con la cabeza escondida entre los brazos, no me atrevo a asomar" [and I'm hiding inside, with my head hidden in my arms, I don't dare look out].[20] Together with her morbid fear of being buried, evoked by the falling walls of the paper castle, comes talk of her perception of fear and cold as "las dos sensaciones más envolventes" [the two most surrounding sensations] of the war years.[21]

As C. describes bombings, refuge in shelters, and the collective fear of dying during the Civil War, another castle appears, corresponding to her later research on eighteenth-century history. This castle's *cielo* [sky] made of research cards, tumbles at the sound of the sirens she remembers from the bombings during the Civil War, and she is trapped beneath.[22] As a result, in the second appearance of a castle image, a childhood fear of literal entrapment under ruins is realized figuratively in relation to her recent past, as it undermines her 'constructed' refuge in historical data.

In C.'s own explanation, *encastillarse,* or to isolate oneself as misunderstood (literally, to defend oneself [in a castle]; to take refuge; to persist in) was "una sensación peligrosa, prohibida por la Sección Femenina, cuando se fomenta conduce al victimismo" [a dangerous sensation, prohibited by the Sección Femenina, when encouraged it leads to feeling victimized].[23] Thus, on one hand in the Sección's terms, the textualized castles C. envisions in *El cuarto* are dangerous because they isolate those who create them, and therefore oppose the conformity encouraged by the regime. On the other hand, they are also dangerous as an image of the self-victimization (through their "falling down" upon her) against which the propaganda warned. Thus, the two castles show her ambivalent emotions with respect to the Sección Femenina's texts, in that a perceived transgressive opposition coincides with a visualization (or "real-ization") of the results predicted by societal norms. In other words, opposition to the univocal text through defense of self leads her to a self-induced victimization based on fear of the societal norms under which C. lived.

In this regard, C.'s castles are uncanny images of her revision of an imposed collective history, or what C. calls, "el machaconeo de aquella propaganda ñoña y optimista de los años cuarenta" [the tiresome insistence on that inane and optimistic propaganda of the forties].[24] Ostensibly, the castles are made out of pieces of personal texts: the first has a base made of notes from a fearless childhood friend and then her own literary writing,[25] and the second is made of ordered cards from her historical research. But Franco and the Sección Femenina had used the castle image for the regime's own purposes, and a graphic example is from one of the Sección Femenina's yearbooks, from approximately 1941.[26] Shown there is the Castle of Mota, which Franco had given to the "Falanges Femeninas" [Women Falangists] to be literally remodeled as their headquarters, or Escuela Mayor [Main School]. Propagandistically, the castle is first verbally 're-constructed' when the Sección receives the gift, as I quote: "Este castillo que veis . . . va a ser testigo hoy . . . de un hecho memorable en nuestra Historia: la proclamación de la mujer en la segunda reconquista de España" [This castle which you all see . . . is going to be a witness today . . . of a memorable occurrence in our History: the proclamation of woman in the second reconquest of Spain].[27] Thus the Castle of Mota is to be the silent witness to the new role given to women under the Sección's Falangist ideal.

C.'s dialogized *encastillarse* in *El cuarto* in effect resemanticizes the castle image to show, first, her historical inner opposition to the role imposed upon her by the Sección Femenina. However, at the same time, when childhood fears and memories of silenced voices return upon Franco's death, her old isolating walls of personal and professional texts shake, as she herself questions the emphasis she has placed on the "la imagen literaria de retirar los puentes levadizos" [literary image of raising the drawbridges].[28] As the falling sky of research cards graphically demonstrates, when a dominant univocal text meets its demise, the orderly text silently created to confront it while based on it, also falls, resulting in both the opening of old defenses and the activation of the fears that undermined their foundation.

Both C.'s talking about Uncle Joaquín and her images of falling castles form a part of the unsteady processing of the "fotos fijas, sin referencia de fecha" [still photos, without references to dates] from C.'s past,[29] uncannily placed in movement within the novel's fantastic present. In this respect, a problematic perception of the world through the senses, in terms of a questioning of the relationship of mind to matter, of dreams to reality, forms an integral part of the literature of the fantastic.[30] In C.'s case, the sensorial imbalance caused by Franco's death creates a conscious attempt to "normalize" through references to the past the strange images which the present brings to her.

As one result, she is capable of assuaging her fear through a conscious negation of vision when confronting the uncertainty of the man in black's identity. C. comforts herself silently by inwardly converting him into a familiar figure: "Así, con los ojos cerrados, me puedo figurar que es un amigo de toda la vida, alguien a quien reencuentro después de una larga ausencia" [So, with my eyes closed, I can imagine that he is a lifelong friend, someone whom I have reencountered after a long absence].[31] Eventually, C. comes to see shadows from her past as being real and doubts the clarity with which she perceives objects in her vacillating present, compared to what she considers normal: "Lo que me resulta sospechoso es lo que veo tan claro cuando abro los ojos. Echo de menos los bultos de sombra que se han ido" [What seems suspicious to me is what I see so clearly when I open my eyes. I miss the shadowy shapes that have left].[32] Soon after, however, when she is about to take a pill from her visitor's little gold box, she returns to "normality": "Es una nube gris que se extiende *ahora* sobre los años de guerra y postguerra, uniformándolos, volviendo imprecisos y opacos sus contornos" [There is a gray cloud that extends *now* over the war and postwar years, making them uniform, changing their outline to be imprecise and opaque].[33]

In her balance between the past and an uncertain future, C.'s altered perception places in movement not only past images but also present objects normally perceived as static. At the beginning of the novel, the startled protagonist looks at a changed, strangely twisted room.[34] Later in the book, during her telephone conversation with Carola, C. is again startled and "las espirales color malva del empapelado de la pared empiezan a girar" [the mauve spirals on the wallpaper start to whirl].[35] This whirling sends her on a "extraño . . . retroceso" [strange return] back to the beach where she saw herself at the beginning of the novel.[36] Shortly thereafter, when Carola leaves the phone, an anxious C. waits for her to return and eventually, as she looks at the large painting above her bed, the static paint starts to move, and returns to another beginning: "el tiempo pintado fluye, se desborda del marco, la luz parece de amanecer" [the painted time flows, it overflows the frame, the light seems like dawn].[37]

In the course of the novel, words "dance," C.'s legs tremble, her head whirls. As she experiences the disorder and uncertainty of revealing hidden memories and the "out-of-control" development of the manuscript on her desk, C. comes to think, "Es que son demasiadas cosas raras" [It's that too many strange things are happening].[38] For C., it constitutes an extraordinary, uncanny effort to verbalize her own text—the hidden, intimate text of her life under Franco— and to perceive the disjoint images that are brought to light in the process.[39]

II. *Extrañar / lo extraño:* The Bodies Behind Franco's Texts and Semantics of the Uncanny

For both Freud and Todorov, the uncanny is intimately linked to re- pression. Secret transgressions, when revealed, are felt as disturbingly contrary to societal laws, again, within the context of an established reality and in terms of both institutional and internalized, individu- alized censorship. That is, the uncanny feeling is the emotional re- sponse of those who experience what, in their normal context, is a disturbing event revealed. It is useful in this sense to return to Freud's linguistic consideration of the uncanny with respect to two defini- tions, of the words *heimlich* and *unheimlich.*

The first word, *heimlich,* is that which "belong[s] to the house, not strange, familiar," and also, that which is "intimate," literally the "home-ly," or homelike.[40] The second, *unheimlich,* means "uneasy, eerie" as well as becoming "the name for everything that ought to have remained [hidden] and secret and has become visible."[41] Ini- tially, then, the adjectives *heimlich* and *unheimlich* are opposites in that the first denotes the "not strange" and the second, the "strange." But, *heimlich*'s signifying of the intimate and homelike ultimately coin- cides with the *unheimlich* when that which is secret, hidden, or out-of- sight is revealed.[42] As Freud concludes, "[t]hus *heimlich* is a word the meaning of which develops towards an ambivalence, until it finally coincides with its opposite, *unheimlich.*"[43]

In Spanish, the indeterminate phrase *lo extraño* ("the strange") cor- responds most closely to the ambivalent coincidence in meaning of the words *heimlich/unheimlich* as Freud defines them to mean the un- canny. In *El cuarto*'s unique textualization of the uncanny, the protag- onist uses various expressions to explain the strangeness she feels. From just the examples I have used above, she sees with startled eyes (*con extrañeza*) the state of her own room at the beginning of the novel, and comments on the "strange things" (*cosas raras*) that are happen- ing to her in her apartment. She also terms the doubling back to pre- vious points in her narrative, "strange" (*extraños*). In C.'s case, like in Freud's definitions, she perceives the familiar as having become un- easily ambivalent when revealed by the occurrence of Franco's death.

In effect, at first C. describes how, after the Civil War, she feels the eminently familiar presence of Franco's image and text in her and others' homes: "Franco es el primer gobernante que yo he sentido en mi vida como tal, porque desde el principio se notó que era unigénito, indiscutible y omnipresente, que *había conseguido infiltrarse en todas las casas*" [Franco is the first ruler whom I have ever felt in my life as such, because from the beginning it was clear that he was the only One, indisputable and omnipresent, that *he had managed to infiltrate every home*].[44] In C.'s reality, Franco's image was omnipresent, producing fear, and deadening laughter and conversation. But at the same time he was an almost incorporeal entity, in his seeming invulnerability to physical ailments: "reinaba de modo absoluto, si estaba enfermo nadie lo sabía, parecía que la enfermedad y la muerte jamás podrían alcanzarlo" [his was an absolute reign, if he was sick no one knew it, it seemed that illness and death could never reach him].[45]

However, one silenced secret in every home was that all, including Franco, were vulnerable to death. The revelation of this intimate truth in the dictator's case was incredible, or literally not believable: "Así que cuando murió, me pasó lo que a mucha gente, que no me lo creía" [So, when he died, the same thing happened to me as to many other people, I just couldn't believe it].[46] Upon Franco's death, his *heimlich*, familiar effigy becomes suddenly a public corpse, lying in state or *de cuerpo presente*, literally, a 'present body'. Thus the extraordinary event of his dying becomes the *unheimlich*, the unthinkable occurrence of what Freud would call the death of the father—in *El cuarto*, in a social sense, that is, the demise of the omnipotent patriarchal text—at the same time as it reveals a common mortality.

In effect, C. considers Franco's collective role of father when she thinks of Franco as the real father of Carmencita, his daughter.[47] She explicitly compares his daughter's situation with that of the rest of the Spaniards, who experienced Franco as the textualized patriarch who defined the discipline of his political family. In this regard, her comparison initially follows the Sección Femenina's teachings. Franco's complicity with the Sección created the text of the subservient woman who deferred to men's initiatives and served her country in the Servicio Social [Social Service]. In order to reinforce this role for young women, the Sección Femenina used Carmen Franco's image together with her father's, to represent the compliant, cheerful daughter of the Caudillo, as seen in *Sección Femenina*.[48] In effect, the regime normalized Carmencita as the image of how all women should follow the dictates of her father and the Falange. Thus a text in an encyclopedia published for schoolchildren explains the responsibilities of Spanish women to serve the Fatherland through their

Social Service, and ends with the ultimate role model: "La hija del Caudillo también lo hizo" [The daughter of the Caudillo also did it].[49]

Yet, when Carmencita Franco finishes the Servicio Social, one text supporting the regime both asks and answers why she would dutifully serve, since as her father's daughter she would not be obliged to do so. The text's propaganda both creates and takes the opportunity to reinforce that Franco is just one more Spaniard among many, and yet an ambivalently exceptional one: "Franco, desde el primer día, ha querido ser, y lo ha sido, un español más, en todo y para todo" [Franco, from the first day, has wanted to be, and has been, just one more Spaniard, in everything and for everything].[50] Here, the daughter's service becomes a reflection of the father's ever-present sense of duty to his country. A particular young woman's forced identification with the fatherland, and through her, all women's, led therefore first to dutiful compliance and then to a loss of self, fading into a reflective shadow of the figure of the omnipresent father, Franco.

It is not unusual, then, that C. would identify herself with Carmencita, but she concretizes their connection, having seen Carmencita Franco in person when they were both very young: "Le vi en Salamanca con sus calcetines de perlé y sus zapatitos negros" [I saw her in Salamanca with her cotton crochet socks and her little black shoes].[51] C. later sees how the little Carmencita's smile, over the years, has turned into a "gesto amargo y vacío" [bitter and empty gesture].[52] Martín Gaite's protagonist then thinks that "hemos sido víctimas de las mismas modas y costumbres, . . . nuestros sueños seguro que han sido semejantes, con la seguridad de todo aquello que jamás podrá tener comprobación" [we have been victims of the same fashions and customs, . . . our dreams for sure have been similar, with the sureness of everything which will never be able to be proved].[53] Thus C. feels that even Franco's daughter has had her dreams crushed by her father's absolute reality.

When C. sees Franco's daughter in the dictator's televised funeral, "la huérfana de ese padre sempiterno" [the orphan of that eternal father] becomes an uncanny image in that she makes C. realize how much "todos envejecíamos con él, debajo de él" [all of us aged with him, under him].[54] While she identifies with the victimization and aging of his daughter, C. proceeds to dissociate again Franco's corporal presence out of the imposed fatherly image, to become a secret force behind the deadened period in which he determined almost every aspect of Spanish life: "Para ella era simplemente su padre, mientras que para el resto de los españoles había sido el motor tramposo y secreto de ese bloque de tiempo. . . , y el tiempo mismo, cuyo fluir amortiguaba, embalsaba y dirigía, con el fin de que apenas se les

sintiera rebullir ni al tiempo ni a él" [For her he was simply her father, while for the rest of the Spaniards he had been the tricky and
secret motor of that block of time. . . , and time itself, whose flow he
dulled, dammed up and directed, with the result that neither he nor
time was barely felt to stir].[55] In a startling, disturbing way, his death
reveals a secret energy and time begins to move again.

In this sense, Dionisio Ridruejo, a key member of the Falange and
Franco's regime, and about whom C. thinks when she sees the
Falangist red berets in Burgos,[56] wrote a significant political piece included in the above-cited Sección Femenina yearbook.[57] In it,
Ridruejo describes an indeterminate time of the Falange's lack of a
natural leader (in unstated reference to the Falange's loss of José Antonio Primo de Rivera) and Franco's lack of an 'organized power'.
After commenting on the inevitable and now-accomplished joining
of the two political forces, he ends with the admonition: "La Falange
y su Caudillo cierran el bloque. . . Bloque de Historia que anda y am-
biciona y que fatalmente dejará laminados en su marcha . . . a los ca-
lumniadores, a los resentidos y a los mediadores" [The Falange and
its Caudillo close the block. . . A Block of History that walks and strives
and which will leave fatally flattened in its march those who slander,
resent, and conspire].[58] Under this historical light, the block of time
under which C. feels she has lived and of which she becomes acutely
aware while watching Franco's funeral, becomes in effect a recognition of the success of Franco and the Falange's proposed goal. At the
same time, the sudden flow in the painting in her bedroom becomes
an uncanny counterimage of powerful movement in the present,
reappropriated from a carefully constructed Block of History that
had menaced to crush its maligned opposition.

III. Estranging the Ideal Woman

While the year 1936 is C.'s expressed dividing line between childhood
and maturity,[59] the paralyzed nature of the time between the beginning of the Civil War and Franco's death precipitates C. in 1975 into
the uncertainty and shadows of a species of second, imposed adolescence. Between 1936 and 1975 there were almost 40 years of personal
growth from child to adult, but under such absolute controls that
change was almost imperceptible. When Franco's death unblocks
time, C. feels the uncanny presence of what was repressed behind the
roles imposed on both women and men during his regime. As Martín
Gaite explains:

El paso de la infancia a la madurez en una época donde en la mayoría de los hogares reinaban el encogimiento, el luto y los problemas económicos, no podía por menos de estar marcado para cualquier adolescente de temperamento sensible por desalientos y miedos. Pero se veía obligado a reprimirlos, lo cual falseaba aún más su verdadera identidad.

[The passage from infancy to maturity in a period of time in which restriction, mourning and economic problems reigned in the majority of homes, had to be marked by discouragement and fear for any adolescent with a sensitive temperament. But he/she was obliged to repress them, which falsified even more his/her true identity.][60]

In this regard, I am specifically concerned with studying how the Sección Femenina's ideal for women contributed to the repression of both mournful, fearful personal experiences and women's sexual expression during the postwar. Other critics have explained how oppositional politics and expressed sexuality are two sides of the same response to repression under Franco's reign, and/or how Martín Gaite shows C.'s simultaneous defiance of and adherence to the role of the Sección Femenina's ideal woman.[61] She outwardly is, as Adrián García has stated, "traditionally feminine in many ways," especially when remembering elements of women's culture under Franco.[62] However, my concern here is to show the ambivalence of C.'s emotions as she confronts the beginning of a necessary estranging—both conscious and unconscious—of some crucial internalized remains of the "feminine" text that, in Martín Gaite's words, "falsified her true identity." In this regard, a close consideration of the meaning of the Spanish verb corresponding to *lo extraño* can help in further clarifying the ambivalence C. feels. In Spanish the verb *extrañar* can mean: 1) to banish, exile; 2) to estrange; 3) to find strange, not to be used to; 4) to surprise; 5) in Latin America, to miss (someone or something); and 6) in the reflexive, to be surprised or astonished.[63] Most of these meanings coincide overtly with the literary functions of the uncanny, insomuch as they describe astonishment, surprise, or a lack of the habitual or normal. There are two additional meanings, however, which are applicable to the uncanny in Martín Gaite's novel: the Latin American meaning of "to miss" and the one which implies a placing at a psychological distance, "to estrange."[64]

In the first instance, *echar de menos* is the more common equivalent for "to miss" in Spain, and Martín Gaite uses this phrase to express C.'s missing what to her are customary shadowy shapes, in the passage I cite above. Intentional or not as the usage may be, the uncanny elements of the novel in general make clear that the death of Franco causes C. to miss his "normalcy." Because her intimate defenses against Franco's dictates depended on both internal opposition and an at least partial compliance, the lack of his impositions produces ambivalent emotion. That is, her confronting his death implies both the revelation of her transgressive opposition to his texts and an uncertain revision of her own internalization of them.

But, as the man in black tells C., "sólo la distancia revela el secreto de lo que parecía estar oculto" [only distance reveals the secret of what seemed to be hidden].[65] Thus the second remaining meaning of *extrañar,* the act of estranging, is an intrinsic part of *El cuarto* in that C. places at a psychological distance, through the uncanny, the texts that resurface from her memory. In effect, the novel shows her inevitable internalization of some of the Sección Femenina's most effective texts as C. carries out a necessary estranging of them, a situating of them in her past and at a certain distance from her present.

In this regard, Martín Gaite states in *Usos amorosos* that she wanted to show how rooted post-war customs had remained.[66] In the same work, she also included herself among the Spaniards who did not consider the postwar era closed until Franco's death in 1975.[67] C., like Martín Gaite, is a part of a significant population who suddenly sees Franco's era as the past upon his death, and the protagonist of *El cuarto* not only perceives the texts under which she lived as now being "strange," but also *makes* them "strange." As an active author of her own and others' stories, she places texts permitted under the regime at both a collective and individual psychological distance, in order to then revise those which have defined her and others.

In the course of Todorov's explanation of the relation to the other in the fantastic, both the uncanny and the marvelous enter into a literary expression of excess, where "the preoccupation concerning death, life after death, and corpses [are] linked to the theme of love."[68] Fantastic literary themes of the self are concerned with perception, consciousness, and the use of altered vision, while themes of the other deal with desire and the unconscious[69] and "are formed out of the relation established between two interlocutors, during their discourse."[70] In these terms, there are two parts to C.'s estranging of the Sección Femenina's text, one in relation to self and therefore to her vision, and another in relation to her interlocutor, her 'other' in discourse, the man in black. Both produce uncanny images of crushed strivings from her past, in the form of an explicit doubling of her self.

The first process of estranging I consider is with respect to the domestic order imposed through the Sección Femenina together with Franco's National-Catholicism.[71] In *Usos amorosos,* Martín Gaite makes clear the regime's repressive postwar admonitions to save both money and energy, especially "el gasto más pernicioso de todos" [the most pernicious expenditure of all], that is, an active sexuality. This last should be saved to uphold the family, "pilar fundamental del nuevo Estado español" [fundamental pillar of the new Spanish State].[72] This was especially important for women, both as domestic guardians and, as C. states in *El cuarto*, "los pilares del hogar cristiano" [the pillars of the Christian home].[73] In this regard and in direct relation to *El cuarto*, Estrella Cibreiro has listed quite succinctly the regime's impositions on women seen in the novel: "order, domestic cleaning and pulchritude, feminine submission, abnegation, repression of instincts and compliance with Catholic doctrine."[74]

Clearly in *El cuarto*, C. as a young girl rebelled inwardly against the excessive domestic order in her grandmother's home in Madrid. Her discourse places the family's apartment in metaphoric relation to Catholic dogma when she describes it as the place "donde se fraguó mi desobediencia a las leyes del hogar y se incubaron mis primeras rebeldías frente al orden y la limpieza, dos nociones distintas y un solo dios verdadero al que había que rendir culto" [where my disobedience to the laws of the home was set and my first rebellion grew against order and cleaning, two distinct notions and only one true god who must be worshiped].[75] She refers to the same home as a "templo del orden" [temple of order], formed by "columnas de ropa limpia" [columns of clean clothes].[76] At the time, she also had the oppositional dream of living in an attic apartment full of dust and clothes tossed everywhere.[77] In the novel's present, she still considers herself an ally of dust, the "enemigo descarado" [shameless enemy], in the 'battle' waged against dirt.[78]

Yet, C. reacts to the disorder produced by Franco's death with an impulse for domestic and literary order. She feels obliged to put her room in order.[79] She thinks that order in her house will make her solitude "más hospitalaria" [more hospitable].[80] When she speaks of her incipient book on postwar customs the idea for which arose when Franco died, she states, "lo ordené todo por temas" [I put it all in order by subjects].[81]

The emotion that provokes her regression to order becomes more apparent when she goes into the kitchen to prepare a drink for her guest. First, she compares inwardly modern, aseptic kitchens with those painted by Vermeer, which have, like her own, "esos muebles usados que . . . rodean (a la figura humana de la mujer) como un recordatorio de su edad infantil" [that old furniture that . . . surrounds (the woman's human figure) like a remembrance of childhood].[82] The familiar childhood memories provided by her kitchen furniture evoke a self-consoling statement: "No hay que tener tanto miedo a las huellas del tiempo" [One shouldn't be so afraid of the marks of time].[83]

A return to a personal past, to both a feminine and literary "order," leads to a normalization of her present situation. At the same time, C. once again reveals a fear of aging, and thus death, in relation to the marks of time and use on her furniture. Thus, as C. calms her fear and cleans the table, two uncanny ghosts appear in the antique mirror in her kitchen. Her own images, as a young girl of eight and then at eighteen, look out at her, resuscitating through a doubling from the depths of the glass like "un fantasma sabio y providencial" [wise and providential ghost]. Her younger selves are a continuing joking reminder to not give in to attacks of domesticity [*las acechanzas de lo doméstico*], and C. reassures them that her domestic order is moderate.[84]

As a result, C.'s feelings of solitude and disorientation within the disordered state of her reality, lead to an apparently non-dogmatic order. But in effect, her new order is not in opposition to, but rather an appropriation of, a significant element (which she now misses) in the regime's construct of domesticity: that of the generalized ideal of moderation, which, according to Martín Gaite, was preached "desde los púlpitos, la prensa, la radio y las aulas de la Sección Femenina" [from the pulpits, the press, the radio and the classrooms of the Sección Femenina].[85] C. again revises official propaganda, here estranging it in order to accept its moderation on her own terms. For this reason, she makes her moderation reasonable in relation to her other, past selves, by affirming that *excessive* disorder crushes you [*te aplasta*].[86]

Thus, precisely after she had attempted to calm her childhood fear of death, C. sees an uncanny ghost from the past, a double that is also doubled. Her moderation of oppositional disorder (which crushes) and the excessive order of past models (which is dogmatic and in itself a 'religion'), leads to the uncanny self-images of past strivings that both familial and postwar feminine ideals had suppressed, in the form of vital, laughing, disorderly selves from both before the war and after. However, C.'s reconciliation of her past selves with specifically her cleaning, or her "picking up" (*recoger*), isolates and resolves only one facet of the postwar repression of women.

The second act of estranging that concerns me here is explicitly another crucial facet of domestic economies: the ultimate excess, C.'s sexual expression. In the postwar years, amorous order, as Martín Gaite amply explains in *Usos amorosos*, became conflated with household economies through the sexualized resemanticization of postwar restriction and rationing and the battle strategy implicit in the language used by the regime's ideology to describe all stages of "making love" (from entering into a relationship to after marriage). Like castles under siege, women were to defend themselves from all attacks. Above all, they were to be passive, waiting at home with their sewing for imagined formal boyfriends, their *novios,* and then their husbands.[87] In this defensive scenario of unfulfillment and disillusion, the young C.'s inner opposition to her grandmother's temple of order and cleanliness is also, in effect, a metaphoric rebellion against the sexual economy enforced by the alliance of Church and State under Franco's regime and Falangist doctrines.

In my reading, then, it is therefore not unusual that C. sees herself in the kitchen mirror precisely while preparing a beverage for the mysterious man in her living room. C.'s past opposition to the Church's institutional order causes her to perceive her interlocutor as smelling slightly of tar, in oblique connection to C.'s Lucifer print on the wall in front of her bed.[88] In this regard, he does reflect desire and sensuality, which are expressed by, among other supernatural figures, the devil.[89] C.'s act of sensorial perception, the smell of a tar "lotion" associated with the devil, enters into her sensualized estranging of familiar Catholic dogma and the Sección Femenina's text. But in C.'s case, the man in black as 'the devil' is above all an uncanny figure, a realization of an image of maximum opposition to Catholic doctrine, in a similar fashion as in her lesser alliance with dust, the enemy of cleanliness. In short, C.'s attraction to the devilish elements in her visitor reflects both past dogma and the resulting "nostalgia de la perdición que se cernía" [nostalgia for looming perdition], which she relates explicitly to the familiar image of Lucifer on her bedroom wall.[90]

The regime's education in absolute Catholic dogma (especially the dichotomy God / Devil) and C.'s intimate opposition estranged through the figure of Lucifer are constitutional elements of C.'s false identity. For the same reason but in a reverse fashion, C. estranges through the man in black a series of authority figures (the judge, the police, and above all, the priest) by her confessional reactions to his questions.[91] But ultimately their dialogue causes her visitor to function as an incorporation of idealized elements of the *novela rosa,* another text intrinsic to falsifying her expression of self. In this regard, García has noted C.'s sexual attraction for the man in black; juxtaposing it with C.'s "childhood fantasy of the typical *novela rosa* hero"; she adds, "[c]learly, although C. critiques [the] *novela rosa* at times, and denounces the Sección Femenina, her behavior is profoundly marked by both."[92] As Isabel Roger further explains, the *novela rosa* functioned as a "decorous literature" (*literatura de recato*), and C. maintains a decorous, restrained attitude with her visitor throughout their conversation.[93]

But, as Roger also states, the man in black does what the *novela rosa* heroes "were incapable of carrying out: the knowledge of the other."[94] Thus, through the disordering of C.'s memory induced by the mauve pill from her visitor's little golden box, she begins to estrange the Sección Femenina's feminine ideal in the form of what she inwardly perceives as a conscious realization of situations from the popular, and permitted, romantic novels. C. then inserts herself into what seems to her to be an uncertain love triangle, a relatively excessive element in her enactment of the *novela rosa:* C.'s bedroom phone rings, and the man in black asks her to tell whoever could be calling him that he is not there. Eventually the caller, Carola, takes C. into her confidence, as frustration in her wait for an Alejandro causes her to confide in another woman.

As Martín Gaite describes women's postwar complicity, "la represión de la sexualidad femenina desaguaba en el ansia de confidencia, de lágrimas compartidas" [the repression of women's sexuality consumed itself in the urge for confidences, of shared tears].[95] However, C., from fear of both her and Carola's uncertain identities, as well as the mysterious Alejandro's, hears herself defensively retreating into the cold rhetoric of the Sección Femenina magazines' advice columns. C. then involuntarily turns away from the woman's confidences to another text that consoles and brings her back to childhood laughter: she begins to think about the school friend with whom she wrote 'their own' *novela rosa.*[96]

In this regard, the appearance of her friend is a result of C.'s fear while confronting the falsifying effects of repression on women and men's identities in the postwar, and forms an intrinsic part of C's estranging of the regime's ideal roles for women. Thus first, the shadow of her Catholic education appears once more, with the devil as the expressed opposition: the two friends fly out a supernatural class window together, while their Religion teacher below laments that they have, "el diablo en el cuerpo" [the devil inside their bodies].[97] Second, the repeated sensation of flying with her childhood friend occurs specifically during C's enactment of the role of the romantic female lead in the *novela rosa* which she is creating *with* the man in black. For C., it is now consciously more normal to enact a role than to express herself freely; the female friend, in a contradictorily laughing version of the complicitous women crying to each other after the war, becomes a necessary ally in order to express her feelings with regard to her estranging of the ideal feminine role.

In this respect, a particularly eloquent passage in *Usos amorosos* explains C.'s difficulties in communicating desire to her interlocutor, and her resulting use of two intermediaries, the *novela rosa* and her friend's ghost. According to Martín Gaite, the most damaging repression in postwar relationships was not the inculcation of physical restraint. It was, rather, the exaltation of a basic insincerity between *novios* and then married couples, which had provoked the continual representation of a role and not "dejarse querer y ver por el otro en su verdad desnuda" [letting oneself be loved and seen by the other in one's naked truth], with desires, fears, deception, and hope.[98] Thus, at the end of her telephone conversation, and faced with going back into the living room and finding her incorporated masculine ideal, C. is fearful of the unaccustomed openness of the conversation she is having there.

As a result, she "forgets her lines," and, as she looks in the mirror in her bedroom, has an uncanny return to another self, from a theatrical presentation in her youth.[99] When she later wants to move closer to her visitor, she again fears she will be left speechless, "reducida al desnudo poder de mi mirada o de mi cuerpo" [reduced to the naked power of my looks or my body].[100] As C.'s thoughts become less and less "orderly," she finds it inexplicable to her visitor that her laughing, *dead* friend is still holding her hand, dressed in "un camisón de fantasma" [a ghost's nightgown] as they fly above the rooftops. In their flight, C. feels a fear of "mirar para atrás" [looking backward].[101]

In general, the erotic attraction to her visitor repeatedly provokes the image of a dead childhood friend, and a fear of the past. At the same time, as if in recognition of past false enactments, the friend's reappearance produces yet another doubling of self. Ultimately, when C. flies with her for the last time in the novel, she does not recognize herself, nor does her friend recognize C., as the woman in the living room below. As they discuss the *novela rosa* which is taking place there, C. asks her friend to not shout because *they* will hear the two friends, and her friend replies, "*ella* ha dicho que es algo sorda" [*she* said that she was somewhat deaf].[102] In short, then, C.'s return to her childhood relationship with her brave friend is to again distance herself from repression, as they as adolescents tried to do by creating their own version of a romantic novel together. Through this uncanny return, C. estranges both the Sección Femenina's imposed sexual identity and idealized literary roles.

When the man in black asks C. whether she can define her past fascination for her friend in terms of lesbian desire, he is met with a heavily veiled reply from C.: she never learned the word, the postwar only provided her with euphemisms, and she was scared to ask because of the ambiguity of the information she received, including in Religion class.[103] Indeed, there was no possible text for the two of erotic love between women when they were friends; they created an idealized, romantic text, which is even more idealized by the loss of the friend through death. As a result, C.'s speaking of her filters out only the ambivalent results of the accumulation of both political and personal omissions.[104]

The vacillation in C.'s identity during the doubling that takes place in her flight becomes perhaps the clearest image of uncertainty in the novel, in that she, like the others in the novel, remain without a 'normal' identity upon the death of Franco's definitions. Especially sexual identity, and the power of sexual desire, remain open to new definition(s). But this revision of old definitions is especially difficult, for what the fantastic confronts most clearly in the case of the old friends' flight over the rooftops and C.'s textualized doubts, is an intimate censorship "which functions in the psyche of the authors themselves."[105]

IV. The Ambivalent Color Black

Like Franco's body lying in state, and the night visitor as an incorporation of ideal romantic texts, *El cuarto* reveals other bodies, buried during the "exaltación del pasado remoto" [exaltation of the remote past] carried out under Franco's reign, at the expenses of the near, traumatic past.[106] In this respect, one vivid corporal image from C.'s memory appears in her description of the transition in her family's back room at the beginning of the war, from being a merry, disorderly playroom to being a very orderly storeroom. In her view, the worst new occupants of the reformed back room were the jars of stewed partridges (*perdices estofadas*) in their vinegar and bay leaf and with their pervasive sour smell.[107] The partridges constitute one of the most uncanny images in the novel, since C. describes them obliquely as if they were embalmed bodies: their jars to her were "sarcófagos panzudos" [fat-bellied sarcophagi].[108] The reference to extraneous, contained dead bodies preserved and inserted into the newly ordered back room in 1936 expresses figuratively the intimate effects of the repression suffered by the playful children of whom C. formed a part before the war. But, as she states when the painting in her bedroom begins to move, "también el cuarto de atrás sigue existiendo y se ha salvado de la muerte, aunque hayan tirado la casa" [the back room still lives too and it has been saved from death, even though the house has been torn down].[109] For C., the memory of those eerie bodies in the back room is part of "making the room live" again, of returning life, at least figuratively, to the controlled bodies that lived there under Franco.

In effect, C.'s estranging of internalized, "normal" texts under Franco is parallel to a process of mourning which takes in *El cuarto*. As Freud describes it, the act of mourning is "the reaction to the loss of a loved one, or the loss of some abstraction which has taken the place of one, such as fatherland, liberty, an ideal."[110] In this sense, more than for specific deaths, C. experiences both an individual and collective mourning of the ideals which governed her identity, both through the regime's controls and through oppositional figures. In *El cuarto*, C.'s reaction is to both miss and to estrange the ideals imposed by Franco's fatherland, and as such constitutes a species of mourning. But she also carries out a delayed process of mourning for pre-war ideals of liberty and modernity, especially for women, which had been silenced; she retrieves from her memory what remains of the now-textualized bodies for which Spaniards could not express mourning in the postwar. As a result, C. inevitably mourns both the texts that had falsified her identity, and those resulting from her own and others' silencing of unrealized ideals from a then-recent past.

In general, one could say that in order for C. to redefine her self, she must first carry out a painstaking recall of elements from her past with which she had become identified, either through others' impositions and her compliance, or her own opposition. In Freud's terms, the act of mourning implies a recognition that in reality the object mourned no longer exists. This is accomplished through a painful drawing up, and concentrating of emotional energy upon, hopes and dreams through which a libidinal attachment was created.[111] Once this gradual process is complete, the psychic and emotional energy it employs can return to active, normal efforts "not related with the thoughts of the dead."[112]

It is in this sense that C. uses a popular saying when she states that, while watching Franco's funeral procession on the television in her neighborhood bar, the group of people there "sentían que en aquel entierro a todos les daban vela" [felt that in that burial everyone had a part].[113] And in this sense, Franco's cadaver is the first body, the first textual *corpus*, which C. "mourns," through her description of the discussion in the bar of the amount of people who filed by Franco's body in the course of the three days he was lying in state, and the reasons, or not, for paying their respects. In C.'s perception, more than a mourning, it is a linguistic autopsy, in which language became open and showed its true self: "Era una polémica libre y relajada, parecía como si las palabras 'regir,' 'destino' y 'patria' se quitasen el uniforme oficial y apareciesen en cueros sobre una mesa de disección para de-jarse hacer la autopsia" [It was a free and relaxed argument, it seemed as if the words "reign," "destiny," and "fatherland" had taken off their official uniform and appeared naked on a dissection table to let an autopsy be performed on them].[114] As the official words of the dictatorship are closely examined, the once-eternal dictator's body is emphatically put to rest: the group discusses the official bulletins detailing every step of his illness, which had "acabado enca-minándole hacia la tumba maciza que le esperaba y cuya losa se mostraba allí en el televisor junto al hoyo vacío" [ultimately sent him on his way to the massive tomb waiting for him, with its slab of stone which was there on television next to the empty hole].[115]

C.'s description of the bar's commentaries shows a collective bringing up and redefining in non-authoritative terms of words for patriarchal authority, once-inevitable direction, and the fatherland. With its detailed revealing and resemanticization of the body behind the abstract texts that had governed her self, the process shows both a loss and the beginning of a necessary detachment from them. Additionally, however, the graphic process in the bar constitutes in brief the social manifestation of another emotional need, that of a public mourning of the texts of a modern freedom of movement and identity suppressed both collectively and in C.'s individual history after the war.

It is precisely her father who carries out the mourning of a symbol of modernity, his late-model black Pontiac requisitioned for the war effort by the nationalists.[116] Still at war, they return the remains of the car to him after his identification of it, during a trip to Burgos in which C. and her cousin Angeles accompany their fathers. C.'s memories of the trip first explain the liberty and joy of sharing an unsupervised room with her cousin and slipping out of the hotel at night with her. On one hand, C.'s elation at the cousins' secret walk and their staying up laughing all night becomes associated with the hotel's modern luxury, with its black bathroom fixtures and C.'s looking in the mirror to put on red lipstick. On the other hand, looking back after the mournful and repressive postwar, to C. her joy at feeling freedom from parental controls seems "loca, inconveniente y egoísta" [crazy, unsuitable, and egotistical], based on her father's sadness.[117]

In her memories of the trip to Burgos, C. mourns a modern freedom and joy that was buried in the war and postwar years. After the excess of happiness she felt at being able to almost get lost on the streets of Burgos, where "andar era casi volar" [to walk was almost to fly],[118] she describes their trip to the junkyard (in Spanish, *cementerio de coches*)—literally "car cemetary", where they were to identify her father's shattered black Pontiac. The cars had been piled up like unruly skeletons; as she looks at the remains there, she imagines the new car her father had taken such pride in maintaining.[119] C. remembers making several mental escapes into fantasy as she describes their careful stepping through what was left of the cars, "con esa especie de temor religioso que nos impide pisar las losas de las tumbas" [with that kind of religious fear which impedes us from stepping on tombstones].[120]

The need to identify the black Pontiac so that they can take possession of its remains becomes a walk through a real collective cemetery, a long one since "allí todo estaba equivocado, la guerra lo había equivocado todo" [everything was mixed up there, the war had mixed up everything].[121] When her father sees what is left of his car, he stands there on the brink of tears and his brother consoles him by saying that at least he is alive. C. then remembers the morning a few months before when her parents had cried together over the death of his brother, Joaquín.

The remains of one modern body that was so important to her father leads again to the ghost of her uncle Joaquín, a laughing, irreverent figure who hid magazines with nude women in her home and said things children weren't supposed to hear. The story of her experiencing of one cemetery created by the war leads to the recognition of not only a shattered symbol of modernity appropriated by Franco, but also the confusion of identities produced by the war and an intimate mourning for the tall, handsome and silenced socialist with his open sexual expression. One figurative cadaver reveals a literal one, and then his hidden images of women's eroticized bodies.

C.'s search with her father for his car becomes her own, in the present, for "bodies" of the modern suppressed by the regime and mournfully brought out from her experience of repression. For C., the "lost women" (*las perdidas*) of whom Concha Piquer sang, become unidentifiable "escombros de la guerra" [ruins of the war],[122] with dark circles under their eyes, the reason for which the words of the songs question.[123] They are dressed in black, but are not in mourning, or so the song speculates: "¿Por qué se viste de negro, si no se le ha muerto nadie?" [Why is she in black, if no one of hers has died?].[124]

Eroticized women floating without a course (*a la deriva*) in C.'s text,[125] they undermine the Sección Femenina's falsely happy feminine image. They are both the lost modern, sexualized woman and images of the sensual woman against which a priest rails in *Medina*, one of the Sección Femenina's principal publications for women, in 1945: "La mujer sensual tiene los ojos hundidos . . . inseguro el paso y triste todo su ser. [Es] como un barco a merced de las olas" [the sensual woman has sunken eyes . . . uncertain step and all her being is sad. She is like a boat at the mercy of the waves].[126] Worst of all, the sensual woman is imaginative, which is not compatible with the Sección Femenina's work for women, nor with their traditional concept of femininity in general: "Sólo la imaginación permanece activa, para su daño, con la representación de imágenes lascivas. [De] la mujer sensual no se ha de esperar trabajo serio, idea grave, labor fecunda, sentimiento limpio, ternura acogedora" [only her imagination remains active, to her injury, with the representation of lascivious images. From the sensual woman one cannot expect serious work, grave ideas, productive effort, pure feelings, welcoming tenderness].[127]

The imaginative C. remembers Concha Piquer's songs about the modern sensual women destroyed by the war, and mourns them by wanting to wrap a black shawl around her shoulders and sing one of their songs to her visitor, also in black.[128] Moved by the memory of the *perdidas* and her father's tears for her irreverent uncle, she in turn feels tears rising to her eyes.[129] Thus in her search for familiar bodies lost in her memories of the shadowy war and postwar years, C. finds and mourns the remains of the sensual body of modern women buried under familial silence and institutional negation.[130]

At the end of his visit, C.'s visitor helps her get her black shawl, and "dócil y voluptuosamente" [in a docile and voluptuous way] she lets him help her put her feet up to rest on the sofa.[131] The shawl she wanted to put around her shoulders in order to sing to the man in black, becomes, in this last scene with him, a shawl he gives her and she herself puts on, and with it, gives in to a sensual, peaceful sleep. Dressed figuratively then literally in black, C. first mourns *las perdidas* and then revitalizes in her own body at least part of their sensual, yet anonymous, identity.

IV. CONCLUSION: THE BODY UNDER THE INITIALS

C. silently dreamed as a young girl of being a woman from a *novela rosa,* walking freely through the night to a modern café called the Negresco, with its "mármoles negros . . . superficies cubistas y . . . espejos envueltos en humo" [black marble . . cubist surfaces and mirrors surrounded by smoke].[132] Towards the end of her conversation with the man in black, she tells the story of her father taking her and her friend (the fearless one with whom she later "flies") to a postwar establishment considered modern. It was one of many that opened under a composite name formed from fragments of two others; in this case, Simu. In the café's back room, the two young girls talk about their imagined island escape, Bergai, a name formed from parts of their own two names.

The last, dark café's name and its black mirrors, like C.'s mirror with its black frame, reflect both the lost 'modern' as well as the confusion of identities which had taken place after the war, starting with the "subversión de valores" [subversion of values] of the black market.[133] But the modern café of which she first dreamed leads, in the end, to one where other, secret identities are encouraged, as well as the elaboration of escapes to an-other "modernity," as an "invención que nos hace sentirnos a salvo de la muerte" [invention which makes us feel safe from death].[134]

This is the last example of how, throughout *El cuarto*, the color black becomes a sign of hidden and mistaken identities, with all the ambivalence provoked by C.'s re-vision of them. It is part of a reflection of places where a suppressed modernity is mourned and uncertainty embraced, even as true identities remain in the fantastic balance. Thus, when at the end of the novel C. says to her daughter that she is neutral with respect to cockroaches, her daughter responds that she should speak sincerely and express the fear she knows C. feels toward them.[135]

Literally, neither the mother nor the daughter want the cockroach to escape, in a familial image of a domestic hunt for an insect the presence of which has become, in the course of this novel, related to uncontrollable change, the conflictively abominable and yet irreverently oppositional dirt, and fear. Ultimately, the end of C.'s text leads to her daughter's text, through the literal reference to the novel *The Thin Man* (*El hombre delgado*), with its "pistas falsas [y] sorpresa final" [false clues and surprise at the end].[136] In effect, at the end of Dashiell Hammett's murder mystery, the detective Nick Charles gives the surprisingly natural, scientific solution which solves the strange case: "So he buried Wynant under the floor, buried him with a fat man's clothes and a lame man's stick and a belt marked D.W.Q., all arranged . . . nobody will discover the grave, and if it is accidentally discovered, then fat Mr. D.W.Q.—by that time Wynant's bones would be pretty bare and you can't tell whether a man was thin or fat by his skeleton—was murdered by Wynant."[137] His wife Nora has the last word in reply to his explanation, at the end of both the latter and the novel: "That may be [but] it's all pretty unsatisfactory."[138]

Similarly, in C.'s text, the natural explanation of the strange remains from the past led not to a solution, but to the reasonable necessity of exhuming other falsely identified bodies, a task belonging to both her and the next generations. In *El cuarto*, it appears as a painstaking and slow process. But only through the bringing to light of these ambivalent, 'buried' bodies, both individual and collective, political and erotic, can the emotional energy focused on them be freed and Franco's idealized texts, including those of the Sección Femenina, definitively be put to rest.

NOTES

1. I will refer from this point on to *El cuarto de atrás* (Barcelona: Destino, 1992) in the main text as *El cuarto,* and for page references as *Cuarto.* All translations here of Carmen Martín Gaite's works, as well as critics' commentary, are mine.

2. Manuel José Ramos Ortega, "Discurso e historia en la novela española de posguerra," *Signa (Revista de la Asociación Española de Semiótica)* 5 (1996): 291. The original Spanish from which I take this quote is: "[la] guerra, la posguerra o como quiera llamársele, aún no ha terminado y [su] fantasma sigue actuando para los herederos de ese episodio histórico."

3. In this sense, I read Freud's analysis according to Todorov's suggestion: as a semiotic act of linking images and interpretation of the function of language in the process, not as a Freudian translation of "ultimate meaning." (Tzvetan Todorov, *The Fantastic,* trans. Richard Howard [Cleveland and London: The Press of Case Western Reserve University, 1973], 150–51).

4. Todorov, 26–27.

5. Ibid., 168.

6. Ibid.

7. Ibid., 166.

8. Ibid., 158–59. Both Joan Lipman Brown ("A Fantastic Memoir: Technique and History in *El cuarto de atrás,*" *Anales de la literatura española contemporánea* 6 [1981]) and Manuel Durán ("*El cuarto de atrás:* imaginación, fantasía, misterio; Todorov y algo más," in *From Fiction to Metafiction: Essays in Honor of Carmen Martín Gaite,* eds. Mirella Servodidio and Marcia Welles [Lincoln: Society of Spanish and Spanish American Studies/University of Nebraska, 1983]) speak to the hesitation intrinsic in the fantastic, among other basic concepts of Todorov's theory. Aleida Anselma Rodríguez refers to Todorov's explanation of breaking of societal rules, in relation to the fantastic in general. (Rodríguez, "Todorov en El cuarto de atrás," *Prisma/Cabral* 11 [1983]: 78, 80–81).

9. As Todorov explains, "In a world which is indeed our world, the one we know, [there] occurs an event which cannot be explained by the laws of this same familiar world. The person who experiences the event must opt for one of two possible solutions: either he is the victim of an illusion of the senses, of a product of the imagination—and laws of the world then remain what they are; or else the event has indeed taken place, it is an integral part of reality—but then this reality is controlled by laws unknown to us" (25).

10. Ibid., 42.

11. Todorov, 46–47. Todorov applies this statement quoted to the pure uncanny, but according to the rest of his theory it is applicable to events of the uncanny within fantastic literature as well.

12. Ibid., 157.

13. *Cuarto,* 128. C. tells the man in black that she thought of writing a book on amorous customs from the nineteen-forties on the day of Franco's funeral, and that

she promised to write a fantastic novel using Todorov's theory the following January, then thinking of a combination of the two.

14. Ibid., 167.

15. Freud, 388. Todorov, on the other hand, describes this literary doubling in a general sense as "the play of dream and reality" (121); in *pathological* terms, as the division of personality, which is emphatically not *El cuarto*'s case. I prefer Freud's description as selected, which so graphically describes the effects of life under Franco's univocal text.

16. As Isabel Roger describes, the 'man in black' "contribuye a reorganizar parte de las imágenes que como un rompecabezas forman la pluralidad del ser de la autora" [contributes in reorganizing part of the images that, like a puzzle, form the plurality of the being of the author], and in recognition of the other (Roger, "Recreación crítica de la novel rosa en *El cuarto de atrás*," *Romance Notes* 27.2 [1986]: 125). I would only change "author" to "protagonist" in the context of my study here. Rodríguez also speaks to the doubling in *El cuarto*, especially with respect to the man in black (79, 84).

17. Freud, 387–88.

18. *Cuarto*, 57.

19. For an excellent analysis on silence from different perspectives in *El cuarto* see Adrián M. García, "Carmen Martín Gaite's *El cuarto de atrás:* A Poetics of Silence," *Romance Languages Annual* 8 (1997).

20. *Cuarto*, 56–57.

21. Ibid., 57.

22. Ibid., 59.

23. Ibid., 120. These definitions are taken from that listed as *encastillar*, with its corresponding reflexive meanings, in the *American Heritage Larousse Spanish Dictionary* (Boston: Houghton Mifflin, 1986), 207.

24. *Cuarto*, 96.

25. Ibid., 57.

26. *Sección Femenina de Falange Española Tradicionalista y de las J.O.N.S.* (Madrid, n.d.), 169. The Sección Femenina yearbook I used lacked a publication date. Its bibliographical listing in the computer source I used, OCLC, listed "1940?" as a suggested, and possible date from the information it contains; however, material from it is cited/reproduced in Luis Otero, ed., *La Sección Femenina* (Madrid: EDAF, 1999), with the date 1941.

27. *Sección*, 168.

28. *Cuarto*, 120.

29. Ibid., 116.

30. Todorov, 120–23. Freud also succinctly states: "For the whole matter [of 'a fear of something uncanny'] is one of 'testing reality', pure and simple, a question of the material reality of the phenomena" (402).

31. *Cuarto*, 38.

32. Ibid., 103.

33. Ibid., 107. Emphasis mine.

34. Ibid., 15.

35. Ibid., 150.

36. Ibid.

37. Ibid., 168.

38. Ibid., 102.

39. Marcela Romano explains C.'s space as being "un territorio donde lo extraño," or the uncanny, "negocia sin pudor con lo 'normal'" [a territory where the

strange negotiates without shame together with the "normal"] (Romano, "*El cuarto de atrás* de Carmen Martín Gaite: una poética del margen," *Confluencia* [1995]: 28). However, the uncanny (or strange), according to both Freud and Todorov, is that which can ultimately be explained in "normally" reasonable terms.

40. Freud, 371.

41. Ibid., 375.

42. Ibid. This last sentence includes a paraphrasing of an illustrative definition of *unheimlich* from Schelling and included in a series of definitions of *heimlich* and *unheimlich,* which Freud cites from a Dictionary of the German Language. Later (375–77) he will emphasize twice the importance of Schelling's words and incorporate them into his interpretation, followed here.

43. Freud, 377.

44. *Cuarto,* 132. Emphasis mine.

45. Ibid., 133.

46. Ibid.

47. Joan Lipman Brown states that C. sympathizes with Carmencita upon her father's death (16).

48. *Sección,* 85.

49. Undated *Enciclopedia escolar,* published in Otero, 170.

50. González, *Francisco Franco, artífice de la Victoria y la Paz,* quoted in Otero, 171.

51. *Cuarto,* 136. In my reading, the diminutive which C. uses for Carmen Franco is not gratuitous, but a recognition of the young girl in the grieving adult daughter in 1975.

52. Ibid.

53. Ibid., 136–37.

54. Ibid., 138.

55. Ibid., 137.

56. Ibid., 111.

57. Sheelagh M. Ellwood explains that Ridruejo was appointed Director-General for Propaganda (National Propaganda Director), specifically, in the Ministry of the Interior appointed in the 1938 Cabinet ("Falange Española and the Creation of the Francoist 'New State,'" *European History Quarterly* 20 [1990]: 217).

58. *Sección Femenina,* 228. For a succinct explanation of the circumstances of José Antonio's death by Republican firing squad and the joining of Franco with the Falange in 1937, see Victoria L. Enders, "Nationalism and Feminism: The Sección Femenina of the Falange," *History of European Ideas* 15.4–6 (1992), 674.

59. *Cuarto,* 187.

60. Martín Gaite, *Usos amorosos de la postguerra española* (Barcelona: Anagrama, 1996), 98. Hereafter I will refer to this work as *Usos amorosos.*

61. As just a sample listing, see: Lipman Brown; Durán; García; Roger; Romano; Silvia Bermúdez, "'Music to My Ears': Cuplés, Conchita Piquer and the (Un)making of Cultural Nationalism," *Siglo XX/20th Century* 1–2 (1997); and Annabel Martín, "Narrative and The Politics of Identity," *Selecta* 13 (1992).

62. García, 481. García states that *El cuarto* attempts to preserve favorable aspects of women's culture, and, "[f]or example, she fondly recalls many aspects of women's culture of the Franco years, including the *novela rosa,* dressmakers, fabrics, clothing, hygiene products, cosmetics, and hair styles" (Ibid., including n.12).

63. *American Heritage Larousse,* 241.

64. I take the succinct and clarifying definition of "to estrange" from the *American Heritage Dictionary*'s definition of *estrange* (*The American Heritage Dictionary of the English Language* [Boston: Houghton Mifflin, 1981], 449).

65. *Cuarto,* 41.

66. *Usos amorosos,* 14.

67. Ibid., 12.

68. Todorov, 138.

69. Ibid., 139.

70. Ibid., 159.

71. See Enders, especially 674–75.

72. *Usos amorosos,* 14.

73. *Cuarto,* 93.

74. Estrella Cibreiro, "Transgrediendo la realidad histórica y literaria: el discurso fantástico en *El cuarto de atrás,*" *Anales de la literatura española contemporánea* 20 (1995): 32. The original Spanish is: "el orden, la limpieza y pulcritud domésticas, la sumisión femenina, la abnegación, la represión de los instintos y el sometimiento a una doctrina católica."

75. *Cuarto,* 75.

76. Ibid., 78.

77. Ibid., 89.

78. Ibid., 87.

79. Ibid., 16.

80. Ibid., 73.

81. Ibid.

82. Ibid., 74.

83. Ibid.

84. Ibid., 75.

85. *Usos amorosos,* 12.

86. *Cuarto,* 89.

87. *Usos amorosos,* 106, 123, 167, 169; and Claudia Schaefer, "A Simple Question of Symmetry: Women Writing in Post-Franco Spain," in *La escritora hispánica,* eds. Nora Erro-Orthmann and Juan Cruz Mendizábal (Miami: Ediciones Universal, 1990), 280.

88. The first mention of the Lucifer print is in *Cuarto,* 18; the smell of lotion is mentioned in *Cuarto,* 36. Blas Matamoro speaks of the man in black in relation to C.'s Lucifer print within his analysis of Freud's *unheimlich,* and states that C.'s visitor "could well integrate" [bien puede integrar] its population ("Carmen Martín Gaite: El viaje al cuarto de atrás," *Cuadernos hispanoamericanos* 351 [1979]: 602). Cibreiro studies the man in black as a 'fantastic' figure, in contrast to the 'real', and in relation to Todorov's theory (36–37). Rodríguez associates the man in black with the devil, and sexual desire specifically, in relation to Todorov's theory and again as a "fantastic" figure in general (81, 85).

89. Todorov, 27.

90. *Cuarto,* 18. The man in black, in that he has elements of the Lucifer from the print hanging on C.'s wall, can also be read as a "supernatural" embodiment of a "future" desire and sensuality, and in this sense his night visit can correspond to the (supernatural) realization "of an ideal love, even if it is condemned by official religion" taking place in the fantastic (Todorov, 138).

91. See *Cuarto,* 34, 68, 122, 126.

92. Ibid., 481.

93. Ibid., 122.

94. Ibid., 125. The original Spanish is: "fueron incapaces de realizar: llevar a cabo el conocimiento del otro."

95. *Usos amorosos,* 143.

96. Rodríguez relates part of the friend's appearance, and notes what she considers the childhood friend's "affinity" [afinidad] with the devil (87).

97. *Cuarto*, 166.

98. *Usos amorosos*, 210.

99. *Cuarto*, 175–76.

100. Ibid., 182.

101. Ibid., 183.

102. Ibid., 184. Emphasis mine.

103. Ibid., 192.

104. Even as their flight reflects their "escapes" (*fugas*) into literature, perhaps the two friends' flight pertains more to the future than to the past, because C., just before flying, explicitly fantasizes about crossing the threshold of the marvelous, where "all is possible and believable" [todo es posible y verosímil] (*Cuarto*, 166). The supernatural qualities of the flights with her dead friend appear to, in Todorov's terms, present C. and us with the image of a "powerful desire" as well as to "life after death" (Ibid., 138–39). In effect, in *El cuarto* the image where both sexual desire and life after death most clearly converge is that of C.'s deceased childhood friend in their journey through the air. The childhood fear of death which C. carries with her throughout the novel together with the uncertainty of changes in the 'feminine' role, combine to bring 'back to life' in a marvelous way the friend who taught C. how to evade fear. In this sense, I agree with Patrick Paul Garlinger when he states, "Desire for the woman [is] what cannot be named. The foreclosure of the possibility of explicit desire between women in the context of Francoist Spain can only be read in Martín Gaite as a loss that never occurred, as a possibility proscribed from the very beginning" ("Lost Lesbian Love Letters? Epistolary Erasure and Queer Readers in Martín Gaite's *El cuarto de atrás*," *Bulletin of Hispanic Studies* 76 [1999]: 527). That is, not a thwarted desire from the past, but an impossible desire, and therefore unable to be thwarted.

105. Todorov, 159.

106. *Usos amorosos*, 23.

107. *Cuarto*, 188–89.

108. Ibid., 189.

109. Ibid., 169.

110. Freud, 153.

111. Ibid., 166.

112. Ibid., 153.

113. *Cuarto*, 134.

114. Ibid.

115. Ibid., 134–35.

116. Debra A. Castillo also uses the term "cadaver" with respect to C.'s father's car. ("Never-Ending Story: Carmen Martín Gaite's *The Back Room*," *PMLA* 102.5 [1987]: 826).

117. *Cuarto*, 110.

118. Ibid., 112.

119. Ibid., 113.

120. Ibid., 114.

121. Ibid., 113.

122. Ibid., 153.

123. *Las perdidas* can mean "prostitutes," but not necessarily; I find it difficult to translate the word in those terms, when Martín Gaite is careful to situate them in the ambivalent, confused postwar.

124. Ibid., 152.
125. Ibid.
126. Quoted in Otero, 49.
127. Ibid.
128. *Cuarto,* 119–20.
129. Ibid., 120.
130. Bermúdez analyzes in different terms both Concha Piquer's songs and the presence of these women in *El cuarto.*
131. *Cuarto,* 200.
132. Ibid., 14.
133. Ibid., 180.
134. Ibid., 195.
135. Ibid., 209.
136. Ibid., 210.
137. Dashiell Hammett, *The Thin Man* (New York: Alfred A. Knopf, 1934), 252.
138. Ibid., 259.

BIBLIOGRAPHY

The American Heritage Dictionary of the English Language. Boston: Houghton Mifflin, 1981.

The American Heritage Larousse Spanish Dictionary. Boston: Houghton Mifflin, 1986.

Bermúdez, Silvia. "'Music to My Ears': Cuplés, Conchita Piquer and the (Un)Making of Cultural Nationalism." *Siglo XX / 20th Century* 1–2 (1997): 33–54.

Brown, Joan Lipman. "A Fantastic Memoir: Technique and History in *El cuarto de atrás.*" *Anales de la literatura española contemporánea* 6 (1981): 13–20.

Castillo, Debra A. "Never-Ending Story: Carmen Martín Gaite's *The Back Room.*" *PMLA* 102.5 (1987): 814–28.

Cibreiro, Estrella. "Transgrediendo la realidad histórica y literaria: el discurso fantástico en *El cuarto de atrás.*" *Anales de la literatura española contemporánea* 20 (1995): 29–46.

Durán, Manuel. "*El cuarto de atrás:* imaginación, fantasía, misterio; Todorov y algo más." In *From Fiction to Metafiction: Essays in Honor of Carmen Martín Gaite.* Edited by Mirella Servodidio and Marcia Welles. Lincoln: Society of Spanish and Spanish American Studies/University of Nebraska, 1983.

Ellwood, Sheelagh M. "Falange Española and the Creation of the Francoist 'New State.'" *European History Quarterly* 20 (1990): 209–25.

Enders, Victoria L. "Nationalism and Feminism: The Sección Femenina of the Falange." *History of European Ideas* 15.4–6 (1992): 673–80.

Freud, Sigmund. *Collected Papers.* Vol. 4. Translated by Joan Riviere. New York: Basic Books, 1959.

García, Adrián M. "Carmen Martín Gaite's *El cuarto de atrás:* A Poetics of Silence." *Romance Languages Annual* 8 (1997): 476–84.

Garlinger, Patrick Paul. "Lost Lesbian Love Letters? Epistolary Erasure and Queer Readers in Martín Gaite's *El cuarto de atrás.*" *Bulletin of Hispanic Studies* 76 (1999): 513–33.

Hammett, Dashiell. *The Thin Man.* New York: Alfred A. Knopf, 1934.

Martín, Annabel. "Narrative and The Politics of Identity." *Selecta* 13 (1992): 39–44.

Martín Gaite, Carmen. *La búsqueda de interlocutor.* Barcelona: Destino, 1982.

———. *El cuarto de atrás.* Barcelona: Destino, 1992 (1978).

———. *Usos amorosos de la postguerra española.* Barcelona: Anagrama, 1996.

Matamoro, Blas. "Carmen Martín Gaite: El viaje al cuarto de atrás." *Cuadernos hispanoamericanos* 351 (1979): 581–605.

Otero, Luis, ed. *La Sección Femenina.* Madrid: EDAF, 1999.

Ramos Ortega, Manuel José. "Discurso e historia en la novela española de posguerra." *Signa (Revista de la Asociación Española de Semiótica)* 5 (1996): 289–305.

Rodríguez, Aleida Anselma. "Todorov en *El cuarto de atrás.*" *Prisma/Cabral* 11 (1983): 76–90.

Roger, Isabel M. "Recreación crítica de la novela rosa en *El cuarto de atrás.*" *Romance Notes* 27.2 (1986): 121–26.

Romano, Marcela. "*El cuarto de atrás* de Carmen Martín Gaite: una poética del margen." *Confluencia* (1995): 23–34.

Schaefer, Claudia. "A Simple Question of Symmetry: Women Writing in Post-Franco Spain." In *La escritora hispánica.* Edited by Nora Erro-Orthmann and Juan Cruz Mendizábal. Miami: Ediciones Universal, 1990.

Sección Femenina de Falange Española Tradicionalista y de las J.O.N.S. Madrid: n/d.

Todorov, Tzvetan. *The Fantastic.* Translated by Richard Howard. Cleveland, OH, and London: The Press of Case Western Reserve University, 1973.

From Post-Francoism to Post-Franco Postmodernism: The "Powers of the Past" in Contemporary Spanish Narrative Discourse (1977–1991)

Ulrich Winter

THIS ESSAY ANALYZES THE REPRESENTATION OF FRANCOISM IN SELECTED narratives from the first fifteen years of the democratic period. These narratives portray Francoism as a hegemonic political, cultural, and socializing power that affects subjects' intellectual and psychosocial formation and determines their relations to their present, past, and to their own selves. My primary purpose is to note certain persistent traits in discourse on Francoism and to reveal an evolution that leads, particularly in the 1990s, to a change in paradigm. In order to highlight this transformation, I limit my study to five novels among the variety of texts directly or indirectly addressing Francoism during this period. Each one represents Francoism as a "power of the past,"[1] that is, each establishes a link with present-day reality, thus reflecting the tensions between the Francoist past and the democratic present, between historical reference and the aestheticizing of history through memory and personal experience.

This essay also details the specificity of literary discourse on Francoism within the framework of postmodernist aesthetics. Outside the significant framework of postmodernism it is difficult to understand this discourse. Furthermore, literary discourse on the issue of Francoism makes the specificity of Spanish postmodernism particularly evident. The basis for this specificity lies precisely in the interweaving of literary aesthetics and the socio-cultural and political situation during the democratic Transition. I contend that the convergence of postmodernity and political post-totalitarianism determines the particular form this discourse takes, for it is a discourse both on Francoism and on postmodernist aesthetics. In order to emphasize its specificity in the context of Spanish narrative and, by extension, of Spanish postmodernism, I use the term *post-Franco postmodernism*. Before proceeding to analyze the novels, it will be necessary to briefly clarify the relationship between post-Francoism and postmodernism.

Postmodernism can be defined as an abandonment of ideological, political, humanistic, and philosophical master narratives, a critique of centered subjectivities, and a textualization of history.[2] As a global cultural paradigm, postmodernism is founded on ideological, political, cultural, and philosophical post-totalitarianism. Robert C. Spires has shown that, in the case of Spain, the expiration of Francoism's ideological power and the transition to democracy created a historical setting that accurately illustrates an epistemological (aesthetic) change, namely, the transition from a "totalitarian episteme" to the "post-totalitarian episteme" of democracy. In the 1980s, Spires explains, "an unexpected connection appeared between General Franco and gender attitudes, between fascism and phallocentrism, while the old polarities, conservatism and communism, suppression and expression, culture and cult, gravitated toward one another." Spires rightfully concludes that "Spanish fiction serves as a register of these discursive events helping to define the post-totalitarian episteme."[3] Other critics, like Paul Julian Smith in his book *The Moderns*, focus even more closely on Spanish postmodernism's specificity and its relation to the Francoist past in various cultural fields during the 1980s and 1990s José-Carlos Mainer has highlighted other essential elements that directly or indirectly clarify the relation between postmodernism and post-Francoism.[4] He puts more emphasis on the connection between the aesthetics of the democratic-period novels and their cultural context. His research elucidates the peculiarities of cultural post-Francoism, showing, for instance, how various authors experience "ghosts of the past" as a historical-social condition, and how discourse on Francoism depends on the generation that given authors belong to. Yet Teresa Vilarós has noted that 1975 signified at one and the same time the disappearance of the dictatorship and of anti-Francoism—the end of the totalitarian regime and also of a Marxist utopia as one of the last remaining political master narratives in Spain: "Franco muere y con él se da fin tanto al franquismo como al antifranquismo. Pero con su desaparición también se va aquella parte de nuestra identidad fatalmente con él implicada tanto desde la izquierda como desde la derecha, y ninguna otra hay disponible para reemplazarla a no ser echando la historia al olvido" [Franco died and both Francoism and anti-Francoism ended with him. But his disappearance also carried along with it that part of our identity, common to both the Left and the Right, which was unavoidably implicated with him, and there is no other available to replace it unless we throw history into oblivion].[5]

Consequently, the disappearance of Francoism not only made democratic culture possible, but created an ambiguous situation, because anti-Francoism had played a significant role in intellectual opposition to the regime (this problem is primarily addressed in novels by Guelbenzu, Montero, Marsé, and Millás). Other novels, such as *El jinete polaco* [The Polish Horseman] (1991) by Muñoz Molina, are further removed from Francoism and, according to critics, fully subscribe to postmodern aesthetics and, more specifically, to the framework of historiographical metafiction. But even in this case, deconstructivism and postmodern negativity regarding the possibility of representing history and constructing the subject have a particular relevance in the Spanish political, social, and literary context. These movements are related to a widespread trend in democratic Spanish narrative, namely, the questioning of the subject and of history; and this questioning is in turn closely related to the experience of Francoism. For this reason one must also analyze Muñoz Molina's postmodernism (e.g., his poetic proposals for history and the subject) in connection with Spanish narrative discourse from previous years—that is, with the specific post-Franco cultural situation. If it is true that, as Vázquez-Montalbán has stated, as a "dictadura modernizadora" [modernizing dictatorship],[6] Francoism produced a "schizophrenic" society, a modern society forced to bear the "superestructura [del] poder franquista" [superstructure of Francoist power],[7] and if it is true that the democratic period's historical amnesia concerning the Francoist decades meant an "imposibilidad de la memoria" [impossibility of memory]—the title of one of J. M. Merino's short stories—then the post-Franco period may be seen as postmodernism's historical materialization, insofar as it forces us to rethink the issues of the subject and the possibility of representing history. Having outlined my focus, I will now discuss five representative texts.

CONSTANTS AND TRANSFORMATIONS
IN DISCOURSE ON FRANCOISM

I. Internalized and Implanted Past

In novels written between 1975 and 1985, Francoism appears primarily as a social power as well as a force shaping the symbolic interpretation of the world. Francoism manifests itself precisely upon its rather sudden disappearance during the transition to democracy.

The famous ironic expression "Bajo (con/contra) Franco vivíamos major" [we were better off under (with/against) Franco] takes on numerous, subtle meanings in these texts. Francoism appears, moreover, as an agent causing traumatic psycho-social, existential, epistemological, hermeneutic, ideological, and moral effects. This is what J. C. Mainer has termed the "interiorización de los fantasmas del franquismo por sus víctimas" [the internalization of Francoism's ghosts by its victims].[8] It takes on broader significance in these novels, however, for they demonstrate that it is precisely the existential internalization of the ghosts of the past that conditions subjects and prevents them from reflecting upon and liberating themselves. The novels under analysis exhibit this process and its consequences on different levels: philosophical-existential, as in José María Guelbenzu's *La noche en casa* [The Night at Home] (1977); psycho-social, as in Rosa Montero's *Te trataré como a una reina* [I Will Treat You as a Queen] (1983); and biographical/historiographical—a reflection on the past—as in Juan Marsé's *La muchacha de las bragas de oro* [The Girl in Golden Underpants] (1978). The "impossibility of memory" cannot be solely attributed to the political transition's historical amnesia, as Juan Goytisolo states; it is also a consequence or symptom of unstable or defeated subjectivities.[9] This does not always lead to the protagonists' physical disappearance, as it does in J. M. Merino's story "Imposibilidad de la memoria" (1989), but it does turn out that support for unorthodox ideas, such as Marxist social utopia or promises of individual happiness (which during Francoism was projected beyond social life), is indirectly determined by Francoist ideology and betrays subjects, hindering their psychic and intellectual liberation. This affects the victorious and defeated sides of Francoism and the Transition equally. The connection between utopia and political action on the one hand and individual self-affirmation and the pursuit of happiness on the other, is one of the most persistent traits in discourse on Francoism. The "naufragio general" [general shipwreck][10] of the political and cultural Left led to the de-realization of politics and history, ironic subversion of leftist discourse, and individual appropriation of history and reality. These features are typical of narratives written during the 1975–1985 decade.

One of the basic, and therefore most consistent, elements in anti-Franco discourse is the personalizing and psychologizing of the Left's commitment, as well as the relation between love and politics—between personal history and social and political history.[11] The idea that active anti-Franco commitment—and a whole series of other attempts to escape a daily life pervaded by National Catholicism—was shaped by Francoism is expressed broadly in José María Guelbenzu's [b.1944] *La noche en casa* (1977), undoubtedly one of the most representative works on the postwar written in the first five years of the democratic period. During the early post-Franco years, the poet Chéspir, "el de los elegantes hexámetros" [the poet of the elegant hexameters], is offered "un papel estelar en el mundillo de la política activista al que su otro yo—un lógico, ruin y zafio producto de la posguerra española—se [aferra] con uñas y dientes" [a star role in the circles of activist politics to which his other self—a logical, mean, and coarse product of the Spanish postwar—desperately clings].[12] He arrives in San Sebastián with the purpose of contacting an underground organization. Once there, he happens to run into his first love, Paula, and they spend the night together. The next morning, she leaves for Denmark in order to meet with her boyfriend. The main plot already posits a thematic link between political action and romance. But there is another love story which has led Chéspir to engage in political action in the first place; his wife Pilar had abandoned him, not coincidentally, at the end of Francoism. Pilar leaves him in order to "autoafirmarse" [assert herself] and live out an ideal Chéspir himself had once shared, before realizing it was only a "myth."[13] What commitment and political utopia, on the one hand, and individual happiness, on the other, have in common, Chéspir describes as "el encauzamiento de los deseos hacia un ideal" [the channeling of desires towards an ideal].[14] This is why political activism becomes a means to compensate for romantic unhappiness. Yet there is no necessary intrinsic relation between the two desires; worse still, neither political ideals nor the pursuit of individual happiness serve as a stable foundation for the subject, because idealism, too, is a part of Francoist education:

El peor daño [que ha causado la educación franquista] no vino de la represión directa del cuerpo, sino del encauzamiento de los deseos hacia un ideal . . . Mal choque es el de nuestros ideales con la corrupción patria, peor aún con la mentalidad insolidaria y franquista que nos ha calado hasta los huesos, vaya la sinceridad por delante; mucho peor esa defensa intelectual que hemos empleado para evadirnos de una realidad áspera y mezquina, perfeccionando una aristocracia de la mollera que ha terminado en escepticismo.

[The worst damage (caused by Francoist education) did not come from direct repression of the body, but from the channeling of desires towards an ideal . . . Our ideals clash with national corruption, even more so with the uncooperative Francoist mentality that has permeated us to the bone, to tell the truth; even more so with that intellectual defense we have used in order to escape a harsh and petty reality, perfecting an aristocracy of the brain that has ended up in skepticism].[15]

As a hegemonic power in the symbolic interpretation of reality, the Francoist system not only defined and determined a repressive reality, but also the opposite stance that subjects chose in protest. In the face of personal and political failure, Chéspir has nothing left but irony, which turns out to be another purely intellectual, and therefore useless, defense.[16] This is why the world order breaks down precisely when power disappears; this power had until then constituted the universal and transcendental signifying order. Chéspir is shown to be a psycho-socially and epistemologically determined subject; Francoist ideology is deeply ingrained into his personality. Searching for the "último fondo" [bottom depth] of "nuestra protesta" [our protest] and for happiness, Chéspir ends up desperately tracing man's entire philogenetic and ontogenetic evolution, and finds the "bottom depth" to be involuntary separation from the mother.[17] But Chéspir is first and foremost a captive of the past. Rather than being an instrument for liberation, the "maldita memoria" [damned memory] is an insurmountable obstacle, because subjects lack a stable and independent perspective from which they might recover history through memory.[18] The existentialist notion of the incompatibility between the self and the world, between consciousness and reality, perfectly fits Spain's post-Franco present.[19] Yet the female character, Paula, "no [tiene] pasado ni memoria" [has neither past nor memory]; she is unable to feel regret, but is able "de volver a duchar[se] y a salir por la mañana a la calle" [to take another shower and go out into the street in the morning], that is, to start anew.[20] Laura in *El desorden de tu nombre* [The Disorder of your Name] and Nadia in *El jinete polaco* also play a decisive role in guiding the protagonists, assisting in their search for reality, and, in a sense, saving them. However, Paula not only ends up abandoning Chéspir, but also Spain in order to seek a life of her own.[21]

Many of the features of discourse on Francoism listed thus far also appear in novels that address, from different perpectives, the so-called lost generation. In *Te trataré como a una reina* (1983), Rosa Montero [b.1951] highlights—albeit without historical references—the primarily psychopathological consequences of sexual repression under the dictatorship, such as paranoia, obsessive neurosis, and so on, the victims of which are both men and women, postwar victors and losers.[22] The characters belong to two different social classes. On one side we have the regular customers at a sleazy bar, significantly named *Désiré*. All the characters' dreams are founded on false promises of happiness: Cuba, the alleged paradise, Bécquer's *Rimas* [Rhymes]. At a certain point, *Désiré*'s bolero singer, Bella, is forced to acknowledge, as were Stuart Pedrell and Chéspir, that she has always been stuck in a blind alley. She is then overwhelmed by the sense of being lost, by a deep emptiness, an "orfandad de sí misma, de su pasado y de su historia" [orphanhood from herself, her past, and her history].[23] As in Guelbenzu's novel—and later in J. J. Millás's *El desorden de tu nombre*—emptiness manifests itself in the form of anxiety attacks. On the other, bourgeois side, we find Antonia, who at age forty is still dependent on her mother and is watched over by her obsessive-neurotic brother Antonio. Only towards the end, when she is abandoned by her first lover, whom she had met by chance, when her brother is in the hospital and her friend Bella is in jail, accused of throwing Antonio out the window—only at this moment of total abandonment does Antonia seem willing to actively confront her situation. Once again, the disappearance of order—the perpetuated Francoist order, indirectly symbolized by her brother Antonio—is what causes psychic breakdown, which is also an epistemological breakdown. When she boards a random train in order to leave, apparently without a concrete destination, she is seized by anxiety attacks; her selfhood collapses and so does the world order. "Reality" becomes "un desorden de impresiones y ella estaba allí, hecha pedazos" [a chaos of impressions and there she was, in pieces].[24] It later turns out that the train is the usual one, taking her once again to her mother's house. Although the characters fail, the key to their identity is ambiguously located in the past.

Juan Marsé [b.1933] offers a different viewpoint in *La muchacha de las bragas de oro* (1978), if only because the protagonist, Luys Forest, fully belongs to the first postwar generation and, furthermore, to the Civil War's winning side. After Franco's death, Forest, the "cronista oficial de la victoria" [official chronicler of victory], devotes himself to revising his past in order to "justificar su vida" [justify his life].[25] He attempts to pose as a secret critic of the regime by means of an autobiography plagued with "poetic licence." Once again, the end of Francoism forces a character to retouch his past. However, unlike the characters on the defeated side, Forest undertakes this endeavor in a self-conscious, rational, and opportunistic fashion, and does not experience the anxiety attacks or permanent anguish that afflicts all the characters in the other novels under discussion. In post-Franco narrative, anguish is evidently an attribute of the Civil War's defeated side and their anti-Franco sons and daughters. Actually, Forest's reconstruction does not follow memory; instead, it is a "prosthesis" that prevents confrontation with the past.[26] Very soon, upon the arrival of young Mariana at his Calafell home, confusion and false perceptions abound. Mariana is a drug addict and belongs to a generation whose members have no parents, or whose parents are absent. From this point on, all references become confused for Forest; Mariana's and her lovers' hesitant sexuality—Forest himself becomes one of these lovers before discovering that he is her father—becomes mass-media illusion. Immersed in an epistemological maelstrom, Forest fails to recognize historical facts and the surrounding reality even when he attempts to do so. The self-conscious subject, who at the beginning of the novel had thought himself capable of falsifying his own biography because he knew the truth, is forced to admit that he is only capable of forging it. Hence his paradoxical statement: "Recuerdo con más precisión al hombre que hubiese querido ser que al que he sido" [I remember the man I would have liked to be more accurately than the one I have been].[27] The self, which had at the beginning been an active subject in the reconstruction of the past, increasingly becomes its object. The Francoist system of interpretation of the world has also affected its own agents. Because in the end Forest is not even brave enough to commit suicide, he is condemned to face the past in his daughter's company.

Furthermore, *La muchacha de las bragas de oro* anticipates the change in discourse on Francoism's determining effects that will become evident in Muñoz Molina's novels. Unlike the aforementioned novels' protagonists, Forest does not imagine a spatio-temporal or ideological utopia, nor does he attempt to materialize one, and, consequently, he does not fail because of an inability to liberate himself from the past. It is true that Forest ends up failing, but he constructs an alternative biography located beyond his real life. The fact that it is a fiction introduces a spatio-temporal discontinuity between life and fictional biography. The reason for this procedure may be that the character is clearly a member of the first Francoist generation; because he does not have a new life ahead of him, he has no choice but to completely withdraw from his real biography. However, Marsé's *La muchacha de las bragas de oro* documents (albeit with pejorative implications) the protagonist's new attitude towards the past, perhaps only because he belongs to the victorious side. The construction of an autonomous universe through the invention of a new biography is as much a poetic procedure as a general historiographical reflection. Both of these features are typical of Muñoz Molina's novels, whose characters nevertheless manage to finally liberate themselves.

II. The Split Subject

On the one hand, Juan José Millás's [b.1946] *El desorden de tu nombre* (1988) resembles Muñoz Molina's novels, especially regarding the characters' attitudes towards the past; on the other hand, the internalization of the ghosts from the past is deliberate and even more radical in Millás. Whereas the reflecting subject in *La muchacha de las bragas de oro* attempts to construct a more convenient biography by reinterpreting his acts and decisions in a more or less poetic light, and this biography slowly breaks down upon the intervention of a different perspective, Millás's protagonist constructs, in writing, an entire fictional universe that parallels his real life. By denying the latter, he settles within a universe founded on the productive and efficient appropriation of ghosts from the past. Unlike the other novels' protagonists, and unlike many of their creators, Millás and his main character belong to a generation whose members experienced directly the most liberal Francoist period and were thirty to thirty-five years old in 1975, that is, young enough to start a new life.

Julio Orgaz, who is forty-two in the late 1980s, is well-settled in the modern free-market world. He has opportunistically climbed up the ranks in a publishing house after failing in his endeavor to become a writer, a result of his lover Teresa's disappearance. However, since her death Julio has suffered from an auditory hallucination; he hears his canary sing the "International" anthem, which leads him to undergo psychotherapy. He falls in love with Laura, not knowing that she is the analyst's wife, and Laura ends up murdering her husband in order to live with Julio. In turn, the latter conceives an imaginary and ideal novel wherein the exact same story takes place. He later settles down within this fiction, which substitutes for real life, and somehow puts an end to therapy; he no longer experiences his self as conflicted, not even recognizing the "International" anthem when he hears it.

Julio is faced with the dilemma of either acknowledging the failure of leftist ideology or conforming to the neoliberalism of the 1980s.[28] The dissonance of personality shared by the protagonists of all the works under discussion takes on psychopathological dimensions in Millás's novel. Reconciliation, professional success, and a positive identity can only be achieved through the denial and repression of the original self. Hence the attempted therapy, and hence the imaginary novel, which turns out to be, as in *La muchacha de las bragas de oro,* another "prosthesis"—Millás uses the same word as Marsé.[29] The procedure for constructing the "prosthesis," that is to complete or replace the mutilated self, is revealing. It is, at one and the same time, poetic, repressive, and psychotic; the novel Julio conceives not only serves to reassemble the self, but *is* in fact a reassembly or construction of the self. It is a universe composed of numerous contradictory fragments which are organized in such a way that the repression of some of the former personality's fragments gives rise to a new personality.[30] This construct makes it possible to abolish guilt, bad conscience, anguish, and history itself: "No tengo culpa, ni memoria de culpa, somos una pasta moldeable y proteica" [I have no guilt, nor memory of guilt, we are a malleable and protean dough], Julio says in the end.[31] Millás's diagnosis is not without cynicism, as Julio and Laura seemingly triumph without being punished. Underlying the appearance of bourgeois normality are personal emptiness, amorality, and psychosis. Instead of facing his past, Julio perpetuates and exploits it in order to triumph in contemporary society. On the question of democratic Spain and its relation with the past, the verdict is definitely pessimistic. Society is made up of men and women who repress their own desires and who, like Laura, fulfill their parents' unsatisfied desires, or else, like Julio, are traumatized by bad conscience because of their inability to do anything against Franco.[32] The unfulfilled father's (Franco's) murder transmutes into the abolition of the former self by means of the ideal novel and the murder of the psychoanalyst, who is a symbol *par excellence* of access to the past. Questioning the past does not cause a breakdown in the personality's schizophrenic structure, but, instead, secures that structure.[33]

El desorden de tu nombre articulates a new paradigm that entails a revised attitude towards the "powers of the past." As was the case with the other novels' protagonists, Julio's relation with the past is at first defined by existential conditioning and psychic-epistemological trauma, and accompanied by feelings of guilt, existential anguish, regrets, and lack of substance. Confrontation with reality leads to a breakdown in his signifying order, in his order of references.[34] He is saved upon becoming the protagonist of a novel where the self, the world, and the past are subject to a de-realization process that isolates them from their historical and psychic context. History, anguish, and the past remain in another world and in another ontology, as does the original self. The construct is founded upon a personality split, which functionalizes and consolidates the original schizophrenia. The self's psychic continuity and history's spatio-temporal continuity are thus interrupted. Having become a character in the novel he has constructed, Julio is simultaneously inside his own world and ontologically removed from it. Naturally, Millás uses this separation to express the protagonist's psychotic state. In Muñoz Molina's novels, by contrast, being detached from oneself and one's own world is a starting-point which forces the characters to establish new, productive relations with their past. Julio and Laura cannot live with the past, whereas Muñoz Molina's characters cannot live without it, that is, without reconciling themselves with a past that needs to be reconstructed. In Muñoz Molina's work, reconciliation of the self and the past is possible, but only through polyphonic memory, not subjective reflection. The characters manage, usually thanks to love, to establish individual reference points within a symbolic universe made up of "non-places."

III. Dialogued Memory and Individualized References

Among Antonio Muñoz Molina's [b.1956] novels, *El jinete polaco* (1991) best illustrates a paradigm shift in discourse about the presence of Francoism, a shift that had already been announced by earlier novels and is, therefore, a logical consequence of them. Whereas in earlier novels psycho-social and epistemological trauma and the existential conditioning by the past had shaped subjects' relations with themselves, their present, and their past, in *El jinete polaco* these problems become an ontological, epistemological, and/or cognitive discontinuity between the reflecting subject, his/her world, and his/her past. Furthermore, in this novel the year 1975 is no longer significant as a setting for the plot. Although the characters live partly or wholly under Francoism, space and time, Spain and the postwar are paradoxically inaccessible, located beyond an impassable border. From the beginning, the characters are outside history, as it were. This explains the discrepancy in age critics have noted between author Muñoz Molina's generation and that of his older protagonists.[35] Through polyphonic or collective memory, the characters are forced to reconstruct history in order for it to exist and for their very selves to exist. The impossibility of objectively representing history and the consequent reconstruction of history from a multiple, de-centered perspective are also typical of postmodern aesthetics and—in the context of post-Franco Spanish literature—of the modes of perception of the aforementioned novels' characters, who are unable to find a perspective that would allow them to confront their Franco-era past. It is therefore necessary to review dialogism and the deconstruction of historical discourse in Muñoz Molina's novels.

El jinete polaco's characters are lost in space and time. Uprooted from their country and having no ties to their own past, Manuel and Nadia are voluntarily locked up in a rented New York apartment during a military conflict (the Gulf War) as they tell each other their life stories. Muñoz Molina's characters have no identity, they cross and inhabit places which the French anthropologist Marc Augé would call "non-lieux" ("non-places"). Augé defines *non-lieu* as "espace qui ne peut se définir ni comme identitaire, ni comme relationnel, ni comme historique" [space that cannot be defined as identitarian, relational, or historical].[36] Non-places are transit places, de-contextualized from their spatio-temporal environment, with no rooting in history and, hence, no identity—places that, as a result, prevent subjects from establishing an identity: hotel rooms, highways, airports, or the New York apartment where Manuel and Nadia tell each other their biographies. According to Augé, non-places are produced by a situation of "surmodernité" (or postmodernity) the essence of which is "excess": excess of time, as the acceleration of history; excess of space, as the superabundance of spatial simultaneities; and, finally, excess of ego and the individual, which gives rise to individualized interpretations of the world.[37] In Augé's view, non-places materialize (and this is particularly evident in *El jinete polaco*) in the acceleration of means of transportation, urban concentrations and a number of other places that partially make up the chronotopes of novels.[38] Spatio-temporal discontinuity not only affects subjects' relations with their present world and the past, but also with themselves. The protagonists travel with ease through landscapes, lives, bodies, voices, and consciousnesses, and their own biography, their own consciousness is but one of the self's possible stopping-places. Places are non-places, and if they lack history and identity, this is also due to the fact that the characters inhabiting them have no identity. The characters themselves are floating non-places, for when they try to appropriate the past, they are unable to find any continuity with it and, therefore, any identity within themselves. *El jinete polaco*'s narrator leaves everything behind, except for his traveling implements (the archetype of the non-place):[39] "Una bolsa liviana de viaje . . . el pasaporte y la tarjeta de crédito, nada más, nadie más, ni siquiera yo mismo, el que he sido y ya no soy" [a light traveling bag, my passport, and my credit card, nothing else, no one else, not even myself, the one I have been and am not anymore].[40]

The relation between subjects' reality and the places and times of the present and past is mediated by voices and photographs, which symbolize the discontinuity between both poles. Even ideological positions are confused, and frustrated love stories are superimposed onto political action. In *El jinete polaco* there is a recurrent memory: Manuel and Nadia in the New York apartment during the Gulf War, looking at the photographs collected in the bottomless trunk given to them by Ramiro, the Mágina (Manuel's hometown) photographer. This scene is emblematic. The trunk full of pictures from Mágina holds these characters' history and the history of others, but in fragmentary fashion, with no chronological order; images co-exist, decontextualized from the time and space they were taken. History is twice removed from the subject; it is not only external, but mediated by photographs. Manuel's and Nadia's biographies tell the story of a banishment, an uprooting, and a lack of identity that spans a long, alienated century. As was the case some fifteen years earlier, in *La noche en casa*, the self seeks "razones más antiguas" [older reasons]— no longer the reasons for desire, or protest, as in Chéspir's case—but the reasons for its uprooting. Chéspir found the phylogenetic abyss; Manuel finds Ramiro Retratista's bottomless trunk and, of course, Nadia. The characters' biographies also symbolically represent Spanish history: the "two Spains" during the Civil War and the postwar, dissidence, exile, isolation, 1960s modernization, Western culture—in sum, the entire history of Francoism. However, the representation of history is still ambiguous. Manuel's biography from the 1960s onward is that of any Spanish teenager, but it is also the biography of any young person in an industrialized country who identifies with pop-culture (e.g., his fondness for the Doors). The other period the protagonist reflects on is his childhood, or even his "prenatal" phase: the Civil War and the previous decades, a "reino de las voces" [kingdom of voices] that are mixed with voices from the present.[41] The "impossibility of memory," of Francoism's historical origins more specifically, is no longer due to trauma, but first and foremost to the fact that Manuel belongs to a different generation. By incorporating the pre-Civil War period, Manuel (Muñoz Molina) attempts to go back beyond the Francoist period in order to "invent himself" and recover an origin other than Francoism that he may declare his own.[42] Rational and personal access to that past is by definition impossible. That period cannot be the object of his own experience; it cannot be verifiable. The relations that mediate between the characters' selfhood, their past, and their present, together with the variety of non-places appearing in this novel, symbolize the spatio-temporal (even ontological, epistemological, and cognitive) gap or discontinuity between the subject, his/her present world, and his/her past, which is aestheticized and deformed by memory and time. Here we also find the principle underlying Muñoz Molina's new aesthetics of historiographical metafiction, which, as critics have well noted, transform history—the Francoist period—into an aesthetic construct.[43] However, even more important is that aestheticizing history to such a degree had not been possible in the other novels I have discussed, precisely because their protagonists remain existentially tied to the past. But for Muñoz Molina's characters the past is somehow invented, with as little reality as Mágina—a time and space that no memory may recover.

Furthermore, in contrast to the other novels under discussion, Muñoz Molina's protagonists find stable references within the historical universe in which they are immersed but to which they do not belong. These references lie between the impossibility of memory and the impossibility of oblivion.[44] The reason is that the places of the past and the past itself are ultimately inaccessible and thus unchangeable. Therefore the characters must use individual references to orient themselves. Once subjects become existentially and psychically detached from their past, the numerous non-places become not another form of conditioning, but a possible way of liberating themselves from Francoist history and giving individual meaning to their own biographies. For Manuel and Nadia, reconciliation with the past, which is also a reunion with each other, cannot take place in the context of Spanish history or through the re-presentation of history. The only place their reunion and, symbolically, their reconciliation with history can occur is precisely another non-place, the New York apartment during the Gulf War. Within the maelstrom of historical references, new fixed points can only be established in a non-place, and they must be individualized, not historical, references. For Manuel, this reference is love—that is, Nadia, who helps to relieve his anguish over an "eterno adiós" [eternal goodbye] and serves as the only means of restoring his identity and his past.[45] Manuel ceases to be a person without a country in order to "no escuchar otra voz que la tuya [la de Nadia] y no tener más patria que tú ni más pasado que los últimos meses" [listen to no other voice but yours (Nadia's) and have no other homeland but you nor any other past but the last few months].[46] Thus, two histories remain at the end of *El jinete polaco*: an external, social, aestheticized history, which takes place between two wars, and an internal, personal history, which has a mythical beginning—the "kingdom of voices"—and an almost marvelous end: love.

This recovery of *El jinete polaco*'s characters' (consciously falsified) biographies entails a constructive and ethical argument that resists postmodern discourse on the deconstruction of the subject and of history. It is worth noting that this ethical choice manifests itself and lies in an act committed in the past by a representative of the parents' generation, the consequences of which determine the protagonist's situation—an act, moreover, around which the novel's narrative structure revolves. In *El jinete polaco*, Nadia's father kills a Nationalist at the beginning of the Civil War; this is an *urszene* [primordial concept] of narrative economy that structures the protagonists' desire for history. The chapter that narrates this event, which is carefully built up from the beginning of the novel, starts with the words, "Un acto . . ." [an act].[47] In the present, acts have become words—words used by the protagonists to narrate their lives to one another—but the only one who acts is the one who narrates and no longer listens. Manuel evinces this change in attitude when he realizes "que por primera vez en mi vida soy yo quien cuenta y no quien escucha" [that for the first time in my life I am the one who tells and not the one who listens].[48] This is the moment when reconciliation (albeit only aesthetic) with the past begins. To narrate means to create identity. The "I" is constructed in the act of narrating, by making itself the subject of ethical charges.[49]

This ethical aspect is linked to a concept of the self that is no longer based on the modern principle of identity—understood as the self's congruence with itself in all its manifestations (the other novels' protagonists failed in this endeavor)—but on the principle of *coherence* which, as described by the contemporary German philosopher Wilhelm Schmid, is an ethical principle that demands that, in order to be itself, the self "shape" existence. According to Schmid, coherence, as a principle for the self, is different from both the modern concept of identity and the postmodern concept of "multiplicity."[50] A coherent self integrates what is fragmentary and contradictory in a perpetual process of self-formation (*Selbstgestaltung*), without thereby ceasing to experience itself as identical. The coherent self is yet to be assembled, not yet to be discovered or maintained. Its coherence is necessarily fragmentary, like the subject itself, and basically narrative, because it constructs itself in the act of telling its history to itself and others, always anew. At the metapoetic or epistemological level, identity is conceived as a narrative and moral process.[51]

CONCLUSION

Schmid's ideas share some elements with the "neomodern" episteme that Gonzalo Navajas describes. According to Navajas, this new epistemic configuration is generally characterized by, among other things, "assertiveness," which contrasts with the negativity inherent in postmodern positions; it thus surpasses negativity without thereby returning to pre-modern or modern paradigms.[52] However, the change in paradigm that I draw attention to in this essay cannot be explained as a general change in "epoch" or "episteme." The close connections between the novels under study allow us to refer justifiably to a discourse on Francoism, which contains certain persistent themes, *topoi*, and viewpoints that change throughout the years. This explains why novels from the 1970s, which are rooted in Francoism, anticipate certain critical attitudes (particularly regarding the representation of history and the subject) underlying the new aesthetic possibilities articulated in novels from the 1990s. It also explains the fact that the "powers of the past" are still present in the later novels, for writers continue to have the same concerns regarding history and the subject. The defining trait of discourse on Francoism—considered as postmodern discourse—lies precisely in the way it questions these two topics, history and the subject.[53]

In three novels—*La noche en casa, Te trataré como a una reina,* and *La muchacha de las bragas de oro*—we see how the subject is de-realized upon the disappearance of the Francoist system because s/he had been dependent on it. In *El desorden de tu nombre,* the subject de-realizes the world in order to survive. In Muñoz Molina's novels, there is not at first an identical self, nor a spatio-temporal world that allows for the self's identity to settle. The de-realized subject, the world, and history realize themselves at the same time—precisely when subjects take responsibility for themselves. Early post-Francoism's psychic and epistemological instability gives rise to doubts about history as a bearer of meaning, and to a profound mistrust of history or at least the possibility of its representation. The self, which was formerly split by schizophrenia, becomes a dialogical self that is ontologically, epistemologically, or cognitively removed from its present and past. If Muñoz Molina's characters—unlike J. J. Millás's—are neither schizophrenic nor psychotic, it is because they are able to secure individual reference points from which to face the "powers of the past" that still prevail. Novels written in the 1990s are assertive regarding the possibility of a constructive identity for the subject and history, without relinquishing mistrust towards the possibility of their representation. Regarding history and regarding the subject, there is both a destructive and a constructive movement.

The persistence and transformation of these particular features of literary discourse on Francoism allow us to state that its origin lies in the convergence of postmodernism and the specifically Spanish version of post-totalitarianism, namely post-Francoism. This concrete situation triggered the urge to rethink two sets of issues: history and the self. The features of this discourse have an aesthetic component, but cannot be understood outside the cultural context of Francoism and early post-Francoism, which for subsequent generations have become an increasingly aesthetic experience.

[Translated by Jacqueline Cruz]

NOTES

Revised and expanded version of an article published in Spanish in M. Albert (ed.): *Vencer no es convencer. Literatura e ideología del fascismo español* [Winning is Not Convincing. Literature and Ideology in Spanish Fascism]. Frankfurt and Madrid: Vervuert / Iberoamericana, 1998, pp. 229–47.

1. José-Carlos Mainer uses this term in his study *De postguerra (1951–1990)* [About the Postwar Period] (Barcelona: Crítica, 1994), 109–42.

2. As explained by Hayden White, *Metahistory. The Historical Imagination in Nineteenth-Century Europe* (Baltimore: Johns Hopkins University Press, 1973); Michel De Certeau, *L'écriture de l'histoire* [The Writing of History] (Paris: Gallimard, 1975); Jean-François Lyotard, *La condition postmoderne* [The Postmodern Condition] (Paris: Minuit, 1979); and Fredric Jameson, *Postmodernism or The Cultural Logic of Late Capitalism* (Durham, NC: Duke University, 1992).

3. Robert C. Spires, *Post-Totalitarian Spanish Fiction* (Columbia/London : University of Missouri Press, 1966), 105.

4. See especially, Mainer, "El otoño del miedo: La imagen fílmica y literaria de Franco" [The Autumn of Fear: The Cinematic and Literary Image of Franco], *Letras Peninsulares* 11.4 (Spring 1998), and *De postguerra*.

5. Teresa M. Vilarós, *El mono del desencanto español. Una crítica cultural de la transición española 1973–1993* [The Hangover after the Spanish Disenchantment. A Cultural Critique of the Spanish Transition] (Madrid : Siglo XXI, 1998), 45.

6. Walther L. Bernecker characterizes Francoism as a "dictadura modernizadora." [A modernizing dictatorship] "El debate sobre el regimen franquista: ¿Fascismo, autoritarismo, dictadura de modernización?" [The Debate on the Francoist Regime: Fascism, Authoritarianism, Modernizing Dictatorship?] in M. Albert, ed., op. cit., 37.

7. Manuel Vázquez-Montalbán, "La novela española entre el posfranquismo y el posmodernismo" [The Spanish Novel between Post-Francoism and Postmodernism], in Yvan Lissorgues, coord., *La renovation du roman espagnol depuis 1975. Actes du colloque des 13–14. février 1991* [The Renewal of the Spanish Novel after 1975. Proceedings from the Conference, 13–14 February 1991] (Toulouse: Presses Universitaires du Mirail), 14.

8. Mainer, *De postguerra*, 124. See also Mainer, "Intervention," in Marie-Linda Ortega, ed., *Le roman espagnol face à l'histoire* [The Spanish Novel and History] (Fontenay/Saint-Cloud: ENS, 1996). Karl-Wilhelm Kreis has a similar focus, but strictly from the viewpoint of psychopathology in *Zur Ästhetik des Obszönen. Arrabals Theater und die repressive Sexualpolitik des Franco-Regimes* [On the Aesthetics of the Obscene. Arrabal's Theater and the Repressive Sexual Policy of the Francoist Regime] (Hamburg: Krämer, 1990).

9. Juan Goytisolo, "Pasado y presente de España," [Past and Present of Spain] *Claves de razón práctica* 50 (March 1995): 56.

10. Mainer, *De postguerra*, 128.

11. This (self)criticism of the Left is already present in literature written during the late Francoist period. A good example is Luis Goytisolo's [b.1935] work, particularly the *Antagonía* tetralogy (1973–1981). It is still repeatedly expressed in Rafael Chirbes, *La larga marcha* [The Long Journey] (Barcelona: Anagrama, 1996).

12. José María Guelbenzu, *La noche en casa* (Barcelona: Destino, 1990), 24–25.

13. Ibid., 117, 115.

14. Ibid., 157.

15. Ibid., 157, 159.

16. Ibid., 40, 48.

17. Ibid., 169–70.

18. Ibid., 170.

19. Regarding existentialist concerns in *La noche en casa*, see Gemma Roberts, "Amor sexual y frustración existencial en dos novelas de Guelbenzu" [Sexual Love and Existential Frustration in Two Novels by Guelbenzu], Ricardo Landeira and Luis

González-del-Valle, eds. *Nuevos y novísimos. Algunas perspectivas críticas sobre la narrativa española desde la década de los 60* [Some Critical Perspectives on the Spanish Narrative from the Sixties] (Boulder, CO: Society of Spanish and Spanish-American Studies, 1987).

20. Guelbenzu, 95; 57.

21. In *Los mares del sur* [The South Seas] (Barcelona: Planeta [Serie Carvalho], 1993), Manuel Vázquez Montalbán represents these issues at the political level. The novel's focus is social reality, which is pervaded by the political transition's "desencanto" [disenchantment]. The lack of reference points causes several of the characters to feel nostalgia for the former period's political and moral order. Like Chéspir, the protagonist, Stuart Pedrell, is a disintegrated subject, another "víctima del puritanismo franquista" [victim of Francoist puritanism] (84). Unlike Chéspir, however, Pedrell is not an inveterate ironist, but, instead—and this has similar implications— a Marxist or "nihilist businessman," another subject with a dual personality who had "distanciado demasiado de sí mismo" [distanced himself too much from himself] by pursuing political ideals incompatible with his social standing (50). The end of the dictatorship has stripped him, too, of identity. Despite belonging—or precisely as a result of belonging—to Francoism's dominant class and surviving the transition without great loss, Pedrell not only fails as a (Gramscian) "intellectual" defending the interests of a social class he does not belong to, but, furthermore, becomes a new victim because he believes in class antagonism as proclaimed by the opposition. The opposition is ultimately inefficient; its ideas hardly correspond to reality since its anti-Franco stance implies that it is still indirectly inscribed within Francoism's symbolic interpretation of the world.

22. Regarding this aspect of Rosa Montero's novels, see Karl-Wilhelm Kreis, "Die Generation der Verlorenen. Zur Psychopathologie der Geschlechterbeziehungen im Erzählwerk Rosa Monteros," [The Generation of the Lost Ones. On the Psychopathology of Gender Relationship in Rosa Montero's narrative] in Christine Bierbach and Andrea Rössler, eds., *Nicht Muse, nicht Heldin. Schriftstellerinnen in Spanien seit 1975* [Neither a Muse nor a Heroine. Women Writers in Spain since 1975] (Berlin: Tranvía, 1992), especially 195–200. Also, Kreis, *Zur Ästhetik*, 113–14, 118, and 125–26. Kreis carefully analyzes, in relation to Arrabal's work, the "patología del católico medio" [pathology of the average Catholic] generated by sexual repression under National Catholicism. He highlights the following elements: sense of sin and guilt, depression, anguish, pathological narcissism; regression to childhood, hysteria, obsessive neurosis, perversions (incest), destructive aggressiveness mixed with hatred, contempt, violence towards objects and oneself; masochism (women), sadism (men); internal dissociation of the self, escapism, longing for authorities that will take on the role of conscience, and so forth.

23. Rosa Montero, *Te trataré como a una reina* (Barcelona: Seix Barral, 1983), 230.

24. Montero, 244.

25. Juan Marsé, *La muchacha de las bragas de oro* (Barcelona: Planeta, 1988), 161.

26. Ibid., 184.

27. Ibid., 170.

28. This dilemma (which, incidentally, is somewhat dichotomous in Millás's novel) is reminiscent of the one facing the group of friends in the first part of Vázquez-Montalbán's *El pianista* [The Pianist] (Barcelona: Seix Barral, 1985), published a few years earlier. These friends are more or less the same age and have had experiences similar to Julio Orgaz's. They have either become, like Schubert's character, according to anti-Franco activist Ventura, ironic "mirones, retóricos, pedigüeños" [voyeurs, rhetoricians, beggars], ungrateful and "sin visión" [without a

vision], or else, like the musician Doria or his 1980s double, Toni Fisas, they are bound to suspect opportunism or intellectual betrayal (*El pianista*, 34).

29. See note 27. And Millás, 172.

30. The selective eclecticism Julio Orgaz applies to his own personality is reminiscent of the mimetic character Julio Rodríguez Puértolas has observed in Francoist ideology. Rodríguez Puértolas, *Literatura fascista española. Vol. 1: Historia* (Madrid: Akal, 1986), 32–33.

31. Millás, 171.

32. Mainer observes this phenomenon in *De postguerra* (114).

33. This is what happens in Millás's novel (131–32).

34. Millás, 15, 20–21, 24, 26, 28, 31, ff.

35. Among them, Thomas Scheerer, "Antonio Muñoz Molina," in Alfonso De Toro and Dieter Ingenschay, eds., *La novela española actual. Autores y tendencias* [Spanish Contemporary Novel. Authors and Trends] (Kassel: Reichenberger, 1995), 236.

36. Marc Augé, *Non-Lieux. Introduction à une anthropologie de la surmodernité* [Non-places: Introduction to an Anthropology of Supermodernity] (Paris: Seuil, 1992), 100.

37. Ibid., 35–56.

38. Ibid., 47–48.

39. Ibid., 110.

40. Antonio Muñoz Molina, *El jinete polaco*, (Barcelona: Planeta, 1991) 395. In a recently published monograph on Muñoz Molina, Christine Pérès observes that his novels' topography is also characterized by the concept of "non-lieux," which are opposed to "lieux de mémoire" [places of memory] (following Pierre Nora), such as, for instance, the fictional city of Mágina. Pérès, Préface d'Antonio Muñoz Molina, in *Le nouveau roman espagnol et la quête d'identité: Antonio Muñoz Molina* [The New Spanish Novel and the Search for Identity: Antonio Muñoz Molina] (Paris: L'Harmattan, 2001). However, I think the presence of *non-lieux* in 1980s novels is not that surprising in itself—we also find it in other Romance literatures, such as French (Jean-Philippe Toussaint) or Italian (Gianni Celati) literature. What I find more interesting is the form and the specific function *non-lieux* take on in personal and cultural identity discourses. On the relation of "non-lieux," and "lieux de mémoire" in the context of post-totalitarian Spanish Culture see my essay in the forthcoming book by Joan Ramon Resina and Ulrich Winter, eds., *Casa encantada: Lugares de memoria e identidades culturales en la postmodernidad ibérica* [Enchanted House: Places of Memory and Cultural Identities in the Iberian Postmodernity] (Frankfurt am Main: Vervuert/Madrid: Iberoamericana).

41. *El jinete polaco*'s first chapter is titled "El reino de las voces."

42. This is also due to the fact that because Franco died a natural death, there is no founding myth for democracy. See Emmanuel Bouju, "Le roman face à la Transition: Défi de l'histoire, réplique du littéraire (1975–1985)," [The Novel and the Transition: A Challenge to History, a Literary Reply] in Marie-Linda Ortega, ed., *Le roman espagnol face à l'histoire* (Fontenay/Saint-Cloud: ENS, 1996), 138.

43. See the work of Scheerer, op.cit.; Maryse Bertrand de Muñoz, "Presencia y transformación del tema de la Guerra civil en la novela española desde los años ochenta" [Presence and Transformation of the Civil War Theme in the Spanish Novel from the Eighties], *Ínsula* (589–590) 1996; and others.

44. The idea that *El jinete polaco* also represents the impossibility of forgetting is developed by David Herzberger in "Oblivion and Rememberance: The Double Desire of Muñoz Molina's *El jinete polaco*," in Joan Ramon Resina, ed., *Disremembering the Dictatorship. The Politics of Memory in the Spanish Transition to Democracy* (Amsterdam/Atlanta: Rodopi, 2000), 127–38.

45. *El jinete polaco,* 403, 419.

46. Ibid., 572.

47. Ibid., 318.

48. Ibid., 180.

49. We find the same mechanism in another novel that, due to space limitations, I am unable to study in depth, namely, Javier Marías's *Corazón tan blanco* [So White A Heart] (1992). In the face of the threat entailed by his father's life and his own biography, the protagonist, Juan, also takes responsibility for his life, somehow reinvents it, and creates new contexts for himself in order to forge an identity of his own. See Ruth Christie, "Self-writing and 'lo que pudo ser' in *Corazón tan blanco* by Javier Marías," in R. Christie, J. Drinkwater, and J. Macklin, eds., *The Scripted Self: Textual Identities in Contemporary Spanish Narrative* (Warminster, UK: Aris and Phillips, 1995).

50. Wilhelm Schmid, *Philosophie der Lebenskunst. Eine Grundlegung* [A Philosophy for the Art of Living. Fundamentals] (Frankfurt am Main: Suhrkamp, 1999), 250–58.

51. For a hermeneutic explanation of this process, see Paul Ricoeur, *Soi-même comme un autre* (Paris: Seuil, 1990), especially 167–98.

52. Gonzalo Navajas, *Más allá de la posmodernidad. Estética de la nueva novela y cine españoles* [Beyond Postmodernity. Aesthetics of the New Spanish Novel and Cinema] (Barcelona: EUB, 1996), 18; 182–84 and *passim.*

53. In the 1980s Mainer used the metaphor of "ghost of the past" in the psychoanalytical or psychosocial sense. This use was perfectly suitable for the novels of the period of the first post-Francoism. For the novels of the 1990s, this metaphor should be extended and understood in the more complex sense articulated by Jacques Derrida in *Spectres de Marx* (Paris: Gallilée, 1993), especially related to the idea of responsibility—assumed or otherwise—to recognize the past as part of the present.

BIBLIOGRAPHY

Augé, Marc. *Non-lieux. Introduction à une anthropologie de la surmodernité.* Paris: Seuil, 1992.

Bernecker, Walther L. "El debate sobre el regimen franquista: ¿Fascismo, autoritarismo, dictadura demodernización? In *Vencer no es convencer. Literatura e ideología del fascismo español,* edited by M. Albert. Frankfurt am Main: Vervuert/Madrid: Iberoamericana, 1998. 29–49.

Bertrand de Muñoz, Maryse. "Presencia y transformación del tema de la Guerra Civil en la novela española desde los años ochenta." *Ínsula* 589–590 (1996): 11–14.

Bouju, Emmanuel. "Le roman face à la Transition: Défi de l'histoire, réplique du littéraire (1975–1985)." In *Le roman espagnol face à l'histoire.* Edited by Marie-Linda Ortega. Fontenay/Saint-Cloud: ENS, 1996. 137–48.

Chirbes, Rafael. *La larga marcha.* Barcelona: Anagrama, 1996.

Christie, Ruth. "Self-writing and 'lo que pudo ser' in *Corazón tan blanco* by Javier Marías". In *The Scripted Self: Textual Identities in Contemporary Spanish Narrative.* Edited by R. Christie, J. Drinkwater, and J. Macklin: Warminster, UK: Aris and Phillips, 1995. 135–52.

De Certeau, Michel. *L'écriture de l'histoire.* Paris: Gallimard, 1975.

De Toro, Alfonso, and Dieter Ingenschay, eds. *La novela española actual. Autores y tendencias.* Kassel: Reichenberger, 1995.

Derrida, Jacques. *Spectres de Marx.* Paris: Gallilée, 1993.

Goytisolo, Juan. "Pasado y presente de España." Interview with Danubio Torres Fierro. *Claves de razón práctica* 50 (March 1995): 56–58.

Goytisolo, Luis (1973). *Antagonía*. Madrid: Alianza, 1987.

Guelbenzu, José María (1977). *La noche en casa*. Barcelona: Destino, 1990.

Herzberger, David . "Oblivion and Rememberance: The Double Desire of Muñoz Molina's *El jinete polaco*." In *Disremembering the Dictatorship. The Politics of Memory in the Spanish Transition to Democracy*. Edited by Joan Ramon Resina. Amsterdam / Atlanta: Rodopi, 2000. 127–138.

Jameson, Fredric. *Postmodernism or The Cultural Logic of Late Capitalism*. Durham, NC: Duke University, 1992.

Kreis, Karl-Wilhelm. *Zur Ästhetik des Obszönen. Arrabals Theater und die repressive Sexualpolitik des Franco-Regimes*. Hamburg: Krämer, 1990.

———. "Die Generation der Verlorenen. Zur Psychopathologie der Geschlechterbeziehungen im Erzählwerk Rosa Monteros." In *Nicht Muse, nicht Heldin. Schriftstellerinnen in Spanien seit 1975*. Edited by Christine Bierbach and Andrea Rössler. Berlin: Tranvía, 1992. 191–204.

Lyotard, Jean-François. *La condition postmoderne*. Paris: Minuit, 1979.

Mainer, José Carlos. *De postguerra (1951–1990)*. Barcelona: Crítica, 1994.

———. "Intervention." In *Le roman espagnol face à l'histoire*. Edited by Marie-Linda Ortega. Fontenay/Saint-Cloud: ENS, 1996. 184–90.

———. "El otoño del miedo: La imagen fílmica y literaria de Franco." *Letras Peninsulares* 11(4) (Spring 1998): 387–412.

Marsé, Juan (1978). *La muchacha de las bragas de oro*. Barcelona: Planeta, 1988.

Merino, José María. "Imposibilidad de la memoria." In *El viajero perdido (Cuentos breves)*. Madrid: Alfaguara, 1989, 58–74.

Millás, Juan José. *El desorden de tu nombre*. Madrid: Alfaguara, 1988.

Montero, Rosa. *Te trataré como a una reina*. Barcelona: Seix Barral, 1983.

Muñoz Molina, Antonio. *El jinete polaco*. Barcelona: Planeta, 1991.

Navajas, Gonzalo. *Más allá de la posmodernidad. Estética de la nueva novela y cine españoles*. Barcelona: EUB, 1996.

Pérès, Christine. *Le nouveau roman espagnol et la quête d'identité: Antonio Muñoz Molina*. Préface d'Antonio Muñoz Molina. Paris: L'Harmattan, 2001.

Resina, Joan Ramon / Winter, Ulrich (eds.). *Casa encantada: Lugares de memoria e identidades culturales en la postmodernidad ibérica*. Frankfurt am Main: Vervuert [forthcoming].

Ricoeur, Paul. *Soi-même comme un autre*. Paris: Seuil, 1990.

Roberts, Gemma. "Amor sexual y frustración existencial en dos novelas de Guelbenzu." In *Nuevos y novísimos. Algunas perspectivas críticas sobre la narrativa española desde la década de los 60*. Edited by Ricardo Landeira and Luis González-del-Valle. Boulder, CO: Society of Spanish and Spanish-American Studies, 1987.

Rodríguez Puértolas, Julio. *Literatura fascista española*, vol. 1: *Historia*. Madrid: Akal, 1986.

Scheerer, Thomas. "Antonio Muñoz Molina." In *La novela española actual. Autores y tendencias*. Edited by Alfonso De Toro and Dieter Ingenschay. Kassel: Reichenberger, 1995. 231–52.

Schmid, Wilhelm. *Philosophie der Lebenskunst. Eine Grundlegung*. Frankfurt am Main: Suhrkamp, 1999.

Smith, Paul Julian. *The Moderns. Time, Space, and Subjectivity in Contemporary Spanish Culture*. Oxford: Oxford University Press, 2000.

Spires, Robert C. *Post-Totalitarian Spanish Fiction*. Columbia/London: University of Missouri Press, 1996.

Vázquez-Montalbán, Manuel (1979). (1979). *Los mares del sur.* Barcelona: Planeta (Serie Carvalho), 1993.

———. "La novela española entre el posfranquismo y el posmodernismo." In *La renovation du roman espagnol depuis 1975. Actes du colloque des 13–14. février 1991.* Coordinated by Yvan Lissorgues. Toulouse: Presses Universitaires du Mirail, 1991, 13–25.

———. *El pianista.* Barcelona: Seix Barral, 1985.

Vilarós, Teresa M. *El mono del desencanto español. Una crítica cultural de la transición española (1973–1993).* Madrid: Siglo XXI, 1998.

White, Hayden. *Metahistory. The Historical Imagination in Nineteenth-Century Europe.* Baltimore: Johns Hopkins University Press, 1973.

Of Good Torturers and Evil Workers:
Antonio Muñoz Molina's *Plenilunio*

Jacqueline Cruz

Twenty-eight years after Franco's death, the prevailing belief among Spaniards—and not only among members of the ruling Partido Popular (PP) [Popular Party]—is that "España va bien" [Spain is doing fine]. According to this view, after two centuries of "lagging behind" its neighbors, Spain is finally a democratic, developed European country, fully integrated into the networks of globalizing neoliberalism and carrying some weight in the international scene. The Franco dictatorship is perceived as a closed chapter that is best forgotten; we do not tend to recall that the celebrated democratic system, and the monarchy that heads it, are its direct heirs. The complicity of many of the current leaders of the Right with the previous regime is thus forgotten, as is—and this is perhaps more serious—the Left's enthusiastic complicity with the neoliberal project and its betrayal of those values that shaped the anti-Franco struggles and the early phases of the Transition. As Jorge Semprún, former member of the Communist Party and former Minister of Culture with the Partido Socialista Obrero Español (PSOE) [Spanish Socialist Workers Party] has noted: "Nuestra transición democrática, que fue ejemplar, *si quiere,* se basa en la desmemoria deliberada, en la amnistía, pero también en la amnesia" [our democratic transition, which *one might say* was exemplary, was based on deliberate forgetfulness, on amnesty, but also on amnesia].[1] This far-reaching amnesia has allowed for the spread of ideological tenets not too different from those of Francoism, albeit conveniently "modernized" in order to facilitate their acceptance by those who, despite their fourteen years in power, still call themselves leftists. One could say, playing with Francoists' common exclamation during the Transition, that, "si Franco levantara la cabeza" [were Franco to raise from the dead], he would heave a sigh of relief and happily rejoin the dead, quite satisfied at his success at leaving everything "atado y bien atado" [all tied up and well tied up]. As Pablo Castellano has expressed it:

Nos guste o no nos guste el actual panorama, a Franco le sucedió el pre-
visto posfranquismo de la restauración monárquica, y éste se ha desarro-
llado, en esencia, con arreglo a la táctica y estrategia de los proyectistas
franquistas y de los realizadores posfranquistas. A su conveniencia . . .
[l]os trabajadores y las capas populares han de sentirse satisfechos: son
explotados, pero ya no son encarcelados.

[Whether we like the new scene or not, Franco was succeeded by the expected post-Francoism of monarchic restoration, and, in essence, the latter has developed in accordance with the tactics and strategy of Francoist
screenwriters and post-Franco directors. At their convenience . . . (w)ork-
ers and the popular classes should feel satisfied: they are exploited, but
they are no longer imprisoned].[2]

Intellectuals have happily joined the chorus of voices praising present-day Spain and have heeded the plea to forget, relinquishing their
independence in return for a role in the mass media.[3] Now that their
success, and therefore their sustenance, depends more than ever on
the market and thus requires their constant presence in newspapers
and on television (to say nothing of massive autograph sessions), they
are almost forced to address political and social issues. However, because the mainstream media have become mega-industries which,
despite differing party allegiances, share an unequivocal respect for
capitalism, intellectuals collaborating with them can hardly be critical of the prevailing socio-economic system.[4] As Manuel Vázquez
Montalbán, one of the few intellectuals who continued to be true to
his Marxist beliefs until his recent death, has noted: "Los políticos
pragmáticos hacen política, los intelectuales pragmáticos la contem-
plan y, a lo sumo, *oponen matices*" [Pragmatic politicians do politics,
pragmatic intellectuals watch it and, at best, *counter nuances*].[5]
In this article, I focus on a writer who is emblematic of the above-
mentioned trends: Antonio Muñoz Molina, author of best-selling
novels, the youngest member of the Real Academia Española, and
one of Spain's most "media-friendly" authors (for several years he
wrote a weekly column in the newspaper *El País*). His stardom is now
shared by his wife, Elvira Lindo, who has made him a character in her
own chronicles for *El País*.[6] At first glance, he appears to be the opposite of the phenomenon under discussion. A self-labeled leftist, he
often embraces progressive causes and, by setting many of his novels
during the Franco era, refuses to submit to the prevailing amnesia he
himself has criticized:

[El] ejercicio de memoria [en la literatura] [cuadra] mal con esa especie
de amnesia posmoderna que nos vienen prescribiendo los poderes políti-

cos y culturales desde que se dio por terminado eso que llaman ahora el régimen *anterior.* [Así] la nueva literatura española debe prescindir de toda referencia al pasado, a menos que prefiera incurrir en delito de lesa posmodernidad.

[The exercise of memory in literature doesn't go well with that sort of postmodern amnesia that the political and cultural powers have been prescribing since the end of what is now called *the previous regime.* Thus, new Spanish literature must dispense with all reference to the past, unless it wants to commit a crime against postmodernity].[7]

Progressive articles co-exist,[8] however, with conservative views more in line with the increasing "rightening" of Spanish society,[9] the most glaring manifestation of which was the PP's victory by absolute majority in the 2000 general elections and, more recently, in the fact that, despite the public outcry and massive demonstrations against the government (particularly against its participation in the Iraqi war), it lost relatively few votes in the 2003 municipal and regional elections.

The following sentence, taken from an article published in *El País Semanal* [*El País*'s weekly supplement], "Los revolucionarios" [The revolutionaries], helps to explain these apparent contradictions: "Las personas de izquierda viven, vivimos, alimentando sueños desprestigiados de igualdad, de instrucción pública, cuando no adorando viejas momias decrépitas" [When not idolizing old decrepit mummies, leftists live, we live, nourishing discredited dreams of equality and public education]. Here, Muñoz Molina defines himself as a "leftist," but it sounds like an afterthought ("they live, we live"); furthermore, he identifies the Left not just with equality and education, but with *decrepitude*—an idea that, as we shall see, is obsessively reiterated in his novels. The message is that leftist ideology is positive, and being a leftist is a source of pride (particularly if one writes for the newspaper that serves as the PSOE's mouthpiece); but it is only an empty label, having little to do with what it formerly represented. This is the same attitude behind the PSOE's recent decision to eliminate the proclamation that had appeared on the party's membership card since its founding in 1879, which, among other things, declared the party's ideal to be the complete emancipation of the working class.[10] According to the party's Secretary General, José Luis Rodríguez Zapatero, this does not entail "renuncias a nada esencial, sino 'innovación' y adaptación al siglo XXI" [giving up anything essential, but rather "innovation" and adaptation to the twenty-first century].[11] Going back to Muñoz Molina's comment, one could ask: "Discredited dreams" for whom? For the triumphant Right? For the Left in power between 1982 and 1996? For Muñoz Molina himself?

In any case, his self-characterization as a leftist is almost too deliberate, as if he were aware that, in light of many of his texts, his leftism is
somewhat questionable and must therefore be made explicit in order
to legitimize his repeated criticism of the Left. As he himself "confessed" in a 1993 lecture: "Formado desde niño en la izquierda y
perteneciente a ella hasta el día de hoy, [me] siento cualificado para
reconocer las variedades de *estupidez* que son estrictamente de izquierdas" [Educated since childhood in the Left and still belonging to it today, I feel qualified to recognize the types of *stupidity* that are strictly
leftist].[12] The type of "stupidity" he most often attacks, incidentally, is
the political commitment of writers, which partly contradicts his criticism of postmodernity and his own public role as intellectual.[13]

It is in his novels, however, where we find his positions most closely
aligned with the Right and where he most clearly rewrites the role
played by Franco's dictatorship and its opponents, thereby legitimizing various aspects of the regime. There are examples of this alignment in most of his works, but it is particularly evident in *Plenilunio*
(1997) [Full Moon], a best-selling novel that was made into a (less
successful) film by Imanol Uribe in 2000. The novel is a mixture of
psychological thriller and detective story, revolving around the murder of a nine-year-old girl in a provincial town, unnamed but identifiable as Úbeda (called Mágina in other novels), and a police inspector's efforts to find the murderer. The third-person narrator
alternately focuses on several of the characters, albeit privileging the
unnamed inspector, who is undoubtedly the hero of the story; his detective skills and his tireless search for the murderer make possible
the latter's capture, thus restoring peace and quiet—or, rather, law
and order—to the town. The murderer (also unnamed), who is the
focus of several chapters, is the perfect antagonist; perverse, without
scruples or remorse, he represents the most despicable elements in
society and is a true monster, the werewolf implicitly alluded to in the
title, whose monstrosity is highlighted on the cover of the Alfaguara
edition, which depicts a fragment of Goya's *El Coloso* [The Colossus].

So far so good. We all agree that, in a child murder case, the bad
guy is the murderer and the good guy is the cop in charge of finding
him. Manicheism is, therefore, almost inevitable. But the ideological
message beneath this apparently straightforward plot is at best problematic. The meticulous and honest inspector who "saves" the small
town is a former member of the infamous Francoist *Brigada Político-
Social* [Social and Political Brigade], whose informing on leftist classmates at the university initiated him into the profession; he was an active member of Franco's repressive apparatus and a three-fold

traitor—to his classmates, to his biological father, a worker imprisoned during the dictatorship, and to his "adoptive father," Father Orduña, the leftist priest in charge of his education at an orphanage. Yet he is never depicted as an *executioner,* but, instead, as a *victim* of the ETA (not coincidentally, given Muñoz Molina's preoccupation with Basque terrorism), which threatened him for years in Bilbao and makes an attempt on his life at the end of the novel (albeit unsuccessfully, thanks to Susana Grey's love):

> Repetía precauciones ahora inútiles, mirar a la calle nada más levantarse, desde la ventana del dormitorio, buscando una presencia inusual, un coche o una persona no familiares en el vecindario, memorizar matrículas, cambiar sus itinerarios entre la comisaría y la casa, volverse cada pocos pasos para comprobar que no era seguido, mirar debajo del coche antes de subir a él.

> [He repeated precautions that were now useless, taking a look at the street from his bedroom window as soon as he got up, seeking an unusual presence, an unfamiliar car or person in the neighborhood, memorizing license plates, changing his itinerary between the police-station and his house, turning every few steps to make sure he wasn't being followed, looking beneath the car before getting inside].[14]

Given his past, we could perhaps compare the inspector with *Beltenebros*'s (1989) sinister Commissioner Ugarte, a "príncipe de las tinieblas, [que] habita y mira en la oscuridad" [a prince of darkness, who inhabits and looks in the dark], who "administraba las potestades del miedo desde un despacho de la Dirección General de Seguridad" [administered the powers of fear from an office at the General Security Headquarters], and who, like God, "[l]o oye todo y lo ve todo" [hears everything and sees everything];[15] or with "aquellos cabrones de sociales" [those bastard social cops] mentioned in *El jinete polaco* [The Polish Horseman]: "jóvenes, eficaces, brutales, de una chulería calculada y grosera, tan estridente como el color de sus camisas y el tamaño de sus corbatas y de las pistolas que esgrimían" [young, efficient, brutal, with a calculated and rude cockiness, as loud as the color of their shirts and the size of their ties and the guns they wielded].[16]

Yet, *Plenilunio*'s unnamed inspector is neither sinister nor cocky. Occasionally his thought processes lead us to believe that he was (or is), but the narrator does not criticize him or give any details about his actions, the tortures he engaged in or encouraged, or the lives he destroyed. Instead, given that he would now use these same methods on the perverse child murderer, they seem to be fully justified:

Tenía que encontrar la cara de un desconocido para castigarlo porque
había matado y para impedirle que volviera a matar pero quería encon-
trarla sobre todo para mirarlo a los ojos y concederse durante unos se-
gundos o minutos un arrebato de amenaza, para atrapar a ese individuo
por las solapas o por el cuello de la camisa y mirarlo al fondo de los ojos
desde muy cerca y *golpearle la cabeza contra la pared, para que se muriera de
miedo, para que se meara,* como se meaban tantos años atrás en las comi-
sarías los estudiantes, los detenidos políticos.

[He had to find the face of a stranger in order to punish him because he
had killed and to prevent him from killing again, but he wanted to find
him primarily in order to look into his eyes and allow himself a few sec-
onds' or minutes' threatening outburst, grab that individual by the lapels
or the shirt collar and look into the bottom of his eyes from very close up
and *hit his head against the wall, so he would die of fear, so he would pee on himself,* the same way students, political detainees, would pee on themselves
at police stations so many years ago].[17]

He is neither cocky nor sinister nor even ideologically convinced of
the necessity of his work. We learn that the inspector is weak and
pusillanimous, marked since childhood by an intense inferiority
complex due to his father's imprisonment; that he is a former alco-
holic; that he is married to a woman whom he has never loved and
who, as a result of the fear she has endured in the Basque Country
(and of his indifference towards her), is now in an insane asylum. Indeed, he is incapable of loving until, as one would expect in a novel
intended for a wide audience, he finds love with a teacher, Susana
Grey. His long history of betrayal and his participation in the *Brigada
Político-Social* are portrayed merely as rather unwise choices resulting
from a lack of initiative and an excess of resentment, as if they were
no more significant than becoming an accountant or a car salesman.
His betrayal of his social class and his fathers (the biological and the
adoptive) are motivated by resentment and shame ("la vergüenza, y
el remordimiento de sentirla, sí eran plenamente suyos, los atributos
íntimos de su identidad personal" [the shame, and the remorse for
feeling it, were fully his, his personal identity's private attributes],[18]
but they are not depicted as overwhelming, tormenting feelings with
which readers might perhaps empathize, nor as the source of a com-
pensatory thirst for power. His choices are almost trivial, inspired by
inertia: "Pensó que a cada uno nos retrata del todo un solo gesto, y
que ése era el que lo retrataba entero a él: parado en el quicio de una
puerta, sin decidirse a dar el próximo paso, por inseguridad o miedo
de no ser aceptado, o tal vez, en el fondo, *por falta de verdadera convic-
ción, de simple impulso de vivir*" [He thought that each of us is fully por-

trayed by a single gesture, and that this was the one that fully portrayed him: standing at the doorway, hesitant to take the next step, due to insecurity or fear of not being accepted, or perhaps, deep down, *due to a lack of real conviction, of a simple drive to live*].[19]

However, the inspector is not an exceptional character in the context of Muñoz Molina's work. On the contrary, most of his characters involved in politics and/or positions of power are equally weak and lacking in initiative, capable of the greatest abjection and the greatest heroism purely out of inertia or habit. This is the case of right-wing and left-wing characters, of the representatives of Franco's repressive forces and the Republican and/or anti-Franco fighters. The inspector has much in common with Mágina's police chief in *El jinete polaco*, a somewhat grotesque character who is "atribulado por el miedo a sus inferiores" [distressed by fear of his subordinates] and publishes poetry under a pseudonym because he is afraid of being considered a "faggot";[20] who dislikes torture, but not out of ethical conviction or for humanitarian reasons, but only because he finds it to be "procedimientos [indignos], de una rusticidad tan lamentable como el arado romano" [undignified procedures, as sadly rustic as the Roman plough], and prefers "suero de la verdad y no bofetadas y amenazas, silla eléctrica en vez de garrote vil" [truth serum instead of slaps in the face and threats, the electric chair instead of the garrote].[21] But he also has a lot in common with *Beltenebros*'s Darman, a Republican fighter during the Civil War who is still involved in the anti-Franco struggle twenty-five years later, but now simply as a mercenary, motivated by money and a lingering inertia, deeply skeptical towards what he supposedly defends, and judging with equal bitterness the suffocating Francoist society and the anti-Franco fighters. This is also the case of *El jinete polaco*'s Commander Galaz, who is considered a hero in Mágina for having refused to second the Franco coup at the beginning of the Civil War, and who was subsequently forced into exile, but who, we discover, had not acted out of ideological conviction, but only because he could not tolerate that his subordinates disobeyed his orders.[22]

The same is true of the protagonist's grandfather, Manuel, who had been confined in a concentration camp after the war and, perhaps not coincidentally, is a violent, wife-beating man: "Si él estaba de parte de algo era del orden, y le gustaron siempre los desfiles y las ceremonias y se emocionaba leyendo en *El Debate* los discursos de Gil Robles, aunque también los de Julián Besteiro y los de Azaña" [If he was in favor of something, it was order, and he had always liked parades and ceremonies and became moved when he read Gil Robles's speeches, but also Julián Besteiro's and Azaña's, in *El Debate*].[23]

We find similar characters in *Beatus Ille* (1986). Jacinto Solana, a member of the Communist Party and author of militant pro-Republic poetry during the war (of which he is ashamed), who spends eight years in Franco's prisons and is later murdered (or so it seems) by the Civil Guard, joins the Republican forces more out of suicidal impulses than anything else:

> Beatriz me dijo que yo no había creído nunca ni en la República ni en el comunismo, que no había traicionado nada porque nunca hubo nada a lo que yo fuera leal, que si en el verano del 37 me alisté de soldado en el ejército dejando mi cargo en el Ministerio de Propaganda no fue para combatir con las armas a los fascistas, sino para buscar la muerte que no me atrevía a darme a mí mismo.

> [Beatriz told me that I had never believed in the Republic nor in Communism, that I hadn't betrayed anything because there was never anything I was loyal to, that if I enlisted as a soldier in the summer of '37, leaving my post in the Ministry of Propaganda, it was not in order to fight the fascists with arms but to seek the death I didn't dare give myself].[24]

Similarly, Minaya, a young anti-Franco fighter in the late 1960s, escapes to Mágina after being arrested by the Brigada Político-Social and, once there, is content to do research on his family's and Solana's past, and to initiate a romantic relationship with Inés.

On a closer reading, what these characters reveal is Muñoz Molina's effort to push back several decades the alleged "End of History and Ideologies," which is normally dated sometime in that vague period called "postmodernity," in particular after the fall of the Berlin wall in 1989; he thus invalidates with one stroke the utopias that shaped the most progressive period in Spanish history, the Second Republic, and kept the fight against fascism alive in subsequent decades.[25] Furthermore, the leftist representatives are portrayed overall in a worse light than the police. In this sense, *Beltenebros*'s Commissioner Ugarte is emblematic, a kind of *lapsus ideologicus* on the part of Muñoz Molina: he is sinister, power-hungry, a rapist, and a murderer, but we learn that, before becoming a commissioner and occupying an office in the infamous *Dirección General de Seguridad,* he had in fact been Valdivia, a member of the Communist party and anti-Franco fighter. The most cruel Francoist torturer thus turns out to be a Communist! Might we extend this conclusion to the Civil War and deduce that Muñoz Molina thinks the greatest atrocities were committed by the Republican side? Perhaps so, if we consider the description in *Beatus Ille* of the lynching of a fascist spy by the people of Mágina. The brutality displayed by these alleged communists and anarchists is unsurpassed by any description of fascist atrocities in any of his works. In any case, the comparison between fascism and communism is repeated throughout his writings and follows a contemporary trend.[26] As Higinio Polo has noted:

> El intelectual pretendidamente apolítico es el modelo que hoy está en el escenario: un intelectual que no tiene relación con los movimientos sociales y que se ha acomodado a la tramposa tesis de la victoria de la democracia sobre los totalitarismos, aceptando la equiparación del nazismo con el comunismo, y admitiendo la entronización de la economía capitalista y la sociedad de mercado como la más razonable, la más eficaz, la menos nociva, la que ha sido capaz de crear mayores cotas de riqueza.

> [The presumably apolitical intellectual is the model that today occupies the center stage: an intellectual who has no relationship with social movements and has given in to the deceitful thesis of the victory of democracy over totalitarianism, accepting the identification between Nazism and Communism, and accepting the enthronement of the capitalist economy and market society as the most reasonable, the most efficient, the least noxious, the one that has been able to create the greatest levels of wealth].[27]

Thus, in *Beltenebros*, 1960s Spain is depicted as a sordid and backward place: "Por los andenes y vestíbulos de la estación cundía un desorden desesperado e inmundo, una angustia de trenes perdidos o interminablemente retrasados que ensombrecía los rostros de fatiga y de insomnio y se adhería a las paredes y al suelo como una suciedad de hollín y de grasa no limpiada en muchos años" [The station platforms and lobbies were filled with a desperate and filthy disorder, an anguish of lost or endlessly delayed trains that gave faces a shadow of fatigue and insomnia and stuck to the walls and the floor like a sooty and greasy dirt that hadn't been cleaned in many years].[28] However, the anti-Franco environment suffers from a similar anachronism and decrepitude. Its members are described as "invulnerables al tiempo y a los efectos de la guerra conmemorada y perdida . . . , vestidos con una rancia pulcritud de maniquíes anacrónicos, muy pálidos, . . . inhábiles como difuntos que vuelven a la vida ignorando todas las cosas usuales" [Invulnerable to time and the effects of the commemorated lost war, dressed with the stale neatness of anachronistic mannequins, very pale, . . . unskilled like corpses who come back to life ignoring all the usual things].[29] They are outside time, oppressive, uniform, disciplined, mere pawns in a political structure that is as hierarchical as the army or the Church. For instance, one of the chiefs, Bernal, is said to have an appearance of "pulcritud eclesiástica" [ecclesiastical neatness]; Darman compares himself to a monk, and the party's di-

rectives are described as "intangibles viáticos en maletas de doble
fondo" [intangible viatica in false-bottom suitcases].[30] This critique
follows a trend initiated in the 1960s and intensified during the Transition years: discrediting the Partido Comunista de España (PCE)
[Spanish Communist Party] either by emphasizing the atrocities
communists committed during the Civil War or minimizing the significance of their opposition to the dictatorship in order to neutralize the enormous political credit they claimed for having led the anti-
Franco fight while other parties simply sat around waiting for the
dictator to die of old age.

Muñoz Molina's portrayal of the Franco period is not free of contradictions. It is true that he always describes it in negative terms, with
special emphasis on the all-encompassing fear: "desterrados, enterra-
dos, presos en las cárceles o en la costumbre del miedo" [exiled,
buried, imprisoned in jail or in the habit of fear].[31] However, while
the author acknowledges the prevailing fear and poverty, he nostalgically idealizes Francoist society, underscoring simple rural life, contact with nature, and family solidarity as "virtues" that have disappeared from today's world. This idealization may be seen in *Beatus Ille*
(precisely what the title alludes to) and *El jinete polaco,* but primarily
in *Sefarad,* in which several of the first-person narrators (one of whom
is the author himself, although many others share his traits) rant
against modernity and technology; by and large the novel revolves
around a nostalgia that is clearly symbolized by the title: "Sefarad era
el nombre de nuestra patria verdadera aunque nos hubieran expul-
sado de ella hacía más de cuatro siglos" [Sefarad was the name of our
true homeland even though we had been expelled from it over four
centuries ago].[32] In a 1991 article, Muñoz Molina noted:

La nostalgia perpetúa la mentira y obra en la memoria como una droga
cuyas virtudes anestésicas son inferiores a su capacidad de destrucción. Al
embellecer el pasado, convierte el horror en heroísmo y la derrota en gloria póstuma y consoladora, y la desgracia en una fatalidad indiferente a
los actos de los hombres que de antemano los disculpa por haberlos des-
encadenado.

[Nostalgia perpetuates lies and acts upon memory like a drug whose anes-
thetic virtues are less significant than its capacity for destruction. By em-
bellishing the past, it transforms horror into heroism and defeat into
posthumous and comforting glory, and misfortune into a fatality that is
indifferent to the acts of men and excuses them beforehand for having
unleashed them].[33]

If we apply this assessment to his own nostalgia, we can conclude that
Muñoz Molina's novels constitute a repeated attempt to *embellish* the

Francoist past, whose negative elements are depicted as mere chance or fate, rather than the result of concrete socio-economic forces and international alliances. However, he does not present defeat as "gloria póstuma y consoladora" [a posthumous and comforting glory]. Instead, there is almost a perverse complacency in his repeated allusions to the Republic's defeat, as if only the communists, and not the Spanish people as a whole, had been defeated: "Como si no hubieran pasado treinta y siete años desde entonces, como si no hiciera media vida que no viste un uniforme y que no tiene una patria y una República a las que mantenerse leal" [As if thirty-seven years had not passed since then, as if half a life had not elapsed since he wore a uniform and had a homeland and a Republic to remain loyal to].[34]

This view of the Left is very much on display in *Plenilunio*, in which the two leftist characters are presented in a very negative light. The most significant is Father Orduña, an anti-Franco priest who is depicted as naïve and decidedly anachronistic, whose faith in utopia is as ridiculous as his attachment to Catholic ritual—perhaps even more so. His home, the old orphanage that hosted clandestine political meetings and is now empty, is described in the following manner:

> [Q]uedaba, sobre todo, como un aire *anticuado* y familiar de *penuria,* las sillas y el sofá tapizados de plástico verde, con quemaduras *viejas* de cigarrillos, como en un piso de *pobres,* un frigorífico sobre el cual había, desde *tiempos inmemoriales,* un jarrón [con] flores *secas,* y al lado, en la pared, un calendario [con] una estampa *rancia* de la Sagrada Familia.

> [There remained, most particularly, like an *outdated,* familiar look of *penury,* the chairs and the sofa upholstered in green plastic, with *old* cigarette burns, as in a *poor people's* flat, a refrigerator that, from *time immemorial,* had a vase with *dry* flowers on top of it and, next to it, on the wall, a calendar with a *stale* image of the Holy Family].[35]

In short, it is permeated by vulgarity and anachronism, and is almost in ruins, a sort of "museo involuntario de otro tiempo, no muy lejano, pero sí muy desacreditado" [involuntary museum from another time, not too remote, but very discredited indeed].[36] Once again we might ask: "Discredited" for whom? And once again, the Church is compared to communism (or vice-versa). Thus Father Orduña displays "una doble obstinación dialéctica de teología y marxismo" [a two-fold dialectical stubbornness, theological and Marxist].[37] And, during a conversation with the inspector, the latter tells him: "Ustedes siempre andaban buscando traidores y apóstatas, gente a la que excomulgar . . . Los dos lados . . . Los curas y los del partido de mi padre. Mi padre consideraba a Stalin o a Fidel Castro o a Ho Chi Minh tan infalibles como ustedes al Papa. Por eso acabaron entendiéndose tan bien, tenían la misma afición a dividir el mundo entre leales y traidores" [You were always looking for traitors and apostates, people to excommunicate . . . Both sides . . . Priests and those in my father's party. My father considered Stalin or Fidel Castro or Ho Chi Minh as infallible as you guys consider the Pope. This is why you ended up getting along so well, you had the same fondness for dividing the world into loyalists and traitors].[38]

The second leftist character in *Plenilunio* is Susana Grey's former husband, a stereotypical 1970s progressive portrayed as an opportunist who uses his leftist ideology to manipulate his partner and who disguises his sexist domination with speeches about free love and open couples, "disfrutando a la vez de las ventajas del matrimonio y del adulterio, de la sinceridad progresista y del engaño de toda la vida, de la paternidad y de la soltería" [simultaneously enjoying the advantages of marriage and adultery, of progressive sincerity and conventional deceit, of fatherhood and singlehood].[39] Deep down, his attitude is not very different from that of the patriarchal bourgeoisie he apparently rebels against: "Todo eran normas . . . habíamos roto con la vida de nuestros padres y con las convicciones burguesas y el resultado práctico era que teníamos muchas más normas que antes, más detalladas y más dogmáticas, una norma para cada gesto y cada instante del día, como los judíos ultraortodoxos" [There were rules everywhere . . . we had broken with our parents' lives and bourgeois convictions and the practical result was that we had many more rules than before, rules that were more detailed and dogmatic, a rule for every gesture and every moment of the day, like ultra-orthodox Jews].[40] This critique of 1970s leftists is all the more effective because it is draped in feminist attire and thus appears to be progressive. Susana is, without a doubt, the most solid character in the novel, the only one who has courageously faced life, who is independent and strong, who knows what she wants and struggles to obtain it; and in the process she manages to save the inspector, first from his emotional stagnation, and later from a terrorist attempt on his life. Consequently, her former acceptance of her husband's revolutionary ideas can only be read as an unacceptable surrender, which, in the final analysis, re-legitimizes bourgeois principles such as religious marriage and parenthood: "En el fondo de sí misma no le habría importado casarse por la iglesia, pero desde luego no le dijo nada de eso a él, que también tenía ideas claras y estrictas sobre la ceremonia nupcial" [Deep down she wouldn't have minded a church wedding, but naturally she didn't tell him any of this, since he also had clear and strict ideas about the wedding ceremony].[41]

However, the most ideologically problematic element in the novel is the character of the murderer. He is clearly a pathological case, but his pathology has serious ideological implications. It is due to two primary factors. The first is class resentment: a fishmonger who has had to work since adolescence, he does not accept his social position and feels envy and hatred towards everybody, including his old parents and, especially, people with economic means:

> [U]no se parte el espinazo trabajando más horas que el reloj y todo se lo lleva luego el gobierno para pagarles pensiones a los viejos que no se mueren nunca, a los inválidos, a los estudiantes, para que los hijos de papá vayan a las universidades y coman con las manos limpias, sin tener que olérselas con repugnancia y lavárselas veinte veces al día, [en] vez de ganarse la vida diciendo a todo sí señor y sí señora y levantándose antes que nadie.

> [One breaks one's back working more hours than the clock and the government then takes it all to pay pensions for old people who never die, for invalids, for students, so that mama's boys can attend university and eat with their hands clean, without having to smell them in disgust and wash them twenty times a day, instead of earning a living by saying yes sir and yes ma'am to everything and getting up before anyone else].[42]

Following the dominant ideology according to which the individual is ultimately responsible for his poverty (a premise shared by neoliberalism, Francoism, and even the *ancien régime*), the low place he occupies on the social ladder appears to be fully justified by his lack of intelligence and moral conscience—and by his physical appearance, which (following the precepts of nineteenth-century naturalism, which condemned the working classes to genetic and physiognomic inferiority) reflects his inability to change: "La cara redonda, [la] barbilla muy pequeña, [parecía] que la cara no estaba terminada de hacer por abajo, el pelo negro, rizado, la frente estrecha, las cejas grandes, casi juntas encima de la nariz" [He had a round face, a very small chin, it looked like the lower part of his face hadn't been completed, black, curly hair, a narrow forehead, big eyebrows, almost joined above his nose].[43] He is similarly condemned by the indelible fish smell, which he cannot erase even if he washes his hands twenty times a day. The message is clear: workers will always be workers, even in those exceptional cases when chance may allow them to climb up the social ladder. As Vázquez Montalbán has put it: "Aquel al que la foto lo haya pillado rigiendo Wall Street, por toda la eternidad regirá Wall Street, y aquel al que lo haya pillado siendo etíope y muriéndose de hambre en Etiopía, toda la vida será etíope y se morirá de hambre en Etiopía" [The one whom the photo captures ruling over Wall Street will rule over Wall Street for the rest of eternity, and the one photographed as an Ethiopian dying of hunger in Ethiopia will always be Ethiopian and will die of hunger in Ethiopia].[44] As for the killer's resentment, the moral of the story is hair-raising: lack of conformity to the *status quo,* namely, transgression of the prevailing dogma, leads to monstrosity and crime. Deep down, the child murderer is not very different from the ETA terrorists who have harrassed the inspector for years: "Ahora imagina que es un terrorista, que saca una pistola del bolsillo de la cazadora y se la pone al guardia delante de la cara y le revienta el cerebro contra la pared" [He now imagines that he is a terrorist, that he takes a gun from his jacket's pocket and puts it in front of the guard's face and smashes his brains against the wall].[45] (Or vice versa: ETA terrorists and, by extension, all Basque nationalists are not very different from child murderers.) Furthermore, and not coincidentally, "la voz, muy educada y suave [le] hacía acordarse [a Susana Grey] de la voz de su ex marido" [his voice, very polite and soft, reminded Susana Grey of her former husband's voice], that is, of a 1970s leftist.[46]

Another factor is the killer's sexual ambiguity. The character has a deep inferiority complex due to the small size of his penis and his erectile dysfunction, and feels threatened by women because he cannot impose his virility on them. This is why he vents his sexual desire and longing for power on defenseless girls: "Le dice las mismas palabras que ha leído en las revistas y escuchado en las películas, las que no se atreve a decir en voz alta ni cuando ha ido de putas, le ordena, le exige, le abre la boca él mismo" [He tells her the same words he has read in magazines and heard in movies, those he doesn't dare to say out loud even when he's been with whores, he gives her orders, makes demands on her, opens her mouth himself].[47] This characterization seems quite reasonable from a psychological (pathological) point of view. However, it is also very dangerous, as noted in the novel by Susana Grey: "No me diga que están enfermos. . . . Que no pueden evitarlo" [Don't tell me that they are sick. . . . That they cannot help themselves].[48] Or, as María Jesús Izquierdo has stated regarding domestic violence: "Algunos hombres se presentan como un ejemplo de inhumanidad, algo *monstruoso,* ajeno al ser humano. Pero de este modo, lo que tiene su raíz en las condiciones estructurales de desigualdad social de las mujeres, y por ello les afecta a todas y no sólo a una parte, e implica a todos y no sólo a una parte de los hombres, se presenta como algo anormal, patológico" [Some men are presented as an example of inhumanity, something *monstrous,* alien to humankind. But in this way, what is rooted in the structural conditions of women's social inequality, and thus affects all women and not only a part of them, and involves all and not only a part of men, is presented as something abnormal, pathological].[49] The ultimate responsibility for the fishmonger's behavior lies in patriarchal ideology, whose obsession with masculinity and sexual potency fosters these kinds of aberrations. Carmen Magallón Pórtolas has used the apparently contradictory expression "pathological normality" to describe male behavior, since "la norma molde de normalidad se asienta sobre una base [patológica y] [e]sta normalidad patológica desemboca a veces en patologías individuales (asesinos, violadores ...) o institucionales (recurso a la guerra, al terrorismo, agresiones al cuerpo de las mujeres ancladas en tradiciones, etc.) agudas" [the standard of normality has a pathological grounding and this pathological normality sometimes leads to acute pathologies, both individual (murderers, rapists ...) and institutional (recourse to war, to terrorism, aggressions against women's bodies anchored on tradition)].[50] But *Plenilunio* does not offer such a profound analysis. The murderer is a monster, period. Moreover, by repeatedly ridiculing his diminished "virility," the narrator becomes complicit with patriarchal ideology and almost empathizes with him on this account (not on account of his class resentment, however): "Pero [la prostituta] enseguida comprendió que iba a ser difícil y acaso imposible, lo había sospechado en cuanto vio lo que había debajo de los pantalones vaqueros y procuró disimular su reacción, su sorpresa, *las ganas de hacer una broma*" [But the prostitute immediately realized that it was going to be difficult and perhaps impossible, she had suspected it as soon as she saw what he had under his jeans and she tried to hide her reaction, her surprise, *the desire to make a joke*].[51]

Within the context of this novel, which depicts independent women in a favorable light, this half-concealed legitimation of patriarchal ideology seems somewhat surprising. Not so, however, when we turn to Muñoz Molina's next novel, *Carlota Fainberg* (1999).[52] Here, the eponymous female character has all the attributes of the *femme fatale;* she is mysterious, tempting, and sexually insatiable, not to mention that she is most likely a ghost (a corpse?). Furthermore—and this is much more significant—feminist literary theory is attacked throughout the novel with an almost unbelievable rage. The Borges-admiring male narrator loses his associate professor position to a lesbian critic, who has the ridiculous name of Ann Gadea Simpson Mariátegui (parodying one of the pre-eminent Latin American Marxist thinkers) and who is described as "la Terminator del New Lesbian Criticism" [the New Lesbian Criticism Terminator].[53] As the head of the department explains, justifying the selection of the "Terminator" over the protagonist:

> Comprende que es una mujer y que es lesbiana. Más del diez por ciento
> de este país es gay y lesbian, Claudio. ¿Y cuántos profesores de este depar-
> tamento tenían hasta ahora esa sexual orientation? . . . [Mientras que tú,]
> ¿[s]obre quién das cursos, qué papers escribes? Siempre la vieja guardia,
> los viejos varones europeos muertos, y desde luego, eso sí, todos straight,
> el viejo machismo español no se rinde.

> [You must understand that she's a woman and a lesbian. Over ten percent
> of this country is gay and lesbian, Claudio. And how many professors in
> this department had this sexual orientation before now? . . . Whereas you,
> who are your courses on, what papers do you write? Always the old guard,
> the old dead European males, and of course, indeed, all of them straight,
> old Spanish sexism does not surrender].[54]

In this novel, feminism and respect for homosexuality are degraded
to mere political correctness and women's and homosexuals' access
to positions of responsibility are mere tokenism. It should be noted,
however, that the novel's attack against literary theory is not limited
to feminism and gay studies. In fact, the novel is a virulent pamphlet
against literary theory in all of its contemporary manifestations, from
Lacanian psychoanalysis to deconstruction to cultural studies (often
ridiculing real critics, such as Paul Julian Smith and Michel Fou-
cault); against what, in a 1997 lecture, Muñoz Molina had defined as
"esos *pervertidos* universitarios del lacanismo, la deconstrucción, el
posestructuralismo y demás *basura* franconorteamericana" [those
perverted academics of Lacanianism, deconstruction, post-structural-
ism, and other Franco-American *garbage*].[55]

Going back to *Plenilunio*, we should note that the narrative technique is also not innocent in ideological terms. All his other novels
have first-person narrators, in addition to one or more secondary narrators whom the former quote or paraphrase.[56] In typical postmodernist fashion, and despite the author's repeated criticism of postmodernism, the faithfulness and veracity of discourse is thus called
into question. Much has been written about the ideological implications of postmodernism, and it is not my intention to try to settle the
debate. Suffice it to say that, depending on the context, the full-blown
questioning of "master narratives" is either reactionary or progressive. This questioning can be reactionary when it is not limited to official discourses, but applies to revolutionary ones as well. This is particularly evident in *Beatus Ille*, where the lack of credibility primarily
affects Solana, the communist poet; what seem to be his memoirs,
also entitled *Beatus Ille*, are later found to be a set-up for Minaya, a
possibly invented version of the events the latter is investigating. This
not only calls into question the specific incidents narrated in the

novel (Solana's and Manuel's relationship with Mariana, and the circumstances of her death at the hands of a would-be fascist spy and subsequently official sculptor, Utrera), but also the description of historical events; perhaps the Civil War and the postwar were not so horrible, after all. At the same time, however, the questioning extends to the novel itself and to what the author apparently conveys, including the negative view of communism and the anti-Franco fight. In *Plenilunio,* the fact that there is an omniscient third-person narrator gives the contents of the novel, including the inspector's "heroism" and the murderer's "villainy," the status of unquestionable truth.

Despite the explicit condemnation of the Franco period, which is always presented as oppressive and suffocating in Muñoz Molina's work, in *Plenilunio,* as in many of his other novels, the author ends up legitimizing many of its ideological ingredients through his denial of the class struggle, his ridicule of the Left, as well as his glorification of an eminently genital "virility." These reactionary leanings are all the more dangerous because they are draped in progressive rhetoric, both within the novels themselves and in the press collaborations that make up the author's public persona.

NOTES

1. Jesús Ruiz Mantilla, "Hoy el compromiso es libre" [Today the Commitment is Free] [Interview with Jorge Semprún], *El País,* 8 August 2001. Emphasis mine.

2. Pablo Catellano, *Por Dios, por la Patria y el Rey: Una visión crítica de la transición española* [For God, for the Fatherland and the King: A Critical Vision of the Spanish Transition] (Madrid: Temas de Hoy, 2001), 11.

3. Montxo Armendáriz's film *Silencio roto* [Broken Silence] (2001), whose purpose is precisely to break the silence enveloping the anti-Franco struggles by the maquis [groups of guerrilla fighters], and Dulce Chacón's book *La voz dormida* [The Sleeping Voice] (2002), a fictionalized collection of testimonies by female political prisoners in the post-war, constitute significant exceptions in the current intellectual landscape.

4. As Manuel Vázquez Montalbán explains: "Si hacemos un análisis de contenido de los medios dominantes se percibe unicidad de motivaciones y finalidades en la transmisión de jerarquía de valores, aunque aparentemente unos medios se enfrenten a otros por las audiencias estrictamente mediáticas o por las audiencias electorales. Un medio puede apostar por una formación política, y los demás por otras, pero la visión de lo humano, de lo histórico, de la finalidad de la relación entre lo humano y lo histórico es esencialmente la misma" [If we analyze the contents of the dominant media, we perceive a unity of motivations and purposes in the transmission of a hierarchy of values, even if apparently some media fight others for strictly media audiences or electoral audiences. A medium may support one political group, and others may support others, but their vision of humankind, of history, of the purpose of the relationship between the human and the historical is essentially the same]. Vázquez Montalbán, *Panfleto desde el planeta de los simios* [A Pamphlet from the Planet of the Simians] (Barcelona: Crítica, 1995), 98.

5. Vázquez Montalbán, 45. Emphasis mine.

6. Elvira Lindo uses her husband for her chronicles, which normally appear in *El País*'s Sunday section (except during the month of August, when they appear daily under the title "Tinto de verano" [Summer Wine]), to make them more prestigious and, by talking at length about their private life as a couple, to give them the same type of sensationalist excitement that informs the tabloids. Although she is a well-known author of children's literature in her own right, she depicts herself as a dumb and frivolous housewife, whom her intellectual, albeit boring, husband attempts to educate.

7. Quoted in Julio Rodríguez Puértolas, "Democracia, literatura, y poder." [Democracy, literature and power] VV.AA., *Del franquismo a la posmodernidad* [From Francoism to Postmodernity] (Madrid: Akal, 1995), 276.

8. For instance, he has addressed domestic violence, comparing it to ETA terrorism and denouncing the complicity of judges and prosecutors ("Otro terrorismo" [Another Terrorism] [*El País Semanal*, October 2000]); he has bitterly denounced the persecution of homosexuality during Francoism ("Un dolor sin historia" [A Grief with No History] [*El País Semanal*, June 2000]); he has attacked the globalizing expansion of neoliberalism, sarcastically indicating that the only "revolution" capable of triumphing nowadays is that of "the rich against the poor"; and has criticized the increasingly widespread racism and xenophobia in Spanish society ("Los revolucionarios" [The Revolutionaries] [*El País Semanal*, July 2001]).

9. In numerous articles he attacks Basque nationalism with the same inflammatory language used by the PP and its followers or fiercely criticizes various communist leaders of the past and present.

10. Quoted in Anabel Díez, "El carné del cambio" [The ID of Change], *El País*, 5 August 2001.

11. Ibid.

12. Muñoz Molina, "La invención de un pasado" [The Invention of a Past], *Pura alegría* [Pure Joy], 216–17. Emphasis mine.

13. This attack is most virulent in his latest work, *Sefarad* (Madrid: Alfaguara, 2001), a hybrid text made up of fiction, autobiography, essay, and historical commentary, many of whose characters are historical figures persecuted by Nazism or Stalinism. Their suffering is depicted in detail. Only one of the victims is shown without any sympathy or empathy, as ultimately deserving his fate, and it is Willi Münzenberg, a member of the Komintern in charge of recruiting Western intellectuals for the communist cause: "Todas las mentiras que él ha contribuido a difundir manipulando y profanando los impulsos más generosos, las vanidades más grotescas, la candidez inextinguible de los inocentes [intelectuales]" [All the lies he has contributed to disseminate by manipulating and desecrating the most generous drives, the most grotesque vanities, the inextinguishable candor of the innocent intellectuals] (222–23).

14. Muñoz Molina, *Plenilunio* (Madrid, Alfaguara, 1997), 100.

15. Ibid., 189, 210, 141.

16. Ibid., 370.

17. Ibid., 15–16. Emphasis mine.

18. Ibid., 126.

19. Ibid., 475. Emphasis mine.

20. Muñoz Molina, *El jinete polaco* (Barcelona: Planeta, 1998), 268, 123.

21. Ibid., 122.

22. Ibid., 219.

23. *Plenilunio,* 115.

24. Muñoz Molina, *Beatus Ille* (Madrid: Seix Barral, 1989), 271.

25. In a 1993 lecture, he attributed the lack of success of *Beatus Ille* to the fact that, in those days, reflections about tradition or memory were not exactly fashionable in Spain. He observed that until a few years before, history and utopia had been the ruling drives among Spanish intelligentsia, but with history finalized, denied, or falsified, and utopia discredited, the Spanish intellectual class enthusiastically chose to limit itself to the present ("La Invención de un pasado," *Pura alegría*, 210). Yet even though he does not restrict himself to the present, he engages in the same "finalization" of History and "discrediting" of Utopia.

26. In a recent article, "Huesos de santo" [Saint's Bones] (*El País*, 12 August 2001), Elvira Lindo notes that her husband has bought the following books: *Hitler y Stalin: Vidas paralelas* [Hitler and Stalin: Parallel Lives]; *Franco, Hitler y los orígenes de la guerra civil española* [Franco, Hitler, and the Origins of the Spanish Civil War]; and *El libro negro del comunismo* [The Black Book of Communism]. This comparison is also the basis for *Sefarad*, which, as I already mentioned, deals with various historical characters persecuted by Nazism and Stalinism. Not coincidentally, Stalin is described in very similar terms to *Beltenebros*'s Commissioner Ugarte: "lo ve todo, lo escudriña todo" [he sees everything, he scrutinizes everything] (Muñoz Molina, *Beltenebros* [Barcelona: Seix Barral, 1989], 187).

27. Higinio Polo, "El intelectual cansado" [The Tired Intellectual], *El Viejo Topo* [The Old Mole] 152 (May 2001), 19.

28. *Beltenebros*, 64.

29. Ibid., 11.

30. Ibid., 47, 14, 29.

31. *Beautus*, 278.

32. *Sefarad*, 167.

33. Antonio Muñoz Molina, "El hombre habitado por las voces" [The Man Inhabited by Voices], *Pura alegría*, 146–47.

34. *El jinete polaco*, 25.

35. *Plenilunio*, 23. Emphasis mine.

36. Ibid., 23–24.

37. Ibid., 27.

38. Ibid., 127.

39. Ibid., 237.

40. Ibid., 227.

41. Ibid., 91.

42. Ibid., 184.

43. Ibid., 394. Perhaps this resurrection of Naturalism is not so surprising after all, given the similarities noted by Castellano between the 1970s Transition and the 1874 restoration of the monarchy (Castellano, 14).

44. Vázquez Montalbán, 47.

45. *Plenilunio*, 212.

46. Ibid., 285.

47. Ibid., 309.

48. Ibid., 140.

49. Ibid., 69–70. Emphasis mine.

50. Ibid., 103–4.

51. Ibid., 408. Emphasis mine.

52. Or when we consider his stance in the controversy that arose in the spring of 2003 over the publication of a collection of misogynous short stories in El Cobre, a publishing house co-owned by Miriam Tey, the director of the Instituto de la Mujer

[Institute for Women]. Hernán Migoya's book, titled *Todas putas* [All Whores], included a short story, "El violador" [The Rapist], considered by many to be an overt eulogy of rape. Numerous public figures called for Tey's resignation, but numerous others, including Muñoz Molina, supported her and the book. Muñoz Molina was among the 130 signers of a manifesto in defense of "freedom of expression" and against what they saw as "el germen de una nueva 'caza de brujas' al más puro estilo fascista" [the seed of a new "witchhunt" in pure Fascist style] (*El País*, 28 May 2003). Elvira Lindo, who also signed the manifesto, wrote a column in *El País* comparing Migoya's short story with, among other classic works, *Plenilunio,* since, in this novel, "el violador de niñas se despacha a gusto" [the child rapist speaks his mind] ("Los Indecisos" [The Undecided], *El País,* 21 May 2003). The comparison is hardly sustainable: *Plenilunio* is a work of fiction and the rapist is a complex, fully developed character, whose motivations are analyzed (and strongly condemned), and whom we would never confuse with the author. By contrast, Migoya's text hardly qualifies as fiction: it does not have a plot and the first-person narrator is not a literary character, merely a "voice" (which could easily be the author's) expressing the "benefits" of rape.

53. Muñoz Molina, *Carlota Fainberg* (Madrid: Alfaguara, 1999), 135.

54. Ibid., 167–69.

55. Muñoz Molina, "Max Aub: una mirada española y judía sobre las ruinas de Europa" [Max Aub: A Spanish and Jewish Look at the Ruins of Europe], *Pura alegría,* 124. Emphasis mine. It is worth noting that Muñoz Molina's critique of the United States academic system is fundamentally ill-informed. For instance, he confuses *assistant* and *associate* professors. The narrator is an associate professor but is being considered for tenure, which associate professors should already have. When an associate professor is considered for promotion to become a "full professor," the outcome of promotion review does not affect his or her tenure within the institution. In the novel, however, as another candidate is hired for his position, the main character has to leave the institution where he works. The novel also represents a poor, and rather tedious, attempt at imitating Spanglish. I wish to thank José B. Monleón for both of these insights.

56. What Muñoz Molina says about Juan Carlos Onetti is perfectly applicable to his own narrative: "Siempre hay alguien que cuenta o alguien que recuerda [y] los mecanismos de la memoria, de la palabra, de la invención involuntaria, de la ignorancia parcial, de la pura desfiguración del tiempo, son una parte de la materia contada" [There is always someone who tells or someone who remembers, and the mechanisms of memory, of the word, of involuntary invention, of partial ignorance, of the pure distortion of time, are part of the told matter] ("Sueños realizados: Invitación a los relatos de Juan Carlos Onetti" [Achieved Dreams: Invitation to the Stories of Juan Carlos Onetti], *Pura alegría,* 167).

BIBLIOGRAPHY

Castellano, Pablo. *Por Dios, por la Patria y el Rey: Una visión crítica de la transición española.* Madrid: Temas de Hoy, 2001.

Díez, Anabel. "El carné del cambio." *El País,* August 5, 2001.

Izquierdo, María Jesús. "Los órdenes de la violencia: Especie, sexo y género." In *El sexo de la violencia: Género y cultura de la violencia.* Edited by Vicenç Fisas. Barcelona: Icaria, 1998.

Lindo, Elvira. "Huesos de santo." *El País,* 12 August 2001.

——— . "Los indecisos." *El País,* 21 May 2003.

Magallón Pórtolas, Carmen. "Sostener la vida, producir la muerte: Estereotipos de género y violencia." In *El sexo de la violencia: Género y cultura de la violencia.* Edited by Vicenç Fisas. Barcelona: Icaria, 1998.

Muñoz Molina, Antonio. *Beatus Ille.* Barcelona: Seix Barral, 1989.

——— . *Beltenebros.* Barcelona: Seix Barral, 1989.

——— . *Carlota Fainberg.* Madrid: Alfaguara, 1999.

——— . "Un dolor sin historia." *El País Semanal,* 11 June 2000.

——— . *El jinete polaco.* Barcelona: Planeta, 1998.

——— . "Otro terrorismo." *El País Semanal,* 29 October 2000.

——— . *Plenilunio.* Madrid: Alfaguara, 1997.

——— . *Pura alegría.* Madrid: Alfaguara, 1998.

——— . "Los revolucionarios." *El País Semanal,* 15 July 2001.

——— . *Sefarad.* Madrid: Alfaguara, 2001.

Polo, Higinio. "El intelectual cansado." *El Viejo Topo* no. 152 (May 2001): 14–21.

Rodríguez Puértolas, Julio. "Democracia, literatura y poder." VV.AA., *Del franquismo a la posmodernidad.* Madrid: Akal, 1995, 267–77.

Ruiz Mantilla, Jesús. "Hoy el compromiso es libre" [Interview with Jorge Semprún]. *El País,* 8 August 2001.

Vázquez Montalbán, Manuel. *Panfleto desde el planeta de los simios.* Barcelona: Crítica, 1995.

www.falange.es: Hyperlinked Fascism

Eloy E. Merino

THE RESURGENCE—OR, INDEED, THE PERMANENCE—OF THE EXTREME Right in Spain has not received much attention in European and North American intellectual circles, especially in the past twenty years. It is assumed that right-wing radicalism in Spain more or less imitates similar movements in other European countries. A specific study thus seems unnecessary, because its research would add nothing to the classical studies on Nazism and Italian Fascism.[1] Another rationalization for not taking note of the radical Right in Spain is the movement's apparent weakness. Its political significance is evidently not a cause for alarm for historians, who prefer documenting other, more worrisome cases, such as the National Front in France or the M.S.I. in Italy.[2]

John Gilmour writes that for the extreme Right in Spain, "the situation has now become more critical than ever . . . the reality is one of ever-quickening decline into obscurity and ineffectuality."[3] The same can be said of modern Falangist groups. This essay aims to indirectly determine some reasons for this obscurity and ineffectiveness. Xavier Casals reports the electoral results of the first three general elections.[4] With varying degrees of success, the six Falangist-inspired groups managed to secure scarcely 125,000 votes between 1977 and 1982. According to the Spanish Ministry of Internal Affairs, in the general election of 1996 the Falangist parties secured 13,406 votes (0.05 percent of the total) nationwide. In the general election of 2000 this figure increased to 21,052 votes (0.09 percent).[5] In neither of the two campaigns, however, was it possible for the groups to place a delegate in the Cortes, the Spanish Parliament. So, as Rodríguez Jiménez argues, the different and consecutive revivals of FE de las JONS, taking place between 1975 and today, pathetically lagged behind in the consecutive electoral contests, each time with fewer militants and fewer votes. Further proof, in short, of the demise of Fascism in Spain.[6]

Neo-fascism and the extreme Right might be moribund, but they clearly manage to survive somehow in Spain. The Falange became officially extinct in April 1977, but it soon returned to the national arena, albeit in disarray, in many manifestations which the democratic process now fosters. It resurfaces in various forms, which all compete to recover José Antonio Primo de Rivera's legacy after the legalization of political parties there were several Falangist collectives that—unable to assemble into a single formation because of their ideological divergences—publicly claimed the use of the abbreviated title, FE de las JONS.[7] One of these collectives, led by Raimundo Fernández Cueta, obtained the legal right to employ the original title, Falange Española de las Juntas de Ofensiva Nacional-Sindicalista [Spanish Falange of the Committees of the National Syndicalist Offensive]. Among the score of groups that professed or profess José Antonio's political and ideological inheritance, this organization consciously strives to be the direct successor of the old Falange. By picking the original title, with no alterations, it drew nearer, or pretended to draw nearer, to the original party and its spirit. Significantly, Casals includes a section on those three Falangist associations which are markedly "dissident" in nature: FE de las JONS Auténtica [Authentic Spanish Falange], the CEDADE, or Círculo Español de Amigos de Europa [Spanish Circle of Friends of Europe], and the FNJ, or Frente Nacional de la Juventud [Spanish Front for the Youth]. The first, formed in 1975, launched a leftist and virulently anti-Francoist rhetoric and presented itself as anti-fascist. CEDADE is the purest "neo-Nazi assemblage that has ever existed in Spain." The FNJ linked itself to European avant-garde neo-fascism.[8]

In the sphere of the more traditional Falangists (whom Casals does not discuss, probably supposing that they do not enter into the scope suggested by his book's title), Falange Española de las JONS is not the only political group to present itself as an inheritor of José Antonio's party. Beside it there appear F.E.A. (Falange Española Auténtica) [Authentic Spanish Falange], the Movimiento Falangista de España [Falangist Movement of Spain], and F.E.I. (Falange Española Independiente—Independent Spanish Falange),[9] according to the "Listado . . ." updated in October 2003. FE de las JONS, F.E.A., and F.E.I. remain active. There are new parties as well, like Falange 2000, Falange Cristiana Democrática [Democratic Christian Falange] (F.C.D.), Falange Española—Frente Nacional-Sindicalista [Spanish Falange—National Syndicalist Front] (F.E.F.N.-S.), and Falange Española Nacional-Sindicalista [National Syndicalist Spanish Falange] (F.E.F.N.). Furthermore, there are two Galician Falangist groups and one from Asturias.

This essay offers a brief analysis of FE de las JONS as it represents itself on its Internet site, *www.falange.es*. In a certain sense this party is one that, through a tacit consensus among the other groups, presents to the Spanish electorate a general framework in which all the modern trends of Falangism would fit. It does so in a manner of a collective forum, without emphasizing differences and without causing major frictions; it is more prudent than some of the other Falangist movements.[10] My purpose is not to explore what distinguishes Falange Española de las JONS from its ideological counterparts, but to analyze some aspects of its ideological corpus in order to ascertain what still survives of the original agenda. I also consider newer aspects that have arisen in response to an obligatory adaptation to the imperatives of the democratic present. These aspects are signs of the party's evolution, as well as its residual contradictions. This essay does not present an exhaustive study of Falange's metamorphosis throughout recent decades. Only those more obvious aspects of the website are touched on, because their very inclusion determines their importance for the party leaders. Examination of these features should also, indirectly, clarify subjects that these leaders openly avoid (the situation of women in a Falangist society, for example). Of course, their website is not the only current textual source for the study of Falange; their *Nosotros* magazine, "Revista de análisis político de FE de las JONS" [Review of Political Analysis of FE de las JONS] and many other publications relay their message in different forms. I concentrate on the website, however, as it is the form with the most universal reach.[11] The party's use of the Internet initiates a new stage in its evolution—to the benefit or detriment of its adherents.

One of the recent European events to arouse anxiety in politicians and intellectuals alike is the rebirth of fascism and the extreme Right, a postmodern "fashogenesis."[12] The old Nazi and fascist parties wear new clothes in order to disguise their message, but they cannot avoid being lumped together. "Neo-fascism" is the one label that can embrace all versions of this revival. Several questions immediately arise: is the generic and modern Falange part of the extreme Right? Is the contemporary Falangist movement an instance of neo-fascism?[13] Or is it simply an inopportune and anachronistic Falangism, now resuscitated as a kind of post-fascism? As we shall see, to the Falangist militants whose writings are published on the website, the word "fascism" is quite an unpleasant term, and some of them reject it outright. For many people "the word *Fascist* is hardly value-neutral. It has become a curse, a term to be hurled at politicians, political parties, or governments that the user finds offensive."[14] The word became a pejorative qualifier after the end of the Second World War and is now used to label people or phenomena deeply disliked. It is both a label and a slogan.[15] Even though the name might not be welcomed by

Falangists, it is presumed in this essay that the foundational Falange is a fascist party. According to Stanley Payne, "there [were] no significant discrepancies between the codified doctrine of mature Italian Fascism and the official program and statements of Falangist leaders that were announced in 1934–35. Ideologically and structurally, historic Falangism was a generically fascist movement."[16] My study establishes how much of it has been transplanted to the present and demonstrates the link as evinced in the title of this essay, hyperlinked *fascism*.

There is a distinction between the terms fascism, neo-fascism, and extreme/radical Right. Paul Hainsworth writes that it could be misleading and unhelpful to apply wholesale the terms "fascism" and "new fascism" to the contemporary extreme Right, for "blanket usage of [such] terms [imposes] a coherence on post-war extreme right forces which misrepresents the diversity."[17] Because the extreme Right announces itself in a wide range of tenors and intensities, Hainsworth suggests that we consider fascism and neo-fascism as peculiar manifestations of the extreme Right, for "undoubtedly, then, [they] play a role within the extreme right and beyond it."[18] As for the differentiation between fascism and neo-fascism—aside from the indispensable updating of their tenets in accord with the historical, social and cultural context[19]—Jill Irvine argues that historical or classical fascism generally manifested a more universal and revolutionary perspective, "or at least a dedication to expanding the Fascist state's dominion over the widest possible territory."[20] Neo-fascism and today's extreme Right substitute for this expansionist approach a "fascism in one country" doctrine whose main concern has been achieving a pure nation-state founded on national exclusivity. Other historians insist on an important difference, for modern neo-fascist movements do not conspicuously reveal themselves to be anti-democratic or totalitarian in their political objectives or programs; instead they "work within the confines of their countries' democratic systems."[21]

Diethelm Prowe cites several critical differences between classical fascism and its modern offspring.[22] What provokes outrage and violence among neo-fascists today is the reality of an emerging multicultural Europe. This issue is of primary importance to voters on the extreme Right. Neo-fascist racism has been molded and nurtured by the process of decolonization and its turbulent aftershocks. The evolution of the extreme Right in Europe has taken place in a prolonged period of peace. Instead of unfolding as a remedial answer to the horrors of the last world war, "its roots [are] in a deep feeling of boredom, alienation and [a] sense of powerlessness."[23] Likewise, if fascism betweeen the wars was fed by generally worsened living conditions and hunger, neo-fascism grows within a politically stable and prosperous consumer society. Rather than being economically motivated, the perceived void is now psychological. The new Western European radical Right "has grown to its own maturity in a society in which democratic norms are no longer questioned by the vast majority of the population. This contrasts with the post-First World War breeding ground of fascism, when European states were still strongly shaped by traditional authoritarian—monarchial—military forces."[24] Neo-fascism is today an urban phenomenon, which no longer feeds on the romanticism of farming or myths of rural innocence. Finally, "transformation of the political culture of Western Europe has also changed the philosophical–ideological discourse of the radical right."[25] Arguments against the effects of the Enlightenment on European societies have faded away: "Holocaust denial has swept aside the fascist preoccupation with the anti-Enlightenment struggle."[26]

It is generally recognized that "no concise or all-inclusive definition of [neo-fascism] as ideology or as political, social, or cultural practice" can materialize. Different notions can be entertained "of what is crucial to a definition of neo-fascism in both historical and contemporary terms."[27] It is pertinent, though, to inquire whether or not modern Falange is a neo-fascist party within the range of the contemporary extreme Right's political affinities. My analysis of *www.falange.es* shows that a significant component of the Falangist political platform is consonant with the description Laqueur develops regarding the peculiarities of neo-fascism.[28] However, Falange does not exhibit some of the other characteristics of European neo-fascism—an alternate way of life, avowed paganism, the fear of immigrants,[29] strong anti-Semitism, denial of the Holocaust, racism—that according to Laqueur define a party as genuinely neo-fascist. Among the three variants Eatwell isolates (recidivist neo-fascism, radical neo-fascism, and hybrid neo-fascism), Falange fits into the third category, that of an "individual or party whose views have some clear links with the fascist past, but who in other ways seems to have broken with central tenets of Fascism."[30] This new hybrid fascism seeks a sort of synthesis of fascism and other ideologies (that of the green European parties, for example), which in a sense hides or camouflages the essentially fascist core. This hybrid character would perhaps explain some of the idiosyncrasies of Falange.

According to Jaroslav Krejçí, there are certain national conditioners in a given country that propitiate and sustain the resurgence and revitalization of neo-fascism:

loss of security: breakdown of law and order / humiliation: offended pride / collapse of the established system of beliefs / relative deprivation, either diachronic (with respect to an earlier period), or synchronic (with respect to other countries abroad) / irritation resulting from contrasting life-styles, possibly based on contrasting codes of behaviour / disputed border: one side longing for its change, the other concerned with the threat to its preservation / leadership losing popularity looks for a target towards which people's discontent could be directed / finally, a sense of frustration may be added as a general characteristic of the prevalent mood.[31]

It is not feasible to think that the situation in Spain at the end of the century would satisfy all of these requirements; democracy is by now firmly established in the country, and Spain suffers from those social conflicts afflicting other European countries on a much lesser scale. FE de las JONS might be better understood, then, as a kind of post-fascism, or as Payne calls it, *neo-Falangism*.[32] Its cyberspace manifestation could more aptly be called postmodern fascism, a label that underscores its hybridity.[33]

Falange today in Spain is thus an amalgam of the new and the old. The original ideological substratum is preserved, but it has also expediently adapted to the realities of today's Spain. At the website this mix of the new and the old, or this updating of the "same," is evident. My primary sources are the texts found in their website link called "Documentos" [Documents].[34] Some are reproductions of essays previously appearing in newspapers and were written by militants or sympathizers of the party. These political compositions in the electronic press serve two primary purposes: indoctrination (a vehicle of political propaganda), and internal and external clarification. A discourse that gradually begins to mark the boundaries, revising and polishing its contents in a parallel process of opening and withdrawal. This discourse is a recapitulation not so much of the old, of what we could call the classical underpinning of Falange, but of the new, the *neo*—of that which is incorporated and bursts into the party's notion of itself as it faces the Spanish and European present, neither of which it has the luxury of ignoring. Falangist discourse also invites controversy in the current Spanish political panorama, for it presents an alternative to what Falange considers ominous or inadmissible trends or facts in society (a nation of nineteen autonomous regions, abortion, secular education, divorce, separatism, etc.). Gustavo Morales censures the modern function of the Spanish press, without realizing that the means he uses to express his thoughts is also used to procure "the obedience of the masses."[35] He writes that *Falange.es*, like its democratic adversaries, behaves in its double capacity as a con-

veyor and a selector of information and judgment, not only as a legitimate candidate for a counterpower. It chooses the information to be
disseminated and the manner of presentation, the approach and the
time resource. The role of informing, of being the face and voice of
a piece of news, of telling the story according to the particular looking glass, cannot be alien to the struggle for control of a society.[36] As
Díaz de Otazú remarks, it is the published opinion creating public
opinion, rather than the other way around.[37] If the website is to get
any benefits for the electoral standing of the party, Morales cautions,
its success will be based more than anything else, on the ability to deliver a message with which the Spanish constituency can identify.[38]

Although texts conveying this message reassess the original ideology and renovate the teachings and premises of the original Falange,
they nonetheless underscore the permanence of the ideas and aspirations of those times. But recycled goods need some touching-up;
the old must be expounded through exegesis. If one of the potential
risks is living the present from a past perspective, professing to a fos-
silized political movement, an equally undesirable danger is "the outrage of judging the past with a mentality of the present, despising not
only the literal context, but the historical framework and the intellectual freedom of the [Falangist] author as well, including his right to
a utopia."[39] Fascist repositioning entails trouble on two fronts. Today's columnist walks a tightrope when he tries to both balance and
denounce two pernicious extremes: the antagonism between the
present (the right to vote) and the past (tradition) is deemed
"false."[40] The columnist looks for a difficult but indispensable compromise if he wants to be noticed by the Spanish electorate; he wants
to appear new without having to change, keeping the essence while
selling an alternate, novel façade. Thus he is occasionally compelled
to defend Falangist dogma from a past perspective in his interpretation of the present, and he has no guarantees of success. It is the price
to pay when the validity of the Falangist option is reasserted seventy-
one years after its birth. On the one hand, Morales argues, it is imperative to recognize and vindicate the notion that *nacionalsindicalismo* was conceived with a critical vision of reality, then, and it set
forth, along its condemnation, some unraveling outlines for most of
the problems of its time and neighboring geopolitical environment.
The ethical, social, and national alternatives articulated by the
founders had a rigorous novelty for the period in which they lived.
Some were even extremely advanced, without a solution of historical
continuity. On the other hand we must bear in mind that "if *nacionalsindicalismo* does not pay heed to the immediate history it will
not have a place in it."[41]

Some of the original ideas of Falange, however, are in no need of postmodern makeup and seem to retain their validity even today. Even when he/she appears to totally engage the present, the Falangist cannot avoid indirectly stressing the original approach. Aguinaga, for instance, disapproves of Falange being equated to ETA in the Spanish press. He is shocked when the press suggests finding an antecedent for the wrongdoings of the Basque *independentistas* in José Antonio Primo de Rivera, for such an assertion represents an "extreme degree of deformation and misinformation." Aguinaga calls it "ill-timed and unreasonable" to compare José Antonio with Basque terrorism just because both are known to have called for the destruction of the electoral ballot boxes. José Antonio's often repeated statement—that destruction is the noblest fate that ballot boxes could wish for—is one of the inauspicious ideas Aguinaga tries to deal with in the best possible way. His strategy is not to discredit José Antonio's assertion (although Aguinaga considers it a mere "splinter" of his discourse). He justifies José Antonio's harsh remark favoring violence against the state as a being commensurate with the behavior of the other political forces that opposed the Spanish bourgeois government of the Second Republic. He has in mind the PSOE [Partido Socialista Obrero Español—Spanish Socialist Workers Party] of Indalecio Prieto and his "dialectics of violence with hyperbolic climaxes."[42] If we are going to condemn the initial brutality of Falange, we should also censure its socialist counterpart in the turbulent 1930s, Aguinaga tells us. He makes the reader believe that in a certain sense Falangist violence could have originated as a reaction to the excesses of the socialists. Furthermore, political terminology had not yet established in the 1930s the now prevalent opposition of democracy and dictatorship; the reigning opposition then was between capitalism and communism. And the latter was unanimously considered a nightmare against which any counteracting violence was justified.

In the 1980s Falange used to openly support a morality of violence in its street propaganda, leaflets, and posters, instructing militants in its practice.[43] In 1995, however, already too conscious of the sour taste this left with the Spanish electorate, Falange officially renounced violence as "political performance."[44] Just the same, as in the case of the Catholic orientation of Falange, this issue remains a contentious one on the website, albeit not expressly stated. Some of the contributors appear uneasy about the need for violence. Others unequivocally praise it as one of the early Falangist tactics that now does not require excuse or attenuation. Antonio Castro reads José Antonio's call for violence "only on the defensive level, as a response to others' aggression, or as a firm and decisive presence in any field"—that is, a passive violence. José María Permuy completely justifies it to deal with abortion, which is viewed as itself a violent attack against the sanctity of life. Other authors do not need any social or political catalyst to advocate violence.[45] Gustavo Morales is very straightforward: negotiating Spanish sovereignty is like predicating that the Constitution the Spaniards passed is wet paper *and that with a gun you get more profitability than with votes.*[46] Böhmler grounds the logic of violence on metaphysical and religious foundations. He opposes man's physiological preoccupation for peace and tranquility or for the sake of his bodily survival to the frenetic struggle for spiritual existence. For Böhmler, consequent affirmation of the worth of violence is but the extreme denial of the anthropological materialism inherent in liberal and socialist ideologies. Violence well-channeled is in the service of order, and order is love, the Augustinian mission to create and protect man's original, sanctified vocation. Thus "without violence there is no order, neither in the individual's life nor in the political community's." Violence is legitimate when an ideal justifies it. It is not arbitrary; it is not the "Hitlerite, Stalinist, and abortionist genocide." The end justifies the means. When reason, justice or the Homeland are attacked with violence, the response is violence.

A deep aversion to abortion is another useful pretext for slipping into an apology for violence. Just as Basque terrorism calls for a strong response ("retributive justice in giving each one what each one deserves"[47]) the destruction of the ballot boxes and the manifestation of party violence are justified as a forceful reaction to the democratic Spanish state, "a devil's deception . . . a derelict association."[48] Through voting—"some ballot papers deposited in a cardboard box and their diabolic obstinacy"—the government allows the absolute crime of abortion. To combat this Satanic philosophy[49] a radical solution is called for, one that would not reside in elections but in violent rebellion, after which a new order (in no way coinciding with the New World Order) would be established, in the judicial, political, and economical fields, replacing the decrepit and unfair contemporary legal arrangement. A new order for a new Spain and for a new civilization of eternal truths and immutable norms.[50] The legalization of abortion alone excuses violence against the reprobate Spanish democracy.

The final corollary (on José Antonio's concept of violence as a *floating idea*) is not a condemnation of violence per se. It is an operative tool set aside for an eventual opportune use. ETA does not have the sympathy of Falange, not because it besieges Spanish society with its customary ferocity, but because it does so for the sake of a taboo aspiration: the dismemberment of the Spanish nation. Violence in Basque separatism is a centrifugal maneuver. Falangist violence, conversely, tries to eliminate everything that might rend the historical fabric of Spain. Falange's is a centripetal aggressiveness that—as in the 1930s, against the political incursion of the socialists—would be amply justified now in order to fight Basques on their own ground.[51] Thus, curiously, and in tune with one of the main worries of the modern Falange, the epithet "fascist," now so feared and dangerous, is cast at ETA.[52] Basque terrorists come to be the comfortable consignee of the explosive adjective, as if proving that any association of Falange with contemporary political extremism would be an oversimplified generalization. Fortunately there is always "somebody" worse than Falangists, "for instance, fascist ETA."[53] When the "Saharian brothers" (those in the former Spanish Sahara who prefer a union with Spain rather than indepedence from occupying Morocco) are defended against the "abominable and despicable act of neglect" on the part of Spain, a question arises at once: "What dreadful crime have they committed[?] Not even the most bloodthirsty terrorist, from the gang of ETA separatist murderers is treated with such cruelty."[54]

The personal worth, ideas, and legacy of Falange's founder, José Antonio Primo de Rivera, constitute some of the party's essential links to the past ("his political and economic ideology is remembered as a splendid sign"[55]). This would explain selecting such an inauspicious political label as "Falange Española de las JONS" in the current Spanish political environment. In reading the documents posted on the web site, one has the constant impression that the past is a vexing residue, a volatile and inflammable ideological deposit that is to be handled with utmost care. Yet for all its risks it is also indispensable because it is the intellectual and political product of the beloved progenitor. The Falangist of today asks himself: How to preserve José Antonio's example and teachings without also embracing the party and its doctrine, both firmly connected to recent Spanish history? It is a bitter pill to swallow, for which no sweet antidote is at hand. With regard to José Antonio, nothing is questioned nor anything debated by today's Falangist commentators. At most they interpret him with the aim of smoothing over his less palatable ideas so as to re-appropriate the national political arena. Through recapitulation of his speeches, writings, and life—an apologetic, explanatory, and clarifying gesture—the original viewpoints are sometimes reaffirmed and sometimes slightly adapted to the present. But the very process of bringing them up to date and the very inclusion of José Antonio as a preeminent star in the current Falangist constellation tell of the strong connection between the movement's two stages. As Böhmler believes, "J.A. is a master of commanding ideas."

One of the ideas that Falange's annotators have emphasized is the *third way* (tercerismo), a notion that was already implicitly interpolated in José Antonio, but that now is expounded openly, under its proper name. Gustavo Morales devotes an entire essay to the topic. First he outlines the idea's properties in the recent past, "in order to define the options that were equidistant from the ideologies of the two big blocs, Anglo-Saxon liberalism and Soviet socialism." Morales perceives *tercerismo* as an offspring of a generic fascist component. Thus he states that *terceristas* "have clear objectives and they carry them out in a direct fashion. Its militants are imbued with an almost religious notion upon which, to achieve the fulfilment of the future's ideals, they must be lived in the present in a socially significant way"— a euphemism for the plea for violence. The *third way* depends likewise on the appearance of an exceptional, charismatic leader. When the party errs it is because the nation fails to produce "a mastermind in each generation." Morales then notes with sadness how European Social Democracy has seized *tercerismo,* making out of it "good merchandise with some clientele in the peripheral territories" upon the banishment of Left and Right during the postmodern globalization.[56] The solution for the Falangists, who have been robbed of the initiative, is a metaphysical *third way,* a hidden and ideal Homeland that would captivate imagination by its brilliance and reason by its purity, generating such energy that it could not be animated by a sensible and comfortable aim, limited by discrepant left and right aspirations and confined to legal, possible, and neutral boundaries. They want the formulation of a national myth, a legend that would unleash insurgent forces.[57]

Another key concept in José Antonio's philosophy is the transcendent power of the Homeland. Again and again in his speeches and writings, the term and its significance are emphasized. Clearly, in the current Spanish panorama of nationalistic fragmentation, his ideas mean to bring together all those Spaniards who, while feeling little sympathy for the resurrected Falangism, are uneasy about or regret the course of events in Catalonia, the Basque country, and Galicia. Starting from José Antonio's often reiterated definition of the Homeland as *a unity of destiny in the universal,* the closest a common citizen comes to such harmony and intelligence is the Homeland—which is first and foremost an intellectual event "because it transcends what is merely sensible, and as such unity is something superior to the sum of individuals." Patriotism is not a pretext for compromise, but is the "elemental impregnation with the telluric."[58] Belonging to a concept of humankind means moving into a limbo, whereas the scope of the Homeland is much more accessible.[59] Equating the concept of Homeland with the mold of an authoritarian state, as detractors of Falange have done, is a fallacy, Castro writes. Another mistake is to accuse José Antonio of investing the duty to the Homeland with the same passion as the duty to God; this instrumentalizes religion and renders it utilitarian. But the Homeland for Falangists of yesterday and today is a potential reality, rather than an actual one. For José Antonio the concept of Homeland, according to Castro, goes beyond the strictly ideological. It is historical, social, and voluntaristic. It is dynamic, resolutely open to the future. It exists as a polestar, but it has to be made, it must be grounded, become earthly. Thus Morales talks about a "hidden and ideal Homeland,"[60] a national myth. Without mentioning it directly, the concept is present in the "Decálogo para las elecciones generales" [Decalog for the General Elections], where there is a demand for the "recognition of a unique national reality, Spain, resulting from the conjunction of peoples, which is resolved in an outcome that is not the mere algebraic sum of factors."

Nationalism in Spain today manifests a very different and more defined image than it did in the 1930s. As a consequence, the Falangist response is more specific and more virulent as well. It begins by labeling Basque separatists as "fascist." Böhmler is blunt: "Being a nationalist is nonsense." In the "Decálogo" they call for more severity in the punishment of terrorists and for comprehensive enforcement of anti-terrorism laws. And they reject "negotiation with ETA. The use of force should never legitimize a political stance." A document from the Spanish Royal Academy of History, reproduced on the website in its entirety, refers to the sorry state of the teaching of Spanish national history in the autonomous regions. A Falangist militant might well share the document's conclusions, especially given his/her concerns for some negative consequences of Catalonian, Basque, and Galician nationalisms.[61] The Academy's approach is transparent: "The chance to study its unique history cannot be denied to each autonomous region. But the drawback is that 'everything that divides us, everything that in the past has led us to fight one another, is stressed', which can induce xenophobia and racism."[62] Falangist militants, likewise, deplore their invisibility in the school curriculum: "Falange is History with the same right to be taught as the others."[63] Morales objects to giving Basque political prisoners, "professionalized murderers," a regal treatment in Spanish penal institutions. Whereas, "if you have stolen anything all the furies of Hell will fall on you. Whether you repent or not, you will serve your time in prison surrounded by all sorts of mafias." Morales distrusts the ability of the Spanish people to prevent the atrocities of the separatists, and he implicitly proposes a retaliatory policy of comparable force ("retributive justice in giving each one what each one deserves"). Violence against violence. "Blood that would not overflow, or youth that would not dare, is neither blood nor youth, it neither glitters nor blooms," concludes Morales, quoting José Antonio.[64]

In the domain of religion there is no substantial evolution within Falange, although Permuy readily acknowledges that the sociological reality of Spain has changed since Falange's founding in 1933. Falange, he writes, is aware that advancement and consolidation of a perverse process of secularization has induced and is still inducing many Spaniards to apostasy, to religious indifference, or to tepidity. To the extent that probably, and sadly, Spain soon could stop being— "if it has not already done so and we do not react with urgency"—a sociologically Catholic nation.[65] The country may want nothing to do with faith, but the Catholic personality of the party has never been questioned since its formation. This religious attribute, Falangists believe, markedly separates them from the Nazis and Italian fascists.[66] But the controversy over the degree and commitment of Falangist Catholicism has crucial importance in the present. On this issue there is, as usual, little uniformity of criteria among the militants. One of the most common accusations leveled against Falange in the 1930s by its enemies on the Right was that it championed a dubious paganism or incredulity.[67] It is true that originators of the movement would have preferred a discernible separation between the two powers, State and Church. Ledesma Ramos, the founder of the JONS, cautioned in 1935 that:

> The national revolution is a task to be fulfilled by Spaniards, and Catholic life is a thing of humans, to save their souls. Let nobody carry their affinity to extremes, intertwine or confuse them, because they are quite different . . . Spain, comrades, does not need patriots that christen her with names. There are many suspicions—and they are more than suspicions— that patriotism gets adulterated under Church wings, it weakens and decays. The yoke and arrows, as a war emblem, would propitiously substitute the cross to preside over the days of the national revolution.[68]

And in his "Norma programática de la Falange" [Programmatic Norm of Falange] José Antonio reiterates what he had already stated on several occasions. He reminds the reader of the Catholic spirit of the future national reconstruction, but also calls for the necessary separation of powers: "The Church and the State will coordinate their respective faculties, without allowing for any meddling or any other activity that might impair the dignity of the State or national integrity."[69]

That today's militants cannot yet agree on this topic is confirmed in the website's own documents. All party members share the identification with and passionate acceptance of the Catholic religion, for not one of the main concepts that sustain the party's ideology can be separated from it without entailing the loss of their *raison d'être* (Homeland, *tercerismo, Hispanidad,* etc.) and risking confusion with the ideology of the opposition or the competitors. But the assimilation of religion into the party's political aspirations leads some to bewilderment and others to exasperation. Permuy is a very firm supporter of National Catholicism, the successful Francoist formula put into practice after the disengagement from European Fascism in 1945. National Catholicism means "that the [Catholic] state, as a perfect society, submits to and registers in its Constitution of Fundamental Laws the commitment to observe and meet the moral duty with Catholicism as the only Church of Christ, to which all societies are bound."[70] Permuy's proposal is based on four factors: 1) the state's public declaration of Catholic worship; 2) a legal codification of Christian inspiration "and the observance of the Authority of the Church as the supreme instance, ultimate and unappealable, in reference to the correct interpretation of moral laws, revealed and natural, grounds and source of indispensable inspiration for civil law";[71] 3) recognition of the Church as a "perfect society" with extensive powers; and 4) re-christianization and re-evangelization of the country. Permuy desires neither a caesaropapism nor a theocracy, though. Böhmler positions himself in the middle of these demands. His model is a country "where the supreme ruler by definition is not a tyrant but a father and servant to all," where the Christian perspective prevails and is the only way towards the consonance of diversity, "the union in the Catholic faith." The youngest among the militants have a more radical vision, more in tune with the original Falangism of Primo and Ledesma Ramos. In his book *Los fundamentos de la Falange* (declared an "official training text" by the party) Miguel Argaya Roca[72] writes that Falange "does not want a confessional State at all."[73] And Permuy strongly reproaches him: "When Miguel Argaya says that Falange does not wish a confessional State, what is he rejecting in a confessional State? Is he rejecting worship of God? Is he rejecting favoring the religious life of its citizens? [Is] he rejecting inspiring its legislation and government operation on the divine law originated from the Church?"[74] Permuy then goes further in locating the germ of Argaya's "incoherence," purporting to identify it in several contemporary Spanish Catholic bishops who have criticized the confessionality of the Francoist state and have warned against its repetition. Because he is exceedingly irritated by the fact that Falange might have been contaminated by this current of opinion (as Argaya's book demonstrates), Permuy suddenly explodes in his review: he believes that Falange needs to rectify itself in this sense because it is closing its doors, or stirring up serious problems of conscience in those of them who are fighting to secure a confessional State. If Falange does not want a confessional State, how would those who do want it fit in Falange? In his judgement, it is urgent that an official declaration from Falange be made with respect to this fundamental issue, in order to end once and for all the confusion today still prevailing.[75]

Falange longs to get hold of political power in Spain through elections, as is demonstrated by the "Decálogo," its political platform for one or both recent general elections in the country (1996, 2000). Here, as in other aspects of its ideology, the party is compelled to consider its discourse very carefully. The irony of a political party determined to abolish political partyism escapes no one. Falange first needs to win the elections, that is, to play the democratic game that nourishes that very partyism. Thus Falange waters down its statements for the Spanish voter. It does not dare to directly postulate the future prohibition of political parties but insinuates this to those who can read between the lines. Falange advocates a republic where the channeling of political participation would be made "through trade unions, professional associations, etc., *in addition to* the parties."[76] It desires the "legalization of other channels of parliamentary representation, dissimilar to political parties." In order to overcome what it calls a "democratic deficit of the current system," it supports a voting system based on listings open to scrutiny. It calls for legal responsibility for those who exercise public posts. It wants to break the "politicians' hegemony." It also demands the abolition of the sixth article of the Constitution.[77] In order to counterbalance the strong presence in the Cortes of nationalistic parties with only local orientation, a reform of the electoral law is included as well. For internal consumption, however, it is not necessary to express such ideas with euphemisms. So Böhmler will quote for his readers José Antonio's teachings with respect to political parties.

Another very peculiar aspect of Spanish fascism is its urgent call to reinforce the cultural, social, linguistic, and political ties with all Spanish-speaking countries in the world, especially in Latin America. The name given to this doctrine was that of *hispanidad,* "a polemic in defense of traditional Hispanic culture and religion, both European and American."[78] It was elaborated in detail by Ramiro de Maeztu in his 1934 work *Defensa de la Hispanidad.* It is one of the characteristics that even more obviously differentiated José Antonio's party from his mentors in Europe. Detractors of *hispanidad* then and now have seen an imperialistic purpose in its aspirations. But supporters argue only for a cultural and spiritual recolonization of Latin America. This doctrine survived the *defalangization* of the Francoist regime after 1945 and was an essential part of its foreign policy, which explains why friendly relations with the Cuban government of Fidel Castro and other leftist Latin American administrations, so incompatible in principle with Franco's right-wing authoritarianism, were maintained during the Cold War.

The concept of *hispanidad* is likewise central to the current political program of Falange. In the "Decálogo para las elecciones generales" it occupies a preponderant place (see below). Four of the twenty-six documents included in the section "Documentos" in October of 2001 dealt directly or indirectly with the issue of *hispanidad*. With one exception, all were signed. Curiously, two articles on brotherly Falangist parties that existed or still exist in Spanish America were included, on Falange Boricua [Puerto Rican Falange] and Falange Socialista Boliviana [Bolivian Socialist Falange].[79] The former participated, together with other Puerto Rican political parties, in a massive protest march against occupation of the island of Vieques by U.S. Marines. In this struggle "you find members of the Partido Independentista Puertorriqueño [Puerto Rican Pro-Independence Party], nationalists, religious citizens, and Falangists, who, despite their ideological differences, in some cases deep, are united in a common cause standing up to the Yankee invader."[80] The editorial calls all "Hispanic comrades" to engage in solidarity with the Puerto Rican patriots, in "their drive to expel gringos from Hispanic lands, which are not limited to Vieques or Puerto Rico, but which extend to places like Malvinas [Falklands] or Gibraltar, where the British still occupy *our* sacred native soil."[81] The leader and founder of Bolivian Falange, Oscar Únzaga de la Vega, is remembered in a text dealing with that party. Únzaga was apparently murdered in 1959 by thugs from a rival party, the MNR [Revolutionary Nationalistic Movement]. He was a militant Catholic, and "possessed a *sui generis* political discourse, based on Italian Fascism and Spanish Falangism, and taught by Iberian priests in Catholic schools." Although it has "few militants," Bolivian Falange has not disappeared altogether. In 2001 a Falangist, Otto Ritter, got elected to the town council in the Bolivian city of Santa Cruz.[82] The universal vitality of Falange also reaches Africa. In Ceuta, one of the two Spanish strongholds on the continent, when Columbus Day was celebrated in 2001, close to four hundred people "gathered on the Plaza de Reyes to vindicate the unity of Spain and the Spanish sovereignty over Ceuta and Melilla."[83] Alejandro Guerra defends the *Spanishness* of Western Sahara, a former Spanish colony: "If anyone would bother to let the Saharian people speak freely, he would be surprised to find that this nation, despite having been betrayed by our current government, would gladly strive to regain its integral place in Spain."

The issues mentioned above represent, to a greater or lesser extent, an actualization of the original Falangist phraseology. One matter absent from the party's program in 1933, however, as it was then literally unthinkable in Spain, is the thorny problem of abortion. Four of the website texts are dedicated to its analysis and condemnation. Argaya Roca's is a statistical account of its practice in the modern world, in order to illustrate its reach at the international level. Díaz de Otazú's, Loma Pérez's and Permuy's are decisively vituperative. I have already cited the latter's vindication of violence in order to fight the "abominable crime." Díaz de Otazú censures both abortion and child gestation in laboratories. For him "a paradox has been perfected. To intimacy without fertility, fertility with no intimacy has been added."[84] Even so, it is abortion, "the bloodiest feature of modernity," that arouses his strongest indignation. Spain, according to him, now has the most hostile legislation to family tradition in all Europe. Díaz deplores the fact that, although Spanish political parties have not made any concessions on the subject of abortion, they have done so regarding more organized minorities like gays and nationalists.

If Díaz disapproves of abortion for religious reasons, Loma Pérez seeks a "purely political approach, as circumstances and effects are involved." For this purpose he first offers a study on the current regulation of abortion by the Spanish legislation and the positions of different political forces with regard to this issue. He also touches upon the methods of Spanish pro-choice groups. Then Loma admits that within Falange, which is not always in accord regarding other, equally controversial matters, a uniformity of criterion exists, "the response given up to now being practically homogenous, with some minor nuances, to the question by the different trends within our movement." Falange's position accords with the Catholic interpretation and is consequently against all kinds of abortion, in a "courageous, clear and totally unambiguous fashion." Loma is making an apology for life, he tells his readers, and thus considers it opportune to refer to other questions tangentially related to abortion (capital punishment, euthanasia, and genetic manipulation). Although the topic of the death penalty is absent from the "Decálogo" it is reasonable to assume that Falange would enthusiastically endorse it to exterminate "irrecoverable individuals." He means those who "treacherously, with premeditation, and in cold blood murder one or several of their brothers," a clear allusion to Basque terrorists. Euthanasia is unacceptable because it turns the state into "an administrator of life and death." On genetic manipulation of human beings, Loma Pérez prefers "to remain on the watch."

It is useful to briefly examine the "Decálogo para las elecciones generales," for it represents, omissions and veiled rhetoric notwithstanding, the political agenda the party displays before the Spanish electorate in order to convince it of the virtues of the Falangist alternative at the start of the twenty-first century. This political platform incorporates some aspects that were also absent from, or minimized in, the original Falangist program in 1933, such as the concern for the environment or the mention of homosexuals. The *decálogo* is a very interesting document, for it reveals some particularities of Falange that are otherwise absent from the website. I have in mind a certain liberal or quasi-democratic (postmodern?) image that appears to contradict the totalitarian spirit but that underscores the populist element in all fascisms. On most issues this element was already implicit in 1933, but now it is made explicit (the declared abhorrence of racism, for example). How much electoral demagogy and how much genuine political vocation there is in this *decálogo* is hard to say, unless Falange wins a parliamentary majority, a possibility that seems now remote, at least in Spain. To summarize my commentary, I have divided the salient issues of the "Decálogo," as they appeared in October of 2001 in *www.falange.es,* in two columns, A and B. Column A shows those aspects from the original Falangism that are still legitimate today. Column B displays those others which signal Falange's adaptation to present conditions in Spain and Europe. I want to call the latter column *suggestive* (the signal of an evolution in Falange; for example, Falange as a green party). Both columns are intimately related, and in many instances their correspondence is merely the updating of Column A (what alludes to *hispanidad,* for example). This juxtaposition clearly demonstrates how much of the old and the new comes into the picture and how modern Falange tries to balance the two, being true to its mixed nature (i.e., hybrid neofascism). Issues not mentioned in the "Decálogo" (role of the army, women's status, the classical features: hierarchy, military / religious service, the essential virtues of the Falangist militant, the value of mythical optimism against modern pessimism, the past-present equation, the concepts of race and caste, etc.) tell of either the convenience of concealing them for fear of a negative reaction in the electorate, or their negligible status on the current political scene.

A Aspects of Original Falangism Still Legitimate Today	B Adaptations of Falangism to Present-Day Conditions
Priority of *Hispanidad*	Opposition to racism
Republican form of government	For the cultural integration of immigrants
Political participation through trade unions and alternatives to political partyism	Dual nationality to Spanish-speaking immigrants
End to hegemonism or dictatorship of politicians	Legal responsibility for politicians
Abolition of article sixth of Constitution	Against representation of nationalist parties in the national parliament
Full employment	Withdrawal of educational competence from the autonomous regions
Against privatization of public companies	Respect for cultural peculiarities of historically Spanish regions
Empowering of social economy companies	Ecological leisure
Universal trade-unionization of Spanish labor force	Official policy to fight drug addiction and delinquency
Limits to foreign capital and investment	Fostering of ecological energies
Protection for small businesses	Reforestation with popular mobilization of an ecological police force
Cooperative exploitation of large landed estates	Total purification of waters
Unification of general education	Systems of compulsory manufacture of biodegradable or recyclable substances
Official and universal celebration of October the 12th (Columbus day)	Rigorous protection of biological and ecological wealth of Spain
Official politization of Spanish youth	Prohibition of abortion

A Aspects of Original Falangism Still Legitimate Today	B Adaptations of Falangism to Present-Day Conditions
Free education	Against child adoption by homosexuals
Proscription of all kinds of nationalism	Harsh punishment for sexual offences
Consistent enforcement of this punishment	Withdrawal from NATO
Acknowledgment of the unique national reality of Spain	Reinforcement of the European Union role
Public disclosure of values of justice and collective effort	Withdrawal of US troops / closing of bases
Against individualism (for a culture of the human being, against a culture of consumption)	Against negotiations with terrorists
Activation of demographic growth	Severe punishment for terrorists
Formation of a Ministry for the Family	
Vindication of sovereignty over Gibraltar	

I have gone over the nature of contemporary Falange based on the documents this political party discloses to the Spanish public on its website. I have also exposed some of the contradictions that, though they might be obstacles inherited from the past, continue to hinder the dissemination of the movement's social and cultural message: "We have been reminded, many times rightly so, that we are lacking in an actualized program, of concrete political solutions, of the ability to reply with celerity in the face of today's economic and social problems. We have been told that new issues have arisen, which could not receive the attention—not even possibly anticipated—in the [classical] times of the foundational Falange and by which we are overwhelmed."[85] Some of the matters reviewed above (violence, Catholic confessionality) conclusively reflect the contradictions burdening Falange—contradictions with no easy resolution. Today, part of this myth, José Antonio, "is the main reference for corrupt politicians who throw his name at each other as if it were a missile. We young Spaniards do claim being *joseantonianos* and we make ours his

legacy of courage, nobility and virtue. The others, the politicians by
trade, are not *joseantonianos*. They wish they were!"[86] Young militants
have let the old ones down. As illustrated by Permuy's reaction in the
face of certain statements found in Argaya Roca's book, the older militants are shocked by the nerve of the young generation. Loma Pérez
depicts the latter's attitude with greater frankness: "That we do not
like to be identified with the prudery, religious bigotry, and qualms
of conscience many of the others exhibit? Yes, it is true, as is true as
well that we feel a long way off from those who fill their mouth with
the word 'Spain.'" These young militants are those who seem to have
a more unobstructed idea about the party's limitations, or have a
sharper awareness of its inevitability. "But we are something else,"
Loma Pérez says in his essay, correcting himself immediately: "we
should be something else, that which, unfortunately or fortuitously,
is still going through a period of formation and regeneration."

Gustavo Morales, among all the authors included in "Documentos," is probably the only one to express himself with more passion
and less caution. He also reflects on the present and future of the
party.[87] Morales reminds his readers that Europe was going through
crucial events in the 1990s, "*glasnost, perestroika,* the fall of the Berlin
wall, and the reunification of Germany . . . a map absolutely unimag-
inable ten years before," events that should have marked a second
turnaround in the history of Falange (the first would probably be the
establishment of the short-lived *nacionalsindicalista* regime in 1939).
But instead of adjusting the historical situation to its advantage, the
party became entangled in a mean-spirited successional squabble,
fated "to be happy about the defeat of communism and then continue the longest and most sterile internal controversy in recent political history." Morales foresees a sad future. The program of 1933,
he says, today lacks the capacity to attract the Spanish populace because of its intellectual boldness. The masses still exist, but now they
do not faint from hunger, for now "they fill their carts in *Pryca* [su-
permarkets] or leave for the country twice a month [and] pay for
their houses with a mortgage loan." Ninety percent of the Falangist
electoral program and political message does not reach this populace. Morales warns that if *nacionalsindicalismo* wishes to be part of history in the twenty-first century in a better and more fruitful manner
than it had been in the twentieth, "it should realize whether in its
message there are any initiatives that, distinguishing the party from
the rest of the options on the political stage, would be understood
and assimilated as their own, and defended as such, by the popular
masses." Without a clear and palatable message for the voters,
Falange will become an antiquarian society, rather than an organiza-

tion with pretensions to political power ("after all today we are closer to the former than to the latter").

Falange formulates its political program in a universal forum, using the latest technology. It lets its adherents and enemies know where it situates itself on controversial issues, and what its weapons are. Certainly, Falange is not the originator of this practice on the Internet. Other European "extreme right-wing and racist groups have used the Internet in a highly efficient and publicly relevant way."[88] The Internet is that ideal propaganda tool José Antonio and the other leaders of the original Falange would have had in their wildest dreams. Goebbels "would have been proud of the many elegant web sites and the use of email to circumvent the many clumsy efforts at censorship."[89] Free use of the Internet by the extreme Right leads one to wonder about its convenience. Is it a panacea or a nursery for new monsters? Now that anyone can use it, it has become a suitable means for proselytizing the "practical ideal" or "practical knowledge," of which Falange is a bearer.[90] There is a peculiar paradox (a derivation of the hybridization effect) in the fact that the proselytization task of Falange, as a neo-fascist party, is carried out in such a democratic medium as the Internet. Falange's insistence—of which this website is a sign—on being taken into account by today's Spanish citizen and voter is a democratic exercise per se. By using the Internet Falange impugns the Internet's essence; the most democratic forum is used to pave the way to the most radical totalitarism. Falange joins its voice to the rich diversity of viewpoints the Internet provides, thus strengthening the democratic process on the one hand, but also threatening it with dissolution on the other. Those who wish to curtail democracy are in their own way helping to build the representative utopian dialogue the Internet is becoming. One of the most important objectives of Falange is to create a stable web of activists and sympathizers through email communication. As Schmidtke argues, Falangists "are able substantially to reduce the costs for a more efficient integration and coordination of dispersed groups which formerly communicated, if at all, rather accidentally via personal contacts."[91] They are nurtured by a sense of belonging through specialized hyperlinks: the computer-based communication has a crucial role in providing the medium through which protest actions can be coordinated and strategies planned. This also applies to an intensified international network among right-wing groups in Europe.[92] The low cost of website maintenance is ideal for enhancing the opportunities for interaction among militants and for the mobilization of allies, which can only be achieved through the dissemination of the Falangist political agenda and the bolstering of its political potency. Whether this can be accomplished remains to be seen in future Spanish general elections. It would not be unreasonable to attribute any boost in the electoral muscle of Falange to the success of its website.

NOTES

1. It is commonplace in works on contemporary Spanish history to write off this imitation (after which it is implicitly or explicitly noted how superfluous it would be to dwell upon the ideology of Spanish fascism) as the mediocre acculturation of others' philosophy. In both cases, apparently, the reader would only need to go to those texts dealing with the peculiarities of Italian and French Fascism in order to gain an approximate idea of the nature of Spanish Falangism. The ritual, "slogans and cries de rigueur, the greeting with the raised arm, the uniform: nothing here was original, as neither the doctrine was, no doubt" (Julio Rodríguez Puértolas, *Literatura fascista española* [Spanish Fascist Literature]. Volumen I [Madrid: Akal, 1986], 31). But Spanish Fascism had its specific peculiarities, which made it into "something very *sui generis* and deeply contradictory" (Ibid., 52). [All translations are mine. I wish to thank Michael Mazzola and Lee Chapman for helping me with the first English version of this paper.]

2. In *Fascism's Return* (Richard J. Golsan, ed. [Lincoln: University of Nebraska Press]), published in 1998, six of the eleven essays included deal with the situation in France.

3. John Gilmour, "The Extreme Right in Spain: Blas Piñar and the Spirit of the Nationalist Uprising," in *The Extreme Right in Europe and the U.S.A.*, ed. Paul Hainsworth (New York: St. Martin's Press, 1992), 227.

4. Xavier Casals i Meseguer, *La tentación neofascista en España* [Neofascist Temptation in Spain] (Barcelona: Plaza y Janés, 1998), 50–51.

5. "Congreso—Resultados por Partidos" [The Congress—Results by Parties], accessed from www.elecciones.mir.ed/MIR/jsp/resultados/index.htm.

6. José Luis Rodríguez Jiménez, *Historia de Falange Española de las JONS* [History of Spanish Falange de las Jons] (Madrid: Alianza Editorial, 2000), 538.

7. Casals, 121–22. This political fragmentation was derived from the divergence in interpretations of José Antonio's thought effected in Falangist circles. The struggle for the party name abbreviations also reflected the expectations based on the supposed magnetism they could exert on the electorate, as Sigfredo Hillers [leader of Falange Española Independiente] recognized in 1973. Upon converting Falange into a political organization he said that an association with the name of Falange Española would recruit more supporters than any other constituting in Spain, thus becoming the most numerous and powerful one (Casals, 123).

8. Casals, 124, 129, 135.

9. Ibid., 50–51.

10. Actually this will for consensus is more factual than imaginary. According to Mariano Sánchez Soler, in order to end the *blue diaspora* (the dispersion of the Falangist movement into antagonistic factions), FE de las JONS publicly called in 1997 for the fusion of the different groups. FE de las JONS was preparing to lead an electoral 'blue front' and be the most potent organizing center in Spanish neo-Fascism (*Descenso a los fascismos* [Descent into Fascisms] [Barcelona: Ediciones B, 1998],172). After the 1996 elections, FE de las JONS has tried to become that "po-

litical nucleus around which turn as satellites all those entities and associations that would contribute to create a public opinion trend akin to Falangism" (Ibid., 177).

11. Sánchez Soler includes a list of thirty-four Falangist publications of very diverse orientation and scope (*Descenso*, 260–62).

12. Richard J. Golsan, "Introduction," in *Fascism's Return*, 1.

13. Emilio Gentile uses the term "neo-Fascism" "to label those postwar movements that: (a) claim to be the heirs of Fascism, (b) assert that the fascist regime was a positive experience in [Spanish] history, (c) praise Fascism as a valid ideology that can still provide solutions to the problems of modern society" ("Confronting Modernity: Italian Radical Nationalism in the 20th Century," *Italian Americana* 15.1 [1997]: 9). Falange claims to want nothing to do with the first and last assertions, but is in implicit agreement with all three. To Roger Griffin the prefix *neo* has a connotation of "offering something new with respect to inter-war phenomena" (*The Nature of Fascism* [London: Routledge, 1993], 166).

14. Leonard Weinberg, "Introduction," in *Encounters with the Contemporary Radical Right*, eds. Peter H. Merkl and Leonard Weinberg (Boulder: Westview Press, 1993), 5.

15. Trond Gilberg, "Ethnochauvinism, Agrarian Populism, and NeoFascism in Romania and the Balkans," in Merkl and Weinberg, 95.

16. Stanley G. Payne, "Spanish Fascism in Comparative Perspective," in *Reappraisals of Fascism*, ed. Henry A. Turner, Jr. (New York: New Viewpoints, 1975), 162.

17. Paul Hainsworth, "Introduction. The Cutting Edge: The Extreme Right in Post-War Western Europe and the USA," in Hainsworth, *The Extreme Right in Europe and the U.S.A.*, 5.

18. Ibid.

19. The new fascism, Laqueur argues, can gather strength only if it adjusts to the changed conditions. As military aggression and conquest are no longer feasible, neo-Fascism has opted for the defense of European values: "Neofascists promise to take tougher action against drug users and pornographers and to restore family values. These 'value conservatives' (Wertkonservative) also invoke the need to do more for the environment; indeed, ecological concerns have become a central issue in their propaganda in the 1990s." Morality is replaced by bioethics, and good is what is good for the planet. There is an ideological affinity between sections of New Age and neo-fascist ideas: "Seen in this light, neo-Fascism could be interpreted as part of a movement trying to fill the spiritual void created by the decline of religion." (*Fascism. Past, Present, Future* [New York: Oxford University Press, 1996], 93–95.) Fascism is not about "to revive as a mass movement in its classic form, typified by jackboots and paramilitary rallies. But a new strand is emerging, which is learning to repackage Fascism for the twenty-first century—a process that is being helped by important intellectual, economic, and political trends" (Roger Eatwell, *Fascism. A History* [New York: Penguin Books, 1996], 352).

20. Quoted in Golsan, 5.

21. Ibid.

22. Diethelm Prowe, "Fascism, Neo-Fascism, New Radical Right?" in *International Fascism. Theories, Causes, and the New Consensus*, ed. Roger Griffin (London: Arnold Publishers, 1998), 312–20.

23. Ibid., 314.

24. Ibid., 316.

25. Ibid., 319.

26. Ibid., 320.

27. Golsan, 14.

28. See note 19; also Laqueur's second chapter, 93–144.

29. It is true, though, that although Falange welcomes immigrants from Spanish-speaking countries, it most probably would reject *en masse* arrival of Arabs or black Africans.

30. Eatwell, 360.

31. Jaroslav Krejčí, "Neo-Fascism—West and East," in eds. Luciano Cheles, Ronnie Ferguson, and Michalina Vaughan, *The Far Right in Western and Eastern Europe*, 2nd ed. (New York: Longman Publishing, 1995), 6.

32. Payne, *Fascism in Spain. 1923–1977* (Madison: University of Wisconsin Press, 1999), 467.

33. Gentile characterizes the "new right as post-modern right-wing 'political existentialism' to distinguish it from the political modernism of Fascism" (16).

34. Some of the texts I found in October 2001—when I started my research for this paper—have been omitted later. Those still found at the time of the paper's final revision are dated accordingly (31 January 2004).

35. Gustavo Morales, "Prensa y poder político" [The Press and Political Power], accessed from www.falange.es. 31 January 2004. Morales is a former national leader of FE de las JONS and briefly was publisher (September 1997 and April 1998) of the right-wing newspaper *Ya*.

36. Ibid.

37. Francisco Díaz de Otazú, "Liberalización, comercios y festivos" [Liberalization, Retail and Holidays], accessed from www.falange.es. 31 January 2004. Díaz is a Falangist from Asturias. He is also a militant of *Comisiones obreras* [Worker Commissions], a leftist labor confederation formed in 1962.

38. Morales, "España, Europa y Falange española" [Spain, Europe and Spanish Falange], accessed from www.falange.es. 31 January 2004.

39. Enrique de Aguinaga, "José Antonio y las urnas" [José Antonio and the Voting Booths], accessed from www.falange.es. 31 January 2004. Aguinaga is Professor Emeritus of journalism at the Universidad of Madrid and board member of the capital's Atheneum.

40. Andreas Böhmler, "Apuntes sobre la filosofía política de José Antonio Primo de Rivera" [Notes on José Antonio Primo de Rivera's Political Philosophy] accessed from www.falange.es. 31 January 2004.

41. Morales, "España."

42. Aguinaga.

43. Through its "Cursos de formación de mandos" (1983) [Courses for Officer Training], where it was recognized that violence in itself is pure barbarity, but "it can be justified when it is used for a noble purpose" (Sánchez Soler, *Los hijos del 20N* [The Heirs of 20N] [Madrid: Temas de hoy, 1994], 106).

44. Sánchez Soler, *Descenso a los fascismos*, 175–76.

45. José María Permuy, "El aborto y la constitución de 1978." [Abortion and the Constitution of 1978], accessed from www.falange.es. 31 January 2004.

46. Morales, "España." Emphasis in original.

47. Miguel Ángel Loma Pérez, "Falange contra el aborto" [Falange Against Abortion], accessed from www.falange.es. 31 January 2004.

48. Permuy, "El aborto."

49. This identification of the ideological enemy with the demoniacal is a tested practice, commonplace in the early Falangist discourse. Then the satanic camp included homosexuals, lesbians, freethinkers, francophiles, spiritualists, the urban workers, converts, Protestants, prostitutes, feminists or liberated women, republican Madrid, among others (see Merino, index: "Satanás").

50. Permuy, "El aborto."

51. In an increasingly atomized Europe, neo-fascism has the job "to rebuild the unity of the world, [and] for those of us here, as the immediate task, the unity of Spain" (Böhmler). We could apply the disquietude José Antonio directed toward to the nineteenth century to the end of the twentieth, which also shows the same pattern of disintegration (Böhmler is quoting José Antonio in order to anchor his statement). In 1935 the founder had warned that Spanish men, the Europeans, had "been disintegrated, [had] been uprooted, [had] been turned into numbers in the electoral lists" (José Antonio Primo de Rivera, *Obras completas.* Agustín del Río Cisneros and Enrique Conde Gargollo, eds. [Madrid: Ediciones de la Vicesecretaría de Educación Popular de F.E. y de las J.O.N.S., 1945], 66). In a liberal allusion to the urgent need to re-cement the pieces of Spain running away (the centrifugal reality then and now) José Antonio called for "the human life to become more tightened and more secure, as it was in past times" (Primo, 119).

52. So writes Permuy on this burning question: "Let us not be deceived by those who pretend to defraud us selling as new, beneficial, and original (even as perfectly assimilable by Falange and pertinent to its doctrine), old and withered, intrinsically perverse ideologies that have been shown to be ineffective to rule societies the right way." On the contrary, he argues, they have given proof of a diabolical capacity to sow the world with the most terrible mistakes and horrors ("*Los fundamentos de la Falange.* Un libro de lectura obligada" [The Fundamentals of Falange. A Book for Required Reading], accessed from www.falange.es. 31 January 2004). Antonio Castro Villacañas for his part reminds the readers that if "it is possible José Antonio's discourse might lack of intellectual refinement to some, certainly it has nothing to do with a net fascist discourse" ("Los discursos de José Antonio" [José Antonio's Speeches], accessed from www.falange.es. 31 January 2004). José Antonio's Falangist ideology "is gradually becoming a political doctrine, that not being at all adverse to Italian Fascism and Mussolini, has nothing to do with them, and much less with Nazism," as José María García de Tuñón Aza, a historian from Asturias, determines ("José Antonio: cita con la historia" [José Antonio: An Appointment with History], accessed from www.falange.es. 23 October 2001).

53. Morales, "Prensa."

54. Alejandro Guerra, "La españolidad del Sahara" [Spanishness of Sahara], accessed from www.falange.es. 31 January 2004.

55. Böhmler.

56. Morales, "Las terceras vías" [The Third Ways], accessed from www.falange.es. 31 January 2004.

57. Morales, "España."

58. Böhmler.

59. Permuy, "*Los fundamentos.*"

60. Morales, "España."

61. This document, perhaps written by an academician, or group of them, with Falangist affinities, curiously regrets that today Spanish nationalisms reject José Antonio's concept of "unity of destiny in the universal."

62. Real Academia de la Historia, "Informe de la Academia de la Historia" [Report of the History Academy], accessed from www.falange.es. 31 January 2004.

63. García.

64. Morales, "España."

65. Permuy, "La falange ante la iglesia y la religión católica" [Falange before the Church and the Catholic Religion], accessed from www.falange.es. 31 January 2004.

66. Böhmler reminds the reader that "religion and politics [are] quite distinct ideals [for] *nacionalsindicalismo,* National Socialism, and fascism. And this is precisely

why Spanish *nacionalsindicalismo* (Homeland, bread, and justice) does not offer any grounds for labeling it together with German nationalism (racial instinct, blood, and land), or with Italian Fascism."

67. See Rafael García Serrano, *Diccionario para un macuto* [Dictionary for a Knapsack] (Madrid: Planeta, 1979), 54. José Antonio also echoed this problem: "Everybody knows they lie when they tell of us that we are a copy of Italian Fascism, that we are not Catholics, and that we are not Spaniards" (Primo, 34).

68. Julio Rodríguez Puértolas, *Literatura fascista española. Volumen II. Antología* (Madrid: Akal, 1987), 8.

69. Primo, 526.

70. Permuy, "La Falange."

71. Ibid.

72. Argaya is a secondary school teacher and a poet. He was founder and director of *Omarambo*, a literary magazine.

73. Quoted by Permuy (*Los fundamentos*), who reviews the book.

74. Permuy, *Los fundamentos*.

75. Ibid.

76. "Decálogo para las elecciones generales", accessed from www.falange.es. 23 October 2001. Emphasis mine.

77. It reads: "Political parties express political pluralism, [they] concur in the formation and manifestation of the popular will and are fundamental instruments for political participation. Their creation and exercise of their activity are autonomous within the respect to the Constitution and the law. Their internal structure and operation will be democratic."

78. Payne, *Fascism in Spain*, 47.

79. According to Rosa Pardo Sanz, author of a study on the Francoist foreign policy in Latin America in the first six years of the regime, "the first sections were created [in the late thirties] in Chile, Argentina, Cuba, Mexico, and Uruguay. Their beginnings were hesitant, with great autonomy vis-á-vis the peninsula and grave leadership problems" (cited by Payne, *Fascism in Spain,* 343). Payne adds that "the largest FET membership, approximately a thousand affiliates, was in Uruguay, whereas the combined membership in all the rest of Latin America was only about four thousand. Nonetheless, the name inspired admirers, leading to the formation of such separate Latin American parties as 'Falange Nacional Chilena' [Chilean National Falange], 'Falange Boliviana,' and 'Falange Socialista Boliviana'" (*Fascism in Spain,* 343).

80. "Gibraltar, Malvinas, Vieques . . . la lucha continúa" [Gibraltar, Falklands, Vieques . . . the Fight Continues], accessed from www.falange.es. 23 October 2001.

81. Ibid. Emphasis mine.

82. "Oscar Unzaga de la Vega (Falange Socialista Boliviana)", accessed from www.falange.es. 31 January 2004.

83. "Falange celebra en Ceuta el día de la Hispanidad" [Falange Celebrates the Day of Hispanidad], accessed from www.falange.es. 23 October 2001.

84. Díaz de Otazú, "Aborto."

85. Loma Pérez.

86. Morales, "España."

87. Ibid.

88. Oliver Schmidtke, "Berlin in the Net: Prospects for Cyberdemocracy from Above and from Below," in *Cyberdemocracy. Technology, Cities, and Civic Networks,* eds. Roza Tsagarousianou, Damian Tambini, and Cathy Brian (London: Routledge, 1998), 73. Sánchez Soler offers a thorough list of right-wing websites en "Una inter-

nacional fascista en internet" [A Fascist International on the Internet] (*Descenso* 269–73).

89. Nicholas Fraser, *The Voice of Modern Hatred. Tracing the Rise of Neo-Fascism in Europe* (Woodstock, NY: The Overlook Press, 2000), 21.

90. Böhmler.

91. Schmidtke, 74.

92. Ibid., 75.

BIBLIOGRAPHY

Aguinaga, Enrique de. "José Antonio y las urnas." Accessed from www.falange.es. 31 January 2004.

Böhmler, Andreas. "Apuntes sobre la filosofía política de José Antonio Primo de Rivera." Accessed from www.falange.es. 31 January 2004.

Casals i Meseguer, Xavier. *La tentación neofascista en España*. Barcelona: Plaza y Janés, 1998.

Castro Villacañas, Antonio. "Los discursos de José Antonio." Accessed from www.falange.es. 31 January 2004.

Cheles, Luciano, Ronnie Ferguson, and Michalina Vaughan, eds. *The Far Right in Western and Eastern Europe*. 2nd. edition. New York: Longman Publishing, 1995.

"Congreso—Resultados por Partidos." Accessed from www.elecciones.mir .es/MIR/jsp/resultados/index.htm.

"Decálogo para las elecciones generales." Accessed from www.falange.es. 23 October 2001.

Díaz de Otazú, Francisco. "Aborto y política." Accessed from www.falange.es. 31 January 2004.

———. "Liberalización, comercios y festivos." Accessed from www.falange.es. 31 January 2004.

Eatwell, Roger. *Fascism. A History*. New York: Penguin Books, 1996.

"Falange celebra en Ceuta el día de la Hispanidad." Accessed from www.falange.es. 23 October 2001.

Fraser, Nicholas. *The Voice of Modern Hatred. Tracing the Rise of Neo-Fascism in Europe*. Woodstock, NY: The Overlook Press, 2000.

"Fundamento y crítica de la globalización." Accessed from www.falange.es. 31 January 2004.

García de Tuñón Aza, José María. "José Antonio: cita con la historia." Accessed from www.falange.es. 23 October 2001.

García Serrano, Rafael. *Diccionario para un macuto*. Barcelona: Planeta, 1979.

Gentile, Emilio. "Confronting Modernity: Italian Radical Nationalism in the 20th Century." *Italian Americana* 15.1 (1997): 8–17.

"Gibraltar, Malvinas, Vieques . . . la lucha continúa." Accessed from www.falange.es. 23 October 2001.

Gilberg, Trond. "Ethnochauvinism, Agrarian Populism, and NeoFascism in Romania and the Balkans." In *Encounters with the Contemporary Radical Right*. Edited by Peter H. Merkl and L. Weinberg. Boulder, CO: Westview Press, 1993.

Gilmour, John. "The Extreme Right in Spain: Blas Piñar and the Spirit of the Nationalist Uprising." In *The Extreme Right in Europe and the U.S.A.* Edited by Paul Hainsworth. New York: St. Martin's Press, 1992.

Golsan, Richard J. "Introduction." In *Fascism's Return.* Edited by Richard J. Golsan. Lincoln: University of Nebraska Press, 1998.

Griffin, Roger. *The Nature of Fascism.* London: Routledge, 1993.

Guerra, Alejandro. "La españolidad del Sahara." Accessed from www.falange.es. 31 January 2004.

Hainsworth, Paul. "Introduction. The Cutting Edge: The Extreme Right in Post-War Western Europe and the USA." In *The Extreme Right in Europe and the U.S.A.* Edited by Paul Hainsworth. New York: St. Martin's Press, 1992.

Krejçí, Jaroslav. "Neo-Fascism—West and East." In Luciana Cheles, Ronnie Ferguson, and Michalina Vaughan, op. cit., 1–12.

Laqueur, Walter. *Fascism. Past, Present, Future.* New York: Oxford University Press, 1996.

"Listado oficial de partidos políticos." Spain. Ministerio del Interior. Dirección General de Política Interior. Accessed from www.mir.es/politint/partpoli.pdf.

Loma Pérez, Miguel Ángel. "Falange contra el aborto." Accessed from www.falange.es. 31 January 2004.

Merino, Eloy E. *El nuevo* Lazarillo *de Camilo J. Cela. Politica y cultura en su palimpsesto.* Lewiston, NY: Edwin Mellen Press, 2000.

Morales, Gustavo. "España, Europa y Falange española." Accessed from www.falange.es. 31 January 2004.

———. "Las terceras vías." Accessed from www.falange.es. 31 January 2004.

———. "Prensa y poder político." Accessed from www.falange.es. 31 January 2004.

"Oscar Únzaga de la Vega (Falange Socialista Boliviana)." Accessed from www.falange.es. 31 January 2004.

Payne, Stanley G. *Fascism in Spain. 1923–1977.* Madison: University of Wisconsin Press, 1999.

———. "Spanish Fascism in Comparative Perspective." In *Reappraisals of Fascism.* Edited by Henry A. Turner, Jr. New York: New Viewpoints, 1975.

Permuy, José María. "El aborto y la constitución de 1978." Accessed from www.falange.es. 31 January 2004.

———. "La falange ante la iglesia y la religión católica." Accessed from www.falange.es. 31 January 2004.

———. "*Los fundamentos de la Falange.* Un libro de lectura obligada." Accessed from www.falange.es. 31 January 2004.

Primo de Rivera, José Antonio. *Obras completas.* Edited by Agustín del Río Cisneros and Enrique Conde Gargollo. Madrid: Ediciones de la Vicesecretaría de Educación Popular de F.E. y de las J.O.N.S., 1945.

Prowe, Diethelm. "Fascism, Neo-Fascism, New Radical Right?" In *International Fascism. Theories, Causes and the New Consensus.* Edited by Roger Griffin. London: Arnold Publishers, 1998.

Real Academia de la Historia. "Informe de la Academia de la Historia." Accessed from www.falange.es. 31 January 2004.

Rodríguez Jiménez, José Luis. *Historia de Falange Española de las JONS.* Madrid: Alianza Editorial, 2000.

Rodríguez Puértolas, Julio. *Literatura fascista española. Volumen I. Historia.* Madrid: Akal, 1986.

———. *Literatura fascista española. Volumen II. Antología.* Madrid: Akal, 1987.

Sánchez Soler, Mariano. *Descenso a los fascismos.* Barcelona: Ediciones B, 1998.

———. *Los hijos del 20N.* Madrid: Temas de hoy, 1994.

Schmidtke, Oliver. "Berlin in the Net: Prospects for Cyberdemocracy from Above and from Below." In *Cyberdemocracy. Technology, Cities and Civic Networks.* Edited by Roza Tsagarousianou, Damian Tambini, and Cathy Brian. London: Routledge, 1998.

Weinberg, Leonard. "Introduction." In *Encounters with the Contemporary Radical Right.* Edited by Peter H. Merkl and L. Weinberg. Boulder, CO: Westview Press, 1993.

Defending the Idea of Spain
against Democracy in the Texts
of Federico Jiménez Losantos

H. Rosi Song

*[P]udiera haber sido patagón o samoyedo, pero, en fin, soy español, que
no me parece, ni en mal ni en bien, cosa del otro jueves . . . Me interrogo—
como incumbe a cada uno—para desentrañar el ser de España. Si este
criterio es válido, y yo lo creo, nada que encuentre en mí podrá parecer,
siendo tan español, intruso en el carácter de la nación.*

*[I could have been Patagonian or Samoyed, but, after all, I am a Spaniard,
which doesn't seem to me bad or good, or something casual . . . I ask
myself—as one should—to unravel the meaning of the essence of Spain. If
this criterion is valid, and I believe it is, nothing that can be found in me,
who is so Spanish, will seem intrusive in the nation's character]*
(Manuel Azaña,"Una Constitución en busca de autor"
[A Constitution in Search of an Author] (1923)

FEDERICO JIMÉNEZ LOSANTOS, A UBIQUITOUS PRESENCE IN SPANISH
media and public opinion, has achieved near celebrity status with the
almost daily publication of his maverick columns in mainstream
Spanish newspapers. His career in journalism, which spans over two
decades, has taken him from media outlets such as *El País, Diario 16,*
and *ABC* to, most recently, *El Mundo,* where he has been delivering
his "Comentarios liberales" [Liberal Comments] since 1997. In addition to publishing many collections of essays, he has been a guest on
political radio shows such as "El primero de la mañana" [First in the
Morning] and "La linterna" [The Lantern], and has appeared on television programs on RTVE, Antena 3 TV, and Tele 5. Since 1999, he
has been collaborating with the triquarterly digital publication *La
ilustración liberal* [The Liberal Enlightenment], and in 2000 he
launched a digital newspaper called *Libertad Digital* [Digital Free-
dom], for which he writes weekly and serves as an editor.

Throughout his career in journalism and writing, this public intellectual, former educator, critic, author, media professional, and po-

litical analyst has criticized both the political Left and Right (although more often the former than the latter) to defend "la idea de España" [the idea of Spain] from what he calls the totalitarian mechanisms that are threatening its existence.[1] He has been extremely critical, in particular, of the cultural policies of the governments of the various autonomous regions of Spain. He sees the educational system of Catalonia and the Basque Country as threats to the entity of Spain. According to Jiménez Losantos, the teaching of local languages and cultures responds to the nationalistic interests of the different regions that instead of working from a comprehensive approach to achieve a harmonious coexistence among the different cultures that comprise Spain, practice policies of exclusion that are divisive and harmful to the rest of the nation.

In a recent effort to defend his idea of Spain, he has published another collection of short essays entitled *Los nuestros* [Our People] (1999). This compilation is especially noteworthy given that the factual tone of his earlier journalistic pieces gives way to a fictionalized view of the country's history, which highlights what he calls the idea of the Spanish nation and the relation to its cultural heritage. With a clear intention to manipulate the frame of the debate surrounding the country's regional politics, Jiménez Losantos introduces in his book a national genealogy structured around brief fictionalized stories of its most distinguished citizens to illustrate the need to preserve the future of Spain as a nation. In *Los nuestros,* he expounds a questionable view of Spanish history, culture, and language that ultimately contradicts his advocacy of civil rights and individual liberties. Taking into account the Spanish state as it stands today amid the dispute surrounding the cultural rights of the autonomies, positions like that of Jiménez Losantos invite closer examination, especially when they seem to resonate with a large audience.

Born in Orihuela del Tremedal (Teruel) in 1951 to a family of educators, Jiménez Losantos moved to Barcelona in 1971 to continue his studies in Spanish philology, which he completed with a thesis on Ramón del Valle-Inclán.[2] Intellectually inquisitive, he engaged in various cultural projects during his youth in this Catalonian city, participating in the creation of a Freudian society and becoming the first translator of François Lyotard's work into Spanish. He published the translation of *Discours, figure* [Discourse, Figure] in 1979. He was also the founding member, with Alberto Cardín, of *Diwan,* the acclaimed cultural magazine of its time. In 1978 his writing career took a fortunate turn when the publisher of the prestigious cultural journal *El Viejo Topo* [The Old Mole] awarded first prize for essays to his "La cultura española y el nacionalismo" [Spanish Culture and Nationalism].

When the same publisher considered printing his collection of critical essays entitled *Lo que queda de España* [What's Left of Spain], Miguel Riera, the principal editor, found the content of some of the essays highly controversial and turned it down. In 1979, the publisher of the competing cultural magazine *Ajoblanco* agreed to publish the compilation, and the first of many collections of Jiménez Losantos's essays appeared on the book market.[3]

Combining writing and politics, Jiménez Losantos ran in the Catalan elections of 1980 as a candidate for the Partido Socialista Andaluz (or PSA, the Andalusian Socialist Party) on a platform defending the cultural and civic rights of all Spanish immigrants. His political career came to an end when his party obtained only two seats, a number insufficient to have any influence in the government of the Catalan Generalitat. This short-lived political aspiration caused the eventual breakdown of his partnership with Alberto Cardín and *Diwan*, because Cardín was opposed to the endorsement of political campaigns in that publication. Parting with the journal, he began to write for *Diario 16,* where he signed the "Manifiesto de los 2.300" [Manifesto of the 2,300]. His signature attracted the attention of the members of the Catalan separatist group Terra Lliure [Free Land], who later kidnapped and shot him in the leg.[4] After the terrorist attack, Jiménez Losantos moved permanently to Madrid, where he has now become a regular pundit, appearing in a variety of Spanish newspapers, on television and radio shows, and on the Internet.

Jiménez Losantos's texts, journalistic and otherwise, are designed for the average citizen. They are clearly and succinctly written, amusing to read for their colloquialism and simplicity. Because they are ever-present in the public domain, this critic has become one of the most visible dissenting voices in Spanish media. His journalistic pieces, which follow Spanish politics as well as international affairs, are often picked up by foreign news sources, most notably by the Cuban American publication *El Nuevo Herald* [The New Herald] whenever this journalist harangues against the Castro regime.[5] His writing, once regarded refreshing for its nonconformist stance and use of slang and expletives, has also been the source of frequent controversies.[6] Along with his dismissive attitude toward contrary opinions, his sarcasm, and his scornful and personally offensive remarks, what is troubling in his writing are the sweeping generalizations he makes in order to hammer into the public consciousness his view of the uncertainties facing Spain in the future. A close review of his books and the texts he has written for newspapers shows a clear preoccupation with the idea of the nation of Spain and its relation to the Spanish language and culture. Jiménez Losantos believes this connection to be absolutely crucial to the continued existence of Spain. He justifies his belief by attaching notions of origin and authenticity to Spain's cultural inheritance and the writing of its history. This perspective, as will become evident throughout this essay, proves to be ultimately incompatible with his belief in individual freedom and civil rights, as the two positions are inherently contradictory.

Jiménez Losantos's ideological evolution throughout the years presents an interesting transmutation: having run the full spectrum from Left to Right, he is today considered one of the most conservative political pundits.[7] In his own words, he is an ultra-liberal interested in individual freedoms, and he considers himself to be a direct descendant of late-nineteenth-century Spanish liberalism.[8] Associated with the resistance movements against Franco's regime, this intellectual, like many others, was once affiliated with the Left—even with the Spanish Communist Party (PCE). He broke ties with this party in the 1970s after his trip to China where he witnessed the suppression of individual liberties. The historical failure of communism, which he recognized after the collapse of the Soviet Union, reaffirmed his earlier conviction to break with this political ideology. He currently defines the political Left as an idea of the past still clinging to distant utopian aspirations, while being incapable of offering any social or economic alternatives that could bring real progress to the country.[9]

Having experienced this change of opinion, Jiménez Losantos identifies himself as an opponent of any political party or ideology that endangers personal freedom. His current attacks on politics, domestic or international, deal with all types of totalitarianism that, in his estimation, assault individual civil rights or what he has termed "cultural rights." He believes that individuals should have the opportunity to preserve his or her original cultural background. By shifting the terms from civil to cultural rights, Jiménez Losantos turns the defense of what can be considered an individual's inalienable rights to a criticism of Spain's current regional politics. Addressing the political efforts made by Catalonia and the Basque Country to implement the cultural tenets of their regions within their respective education systems, he condemns these measures for the potential they have to curtail the freedom of the individual. He uses as an example the case of immigrants to Catalonia from other Spanish-speaking regions of the country, who, without leaving the nation's borders, are nevertheless obliged to function in a different language. A closer examination of his criticisms, however, reveals that Jiménez Losantos bases his opposition to these policies more on political grounds. His opinion that these policies are a direct affront to the cohesion of the nation comes from his belief that the compulsory use of different languages within the country will be disastrous for the future unity of Spain. He reckons that a common language shared by all communities is one of the most important elements to maintain Spain's national identity. He blames the regional politics that, in his view, are threatening Spain's future on the inability of the socialist government to recognize the importance of preserving the commonalities that exist between the different regions and cultures of the country.[10]

This criticism and concern for Spain are apparent in Jiménez Losantos's various collections of essays. In these writings he examines what he calls a particular idea of Spain and a particular idea of freedom to defend the preservation of the cultural legacy of Spain. The need for this defense comes, according to his viewpoint, as the result of the totalitarian practices of the Spanish socialist party (PSOE) and its president, Felipe González. His books, from *Lo que queda de España* (1979, 1995),[11] *La dictadura silenciosa. Mecanismos totalitarios en nuestra democracia* (1993), and *Contra el felipismo* [Against Felipism] (1993) to *Crónicas del acabóse. Contra el felipismo II* [Chronicles of the Limit: Against Felipism II] (1996), offer a description of purportedly antidemocratic policies that were put in motion beginning in 1982. Jiménez Losantos explains in his books how Spaniards reacted vigorously in 1996 against these practices by voting for the Partido Popular.[12] The criticism surrounding the politics of post-Franco Spain and the democratically elected socialist government of 1982 centers around three topics: what Jiménez Losantos calls "felipismo," nationalism, and "polanquismo." These terms refer, respectively, to the multiple financial scandals of the socialist government under Felipe González, the persecution of Spain and its language, and the limitation of freedom in the communications industry by the media and business mogul Jesús de Polanco.[13] His overarching concern, however, has to do with Spain and its future as a nation, where the only commonality that unites all communities is the Spanish (or Castilian) language. He believes that the inability of the government during the 1980s to recognize the importance of preserving a common heritage has been threatening the future cohesion of Spain.[14]

One of the pressing matters in the current politics of this Iberian country, as regional autonomies deal with their own cultural identities and the future of their own self-determining governments, is the relationship between the central state and its peripheries. This concern was evident in a recent issue of *Cambio 16,* where the question "What is Spain today?" was put forth in an editorial: "What do we call Spain? Is it a plurinational state? An autonomous state, comprising different nationalities and regions? A state without a nation? A nation of several states? It is becoming more and more difficult to know where we stand."[15] The texts of Jiménez Losantos hinge precisely on this apprehensive feeling that what traditionally was regarded as Spain, either in terms of history or of culture, is in dire need of revision or, even worse, no longer applies. He expresses this clearly in the introduction to one of his best-selling titles, *La dictadura silenciosa,* where he asks "¿Seremos capaces de reinventar, sin esperar a que lo intente el Gobierno, una España nueva y una nueva libertad?" [Will we be able to reinvent, without waiting for the Government to try, a new Spain and a new freedom?].[16] Despite the novel adjectives with which he chooses to present these concepts, an examination of his reasoning reveals that the "reinvention" of a "new Spain" and a "new freedom" can only come at the expense of putting into place old practices regarding issues of national identity. Jiménez Losantos recognizes that the regional governments have the freedom and the right to preserve their own cultural legacies, but he is convinced they should do so only while safeguarding the language of Castile and its culture that unites the entire nation. However, his argument to preserve these cohesive bases becomes problematic as he leaves unquestioned the origin of the primacy of the Spanish language and culture in the country's history. Advocating a problematic concept of cultural identity, whose legitimacy rests overwhelmingly in its own historicity and a nostalgic view of yesteryear, he defends a hegemonic cultural legacy amid the new organization of states and powers that replaces past centripetal practices.

Postmodern theories have facilitated the understanding of our relationship with the past. As Linda Hutcheon has observed, postmodernism, in the process of studying the politics of representation and the writing of history, has helped us recognize culture as a product of representation and not a source of origin.[17] Moreover, the theorization of the past from the post-colonial perspective, which looks critically at the articulation of national cultures and official languages, has enhanced our comprehension of how these discursive practices have been used throughout history as means of subjugation.[18] It has also helped us understand how concepts such as "tradition," "truth," and "originality" are used to shape our concept of an acceptable and "ordered" reality. As we attempt to recognize the mechanisms that are at work behind the articulation of concepts such as tradition and history, and the way authority becomes legitimized, post-colonialism offers a useful theoretical model to study modern nations as well. It is particularly relevant when analyzing Spain, which is currently struggling to find its "core" identity while mapping its future as a unified nation, and in so doing, is having to rely solely on its history. By shifting our attention to the intention behind the discourses that seek to legitimize or authenticate notions of national identities, we are able to discern their correlation with foundational issues. This intent can be regarded as a conscientious effort to inhabit the collective imagination, creating an illusion of communal legacy that appeals to culture and tradition and the need for their preservation. Studies that address the concept of "nation" as a shared community, termed by B. Anderson an "imagined community" and shown by H. K. Bhabha to rely on a necessary fictionalization of the past, propose a critical angle from which to revise existing efforts to avow the idea of nation.[19] As the writings of Jiménez Losantos reveal, these endeavors, once closely examined, still operate with underlying assumptions about categories of cultural identity and values. They are assumptions that, while superficially embracing pluralism, ultimately perpetuate intolerant attitudes regarding difference.

The political period that began after the death of Franco and the end of his dictatorship in 1975, known as the Transition, and the later government of the PSOE under the presidency of Felipe González, was a critical time in the development of Spain's national identity. As the country rapidly modernized politically and economically while reintegrating itself into the European and international political arena through membership in the European Union and NATO, it became radically regionalized, experiencing a process of political devolution from 1978 to 1983 that moved the country quickly toward a form of federal state.[20] Beneath all these modernizing changes, however, it was evident that the political transition was not an easy period; nor was it free of controversy. As the attempt in early 1981 to overthrow the government revealed, the transition to democracy was not a move that pleased all sectors of Spain's social and military order. Referring to the coup led by Lieutenant-Colonel Tejero, Teresa Vilarós has pointed out that the political process of the Transition failed in its original purpose of serving as a social and political revolution, becoming instead a mere compromising pact between the Right and the Left.[21]

A sentiment of disenchantment settled in among Spaniards after the failure of the Transition to revolutionize Spain, with the international and national economic hardship of the 1980s as a backdrop. At the same time, negotiations between the central and peripheral states that questioned relations between national and regional identities also raised questions about the future of the country. The political and economic changes also resulted, as Jordan and Morgan-Tamosunas observe, in new challenges concerning the effects of multiculturalism and ethnicities, not only within the different Spanish regions but also from the increasing numbers of immigrants and refugees arriving from North Africa, Latin America, and, more recently, Eastern Europe.[22] Considering these circumstances, and factoring in the context of globalization, it is not surprising that Spaniards are having difficulties understanding their place, and their identity, within their own country and the world. It could be argued that Jiménez Losantos's criticism of Spanish politics is merely symptomatic of these issues. His writing of *Los nuestros,* in fact, could be seen as a conscientious attempt to provide the missing commonality between the different communities that comprise contemporary Spain.

Jiménez Losantos believes that it was during the period of the Transition that the foundations for the future degeneration of Spain were established. According to his analysis, the local governments, faced with the weakness of a newly elected socialist government, used the democratic Constitution of 1978, which granted the right to regional autonomy, to put into practice extreme measures regarding language and culture.[23] He claims the mandatory inclusion of regional languages within the education systems creates a situation that mirrors, in reverse, the discriminatory practices of Franco's regime toward Spanish speakers. According to him, the linguistic policies of the Catalonian and Basque nationalisms affect the lives of millions of people who will be condemned to second-class citizenship, but more important, the policies will have fatal consequences for the Spanish nationhood.[24]

Reminding his readers of the number of Spaniards who immigrate transnationally, Jiménez Losantos points out the injustice that is being done when the descendants of these individuals, without even having moved outside their own country, are obliged to learn and function in a language different from the one spoken by their parents. Furthermore, he suggests that by mandating that these people function in a language they do not know, they will be inexorably stigmatized and eventually face discrimination. In truth, however, his criticism of the linguistic immersion program designed by the Generalitat in 1994 has more to do with what he sees as an irreversible movement toward the loss of a collective national identity than with any actual discrimination that is practiced against, for example, non-Catalan speakers in Catalonia. Likewise, his worries about the creation of second-class citizens in the region has more to do with the consequent future handicap facing the descendents of these immigrants, who he fears may be unable to function in the rest of their own country, than with the possibility they will adjust to their new culture through their newly imposed educational system.

By offering documentation of the different pieces of legislation that foment the use and implementation of regional languages,

Jiménez Losantos claims to demonstrate that the apparent "pluralistic" ideology driving laws trying to balance official and regional languages is in reality only an illusion. In practice, he argues, they respond to nationalistic interests and are extreme in their application. He illustrates this point by offering the results of a survey commissioned by the newspaper *ABC,* which found that 91% of Catalonian elementary schools do not teach anything that is Castilian.[25] Through an analysis of individual cases, consultation with specialists, and statistics on the shift in numbers between Castilian and other regional language speakers, Jiménez Losantos portrays a radical trend to impose and create a regional identity, even if that means suppressing part of the region's own history. As a key example, he refers to a brochure designed by the Generalitat introducing Catalonia to the rest of the world and distributed among international journalists in which there is no mention of Spain in any part of the region's history. He also complains about an advertisement for the 1992 Olympics, which, even though funded by the Spanish government and Spanish taxpayers' money, contained references to Barcelona and Catalonia but not to Spain.[26] What he wants to illustrate with these examples is how these practices threaten the future of Spain and its collective identity as a nation, and even more so when a common language that sustains its own existence is being driven out of study plans by "extreme" regional educational policies.[27]

The persecution being suffered by Spain's official language can be understood, according to Jiménez Losantos, as a reprisal from the political Left, based on the affiliation of Castilian with the Right, and therefore with Franco, that unavoidably surfaces when talking about the past 40 years of Spanish history.[28] It is his opinion that this blind hatred needs to be denounced, because the inability of intellectuals and politicians to unbind the idea of Spain from right-wing politics is endangering the future of the nation while they could be enabling its potential dissolution. Jiménez Losantos points out how the idea of Spain, ideologically objectionable due to its past political affiliation, cannot be embraced or even defended by the official government. Although his position has been harshly criticized or dismissed as unreliable overstatement by media outlets such *El País,* his arguments have connected with the Spanish public, as the success of his books and their multiple printings attest. *Los nuestros,* for instance, went through six consecutive editions in the year of its publication, and *La dictadura silenciosa* and the expanded edition of *Lo que queda de España* went through twelve and three printings, respectively, within the first months of their publication.

The relationship between the idea of "Spain" and the country's fascist past is, indeed, difficult to avoid, given the historical proximity of the term to its use by the Falangist party and Franco's dictatorship. One need only glance at the document "Fundación de Falange Española" [Foundation of the Spanish Falange] to witness an example of insistence on the idea of Spain as a unified fatherland and evidence of the desire to recover "el sentido universal de su cultura y de su Historia" [the universal meaning of its culture and history].[29] Under the leadership of José Antonio Primo de Rivera (1903–1936), fascism in Spain sought to employ the ideological framework of nationalism to enlist moral enthusiasm. In order to attain cultural and ideological hegemony over post-Civil War Spain, Francisco Franco (1892–1975) in turn adopted the idea of national unity and of traditional Spanish values as the foundation of his political cause. That this affiliation has influenced the shaping of later democratic governments is clear from the efforts they have made to achieve a clean break with the past while rendering obsolete any discursive markings or allusions that could remind the populace of past rhetorical practices.

Given this historical burden, Jiménez Losantos understands the need to disassociate the idea of Spain from this past. He argues, however, that the socialist government of Felipe González was unable (or unwilling) to accomplish this task, thus placing the future of the country in danger. It is for this reason that he makes an effort in his writing to articulate the basic features that define a nation and its identity and to promote the idea that, despite the political ideology or government of the moment, there are tenets that should remain essential and common to a specific group of people and location. For Jiménez Losantos, the importance of resisting the conflation of nation with politics—and, more specifically, of "Spain" with right-wing politics—is of utmost significance for the survival of the country. Distinguishing national identity from politics, he argues the importance of understanding the former as a product of a nation's culture and tradition that are fundamental to the comprehension of its history and the improvement of its future.[30] With the conviction that culture is made manifest in the fostering of its language and literature, he also believes that knowledge of that culture's history becomes indispensable to the effort to ground a civic conscience among its population:

No se puede tener una idea clara de los derechos ciudadanos sin conocer qué es y cómo se ha hecho la comunidad en la que uno vive, y eso es precisamente lo que viene sucediendo en España desde hace quince años: se tergiversa la historia y no se respeta la lengua común, sin las que toda educación colectiva queda al aire.

[One cannot understand the rights of the citizens without first understanding what these are and how the community in which one lives was made, and that is precisely what has been happening in Spain for the last fifteen years: history is being distorted and the common language is no longer respected, and in the absence of this, all collective education is being abandoned.][31]

Understanding and recognizing one's national identity has to do, in his estimation, with the embrace of its culture and the legacy of its literary tradition. For him, Spanish literature, backed by the "generous" tradition of Cervantes, "always" embodied a spiritual freedom (*Lo que queda* 159). He is the first one to denounce earlier abuses that were committed in the name of fanatical and excluding "españolismo" [Spanishness] because, according to him, this freedom needs to be protected and kept free of any material or ideological interest.[32]

The defense of Spain in the name of culture and tradition, however, should be questioned. Jiménez Losantos believes that difference can be achieved and embraced only when a common base is shared and acknowledged. In the case of Spain, the obvious element of cohesion is its language, which, vouchsafed by historical tradition and a rich cultural legacy, makes it "el único vínculo que permite re-llenar los soberbios baches históricos de la nueva nación" [the only bond that lets us compensate for the arrogant historical breaches caused by the new nation].[33] However, what becomes evident in this rhetoric is that the author fails to examine how this commonality is achieved. Culture and language are never gratuitous outcomes in themselves but the end products of the relentless practice of determinate social configurations that respond to the specific interests of a community or a nation. As Derrida has reasoned, language, in the form of monolingualism, is always colonial, because it "tends, repressively and irrepressibly, to reduce language to the One, that is, to the hegemony of the homogeneous."[34] But in Jiménez Losantos's view, a national culture, along with its official language, does not need to be questioned as much as it needs to be valued and preserved as a legacy of the past. Especially now when the linguistic, idiomatic, cultural reorganization, and the changes in the Constitution have caused a resurgence of nationalistic feelings and

[la] presión ideológica, harto primaria, del catequismo supuestamente progresista de los últimos tiempos está imponiendo—y, lo que es peor, acostumbrando para luego legislar—distorsiones gravísimas en el modo

de encarar la Historia y la Cultura de todos, repartidas cuidadosamente según el acta de bautismo de los protagonistas.

[The ideological pressure exerted by the supposed progressives of the recent past through their most basic catechism—and, what is worse, becoming accustomed later to legislate—is imposing serious distortions to the way we look at history and the common culture, distributed carefully according to the birth certificates of the culprits of these changes.][35]

Although he seems to grasp the procedure that puts political ideologies into practice ("acostumbrando para luego legislar" [becoming accustomed later to legislate]), he chooses to ignore the process by which the "todos" [everybody] to which he refers have received the historical and cultural legacy he is so keen to preserve.

Even as Jiménez Losantos admits to past abuses and injustices committed throughout Spanish history, he believes that its heritage, which he defines as its language, should not be demonized for earlier sins but embraced as a surviving lesson from the past for the benefit of the present. However, he never acknowledges the fact that the conservation and continuation of this language was achieved only through the self-perpetuating process of its own institutionalization. The "national" interest that drives him to write his journalistic pieces and essays about the current state of Spain and its future is not, in truth, too different from the very nationalistic extremes he denounces. His take on history and national identity and his consideration of language as the core component of a nation shares the very impositional qualities that he denounces in the regional cultural policies. If the future of Spain depends on its language and its cultural tradition, these can be fully preserved only to the extent that they are endorsed and supported by the official and authorizing institutions of the nation, which in turn can be translated only into the imposition of a set of cultural tenets with the purpose of advancing their eventual naturalization.

Bestowing superior importance to the cultural characteristics of a nation by considering them the source of its identity, as Jiménez Losantos does, responds to what Anthony Smith would explain as the perennialist approach to the understanding of nation and national identity. Holding the idea of nation as the "bedrock of human society," this perspective grants it a "primordial" natural order (which may need to be reasserted) as the result of "the power and enduring quality of the fundamental" cultural ties.[36] The perennialist perspective has contributed to fanatical stands surrounding the concept of nation because it upholds the notion of "our people," a community of any collective cultural identity that is seen to have survived throughout time immemorial.[37] History written from this perspective is often conflated with myth and "kernels of historical fact, around which there grow up accretions of exaggeration, idealization, distortion and allegory."[38] This practice is certainly reminiscent of Francoist historiography, which David Herzberger had characterized as a glorious epic narration of the past, centering in the heroic figure of Franco the fulfillment of Spain's historical destiny.[39] Although Jiménez Losantos is very critical of such practices and is the first to recognize the danger of extreme nationalisms, his essentialist view of culture and language is not very distant from the historical perspective of the perennialists. As an intellectual, he places value on the essence of culture, which he deems crucial to the perpetuation of Spain, for unless people assume "el hecho nacional-español como base o herencia del límite cultural que intentamos definir o incluso como clave esencial del pasado de esa cultura que hacemos o queremos nuestra" [the Spanish-national reality as the foundation or inheritance of the cultural limit we are trying to define or even as an essential key to the past of that culture that we make or want as ours)], there will be no future for this nation.[40]

It is from this perspective that Jiménez Losantos seemed to have compiled a chronicle of notable figures in the history of Spain and entitling it *Los nuestros*. Smith observes that intellectuals, as well as the wider stratum of the professional or intelligentsia classes, play an important role in the production of "mythistoire" and in the process of its legitimization, for as they become interested in rediscovering their past they reappropriate historically what has been traditionally handed down from generation to generation.[41] Through the narrativization of the past and the exaltation of its language, this process represents an evident interest in laying down the signs that "clearly [mark] off those who speak [the language] from those who cannot [because] it evokes a sense of immediate expressive intimacy among its speakers."[42]

Echoing the beliefs of Manuel Azaña, a man he greatly admires, Jiménez Losantos looks for a way to discuss and uphold, simultaneously, the ideas of freedom and devotion to the Spanish nation. He appreciates the manner in which Azaña was able to define a way to achieve freedom for the Spanish individual without having to question his or her Spanishness or the future of Spain. Jiménez Losantos's own writing can be interpreted as an effort to advocate the same ideas in the present. He has written, as mentioned earlier, that in order to save Spain, it was fundamental to assume "el hecho nacional-español" [the Spanish-national reality] as a base or cultural legacy that the community could opt to appropriate as its own.[43] *Los nuestros* could be interpreted as his conscious gesture to provide proof and foundation for this cultural and historical base. What is interesting about his collection, however, is that it reveals the paradoxical nature of his understanding of Spain's cultural legacy: while he perceives it as a phenomenon that takes precedence over politics or any type of ideology, he regards it as a choice that a community can make about its past.

Jiménez Losantos's remark implies that the essential nature of a cultural identity is not given, it cannot be automatically granted; instead, a cognitive effort must be made to recognize and preserve it. The origin of culture can be seen as arbitrary when its components seem to fit a purposeful reading of history and reality. As Edward Said explains, the term/concept "beginning" signals simultaneously to the idea of a continuity that flows from its inception while challenging that same continuity because it is "a creature of the mind" and "something of a necessary fiction."[44] Building on this observation, H. Bhabha questions, for instance, the nature of the discourse of literary history, pointing out how this type of narrative seeks to establish its legitimacy as it progressively works to distinguish the past from the present in a process where the "authority of the past is finally authored (and authorized) in the present."[45] On the one hand, the ordering of the past from the present implies a historicist and teleological perspective that finds, in its chronological organization and writing, "an organic, progressive approximation of reality, the accuracy of reflection."[46] On the other hand, the writing of the past "enables a perspective of essential order, coherence, culmination and Culture."[47] This "act of writing" establishes the possibility of offering a unified perspective of the past that can be used as a point of reference, either to emulate that past or to preserve it as part of a national inflection.

Jiménez Losantos's search for a sustainable Spanish identity that could uphold the idea of a unified nation is seen in his writing of *Los nuestros*. What he tries to offer in this collection are the stories of one hundred notable characters who played a significant role in the creation of "the entity of Spain." Originally part of a series called "Crónicas" [Chronicles], these noted biographies were first published in the Sunday section of *El Mundo*. They were designed to revive the liberal tradition of Spain by emphasizing its notion of individual freedom while providing a defense of the idea of Spain.[48] As the author explains it, given the lack of interest demonstrated by the official government to preserve the official culture and language, he published this compilation as a counteraction to its institutional passivity. Through a compelling and nostalgic view of the past, Jiménez Losantos tried to reassert its validity. The chronological weaving of history in these texts can be interpreted as a conscious effort to unite the present by validating its past.

According to the author, when the *El Mundo* chronicles appeared, they became extremely popular and garnered an incredible response from the editorial board and the public. Jiménez Losantos interpreted the substantial feedback he received from his readers as evidence of the pressing need to talk about *Spain*. In the introduction to the compilation, he explains that the enthusiasm for these texts emerged from people belonging to the full spectrum of political ideology: from right-wing ideologues who wanted to read about heroic historical actions of individuals to leftists showing nostalgia for a "national component" in the current study of Spanish history. Both groups, he contends, coincided in their desire to "*leer historias* de personajes *nuestros*" [read stories of our people].[49] The concept of "ours" and "story" is emphasized in his introduction, where he presents the collection as a joint venture in which fiction is used to defend the nation. He claims that when the texts were published in the newspaper, they became something of a public exercise in the understanding of "History" and "Spain," exploring what he calls the forgotten "Spanish dimension" in the study of the Spanish past. Through these chronicles he wanted to convince the public to see and comprehend Spain as a historical product that was intimately related to its individuals and not simply something entangled with politics.[50]

Blending the biographical element into the larger framework of Spain, Jiménez Losantos explains his desire to avoid discussion of the traditionally studied historical conflicts (topics of war and oppression, class tensions, regional rivalries, etc.) and to concentrate instead on the three main topics suggested by his readers: nation, individual, and narrative.[51] Armed with these paradigms, he delves deep into the past to move beyond the concept of nation to the myth itself. It is revealing how in "Argantonio. El mito real" [Argantonio: The Real Myth], before embarking on a narration about the first known king of the Iberian Peninsula, Jiménez Losantos chooses to start the story by recreating the mythical story of Spain, abandoned child and nursing animals included.[52] His emphasis on this "beginning" at the start of his compilation sets up the chronological ordering of his texts and the historical characters. The purpose behind this organization is to demonstrate how they all, at the end, shaped today's Spain despite having belonged to different ethnic and cultural communities, different professions, ideologies, religions, and gender.

On the one hand, the narrative nature of these texts is acknowledged by Jiménez Losantos, who confesses that his view of history is that of the aficionado, who is not interested in historiography so much as in seeing "la Historia como un río de orígenes remotos y subterráneos, nacido en las fuentes anónimas y en neveros lejanos más que en el bautismo institucional; *nos gusta* asomarnos a esa corriente alimentada por afluentes tumultuosos y regatos pequeños" [History as a remote and subterranean river of origins, born from anonymous fountains and far-away ice fields rather than from institutional baptisms; *we like* looking into that current, fed by tumultuous tributaries and small streams].[53] Employing the general "us" to show he is part of a majority, he expresses his desire to see in history "su fluir como el río que nos lleva" [its flowing, like the river that carries us].[54] In turn, the fluidity of the events of the past showed this novice historian that in each slice of history "[s]omos nosotros mismos, cuando los que nos siguen salten sobre nuestro recuerdo para seguir su propio curso en la corriente común" [we are ourselves, when those who come after us will jump over our memories to continue their own course in the common stream].[55] He writes how he yearned to communicate through these texts the sense of continuity he felt when working on them, in communion with "el fresco río de España" [the fresh river of Spain] and the sense he had of being carried by its force.[56] Hence, it is not by chance that the title he chooses for his introduction is, appropriately, "La España que nos lleva" [The Spain that Carries Us].[57] From this perspective, individuals seem incapable of reacting to the power of history and its influences. Jiménez Losantos recognizes this powerlessness, but he accepts it because of the identity it gives him: "No sabría explicarme sin España. Tampoco quiero" [I would not know how to explain myself without Spain. I wouldn't want to, either].[58] To embrace history and the idea of Spain, and particularly Spain seen from this perspective, becomes paradoxical for a man whose creed is "[detestar] cualquier idea de nación que pase por encima del individuo, de todos y cada uno de ellos" [to detest any idea of nation that surpasses the individual, each and every one of them].[59] When he holds the writing of history to be a necessary fiction for exploring the source of identity and cultural legacy that can influence one's own self-identity, it is quite puzzling that he can make this perspective coexist with a universalizing and transcendental conception of the past.

If, as Hutcheon has argued, the postmodern position asserts that "[k]nowing the past becomes a question of representing, of constructing and interpreting, not of objective recording," this endeavor should entail an understanding of its limitations as well as its power. Accordingly, the construction of the past cannot escape an examination of its intentionality, for "it is more an attempt to comprehend and

master it by means of some working (narrative/explanatory) model
that, in fact, is precisely what grants a particular meaning to the
past."[60] For Patricia Waugh, the consequence of this knowledge is:

> History becomes a plurality of "islands of discourse," a series of metaphors
> which cannot be detached from the institutionally produced languages
> which we bring to bear on it. Alternatively, history is a network of agonis-
> tic language games where the criterion for success is performance not
> truth. The implication of this is that "truth" cannot be distinguished from
> 'fiction' and that the aesthetic has thus incorporated all.[61]

The intentionality of this construction, especially in those efforts
dealing with the narration of a cultural legacy, a national identity, or
even a history of national literature, is revealed by the post-colonial
reading paradigm, which perceives in the imposition of such narratives a way of continuing the *status quo*. Commenting precisely on the
importance attached to national culture, Frantz Fanon pointed out
that making claims to a national culture in the past not only rehabil-
itates the nation to which the culture belongs but also "serve[s] as a
justification for the hope of a future national culture."[62] Along the
same lines, Bhabha has explained how organizing the past chrono-
logically through narrative can be compared to "[w]riting as the fill-
ing of a gap," because it provides a "linear time consciousness . . . tele-
ology and unity, progression and coherence" that gives the writing
materiality, not as fiction but as a necessity.[63] Considering this intentionality, it becomes clear how Jiménez Losantos's effort to communicate a teleological sense of history prevails beyond the fictionality
of his work. As Bhabha pointed out, these type of texts are ideological in nature because they deny their material and historical construction and "[t]heir practices can be seen as unmediated and universal
because the unity of tradition lies in an absolute presence."[64]

The ideological imperative is obvious in Jiménez Losantos's *Los
nuestros*. Even though he includes historical characters from both the
Left and the Right to demonstrate the diversity of country's cultural
and historical identity, the book cannot hide its essentialist view of
Spain.[65] This becomes evident in the choice he makes for his final
piece, which at the end, questions the ideological position of the
book itself. The last text is a tribute to Miguel Ángel Blanco Garrido,
a councilman from a small town in the region of Vizcaya who was kidnapped and later executed by ETA in July 1997. The Spanish public
grew increasingly frustrated during the forty-eight hours that ETA
gave the Spanish government to free incarcerated terrorists in exchange for the councilman's life. When the deadline passed and

Blanco's body was found on the side of a road, the public staged an unprecedented demonstration. More than five million Spaniards took to the streets to protest his death and to condemn terrorism.[66] The author selected Blanco as his subject because, for him, the young councilman represented better than anyone the average person: one of *us,* one of the many in Spain who wants only to "andar por casa, por la casa grande de nuestro pueblo, sin tener ni temer, sin morir ni matar" [go about in his home, the large home of our people, without wanting or fearing, without dying or killing].[67] Blanco's ordinary life and background placed him close to the people, making his perils identifiable with those of the community. That is why Jiménez Losantos described him as a martyr of the "fe española" [Spanish faith] and recognized his agony with that of Spain:

> Porque durante dos largos, larguísimos días, España vivió la agonía de Migue como suya. Y cuando llegó su muerte, la vivió como si fuese suya, personal e intransferible. De ahí el llanto, el río inmenso de llanto que anegó la cara antigua y hermosa de la patria. De ahí los millones de personas que salieron a la calle a llorar su propia muerte y a agradecer a Miguel Ángel que hubiera muerto por ellos. Porque así se ha entendido y si no es así, no se entiende: el pueblo español ha sentido que Miguel Ángel ha muerto por todos los españoles. . . . Miguel Ángel Blanco no pertenece ya sólo a nuestra historial política sino a nuestra historia religiosa, si puede hablarse de religión en el sentimiento nacional. Unamuno, su paisano y maestro, diría que sí.

> [Because during two long, extremely long days, Spain lived Migue's agony as his own. And when his death arrived, he lived it like it was his, personal and nontransferable. Hence the cry, the immense river of tears that drowned the old and beautiful face of the fatherland. Hence the millions of people that came out into the streets to cry their own deaths and to thank Miguel Ángel for having died for them. Because that is how this incident was understood; and if not that, it would not have been understood: the Spanish people felt that Miguel Ángel had died for all Spaniards. . . . Miguel Ángel Blanco no longer belongs only to our political history but to our religious history, if one can speak of the religion of national sentiments. Unamuno, his country fellowman and teacher, would have agreed.][68]

This portrayal of Spain as a victim of terrorism, encapsulated in the tragedy of this councilman, cannot hide its emotional manipulation when the account of the fatal incident acquires religious connotations. If Jiménez Losantos denounced the conflation between history and politics, he, in turn, is guilty of conflating national history with religion. The author's account of Blanco's death borrows from the story in the New Testament of Jesus and Lazarus, in which the former calls the latter from his death. For Jiménez Losantos, the death of Blanco was a call to Spain: "levántate y anda" [get up and walk].[69] In his interpretation, this call not only led to the massive protest that followed the assassination and triggered the dialogue that would bring a temporary cease-fire between ETA and the Spanish government but implied a call for action: a call to unite against those that attack "us," to defend what "we" regard as "our home." Rendering Blanco's murder and suffering as "ours" and presenting the conflict as an antagonism between aggressor and victim, the author makes it easy for readers to interpret this fable as a clash between "us" and "them." This separation further reinforces the existing division in Spain—a division that, in the end, the title of the compilation seems to address: "*Los nuestros.*"[70]

As Jiménez Losantos sets the parameters of the debate surrounding regional politics from this perspective, several questions arise: if one can know who "us" is or what is "ours" by the language we speak and the culture we share, how do we define "them" or what is "theirs"? Moreover, what are the ramifications of the author's calls for the preservation of the common cultural markings, even as he opposes the vigorous implementation of the regional ones, if it is through these markings that a community can be defined? And even when he recognizes and accepts the right of the different autonomous regions to access and nurture their own cultures, how can this perspective be regarded as innocently inclusive, when what he proposes is to insist on continuing the markings of difference (i.e., the markings of culture or language)? How can this attitude fail to embody or perpetuate the expansive and compulsory nature of official institutions and culture? How do we reconcile personal freedom within this greater "us" without conforming to the larger and more general characteristics imposed on us, as individuals, by history? And finally, considering these issues, what is really entailed in upholding and preserving the idea of Spain when the proposed validity of this concept is conditioned solely by tradition and its own historicity?

The publication of the essays that constitute the collection *Los nuestros,* which appears in the literary career of Jiménez Losantos as an active gesture for counteracting what he sees as the gradual disappearance of Spain, reenacts the unavoidable essentialist gesture of nationalism, despite providing denial and criticism of such practice. The tensions in the current political situation in Spain are manifested in the relationship between the central state and the regional autonomies concerning cultural and educational policies. What cannot be ignored, however, is that these tensions respond to a desire to preserve a certain way of life and to a particular idea about national identity and reality that finds its *raison d'être* in its own institutionalization and continuity. The foundational tenets of this identity, located in its culture and language, acquire transcendental significance in the texts of this writer, a transcendence that clouds our awareness of the imposed nature of these elements as they are assimilated into our perception of the concept and idea of nation.

Although Jiménez Losantos claims that the legacy of Spanish culture continues into the present and that this culture is what it is today because of its detachment from nationalist interests, it becomes impossible to distinguish between these two ideas within the framework of his argument. The signifier "Spain" is irrevocably associated with a geographical and communal context that is naturally inclined to preserve the very characteristics that are used to define it as a nation in the first place. It cannot be ignored that the success of his project, as he pursues the idea of "Spain," can only be measured by the continuation and preservation of the social and political conditions that correspond specifically to the preexisting boundaries he has set. Ultimately, the validity of his claim can be questioned because, despite its "inclusive" politics, the basis for a new idea of Spain still includes, rather than a simple expansiveness, a culture imposed by the past and the history of the population that produced it. What becomes obvious is that the layers of historical sediment that make up a particular culture should not be preserved just for the sake of continuity or its survival through the passing of time. Taking into consideration the interests and effort put into preserving it, the dynamics of power that contributed to its sedimentation should not remain uncontested.

Although we might agree with Jiménez Losantos on the necessity of the term "Spain" and recognize all the regions and cultures that constitute it, we should be aware of the fictionality of such formulation. In his effort to preserve the idea of a coherent nation, however, this author seems to willfully ignore this aspect of its articulation. Even though he correctly intuits that discussions around the concept or idea of Spain will be crucial for its future, should he participate in the mythical recreation of its particular inflections? There should be a recognition that upholding a set of cultural characteristics because it belongs to a majority will inevitably lead to the institution of systems of categorization, engendering policies that discriminate between the groups that belong to this majority and those who do not. Checking the pulse of the debate concerning the future of this country should always entail an awareness of what is really at stake when individuals and institutions search for commonalities between themselves and their nation, and should seek an understanding of the extent to which the values espoused are rather impositions than free choices.

NOTES

The epigraph is contained in the first volume of a two-part anthology that includes the works of Manuel Azaña (1880–1940), the last president of the Second Republic. The anthology was edited by Federico Jiménez Losantos and published in 1982 by Alianza Editorial. The first part contains Azaña's essays, and the second, his public speeches. All translations in this essay are mine, unless otherwise noted. A shorter version of this essay was published in Catalan with the title "Revisar la historia, rescatar la cultura" in *El Contemporani* 28 (Jul–Des 2003): 67–73.

   1. These are words that Jiménez Losantos uses to explain his position in his introduction to *La dictadura silenciosa. Mecanismos totalitarios en nuestra democracia* [The Silent Dictatorship: Totalitarian Mechanisms in our Democracy] (Madrid, Temas de Hoy, 1993), iii.

   2. The biography of Jiménez Losantos offered in this essay is an amalgam of data culled from his book jackets and from the compilation by Corpus Ruiz posted on the Internet at www.arrakis.es/~corcus/inicio.htm.

   3. The editors of *El Viejo Topo* deemed unprintable the following texts of the collection: "La mayor barbaridad" [The Biggest Atrocity] and "Escribir en castellano en Cataluña" [Writing in Castilian in Catalonia], which are harsh attacks on the linguistic policies of the Autonomy of Catalonia. Jiménez Losantos explains that the topic of "Castilian in Catalonia" has been taboo for a long time and in *La dictadura silenciosa* (161–62) recounts how editor Miguel Riera of *El Viejo Topo,* the leading left-wing intellectual magazine, backed out from the promised publication. Curiously, he reflects, it was an anarchist publisher, responsible for the publication of *Ajoblanco,* who ultimately agreed to publish his book criticizing the Generalitat (163).

   4. Besides signing the much publicized manifesto against the standardization of the Catalan language in Catalonia's education system, Jiménez Losantos came to the attention of the terrorist group because of his harsh criticism of the cultural policies of the governments of Catalonia and the Basque Country. The document, known as the "Manifiesto de los 2.300" for the number of signatures collected, called for the equal rights of all languages spoken in Catalonia (specifically, Castilian) and argued for the recognition of immigration into the Catalan region from other Castilian-speaking parts of the country, including calls for the preservation of the immigrants' original language and culture. Published in January 1981 by *Diario 16,* it counted among its signatories Alberto Cardín, Carlos Sahagún, and Amando de Miguel. Jiménez Losantos writes in his book *Lo que queda de España. Con un prólogo sentimental y un epílogo balcánico* (Madrid: Temas de Hoy, 1995) about the persecution he and the other signatories suffered after the publication of this document, which resulted in the departure of all 2,300 involved, and more than 14,000 Castilian-speaking teachers, from Catalonia.

   5. Most recently, the case of Elián González, the Cuban boy who was returned to his father on the island, was the target of his criticism. See, for example, his article "Elián volvió a casa" [Elián Returned Home], published by *El Nuevo Herald* on 11 July 2000. Jiménez Losantos depicts the boy as the latest victim of Fidel Castro.

6. Characteristic of the belligerence in his writing is this comment regarding the bombing of the World Trade Center in New York City by Muslim terrorists in September 2001: "Eso de que la pobreza la producen los países ricos es, insisto, una vieja majadería marxista-leninista que ahora se presenta disfrazada de conmiseración universal y que solo pueden creer los que íntimamente odian a los pobres, no a la pobreza. [Los] niñitos palestinos y los cabritos de sus papás que bailan celebrando la masacre de Nueva York viven de la limosna estadounidense y europea o de un salario israelí. Viven mal porque Arafat y sus colegas criminosos lo roban casi todo y no tienen las instituciones de Florida o Almería" [The notion that poverty is caused by rich countries is, I insist, an old Marxist-Leninist lie presented to us, at the moment, disguised as universal commiseration, and which can only be believed by those who secretly hate the poor, not poverty. The little Palestinian children and their bastard fathers who dance, celebrating the massacre in New York, live off of American and European charity or the wage of an Israeli. They live poorly because Arafat and his criminal colleagues steal almost everything and have neither the institutions of Florida nor Almería] ("¿Pagar al terror?" [To Pay Terror?], *El Mundo,* 14 September 2001).

7. It is interesting that Julio Rodríguez Puértolas portrays the ideology of Jiménez Losantos as neo-fascist in the first volume of his book *Literatura fascista española* [Spanish Fascist Literature] (806–9).

8. It should be noted that whereas liberalism is generally associated with the Left in the United States, in Europe it is linked with the political Right. Self-described liberals in the U.S. are generally cultural liberals who emphasize the importance of preserving civil liberties but who in economic matters believe in a relatively greater role for the State in the regulation of markets, as well for economic redistribution. Liberalism in Europe is economic liberalism, with a greater embrace of free-market ideology. This brand of liberalism is more akin to conservative libertarianism in the U.S., with its emphasis on economic, rather than personal, freedoms. Jiménez Losantos, proclaiming the right to cultural freedom for each individual, is definitely in support of unfettered markets and is ideologically aligned with the political Right.

9. His political disillusionment is explained in the introduction and the first chapter of *La dictadura silenciosa* (11–75). He does not spare harsh words when it comes to assessing the political Left in his other writings: "La izquierda ya no tiene un modelo político alternativo al del capitalismo liberal, tampoco tiene una alternativa clara e identificable al Estado democrático burgués, ni puede exhibir ninguna moral particular con pretensiones generales. Tras la caída del Muro, la izquierda sigue presumiendo del monopolio de los buenos sentimientos, es la conciencia autosatisfecha de la especie, la vanidad sin motivos y el orgullo ridículo, pero objetivamente no tiene ninguna alternativa económica, política o moral al liberalismo salvo perfeccionarlo y mejorar el funcionamiento de sus instituciones, que es precisamente la esencia misma de ese sistema, perfectible por definición" [The Left does not offer an alternative political model to liberal capitalism, has no clear and identifiable alternative to the democratic bourgeois State, and cannot even exhibit a particular moral position with some general pretexts. After the fall of the Wall, the Left, as the self-satisfied conscience of our species, continues to assume a monopoly on good sentiments, possessed of a vanity that is without motives and of a ridiculous pride, but, objectively, it does not offer any economical, political, or moral alternative to liberalism and can only perfect and improve the functioning of its institutions, which are precisely the essence of that system, improvable by definition] ("Lo abyecto" [The Wretched], *El Mundo,* 13 September 2001).

10. *Lo que queda,* 165.

11. *Lo que queda* was published in a revised edition in 1995 with the added subtitle "*Con un prólogo sentimental y un epílogo balcánico*" [With a Sentimental Prologue and a Balkan Epilogue]. In the new texts included in this new edition, a prologue and an epilogue, he restates his earlier opinions and suggests that time has proven him right in his criticism of the cultural policies of the autonomous regions, especially Catalonia.

12. *La dictadura*, viii.

13. Ibid., iii. According to Jiménez Losantos, the degradation of democracy at the hands of the Socialist government revolved, among other things, around its financial scandals, as he demonstrates in writing about the Roldán, Filesa, GAL, Renfe, AVE, Intelhorce, BOE, Red Cross, and CESID cases, and about the blackmail and spying of the King (*Crónicas del acabóse. Contra el felipismo II.* [Madrid: Temas de Hoy, 1996], iv).

14. Updating this discussion, I would like to point out the current political debate surrounding the term "constitutional patriotism." Adopted by the conservative Partido Popular as the perfect solution for the future of Spanish state, it emphasizes on the importance of the country's cultural heritage to maintain a unified national identity. For an analysis of this debate, see Song's "Cap una España unida: La producció del patriotisme constitucional" [Towards a United Spain: The Production of Constitutional Patriotism] in *Les mentides del PP* [The Lies of the PP] (Barcelona: Angle Editorial, 2003), 26–41.

15. From the editorial published on 12 September 1999 in *Cambio 16,* cited in Barry Jordan, "How Spanish is it? Spanish Cinema and National Identity," in Contemporary Spanish Cultural Studies, ed. Jordan and Rikki Morgan-Tamosunas (London and New York: Arnold and Oxford University Press, 1999), 68. I borrow from Jordan's own translation of the original cited in his article. Jordan's essay explores, among others, issues regarding Spanish identity and the idea of the Spanish nation. The original editorial of *Cambio 16* reads: "¿A qué llamamos España?: ¿Estado plurinacional, estado autonómico, de nacionalidades y regiones, estado sin nación, nación de varios estados . . . ? Cada vez resulta más difícil saber donde estamos."

16. *La dictadura*, viii.

17. Linda Hutcheon, *The Politics of Postmodernism* (London: Routledge, 1989), 7.

18. For a brief introduction to the critical perspectives of post-colonial theory, see the introductory pages of Bill Ashcroft, Gareth Griffiths, and Helen Tiffin, *The Empire Writes Back: Theory and Practice in Post-colonial Literatures* (London: Routledge: 1989).

19. See Anderson's *Imagined Communities: Reflections on the Origin and Spread of Nationalism* (London and New York: Verso, 1991), 5, and Bhabha's "Representation and the Colonial Text: A Critical Exploration of Some Forms of Mimeticism" in *The Theory of Reading,* ed. Frank Gloversmith (Norfolk, VA, and Totowa, NJ: The Harvester Press, 1984), 93–97.

20. Jordan and Morgan-Tamosunas, 16.

21. Teresa Vilarós, *El mono del desencanto. Una crítica cultural de la transición (1973–1993)* (Madrid: Siglo XXI, 1998), 8–10.

22. Jordan and Morgan-Tamosunas, 16.

23. He understands the degradation of the government of Felipe González and the PSOE (with its multiple financial scandals and corruption) to have been part of the weakening process of the Spanish central government, which would result in its feebleness in dealing with cultural policies regarding the autonomous regions (*La dictadura*, iii–iv).

24. *La dictadura*, 13.

25. *Lo que queda*, 432. Jiménez Losantos refutes the assumption that the majority of people who live in Catalonia derive, in fact, from the region and its culture. He cites a survey to demonstrate that in fact, Castilian is spoken as a family language by 29.5 percent in the capital, compared with 47 percent who are Catalan speakers. He also notes that in the province of Barcelona, this difference increases, comparing 60.9 percent Castilian speakers with 38.5 percent Catalan speakers. He acknowledges that despite these numbers, Catalan is the language that is understood and used in social situations by 83 percent of the population living in the capital, even if only 19.1 percent can speak and write it, and 12.9 percent cannot understand it at all; compared with the provinces, where only 11.5 percent can speak and write it, whereas 68.4 percent can understand it and 31.3 percent cannot (*Lo que queda* 209).

26. *La dictadura*, 179–83.

27. Ibid., 13, 145–83; and *Lo que queda*, 431–94.

28. He writes: "Pero no, todos los españoles ilustrados conocen de uno u otro modo el pecado: Franco hablaba castellano, la derecha ha hablado castellano estos últimos cuarenta años y como la izquierda no podía hablar lo que quería, su mudez simbólica condena a la lengua por fascista" [But no, all learned Spaniards, one way or another, recognize the sin: Franco spoke Castilian, the Right has spoken Castilian for the last forty years, and because the Left could not speak what they wanted to, their symbolical muteness condemns this language for being Fascist] (*Lo que queda*, 178).

29. Quoted in Stanley G. Payne, *Falange: A History of Spanish Fascism* (Stanford: Stanford University Press, 1961), 39.

30. This position has been analyzed as part of nationalistic discourse by Xosé-Manoel Núñez in his essay "What is Spanish Nationalism Today? From Legitimacy Crisis to Unfulfilled Renovation (1975–2000)" in *Ethnic and Racial Studies*, Vol. 24: 5 (2001): 719–52.

31. *La dictadura*, 13.

32. Ibid.

33. *Lo que queda*, 198.

34. Jacques Derrida, *Monolingualism of the Other; or, The Prothesis of Origin*, trans. Patrick Mensah (Stanford: Stanford University Press, 1998), 39–40. The relationship between the individual and his or her language is always complicated, especially in terms of how this individual takes possession of it: "Because the master does not possess exclusively, and naturally, what he calls his language, because, whatever he wants or does, he cannot maintain any relations or property or identity that are natural, national, congenital, or ontological, with it, because he can give substance to and articulate *[dire]* this appropriation only in the course of an unnatural process of politico-phantasmatic constructions, because language is not his natural possession" (23).

35. *Lo que queda*, 212.

36. Anthony Smith, *Nations and Nationalism in a Global Era* (London: Polity Press, 1995), 5. Although the perennialist perspective, as explained by Smith, has been the source of ardent nationalist movements when its members saw themselves as victims who had been forced "to 'forget' their nation and its (usually glorious) history" and fought to recover its "natural order," it has also been responsible for articulating and grounding the importance of cultural ties within a community.

37. Ibid., 53–55.

38. Ibid., 63.

39. David Herzberger, *Narrating the Past: Fiction and Historiography in Postwar Spain* (Durham, NC: Duke University Press, 1995), 45.

40. *Lo que queda*, 166.

41. Smith, 65. Smith defines "mythistoire" as the representation of "an amalgam of selective historical truth and idealization [to] present a stirring and emotionally intimate portrait of the community's history, constructed by, and seen from the standpoint of, successive generations of community members" (63).

42. Ibid., 66.

43. *Lo que queda,* 166.

44. Edward Said, *Beginnings* (Baltimore and London: The Johns Hopkins University Press, 1978), 76–77.

45. Bhabha, 93.

46. Ibid., 94.

47. Ibid.

48. *Los nuestros. Cien vidas en la historia de España* (Barcelona: Planeta, 1999), 11.

49. Ibid.

50. Ibid., 12.

51. Ibid.

52. This is the myth of Spain as rendered by Jiménez Losantos:

"Vivimos en un lugar de sol y sombra que los fenicios llamaron Ispania; los griegos, Hesperia; otros pueblos, Ophixia; los cartagineses, Iberia; y finalmente los romanos, de vuelta a los orígenes fenicios, Hispania, con elegante H latina que no oculta su significado de *tierra de conejos;* por cierto, mejor que Ophixia, que significa *tierra de serpientes.* Y este lugar, desde antes de ser España, que es el nombre que resume todos los anteriores, tiene, entre otros, tres reyes míticos: Gerión, Gárgoris y Habis. Gerión, según el mito griego, pastoreaba bravos toros y pacientes bueyes, era fuerte y rico, y vino a matarlo Hércules, que se quedó con las Columnas y con el Estrecho. Gárgoris, además de pastor, fue apicultor; descubrió la miel y con ella el vicio, porque tuvo con una de sus hijas un crío, obviamente incestuoso, llamado Habis. Arrepentido o avergonzado, pero políticamente irresponsable, Gárgoris dejó a su hijo en el monte para que las fieras proveyeran, pero unas ciervas, incomparablemente más gentiles que la loba que tuvo que hacer otro tanto con Rómulo y Remo, lo amamantaron. Este Habis, superado el pequeño problema de su crianza, estaba tocado por la mano de todos los dioses: se bañaba cubierto de tatuajes y no perdía los colores; seguía a los ciervos, sus parientes, corriendo por el monte; era sabio y siempre joven; la suerte sonreía a cuantos se le acercaban . . . Lo que ya realmente lo consagró en el empíreo mediterráneo fue que acertó a inventar el arado, que, con el yugo de Gerión, hizo feraz y mítico el Jardín de las Hespérides, Hesperia, Iberia, Hispania o Ispania."

[We live in a place of sun and shadow that the Phoenicians called Ispania; the Greeks, Hesperia; other people, Ophixia; the Carthaginians, Iberia; and finally, the Romans, in return to the Phoenician origins, Hispania, with the elegant Latin H, that does not hide its meaning of *land of rabbits;* which is, by the way, better than Ophixia, which means *land of snakes.* And this place, before it was to become Spain, which is the name that summarizes all the previous ones, had, among others, three mythical kings: Geryon, Gargoris, and Habis. Geryon, according to the Greek myth, tended to brave and patient oxen, was strong and rich, and Hercules, who took possession of the Columns and the Strait, came to kill him. Gargoris, besides being a shepherd, was a beekeeper who discovered honey and with it vice, because he had by one of his daughters a child, named Habis. Regretful or embarrassed but politically irresponsible, Gargoris left his son in the mountains so the beasts would devour him, but some does, incomparably more kind than the she-wolf that saved Romulus and Remus, fed him. This Habis, having overcome the small problem of his upbringing, was touched by the hand of all the gods: he bathed, covered in tattoos, and didn't lose the colors; he followed the deer, their relatives, running around the mountain; was wise and always young; luck always smiled on those who approached him . . . What really consecrated him among the Mediterranean divinity was that he invented the plow, which, with Geryon's yoke, made fertile and mythical the Garden of Hesperidia, Hesperia, Iberia, Hispania, or Ispania.] (*Los nuestros,* 19–20)

53. *Los nuestros,* 13. Emphasis mine.

54. Ibid., 13–14. He uses the title of the work of José Luis Sampedro to characterize his view of history.

55. Ibid., 14.

56. Ibid., 15.

57. Ibid., 11.

58. Ibid., 16.

59. Ibid.

60. Ibid., 58, 64.

61. Patricia Waugh, *Postmodernism. A Reader* (London: E. Arnold, 1992), 6.

62. Frantz Fanon, "National Culture," in *The Post-Colonial Studies Reader,* eds. Bill Ashcroft, Gareth Griffiths, and Helen Tiffin (London and New York: Routledge: 1995), 154.

63. Bhabha, 97.

64. Ibid.

65. Among the characters he includes in his book are Francisco Franco, La Pasionaria, Manuel Azaña, and Manuel Machado.

66. The magnitude of the public outcry at the death of this town councilman played a role in the subsequent cease-fire between ETA and the Spanish government, which ended without solution to their disagreement in July 2000. Since then, ETA has returned to their attacks and has killed more than twenty people.

67. *Los nuestros,* 414.

68. Ibid., 415–16.

69. Ibid., 418.

70. Although Jiménez Losantos explains in the introduction to his book that the title is a private joke that refers to past political affairs and the induction of the ex-director of the newspaper *El País* into the Real Academia Española [Royal Spanish Academy], the use of this title offers an explicit message about the true discriminatory and arbitrary practice of history. In fact, the joke is wasted when readers who agree with the author's propositions look into the texts that constitute the book in search of the commonality that the critic has denounced as missing or on the verge of disappearance.

BIBLIOGRAPHY

Anderson, Benedict. *Imagined Communities: Reflections on the Origin and Spread of Nationalism.* London and New York: Verso, 1991.

Ashcroft, Bill, Gareth Griffiths, and Helen Tiffin. *The Empire Writes Back: Theory and Practice in Post-colonial Literatures.* London: Routledge, 1989.

Azaña, Manuel. *Antología. Ensayos y Discursos.* Edited by Federico Jiménez Losantos. 2 vols. Madrid: Alianza, 1982.

Bhabha, Homi. "Representation and the Colonial Text: A Critical Exploration of Some Forms of Mimeticism." *The Theory of Reading.* Edited by Frank Gloversmith. Norfolk, VA, and Totowa, NJ: The Harvester Press, 1984.

Derrida, Jacques. *Monolingualism of the Other; or, The Prothesis of Origin.* Translated by Patrick Mensah. Stanford: Stanford University Press, 1998.

Fanon, Frantz. "National Culture." In *The Post-Colonial Studies Reader.* Edited by Bill Ashcroft, Gareth Griffiths, and Helen Tiffin. London: Routledge, 1995.

Herzberger, David. *Narrating the Past: Fiction and Historiography in Postwar Spain.* Durham, NC: Duke University Press, 1995.

Hutcheon, Linda. *The Politics of Postmodernism.* London: Routledge, 1989.

Jiménez Losantos, Federico. "Lo abyecto." *El Mundo,* 13 September 2001.

———. *Contra el felipismo.* Madrid: Temas de Hoy, 1993.

———. *Crónicas del acabóse. Contra el felipismo II.* Madrid: Temas de Hoy, 1996.

———. *La dictadura silenciosa. Mecanismos totalitarios en nuestra democracia.* Madrid: Temas de Hoy, 1993.

———. "Elián volvió a casa." *El Nuevo Herald,* 11 July 2000.

———. *Los nuestros. Cien vidas en la historia de España.* Barcelona: Planeta, 1999.

———. "¿Pagar al terror?" *El Mundo,* 14 September 2001.

———. *Lo que queda de España. Con un prólogo sentimental y un epílogo balcánico.* Madrid: Temas de Hoy, 1995.

Jordan, Barry. "How Spanish is it? Spanish Cinema and National Identity." *Contemporary Spanish Cultural Studies.* Edited Barry Jordan and Rikki Morgan-Tamosunas. London and New York: Arnold and Oxford University Press, 1999, 68–78.

Jordan, Barry, and Rikki Morgan-Tamosunas, op. cit., 13–16.

Núñez, Xosé-Manoel. "What is Spanish Nationalism Today? From Legitimacy Crisis to Unfulfilled Renovation (1975–2000)." *Ethnic and Racial Studies* 24.5 (2001): 719–52.

Payne, Stanley G. *Falange: A History of Spanish Fascism.* Stanford: Stanford University Press, 1961.

Rodríguez Puértolas, Julio. *Literatura fascista española.* Vol. I. Madrid: Akal, 1986.

Ruiz, Corpus. Federico Jiménez Losantos. Biografía. Accessed from *www.arrakis.es/~corcus/inicio.htm.* 30 October 2001.

Said, Edward. *Beginnings.* Baltimore and London: The Johns Hopkins University Press, 1978.

Smith, Anthony D. *Nations and Nationalism in a Global Era.* London: Polity Press, 1995.

Song, H. Rosi. "Cap una España unida: La producció del patriotisme constitucional." *Les mentides del PP.* Barcelona: Angle Editorial, 2003, 26–41.

Vilarós, Teresa M. *El mono del desencanto. Una crítica cultural de la transición (1973–1993).* Madrid: Siglo XXI, 1998.

Waugh, Patricia. *Postmodernism. A Reader.* London: E. Arnold, 1992.

Postscript
Remaking Memory: Culture and Fascism in Spain

Jordi Gracia

They have disappeared from bookstores but can still be found in libraries. Half a century ago their works and portraits filled the pages of newspapers and magazines, and now they take up only small spaces in specialized journals devoted to certain emotionally charged anniversaries. They had resounding names and boldly trod the earth in uniform. And little could they have guessed that their books and names would end up covered in ashes. They are Rafael Sánchez Mazas, Agustín de Foxá, and Rafael García Serrano: the writers of Spanish fascism.

The place Spanish fascist literature occupies in the culture of democracy is almost a non-place, a position that remains diffuse and confused. Or, to state the matter differently, academic criticism has barely begun to assess its literary value and describe its aesthetic contributions. Javier Cercas's latest novel, *Soldados de Salamina* [Salamina's Soldiers], which has sold 100,000 copies, has allowed many readers to revive something like ethical and historical emotions, but also to discover some basic facts of which most Spaniards were completely unaware;[1] for example, that Rafael Sánchez Ferlosio, author of *El Jarama* [The Jarama], a reference work in high school and university curricula, is the son of Rafael Sánchez Mazas, whose textbooks we have managed to ignore, but who is well-known as founder of Falange Española [Spanish Falange], co-author of the "Cara al sol" [Facing the Sun] anthem, and minister without portfolio in Franco's government during the early post-war period. Cercas's academic work as a literature professor includes a lengthy essay about the young Gonzalo Torrente Ballester's fascism. To a great extent, the origin of *Soldados de Salamina* can be found in the puzzling critical questions he confronted some years earlier: What would Manuel Machado's future have been like had he spent the war in the Republican zone? Should

we not now disregard rigid affiliations and look back to a past that
has been sharply and unfairly divided into good guys and bad guys?

Andrés Trapiello asks himself a similar question in a prologue to
Manuel Machado's poems; neither he nor Cercas recalls certain
verses, published by Antonio in volume eighteen of *Hora de España*
[The Hour of Spain], that describe the shadow of an uncertain future. Antonio's remembrance of his childhood in Seville calls forth
Manuel's memory: "Aviva tu recuerdo, hermano. / No sabemos de
quién va a ser el mañana" [Revive your memory, brother. / We don't
know whose future it will be]. The verses woefully express the sense
of being a puppet in somebody else's play, a puppet whose strings go
beyond feelings and biography—as if history's violence were already
irreversible or could only intensify. It is less surprising that Max Aub
would recall some of these verses when he evoked, from exile, his
meetings with Antonio Machado during the war, quoting the last
line—"No sabemos de quién va a ser el mañana"—together with Antonio's naïve answer to his request for a comedy he wanted to stage:
"Es la historia de un soldado. Pero no tengo el original. Lo tiene mi
amigo Juan Cassou. Tiene usted que pedírselo. Sabe usted: es de mi
hermano y mía, naturalmente la firmaría yo solo" [It's the story of a
soldier. But I don't have the original. My friend Juan Cassou has it.
You have to ask him for it. You know: it's my brother's and mine; naturally, only I would sign it].[2]

Why should we re-read Manuel Machado today, and appreciate *el
mal poema* [the bad poem]? Why should we stop squeamishly avoiding his jokes and minor villainies, and the fact that he was simultaneously a bad person and a good poet? Would anyone still consider such
an opinion some sort of political complicity or propaganda for this
or that ideology? Is re-reading Manuel Machado as a poet today
merely a consequence of the passage of time, or rather an example—
and a clear one indeed—of a general neutralization of politics, which
is now considered a pathogen for literary reading? Thirty years ago,
the only good Machado was Antonio, and Borges himself felt compelled to call attention to Manuel with a well-known witty remark. But
since then literary politics have grown less fractious. If no one has
ever seriously questioned Antonio Machado's value as a poet and es-
sayist, now no one denies Manuel's value either. We can even find
echoes of his poetry in high-quality democratic period authors, such
as Miguel d'Ors or Carlos Marzal, who in the wake of a necessary but
belated resurrection (annotated editions, monographic studies, doctoral dissertations, editions of previously unpublished documents)
have positively re-evaluated him.

Javier Cercas, like many of his contemporaries, such as Marzal or Felipe Benítez Reyes (another poet who echoes Manuel Machado), does not read the war and its consequences as a simple equation. Half a century is plenty of time to allow us to turn to the past and look at it ourselves, not through the lenses of others who experienced the difficulties of anti-Franco militancy or were forced to modify their readings and criteria so as to avoid playing up to a power or counter-power. We have started to read Spanish fascist literature using criteria that are less biographically conditioned and thus freer from the hostility personal experience previously projected on it and its practitioners. Our elders' authority is no longer sufficient reason for us to unquestioningly accept that Manuel Machado was a bad guy just because the new regime enthroned him as the true, good old Machado.

Perhaps what I have outlined is a false perception. The place fascist literature occupies might be simply the one it deserves: oblivion. After all, it sprang from an ideological and political fever that aesthetically intoxicated writers. It is as if the sporadic commemorations of one author or another were the only possible place for this literature today, or stock for eccentric or disoriented philologists' libraries were its only possible use. Maybe it did not yield much more than learned recreation or boastful erudition; in the end, Francisco Umbral's precocious diagnosis may turn out to be the most lasting: that overall these authors wrote a tidy prose with style but had no literary ambition, or were prevented from achieving higher aesthetic aims for historical, ideological, or ethical reasons.

This judgment is presumably accurate, but also insufficient. It is adequate in order to gauge the value of a prose style Umbral himself inherited, one that served as a clear reference point in his own training as a writer and that explains his distaste for the novel as a genre. Falangist journalism has been useful to him as a prose model for a type of literature that dissolves genres, or else aspires to disobey their rules while knowing them well. And he is not the only author to be tempted by this type of prose: authors such as Juan Perucho or Álvaro Cunqueiro are very indebted to this learned and whimsical mode of writing (although the common source for all of them are Eugenio d'Ors's brilliant, intuitive filigrees). What is less certain is whether a different type of critical approach can judge fascist literature on less practical grounds, or independently of the interests of individual writers who need to reinvent and dignify their own literary traditions. Umbral found one of his many literary lineages in Falangist prose, but most likely he found what he was already looking for, as usually happens when we search for something. He failed to look, so to speak, in that other possible place—namely, the novel—of which Foxá, Sánchez Mazas, or García Serrano had managed to create some valuable examples.

My hesitant reflections do point towards a certainty, which is that Spanish literature has not yet found a way to give literary and historical coherence to a set of works radiating aesthetic as well as political and literary complicity. The facts we need in order to draw the picture are there, but we still cannot articulate a theory or interpretation that would will give them meaning. We cannot distinguish minor and major accomplishments, nor can we narrate the maturation of fascist literature, signal its internal rhythms, and define the creative impotence that led to oddly creative results. We have yet to explain its internal links with the avant-garde and Italian, German, and Portuguese fascisms, taking note of the complicities that were built into *tertulias* [literary coteries] and magazines of the 1930s, separating urgent historical interests from more significant literary ambitions, and recomposing the dispersed unity of works produced by authors with unique fascist-leaning sensibilities. Between Sánchez Mazas's aseptic aristocratism and García Serrano's sense of honour and trench instinct, we can see many shades of a common sensibility. I do not know if these two authors stand at opposite poles of Spanish literary fascism, but they do represent two different, hostile ways of understanding the aesthetic adventure of fascism in Spain.

A recent book by María Ángeles Naval is sensible enough to reflect upon these distinctions. Such reflection helps to better understand good and bad fascist literature, and also to determine what fascism's literary expression could have been, both as a sensibility and an ideology, and what it really was: no more, or little more, than a politically militant literature. However, the academic world is evidently not the sphere most interested in the interpretation of the literature of fascism, if we consider the scant attention devoted over the past twenty years to this ocean of dispersed and still largely unreprinted literature. Some of the lengthiest studies were based on outdated or scarcely operative analytical premises—the lengthiest example being Julio Rodríguez-Puértolas's *Literatura fascista española* [Spanish Fascist Literature]—and very few have attempted to develop the solid insights found in Mainer's classic anthology, *Falange y literatura* [Falangism and Literature], which goes all the way back to 1971. Victoriano Peña's *Intelectuales y fascismo* [Fascism and the Intellectuals], published in 1995, focused once again on Giménez Caballero, one of the best-known figures in Spanish fascism, but is too whimsical to serve as a stable reference on the subject. A year earlier Juan Cano

Ballesta, who not coincidentally is very knowledgeable about 1930s Spanish literature, had collected critical essays about Falangist rhetoric in another volume, *Las estrategias de la imaginación* [The Strategies of the Imagination]. Part of the criticism and literary theory written in the early postwar period was examined in Sultana Wahnón's volume, but I believe that the most valuable contribution, and the one which overall provides the best and most comprehensive survey of fascism and literature, is the volume edited by Mechthild Albert. Not the least of its merits is its break with the war chronology in order to accommodate literature into its historical context. The book begins with the 1930s, goes through the war on its way to the 1940s, and towards the end jumps to fascism's sequels in democratic Spain, including both Vizcaíno Casas's coarse predictability and the greater depth with which authors such as Antonio Muñoz Molina or José María Guelbenzu has approached the past.

Unfortunately these publications and other similar studies have had a very limited impact, thus involuntarily bearing witness to the oblivion in which literary fascism finds itself. Within the realm of ideas, it may be useful to recall that the last chapter of Javier Varela's *La novela de España* [The Novel of Spain] chooses to linger on José Antonio Maravall's trajectory as a vocational interpreter of the origins of modernity—a modernity he had ideologically and politically fought against during the war and early postwar. It is almost as if this biographical episode—the euphoria and the sentry duties in Burgos, Salamanca, or Pamplona—had been something akin to a collective bond that gave meaning to his work as part of a team, despite the fact that his writing ended up drifting very far from the earlier feeling of unity and camaraderie, as was also the case with Luis Díez del Corral's work (and with that of some more obviously political figures, such as Ridruejo, Laín, or Tovar).

It is quite possible that the academic activity of Hispanists is not the most reliable source for determining the presence or survival of fascist literature and some of its authors. Creative writers may be better suited for this task. In the 1970s literary fascism became a part of some authors' intellectual interests. The highly politicized literary environment wrought a new type of author who undid the knots of prejudice or commenced tying them up in a different way, that is, who aspired to create his own marks of identity on the margins of official history, far from commonly accepted truths. Not surprisingly, one of the most sensitive issues was the value of the fascist literary heritage, which was still so close, and in some cases still so alive. Also not surprisingly, one of the forms adopted by literary rebellion and rebellion against the conventional truths of political resistance was the un-prejudiced—or non-political—reading of authors who were afforded primarily a political label and only secondarily a literary identity.

The unbiased judgment exhibited by some democratic-period authors became contagious, as if there had been an agreement based on a generational or historical imperative to take a fresh look at a literature loaded with political toxins. These authors agreed to re-read it, reducing its political charge, albeit not denying its historical significance. Thus, they started to notice some specific things, to highlight forgotten titles, to emphasize some failures pregnant with literary meaning. They started to point beyond the tidy prose which Umbral defined and in which, as a writer doubling as critic, he probably remained stuck. They started to believe that not all fascist literature was the adulterated or Manichean by-product of an ideological disease. The cultural establishment of the 1970s viewed their attitude as a suspicious reassessment manoeuvre and was concerned that the presumption of a democracy or its very fragile constitution before 1982 might be enough to absolve fascists of their historical sins, or that the time had come to look at the better known authors with different prejudices, ones fuelled not by political fury but by learned curiosity towards other people's adventures.

In fact, the writers who sought to recover fascism's lost literature were of a specific type. They were professional writers but none were professors. Most were more than mere novelists, usually columnists and essayists attentive to the present and recent past, who were attracted to the dynamics of literature but also eager to form an independent judgment, which was to become their greatest asset. Even though they were all younger than Umbral, deep down their activity was shaped by the same stubborn independence normally exhibited by the author of *Las palabras de la tribu* [The Words of the Tribe]. And even though they did not share Umbral's devotion to César González Ruano, they learned a way to practice literature based on personal choices made as a result of their biographies, their experiences, and often their family libraries—the type of library that could bring together at home the titles that a certain period and social class once considered essential. Most of the writers who engaged in this critical reading exercise (restraint from historical and political condemnation), had been regular browsers of dusty and forgotten editions at second-hand bookstores, as if returning to the past was also a way to signal their attitude towards the present. Leftist militancy and democratic sensibility lacked literary color or, at the very least, aspired to neutralize political prejudices in order to emphasize aesthetic and literary ones. The authors who engaged in this endeavor of recovery were of widely varying ages; the list is somewhat incomplete and arbitrary, but I think those who made an effort to learn to read fascist literature better—and restructure postwar literary history—include, very prominently, Umbral himself, in addition to authors with a peculiar literary marginality, such as Joan Perucho and Carlos Pujol, learned journalists with literary inclinations as well as their comrades like Juan Ramón Masoliver, and much younger writers who promoted publishing houses or critical sections in magazines and newspapers in the 1970s and developed their own personalities in the 1980s: Andrés Trapiello, Miguel Sánchez-Ostiz, Juan Manuel Bonet, Miguel d'Ors, and José Carlos Llop, among others. Obviously, none of them can be characterized by any form of literary fascism, nor is such an affinity a major component of their work. What they all share is a critical attitude towards the official Left's cultural prejudices and also the intuition of a parasitic, dubious, controversial and intentionally noisy form of identity. This is how allergy to oblivion and the desire to repair historical injustice tend to manifest themselves.

The following comment about the Trieste publishing house was signed by a balanced man, one not inclined to hyperbole. Juan Manuel Bonet stated that publishing Sánchez-Mazas, Ruano, or Miguel Villalonga in the 1980s, when "nada estaba claro, . . . implicaba, pudo comprobarse enseguida, excomunión automática por parte de algunos" [nothing was clear, . . . (it) entailed, as was soon proven to be the case, automatic excommunication by some].[3] It is not difficult to imagine what publishing those same authors could have meant some years earlier, when Franco was still alive and issues in literary culture were also, very fundamentally, issues in the politics of resistance or complicity. Ocnos, a high-quality, ambitious collection edited by Joaquín Marco, was the first to publish two very shocking works whose coexistence was not well-received by the person in charge of distribution in Madrid, who suffered from the very rigidity Bonet mentions. Publishing García Lorca's *Poeta en Nueva York* [Poet in New York] was one thing; publishing Rafael Sánchez-Mazas's poems was quite another. The juxtaposition was indeed explosive at the time, just as it still was, according to Juan Manuel Bonet's testimony, ten or fifteen years later, even though the threat to democracy posed by the 23 February 1981 attempted *coup d'état* was much diminished after the 1982 Socialist victory and Minister of Defence Narcís Serra's subsequent control over the Army.

Nothing is completely fortuitous. The Trieste collection, which Trapiello headed after 1982, was the gathering point for several people who were somehow or other connected with Spanish fascism's past. Carmen Martín Gaite published *El cuento de nunca acabar* [The

Never-ending Story], but she may also have had something to do with her friend Trapiello publishing her former father-in-law, Sánchez-Mazas, who died in 1966. His unfinished novel *Rosa Krüger* appeared in this collection, following an anthology of narrative texts and vaguely evocative, stylish articles, titled *Las aguas de Arbeloa* [The Waters of Arbeloa]. The same collection hosted—alongside Martínez Sarrión's poems a novel by Miguel Sánchez-Ostiz and a diffuse essay by Rafael Conte—Miguel Villalonga's *Autobiografía* [Autobiography] and César González-Ruano's poems. It also made room for Alberto Jiménez Fraud's liberal neatness in *Visita a Maquiavelo* [A Visit to Maquiavelo].

It is not too surprising that the author to best and most programmatically interpret some fascist authors is Trieste's director himself, Trapiello, years after putting an end to this publishing venture. In 1994 he published a book written, as he has confessed in his diaries, with remarkable speed but with a definite intention camouflaged as an unwary and irresponsible spontaneity. If we re-read *Las armas y las letras. Literatura y guerra civil, 1936–1939* [Arms and Letters: Literature and the Civil War, 1936–1939] today, we get the impression that it was the one book to crystallize many of the changing attitudes towards the war and the literature it bred, not so much because it fictitiously inflated the quality of a group of authors lacking a substantial corpus of works, but because it restored human and historical complexity to a picture that had often been simplified on the basis of generic and mutilated truths. Little of the material had never been seen before; what was novel was the focus of an author willing to lay the foundations for new prejudices, rather than fossilize inherited ones. One need only to read without a spirit of historical revenge, exhibiting instead a willingness to pinpoint paradoxes or complexities in what history had lazily taken to be stable and clear. There was not much more of a purpose, at least a declared one, but this was enough to start anew.

This is what another author also did, one with a different history and of a different age, but with a similar desire for freedom of judgment and for bringing fresh air into the field. Around the same time in Spanish university classrooms, specifically Barcelona's, other facts were being connected with the purpose of reducing historical perplexity. Antonio Vilanova, who had been a regular literary critic at Destino (a Spanish publishing house) and the best interpreter of postwar neo-realism, devoted a few hours in his courses to, once again, Rafael Sánchez Mazas, specifically to his *La vida nueva de Pedrito de Andía* [The New Life of Pedrito de Andía], because *Rosa Krüger* still did not exist as a published novel. The editions of Sánchez Mazas's works on the market had not been published by Destino, where Vilanova served as Nadal Award jury member, nor by Lumen, where he put together an excellent collection, but rather by Planeta. The latter published Sánchez-Mazas in pocket editions and launched a complex, sizeable collection of testimonials and autobiographical texts and memoirs in the 1970s. During the 1980s and 1990s, its director, Rafael Borrás Betriu, managed to publish practically all the war survivors who could weave together memories of any historical interest. This autobiographical literature included Franco's personal secretary, Francisco Franco Araújo, as well as the good novelist and Falangist Rafael García Serrano, who published his valuable memoirs, *La gran esperanza* [The Great Hope], unabashedly subtitled *Nosotros, los falangistas* [We, the Falangists], in this collection.

It is García Serrano, who is relatively accessible in Planeta, whose work makes the reader most uneasy (along with some of Foxá's and Sánchez Mazas' novels)—not because of his ideological stubbornness, but because of the personal and professional honesty displayed by a Falangist who never cheated. The quality of his lively and intimate prose, his uncompromising loyalty to a certain notion of camaraderie and life, and the Barojian lineage of a novel that had not fared well with Francoist audiences either (because it outrageously and impudently exceeded the bounds of bourgeois conventions in and outside Pamplona) add to his reputation. Garcías Serrano's case is the least explicable of all because the quality of his work is well above the contempt and neglect that befell it and because, unlike others, he was unable to profit from his provincial rooting. Most of his work has not yet benefited from careful reading, even though his significance in literary history is comparable to Cela at his best and to a Barojian tradition enlivened by convictions and human warmth. But García Serrano has yet to find his own Umbral, Trapiello, or Sánchez-Ostiz.

Does this re-evaluation have to be such a tortuous labyrinth? Perhaps not, considering the slow process of maturation that history reserves for some things, and particularly the skill with which contemporary criticism assesses high-culture forms, even when these are draped in fascist ideas and paraphernalia. 1937's Pamplona, war-era Pamplona, was a source of camaraderie and complicity for hard and soft fascists alike, who came together with a literary and aesthetic purpose. Many of the new postwar authors, some of them born in Pamplona, participated in the founding of *Arriba España* [Go Spain] and *Jerarquía* [Hierarchy],[4] and it is perfectly understandable that an important current author, Miguel Sánchez-Ostiz, has reacquainted us with shadows from the past like the exquisite typographer, columnist and writer, Ángel María Pascual. Sánchez-Ostiz has devoted many hours of reading and writing to outlining the origins of this portrayer of provincial customs and disillusionment. This is why he was entrusted with editing Pascual's poems, *Capital de tercer orden* [A Third-rate Capital], and also the widely-read *Glosas a la ciudad* [Comments about the City], both published by the Diputación de Navarra (Navarra's local government). Similar reasons have led José Carlos Llop to approach other historically and literarily culpable authors, such as Lorenzo Villalonga, author of the excellent novel *Bearn*, whose unpublished *Diario de guerra* [War Diary] he prefaced and edited after translating and studying Miguel Villalonga's *Autobiografía*.

Such are the labyrinthine paths taken by a literature that had some quality moments, but, as noted above, is not yet sufficiently appreciated. Still missing is the broader picture tracing the growth of a fascist sensibility liberated from the immediacy of the political. An attempt to separate the fascist molds and mists from the urgency of war-and-victory Falangism is also lacking. Perhaps only when this is accomplished will we, following in the footsteps of María Ángeles Naval's book, be able to re-read this literature, which did not produce a Céline or a Curzio Malaparte, but did include a handful of authors who were sometimes enveloped by nostalgia, other times saturated by a culture sterilized by the *uchronie,* and more often who conspired to build a literature that, after 1939, was not exactly one of victory, but one glorifying social norms and ideas—a reconstitution of sensations and feelings that deserves the thoughtful calligraphy of meticulous study. It may be worth re-reading *Madrid, de corte a cheka* [Madrid, from the Court to the Coop], *La vida nueva de Pedrito de Andía* and *Rosa Krüger, La fiel infantería* [The Faithful Infantry], or *Diccionario para un macuto* [A Dictionary for a Knapsack] in this new light. Such a reading may wind up proving right those who stress, in elitist book collections or luxury, institutional re-editions, the value of what is still seen as an inert and useless mass of literature.

The postwar is surely that "ámbito moral" [moral sphere] mentioned by Mainer in *De postguerra* [On the Postwar Period], as well as an aesthetic realm. This may also mean that the generations raised in the democratic period see the postwar era and Francoism itself as a piece of old history analogous to the turn-of-the-century crisis or the liberal triennium. Francoism's historical proximity still affects them directly in everyday life—their elders' memories, evocative literature, memoirs, the pitfalls of nostalgia—but this past is not part of a lived biography or personal experience. The type of historical emotion—or intellectual fever—induced by exercises in evocative history is no different from that awakened by Jovellanos's banishment, Blanco

White's exile, or Clarín's rebellious sadness. The latter are more remote, yes, but that is all. Starting with the transition to democracy, writers and intellectuals lack the feeling that marked previous generations, of having had history usurped or their own biographies irreversibly confiscated. They perceive Francoist repression as a historical fact, not as an experience that shaped their own lives; as something they have heard, read, and vicariously suffered, with a melancholy and compassion essentially no different from what is elicited by Moratín's letters.

This is why I draw attention to sources that can be used to rewrite a chapter of twentieth-century literary history. Clearly, the first impetus for revision grew out of the very literary vitality of democracy, not from an inquisitive urgency on the part of academia. Moreover, the impact of these revisions may be hard to gauge, because they also affect other phenomena, such as the liberal exile. The current revitalization of the work of Max Aub, Arturo Barea, or Ramón J. Sender is indebted to commemorations which the university has used and which may eventually lead to a restructuring of the canon. Perhaps some of Max Aub's *Campos* [Fields] or an extremely original novel such as Paulino Masip's *Diario de Hamlet García* [Hamlet García's Diary] will take the place of seemingly unshakable canonical works such as *Nada* [Nothing] (though this novel probably won't lose much of the humble truth it embodied, being as it was a shipwreck or survivor within a huge lie). But revision may come via other routes which are worth summarizing here, despite their obviousness. The first is, of course, the neutralization of political instinct or ideological revenge as a critical criterion for literary history. The second is the slow transformation of reading prejudices and the ensuing harvest of valuable texts previously buried by negligence, such as Julián Ayesta's *Helena, o el mar del verano* [Helena, or the Summer Sea]. The third could very well be the mentality of today's readers, who are insensitive to art's consolation value at a time of resistance and are captivated by less transient or immediate values, or perhaps only attentive to literary meanings that do not revolve around crying over defeat or vindicating the defeated.

With regard to fascist literature in particular, the current situation may invite us to re-read it for an additional reason. The time is already past for vindicating a literature that won the war but, as Trapiello brilliantly summarized it, lost the history of literature. Those who hesitantly approach fascist literature today do so without the burden of believing it to be the literary expression of power; it no longer symbolizes a political victory, nor is it an attic where intrepid democrats and writers may find corpses useful for their own purposes of literary affirmation. Those who approach it today probably do so equipped with nothing other than their own historical and generational prejudices, and without considering retaliation or vindication as a factor in the making of literary history. Perhaps this criticism will sensibly take this new route, more aseptic but not at all unwary. This could also be the way to determine whether Francisco Umbral, Andrés Trapiello, and Miguel Sánchez-Ostiz were right when they attempted to carry out their own analyses of literary history, even if they were only recreative, or *erudipausal*.[5] Often it is this type of honest, noble, "writerly" reading that teaches us how to re-read what was poorly read before, or was read with preconceptions that muted the voice of a literature all too damaged by its own historical context.

[Translated by Jacqueline Cruz]

NOTES

1. By 2003 this novel has sold more than half a million copies. Since the preparation of this essay in 2001, other titles on the topic have been published, including one earlier title I unfortunately omitted from the article, Enrique Selva's *Ernesto Giménez Caballero. Entre la vanguardia y el fascismo* [*Ernesto Giménez Caballero. Between Avant-Garde and Fascism*] which was published in 1999 in Madrid (Pre-Textos). Mechthild Albert has published a study on fascist literary aesthetic, *Vanguardistas de camisa azul* [Blue Shirt Avant-gardists] in 2003 (Madrid: Visor) while Mónica and Pablo Carbajosa have published *La corte literaria de José Antonio* [*The Literary Court of José Antonio*] (Barcelona: Crítica, 2003). The fascist nationalism has also found a excellent interpreter in Ismael Saz, *España contra España. Los nacionalismos franquistas* [*Spain against Spain. Francoist Nationalisms*] (Madrid: Marcial Pons, 2003).

2. Max Aub, *Cuerpos presentes* (Segorbe: Fundación Max Aub, 2001), 171.

3. Eloy Sánchez Rosillo, *Andrés Trapiello* (Madrid: Calambur, 1994), 74.

4. This story has been told many times. An unusual, recent version is Miguel Sánchez-Ostiz's *Barruntos de la botica* [Suspicions from the Drugstore], in the collection *El coqueto Don Sancho Sánchez* [The Flirt Don Sancho Sánchez] (Pamplona: Diputación de Navarra, 2000).

5. "Erudipáusico" is a term coined by Cela, which combines "erudition" and "menopausal", and refers to the physiological disorders caused by excessive erudition. [Note of the Translator.]

BIBLIOGRAPHY

Albert, Mechthild. *Vanguardistas de camisa azul.* Madrid: Visor, 2003.

———— . ed. *Vencer no es convencer: literatura e ideología del fascismo español.* Madrid: Vervuert Iberoamericana, 1998.

Aub, Max. *Campo de los almendros.* Edición de Francisco Caudet. Madrid: Castalia, 2000.

————. *Campo abierto*. Madrid: Alfaguara / Santillana, 1997.

————. *Campo cerrado*. Madrid: Alfaguara, 1997.

————. *Campo francés*. Madrid: Alfaguara, 1998.

————. *Campo de sangre*. Madrid: Alfaguara, 1998.

————. *Campo del moro*. Madrid: Alfaguara, 1998.

————. *Cuerpos presentes*. Edited, with an introduction and notes by José Carlos Mainer. Segorbe: Fundación Max Aub, 2001.

Ayesta, Julián. *Helena o el mar de verano*. Barcelona: Acantilado, 2000.

Cano Ballesta, Juan. *Las estrategias de la imaginación: utopías literarias y retórica política bajo el franquismo*. Madrid: Siglo XXI de España, 1994.

Carbajosa, Mónica y Pablo. *La corte literaria de José Antonio*. Barcelona: Crítica, 2003.

Cercas, Javier. *Soldados de Salamina*. Barcelona: Tusquets, 2001.

Foxá, Agustín de. *Madrid de corte a cheka*. Barcelona: Planeta, 1993.

García Serrano, Rafael. *Diccionario para un macuto*. Barcelona: Planeta, 1980.

————. *La fiel infantería*. Barcelona: Planeta, 1980.

————. *La gran esperanza: nosotros, los falangistas*. Barcelona: Planeta, 1983.

González Ruano, César. *Poesía*. Madrid: Trieste, 1983.

Jiménez Fraud, Alberto. *Visita a Maquiavelo*. Madrid: Trieste, 1984.

Machado, Manuel. *Poesía*. Selections, introduction, and notes by Andrés Trapiello. Barcelona: Planeta, 1993.

Mainer, José Carlos. *De postguerra (1951–1990)*. Barcelona: Crítica, 1994.

————. *Falange y literatura*. Barcelona: Labor, 1971.

Martín Gaite, Carmen. *El cuento de nunca acabar: apuntes sobre la narración, el amor y la mentira*. Barcelona: Destino, 1997.

Martínez Sarrión, Antonio. *Horizonte desde la rada*. Madrid: Trieste, 1983.

Masip, Paulino. *El diario de Hamlet García*. Madrid: Visor, 2000.

Naval, María Ángeles. *La novela de vértice y la novela del sábado*. Madrid: CSIC, 2001.

Pascual, Ángel María. *Capital de tercer orden: versos del amor de disgusto*. Pamplona: Diputación de Navarra, 1997.

————. *Glosas a la ciudad*. Pamplona: Gobierno de Narvarra, 2000.

Peña Sánchez, Victoriano. *Intelectuales y fascismo: la cultura italiana del 'ventennio fascista' y su repercusión en España*. Granada: Universidad de Granada, 1995.

Rodríguez Puértolas, Julio. *Literatura fascista española*. 2 vols. Madrid: Akal, 1986–1987.

Sánchez Ferlosio, Rafael. *El Jarama*. Barcelona: Destino, 2001.

Sánchez Mazas, Rafael. *La vida nueva de Pedrito de Andía*. Barcelona: Planeta, 1995.

————. *Las aguas de Arbeloa: y otras cuestiones (relatos)*. Madrid: Trieste, 1983.

————. *Poesías*. Edición de Andrés Trapiello. Granada: Editorial Comares, 1990.

————. *Rosa Krüger*. Barcelona: Ediciones del Bronce, 1996.

Sánchez Ostiz, Miguel. *Barruntos de la botica*. In the collection *El coqueto Don Sancho Sánchez*. 3 vols. Pamplona: Diputación de Navarra, 2000.

Sánchez Rosillo, Eloy. *Andrés Trapiello*. Madrid: Calambur, 1994.

Saz, Ismael. *España contra España. Los nacionalismos franquistas*. Madrid: Marcial Pons, 2003.

Selva, Enrique. *Ernesto Giménez Caballero. Entre la vanguardia y el fascismo*. Madrid: Pre-Textos, 2000.

Trapiello, Andrés. *Las armas y las letras: literatura y guerra civil (1936–1939)*. Barcelona: Planeta, 1994.

Umbral, Francisco. *Las palabras de la tribu: de Rubén Darío a Cela*. Barcelona: Planeta, 1996.

Varela, Javier. *La novela de España: los intelectuales y el problema español*. Madrid: Taurus, 1999.

Villalonga, Llorenç. *Bearn, o la sala de las muñecas*. Madrid: Aguilar, 1998.

——— . *Diario de guerra*. Valencia: Pre-Textos, 1997.

Villalonga, Miguel. *Autobiografía*. Madrid: Trieste, 1983.

Wahnón, Sultana. *La estética literaria de la posguerra: del fascismo a la vanguardia*. Amsterdam: Rodopi, 1998.

Contributors

Louise Ciallela is Assistant Professor of Spanish at Northern Illinois University, DeKalb. Her essays have been publishedin *Cervantes* and *Feminist Media Studies*. She received her doctoral degree the University of Wisconsin-Madison in 2000, and has recently completed a book on reading gender in Spanish narratives from the turn of the nineteenth to the twentieth century.

Jacqueline Cruz earned her Ph.D. from the University of California, Los Angeles in 1993. She is currently affiliated with the *Instituto de Estudios Internacionales*, Seville (Spain). She is the author of *Marginalidad y subversión: Emeterio Gutiérrez Albelo y la vanguardia canaria* (1995) and co-author of the volume *La mujer en la España actual: ¿Evolución o involución?* (2004) with Barbara Zecchi. She has also published over twenty articles in academic journals in Spain and the United States, and the translated several books for Cátedra's "Feminismos" collection.

Patrick Paul Garlinger is Assistant Professor of Spanish at Northwestern University. His articles have been published in journals such as *Revista de Estudios Hispánicos, Revista canadiense de estudios hispánicos, Bulletin of Hispanic Studies, Diacritics,* and *Revista Hispánica Moderna*. His book entitled *Confessions of the Letter Closet. Epistolary Fiction and Queer Desire in Modern Spain,* is forthcoming from the University of Minnesota Press.

Ana Gómez-Pérez teaches at Loyola College in Maryland, where she is Assistant Professor of Spanish. She received her Ph.D. from the University of Pennsylvania in 1997. She has published several articles on Spanish narrative of the nineteenth and twentieth centuries, including studies of Galdós, Rosa Chacel and Torrente Ballester. She is currently working on a book manuscript on the importance of memory and its relationship to an apocalyptic strain of contemporary political and philosophical thought in modern Spain.

JORDI GRACIA teaches at the University of Barcelona, Spain, and is the author of *Estado y Cultura: el despertar de una conciencia crítica bajo el franquismo* (1996), *Los nuevos nombres. 1975–2000* (2000), *Hijos de la razón* (2001), and *La resistencia silenciosa. Fascismo y cultura en España* (2004). He has also coauthored *El ensayo español* (1996–97), and *La España de Franco* (2001). His many articles have been published in academic venues both in Spain and the U.S.

RICARDO KRAUEL received his Ph.D. from Brown University in 1999. He published *Voces desde el silencio: heterologías genérico-sexuales en la narrativa española moderna, 1875–1975* in 2001 and has authored several articles that have appeared in *Anales Galdosianos, Anales de la literatura española, Revista canadiense de estudios hispánicos, Monographic Review,* and other academic journals. He is presently teaching at Princeton University.

ELOY MERINO published a book, *El nuevo* Lazarillo *de Camilo J. Cela. Política y cultura en su palimpsesto* in 2000. He is also the author of six other essays that appeared in *Letras Peninsulares, Chasqui, Ojáncano,* and *Monographic Review.* He is Assistant Professor of Spanish at Northern Illinois University, De Kalb. He received his Ph.D. from the University of Miami, Coral Gables, in 1998.

CARMEN MORENO-NUÑO has published a monograph (*El discurso cartográfico, filosófico y postcolonial en* Mesagem de Fernando Pessoa, 1998) and has also authored three articles in the *RLA: Romance Languages Annual* Bulletin. She is Assistant Professor of Romance Languages at Wesleyan University. She received her Ph.D from the University of Minnesota in 2000.

H. ROSI SONG is Assistant Professor of Spanish at Bryn Mawr College. She has authored several articles published in the *RLA, Romance Notes, Inti, Hispamérica, Hispanic Journal,* and *Journal of Spanish Cultural Studies.* She is currently finishing a manuscript on Spanish intellectuals and their political commitment under Francoism.

DIONISIO VISCARRI received his Ph.D. from Ohio State University in 1996, where is now Assistant Professor of Spanish. He has published his essays in *Letras Peninsulares, Boletín de la Biblioteca de Menéndez Pelayo* and *RILCE: Revista de Filología Hispánica.*

ULRICH WINTER is Professor of Spanish and French Literature at Phillips-University Marburg, Germany. He is the author of *Der Roman im Zeichen seiner Selbst,* a book on the literary self-representation in the Spanish novel from the fifteenth through the twentieth centuries. He is the editor of a special volume for the academic journal *Iberoameri-cana* (2004) and co-editor with Joan Ramon Resina of the forthcoming book *Casa encantada,* a collection of essays on memory.

Index